THE **STARTER** COOK

A Beginner Home Cook's Guide to Basic Kitchen Skills and Techniques

LINDA JOHNSON LARSEN

LYONS PRESS
Guilford, Connecticut

An imprint of Globe Pequot Press

**To my dear nieces Grace and Maddie, and my sweet nephew Michael.
I hope this book helps you and all beginning cooks love the kitchen!**

To buy books in quantity for corporate use
or incentives, call **(800) 962-0973**
or e-mail **premiums@GlobePequot.com.**

Copyright © 2012 by Morris Book Publishing, LLC

Lyons Press is an imprint of Globe Pequot Press.

Text design: Maggie Peterson
Project editor: Julie Marsh
Layout: Maggie Peterson

Library of Congress Cataloging-in-Publication Data

Larsen, Linda Johnson.
 The starter cook : a beginner home cook's guide to basic kitchen skills and techniques / Linda Johnson Larsen.
   p. cm.
 Includes index.
 ISBN 978-0-7627-7448-7
 1. Cooking. I. Title.
 TX651.L37 2011
 641.5—dc23

                                                                              2011034650

Printed in the United States of America

10 9 8 7 6 5 4 3 2 1

Contents

Introduction

Learning how to cook is one of the most important skills you can develop. Many people just don't cook. Either they never learned how to, or they are intimidated by the thought of preparing meals. Cooking isn't difficult; like most other skills, it just takes practice. Start by teaching yourself the basics of food and the kitchen and you'll soon find yourself making whole meals with ease. Cooking is one of the best things you can do for yourself. Not only is it satisfying to the soul, but it's often healthier than restaurant or take-out fare, and it's far less expensive.

Salads and simple side dishes are probably the easiest foods to make. Salads, which are just combined and tossed with a dressing, can be an entire meal. Following these easy recipes will give you a lot of confidence. And a side dish, like roasted potatoes or scalloped corn, is perfect for accompanying a rotisserie chicken from the deli or one of those marinated salmon fillets you just bake and eat.

If your family loves beef, start by cooking simple beef recipes. Marinated and grilled or broiled steak, beef stir-fries, and casseroles are good recipes to choose. A meat pasta sauce, served over linguine or penne, and a classic meat loaf are easy to make too.

For chicken lovers, look for recipes using baked, panfried, or broiled boneless, skinless chicken breasts. This cut of poultry is the easiest to work with, it cooks very quickly, and it's adaptable to many cuisines and flavors.

For seafood lovers, boneless fish fillets are the easiest to handle and cook. This type of fish cooks very quickly and is so mild you can use it in almost any recipe. Fish soups, grilled fish, and broiled fish are the fastest quick-cooking seafood recipes.

And for pork lovers, look for simple recipes that use pork tenderloin and pork chops. Both of these cuts of meat cook quickly, are easy to work with, and again pair well with almost any ethnic cuisine flavors.

Once you've become comfortable making the basic recipes for each different cut of meat and the different categories of recipes, you can start having fun. Create your own recipes using your favorite flavors and foods. For instance, once you've mastered broiling fish fillets with a simple mustard glaze, make your own glaze using Tex-Mex ingredients like chili powder, serrano peppers, and salsa. Or add a Spanish flair by using paprika, ground almonds, some chopped olives, and a lemon sour cream glaze.

When you are comfortable making a basic recipe, it's time to branch out! Use the same type of food, proportions, and cooking times as in the original recipe but add your own touch. Use your family's favorite ingredients, or change the seasonings, spices, and herbs to the ones you like best. Substitute mushrooms and green bell peppers for cherry tomatoes and zucchini in a chicken quiche, or use a sauce you love for chicken to cook pork chops.

Cooking recipes, like soups, stews, salads, casseroles, pasta dishes, and sandwiches, are much easier to learn than baking recipes. Although there are some baking tips and descriptions in this book, if you want to bake, be sure to invest in a good baking book. Baking recipes are scientific formulas specifically designed for a particular result. Simple baked recipes like brownies or quick breads are the best choices for beginners. When you understand how to measure, mixing skills, and doneness tests, you can expand to cookies, cakes, and pies.

When you create a recipe that you and your family love, be sure to write it down. It's hard to re-create a successful recipe from memory, even if it's very simple. Keep notes as you work, and your cooking skills will get better and better as your repertoire increases.

The most important advice I can give you is to start slow and enjoy every minute. Don't jump in with a complicated recipe that takes hours of preparation and has a twenty-item ingredients list. Small steps will lead to complicated recipes, I promise you. Build on your successes, enjoy learning about new foods, and enjoy sharing these foods with your family and loved ones. If you haven't cooked much before, you are learning an incredibly valuable skill that will serve you well now and in the future. Nothing is more satisfying than creating a delicious recipe that you can serve to friends and family. You'll save money, your health will improve as you wean yourself from fast food and processed food, and your confidence in every part of your life will grow.

Now let's get starting cooking! The initial work and preparation to learn the language of food, how to shop, and how to transform and stock your kitchen may seem daunting, but once you've accomplished that, you'll be able to get an excellent and delicious dinner on the table with not much effort. The rewards are legendary!

① STOCKING THE KITCHEN

Once you have a well-stocked pantry, the necessary cooking tools, and basic snack-packing accessories, it will be easy for anyone in your household to prepare a healthy snack in minutes for on-the-spot consumption or later in the day. And it will be easier for you to learn how to cook!

Your first step into the cooking world starts with stocking your kitchen. Without food, you can't make a meal! There are two parts to your stock of food: staples and perishables. Staples are foods such as oil, flour, and spices that you should have on hand at all times. Perishables are foods that you buy weekly (or daily), including fresh fruits and vegetables, dairy products, and fresh meat.

Food is stored in a pantry (or shelves), the refrigerator, and the freezer. Each one should be organized so food doesn't go to waste, and so you don't stand at the freezer staring at a bunch of unidentified packages containing mystery products. More about that in a bit! First, let's learn about the foods you should have in your kitchen.

Buy fresh, local produce whenever possible, and in as wide a variety as possible. Of course, we should try to eat seasonally. There is something quite beautiful about organizing the way your family eats around the year's cycle: French onion soup in winter, rhubarb pie in the spring, tomato salad when the sun is high, and apple crisp in the fall. That being said, if you are a busy, working parent, you are not going to have time to buy local greens every day at a farm stand. Buy fresh whenever you can, and make smart decisions about staples, canned food, and frozen food when you can't.

STAPLES AND VALUE-ADDED FOODS

Every kitchen should have a variety of long-life and shelf-stable foods on hand. These are the foods that last for months that help you bake and cook. They can get you out of a jam by inspiring quick meals and will be there if you are housebound for any reason. And value-added foods, which combine two or more ingredients, can save valuable time in the kitchen and make cooking easier. Salad dressings are also great marinades. A pasta sauce can be used as a quick pizza sauce. And frozen vegetable blends can be added to a stew or soup to stretch it at the last minute and save preparation time.

Pantry Staples and Value-Added Foods

A properly stocked pantry is essential not only for quick and efficient cooking, but for assisting the creative process. When you have a pantry stocked full of essentials, creating new dishes becomes much easier and can get you out of the same old food rut. And if you have food on hand, you will be more apt to cook it when pressed for time, as opposed to making a frantic call to the pizza parlor. As an example, if you have dry pasta, a jar of capers, and a can of tuna on hand, the addition of some fresh tomatoes can make a quick, healthy, and elegant dinner. Your only limitation is your own creativity. In fact, sometimes the best dishes are created when there is seemingly "nothing to eat" in the house and a quick search of the pantry reveals a treasure trove of ingredients.

Before refrigeration, the pantry was limited to dry goods, root cellar foodstuffs, and home-canned items, as these were the only way to preserve foods. Today's pantries are not just a cupboard full of dry ingredients but have expanded to the refrigerator and freezer and maybe even the windowsill if you can keep certain essential herbs growing all year.

There are some items you should never be without. Some of these recommendations come from a sheer sense of survival. In case you are snowed in or worse and need to eat, these items will save the day. And others are nice to have on hand to make your meals more exciting and to put the perfect finishing touch on any meal.

Baking mixes. These are a beginning baker's best friend. Baking mixes teach you how to measure, what a batter should look like when it's ready to be poured into the pan, and how baked goods should look. Don't be ashamed to use baking mixes. You can dress them up with your own additions (more chocolate chips in a brownie!) when you get a bit of experience.

Baking supplies. You'll need all-purpose flour; whole wheat flour; baking powder and soda; cornstarch; cocoa; baking chocolate; marshmallows; corn syrup; both regular and kosher salt; granulated, brown, and powdered sugar; honey; maple syrup; baking mixes; cornmeal; cornstarch; and dry yeast to make cakes, cookies, pies, breads, and desserts.

Beans and legumes. Canned beans are good to have on hand for quick meals. Stock black beans, kidney beans, pinto beans, chickpeas, cannellini beans, and white beans.

Helpful Tip

Since many items in the pantry are long lasting, do not require refrigeration, and may not have expiration dates, it is a good idea to mark them with the date you purchased them. This lets you make sure the freshest items get used first and that foods do not sit too long or get buried in the back of the cabinet or shelf.

These can be turned into quick soups with the addition of broth and vegetables. A quick whirl in the blender can make an appetizer spread. Canned beans are a delicious addition to salads, too. Lentils are quick cooking. Dried beans and split peas are great for Crock-Pot cooking or those days when you want a long-simmering soup on the stove.

Bread. Some breads are stored in the pantry; others in the fridge. Premade pizza crusts, some sliced breads, and tortillas can be stored in the pantry. Read labels for the proper storage instructions. Most breads, when stored in the fridge, dry out more quickly because the cool air makes the starches cold so they become dry. And be sure to watch out for mold. If bread gets moldy, it must be discarded.

Canned fruits. Pears, apricots, and peaches are the most common canned fruits. They can be used to make quick desserts and are also used as baking ingredients to reduce fat content. The packing liquid is used in stir-fry recipes and as glazes for cookies, cakes, and breads. Buy fruit packed in light syrup, unless the recipe calls for fruits packed in heavy syrup. Nobody needs that extra sugar!

Canned meats. Canned meats make excellent last-minute sandwiches and salads. And they can be added to soups and casseroles. Use canned, drained meats to make crisp little cakes for a fast dinner. You can now find many meats packaged in pouches instead of cans. Many of these products are flavored. Pouch meats have less liquid and are high quality. Stock canned tuna, chicken, salmon, dried beef, and deviled ham. And if you're a fan, beef or turkey jerky can be a delicious quick snack.

Canned soups and sauces. There's nothing wrong with canned soup. It can save you when you are sick and just can't face cooking anything. Soups are also an important ingredient in many recipes, especially casseroles. Chicken stock, beef stock, and vegetable broth are the base for many homemade soups and sauces. Canned sauces include mayonnaise, salsa, Tabasco sauce, sweet-and-sour sauce, stir-fry sauce, barbecue sauce, and ethnic goodies like tahini, Jamaican jerk sauce, chutney, teriyaki sauce, chile paste, and oyster sauce.

Canned vegetables. Canned vegetables are another pantry staple. Canned corn, green beans, and tomato products should be kept on hand at all times. Tomato paste, tomato sauce, diced tomatoes, tomato puree, and whole tomatoes packed in juice are all used to make pasta sauce, barbecue sauce, soups, and pizzas.

Condiments. Condiments play an essential role in cooking. Sometimes they are the main actor; other times they are the unseen understudy that saves the day. Stock ketchup, mustard, pickles, relish, salsa, Worcestershire sauce, soy sauce, capers, olives, sun-dried tomatoes, and other ethnic favorites. Ketchup can be used to make barbecue sauce and to flavor casseroles. Mustard is used in salad dressings, barbecue sauces, and marinades. Pickles and relishes add flavor to many dishes. And salsa has become as ubiquitous as ketchup! Once opened, many of these condiments must be refrigerated. Read labels to make sure that you are storing each one correctly.

Dried fruits. Dried fruits not only make an excellent last-minute snack but are delicious added to cookie, quick bread, and cake batters. They are also important components to many ethnic dishes and are delicious stirred into sandwich spreads and salads. Stock raisins, currants, dried cranberries, dried cherries, and coconut.

Marinades and salad dressings. There are many types and flavors of marinades available. They can be used as the sauce for a stir-fry or used to marinate meats before they are grilled. You can find salad dressings ranging from the basic oil-and-vinegar mixture to Caesar salad dressing and all kinds of mayonnaise. Use them as marinades too, or as the base for a stir-fry sauce.

Nuts and seeds. These little nutrition powerhouses have a place in every diet. Stock walnuts, pecans, pistachios, almonds, pine nuts, sesame seeds, poppy seeds, caraway seeds, fennel seeds, and sunflower seeds. If you live in a hot climate, you may want to store these items in the freezer, because they can go rancid quickly.

Oils. Cooking oils like peanut oil, canola oil, and safflower oil belong in every pantry. You should have several types of olive oil, including regular olive oil for sautéing and extra virgin olive oil for salad dressings and to toss with pasta for a fast dinner. Specialty oils include sesame oil for flavoring stir-fries and flavored oils for fast cooking. Don't make your own flavored oils; they can be a safety hazard.

Pasta. Dried pasta is another lifesaver. Rather than order pizza, cook some pasta al dente and toss with butter and cheese for an almost-instant dinner. The types of pasta now available will boggle your mind. At the very least, have spaghetti, fettuccine, linguine, penne, ziti, farfalle, elbow macaroni, orzo, lasagna, manicotti, gemelli, rotini, and wagon wheels on hand. Today there are many gluten-free pasta varieties on the market.

Pasta sauces. You can make a quick meal out of dried pasta and canned tomato pasta sauce. Stock all different kinds of tomato-based pasta sauces, including marinara, tomato and cheese sauces, and meat sauces. Alfredo or white sauce is an excellent short-cut ingredient. And pesto can make an instant dinner with some cooked spaghetti and Parmesan cheese.

Peanut butter. What's a pantry without peanut butter? Stock both creamy and chunky types for use in sandwiches, baking, desserts, and sauces. It's an inexpensive substitute for tahini when making hummus, can be blended with oil and seasonings for a pasta sauce, and is the key ingredient in Indian satay.

Rice. Rice has sustained populations for generations and has a place in every pantry. Stock long grain white rice for pilafs, short grain Arborio rice for risotto, brown

Helpful Tip

Potatoes, onions, and garlic should be stored in the pantry, not the freezer. Cool air forces the starch in potatoes to convert to sugar. Onions and garlic can become mushy when chilled. Keep potatoes and onions separate, because they each emit chemicals that make the other ripen too quickly.

rice, and wild rice (this is actually a grass seed). Experiment with exotic rice like basmati, jasmine, and Texmati. These grains have wonderful texture and smell deliciously fragrant when cooking. Mixing rice with beans makes an almost perfect protein for vegetarian meals.

Spices and seasonings. A good supply of spices and seasonings can transform your cooking into something special. Depending on the ethnic cuisines you enjoy, you should have dried herbs and spices in your pantry. Stock oregano, basil, Italian seasoning, marjoram, mint, celery salt, garlic and onion powder, bay leaves, chives, rosemary, sage, thyme, curry powder, allspice, turmeric, cinnamon, cardamom, chili powder, ground ginger, cloves, mustard, nutmeg, and paprika. And don't forget flavorings! Vanilla, peppermint extract, and almond extract are the basics.

Vinegars. The three basic vinegars include balsamic, cider, and wine. Balsamic vinegar is used for making salad dressings and drizzling over finished Italian dishes. The real stuff is expensive; treat it carefully. Cider vinegar is used in baking and cooking. And red and white wine vinegars are used in salad dressings and sauces.

Whole grains and cereals. This list includes oatmeal, quinoa, cracked wheat or bulgur, barley, millet, and popcorn. These foods can be used to make a quick breakfast or easy pilafs and are delicious added to casseroles and soups. Quick-cooking grains can be used to make a fast salad with vegetables and cooked meats. Dry breakfast cereals, of course, have a place in any pantry. They can be used in baking, too.

Wines. These alcoholic beverages make an excellent flavoring. Red and white wines that are good enough to drink are good in small amounts in soups and stews. Remember that not all of the alcohol will cook off when heated. Sherry and Marsala have strong flavors and should also be used sparingly. Cooking wines should be avoided, as they are heavily salted (to be undrinkable) and are usually of poor quality.

Don't be afraid to buy certain foods in bulk. If you know that you use lots of olive oil or basmati rice that you'll use up in a reasonable period of time, stock up. Just make sure to label the purchase date on the product and that you store it in a proper container. You may want to decant rice, grains, pasta, flour, and sugars into storage containers instead of keeping them in their original packaging.

The beauty of pantry staples is that they almost never spoil, so your monies are safe in these food investments. (Some staples like whole wheat flour, nuts, and seeds can spoil or turn rancid because of their high fat content, so be sure to follow expiration dates to the letter!) And you can store them anywhere, so if you don't have a pantry, a hall closet or space in the basement can be converted into an auxiliary pantry. Use wire risers on your shelves, if necessary, so you can see all of the foods in the pantry.

Clean out your pantry once every month or two. Remove all items, reorganize if necessary, wash down the shelves, and replace food. Take the time to look at all of the expiration and 'best if used by' dates on the products. Use foods close to the dates, or give them to a food pantry if you know you won't use them. Never give expired products away for someone else to use, though; just toss those.

Refrigerator Staples and Value-Added Foods

The refrigerator is a kitchen basic. Before refrigeration, shopping (or harvesting) was a daily occurrence. Mechanical refrigerators are a very new invention, and while people

figured out a long time ago that cold temperatures keep food fresh longer, they were limited to ice boxes and winter weather. Even then, those who lived in warm climates and had no access to ice at any time of year had to find other solutions to food preservation challenges.

A well-organized fridge is key for any cook; it allows for items to be found more quickly and minimizes the chances that foods will go bad while sitting hidden in the back of the fridge. Foods should be organized with like foods (veggies with veggies in crisper drawers, for example) and, if opened, should be labeled with expiration dates. Be sure to check expiration dates regularly to ensure that you use fresh foods.

Keeping a running grocery list will ensure that you never run out of a key ingredient right when you need it most. When you discover that you're running low on a certain item, add it to your list for the next time you go grocery shopping.

The basics of managing cold storage are simple: Know what is in your fridge, when you put it there, and how long it can last. There are high-tech list-making machines you can keep on your fridge. Just enter the foods you want to add and print out a list before you go to the supermarket.

There are many variables to determine how long food items can last in the fridge. What is the temperature of your fridge? Is the door opened a lot? How crowded is your fridge, and is there adequate airflow inside the unit? The optimal temperature for your fridge is around 38°F, but anything under 40°F is generally considered safe. Train your family to open the fridge door as little as possible. Don't overcrowd the fridge, and make sure it's kept clean, inside and out.

Now that you understand your refrigerator and its nuances, you need to pack it to store foods efficiently and safely. There are a few tricks and techniques to use so you don't waste food and get the longest shelf life for your foods. You'll be amazed how simple these techniques are and what a huge difference they can make.

The following items will last longer than a couple of weeks, so they are considered staples for the fridge. But remember: Many of these items still have expiration dates!

Cheeses. Hard cheeses usually last up to a month in the fridge if kept in their original packaging. Pay attention to expiration dates. Once you open a block of cheese, it may mold or dry out before the expiration date is reached. Always repackage opened blocks of cheese in plastic wrap, plastic bags, or foil. The fridge is a dry place, and cheese will dry out if not tightly wrapped.

Condiments. Most condiments need to be put into the fridge after they are opened. Read the label to make sure. Ketchup, mustards, mayonnaise, preserves, jams, jellies, capers, pickles, olives, horseradish, salsa, soy sauce, hoisin sauce, plum sauce, oyster sauce, and Tabasco sauce are all staples that should be refrigerated, along with salad dressings and cooking wines.

Dairy products. Some dairy products, including sour cream, buttermilk, butter, and eggs, last for weeks in the fridge. Follow expiration dates and be sure to tightly cover these products so they don't absorb flavors from other foods.

Deli foods. Don't forget the deli for great convenience foods! Rotisserie chicken is one of the most popular deli convenience foods. Prepared salads and casseroles, sliced meats and cheeses, and desserts can help round out a meal when you're just starting to cook.

Refrigerated doughs. Refrigerated doughs are great choices for making quick meals. They can be used to make breads for sandwiches, wrap leftovers for quick calzones, or as breadsticks or crescent rolls to add some heft to your meal. These doughs are easy to dress up, too; sprinkle them with dried herbs or cheeses before baking.

> ## Helpful Tip
>
> Keep your fridge clean. Wash it out every two months by removing all food. Then wipe down the shelves and door with a solution of dish detergent, white vinegar, and one teaspoon of baking soda. Remove the veggie drawer and wash it thoroughly. If there is mold in your fridge, you'll breathe spores every time you open the door. Dry everything, then restock the fridge, making sure to keep the oldest items at the front so they get used first.

Some fresh fruits. Pears, apples, and bananas do not have to be refrigerated if they are going to be used promptly. If you have a cool pantry, place pears, apples, and bananas there. Prepared fresh fruits, often packaged with dips, are super easy and convenient.

Fresh pasta. Many fresh pastas are now available. They range from fresh fettuccine to stuffed ravioli. Follow expiration dates and make sure you use them fairly quickly. They cook in 2 or 3 minutes, so they can save you time in the race to make dinner.

Pasta sauces. Lots of new types of fresh pasta sauces are available in the refrigerated section of the supermarket. These items, including basil pesto and sun-dried tomato pesto, tomato-based sauces, and white sauces, last for weeks in the fridge and are perfect for last-minute meals.

Fully prepared meats. Properly braising a pot roast is a long process. You can buy a fully prepared pot roast with gravy in the meat section of the supermarket. Just heat and eat! You can also find stuffed chicken breasts, fish fillets, and braised short ribs.

Fresh vegetables. Some produce will last for quite a while in the fridge. Carrots, broccoli, summer squash, brussels sprouts, zucchini, and other produce can last up to a week in the fridge. Think about using specialty produce storage bags to keep them fresher longer. Fully prepared vegetables and fruits are very convenient. Stir-fried blends are fully prepared and ready to go in the wok.

Freezer Staples and Value-Added Foods

Freezers are a great place for long-term storage, but frozen items do not last forever, even though it may seem like it! The freezer is a hostile place; freezer burn can ruin just about any frozen product. Freezer burn is dehydration of frozen foods. It looks like a dried-out spot or patch on the food. Food that has freezer burn is still edible, but the texture is unpleasant. You can use meats or vegetables that have freezer burn in soups; they may rehydrate during the cooking process, but that's not guaranteed. To avoid freezer burn, wrap all packages tightly using plastic wrap and bags specifically marketed for freezer use.

If you use a vacuum packer to freeze foods, you'll find that they do last months longer than if they are simply wrapped in plastic. The vacuum packer is especially good for individual servings of meats, fish, fruits, potatoes, and other produce. Be sure to follow instructions for using this appliance, and never substitute other bags or containers for the ones specifically developed for the vacuum sealer.

Freezer items need to be packed certain ways. Always use freezer wrap and freezer bags. And organize your freezer so you can find food when you need it. Keep a small notebook nearby with a list of the foods your freezer contains. And regularly update that list so you know when you need to replace something.

Breads freeze well. You may want to slice unsliced bread before freezing it so you can take out a few portions at a time for toasting. Don't freeze bread in the package it came in; transfer to freezer bags.

Freeze condiments or other flavoring items like minced garlic, pesto, or peeled and grated

BUDGET TIP

Food waste is one of the biggest budget busters. But how do you know how long a food has been in your fridge? You need to know what you have on hand and use it or freeze it while the food retains quality. Designate a special shelf or spot in your refrigerator and pantry for these fresh foods. Look through this shelf every day and rotate foods so you use older foods first.

fresh gingerroot by tablespoons in small bags. You can freeze lime and lemon juice in ice cube trays, then place them in freezer bags.

Fruits are a great item to freeze. You can buy lots of prefrozen fruits, or freeze your own. To freeze berries, rinse off the fruits, then place them in a single layer on a cookie sheet. Freeze until hard, then package into hard-sided freezer containers. Peaches can be frozen after they are peeled; blanch in boiling water for 30 seconds, then place in ice water. Slip off the skins, slice the peaches, and sprinkle with lemon juice. Freeze in a single layer until hard, then pack into hard- sided containers. Frozen fruits make excellent pie fillings and are also great for smoothies. Don't thaw the fruit before pureeing so your smoothies will be thick and cold.

Herbs freeze beautifully. To freeze, first rinse them and shake dry. When they're dry, line a cookie sheet with parchment paper. Place the herbs on the paper in a single layer and freeze for 1 hour. Then place into freezer bags.

Ice cream should be in everyone's freezer! Low-fat ice creams and frozen yogurts are available for the health conscious, as well as sorbets and sherbets. In the summer, make your own popsicles out of juice for a healthy treat. Ice cream is also wonderful to use for a last-minute dessert with a homemade topping.

Liquids should be stored in hard-sided plastic freezer containers with tight-sealing lids. Chicken, beef, and vegetable broth should be stored in 2-cup or 4-cup containers for easy measuring into soups, stews, and sauces. Leave some headspace (air space) in the container when freezing liquids, because they will expand when frozen.

Frozen meals you buy in the grocery store are great, but you can also make and freeze your own! Meal starters are ready to go; you just cook them and add meat. Frozen pizzas are an instant dinner; you can dress them up with more veggies, meats, and cheeses.

Frozen meats make up one of the biggest sections in the frozen-food department. Frozen precooked meatballs, seasoned fish fillets, seasoned hamburger patties, frozen fish and shellfish, seasoned chicken breasts, and ready-to-cook steaks are just a few of the options.

Uncooked meats should be divided into smaller portions (so they thaw quickly) and then wrapped in freezer-safe packaging. Divide ground beef into patties, separate the patties with freezer plastic wrap, then package in hard-sided containers. Cut up a whole chicken before freezing for faster thawing. Never freeze meat in the packaging from the grocery store; that wrapping isn't freezer safe, and the meat will develop freezer burn.

Helpful Tip

Every three months or so, it's a good idea to go through your freezer and make a "surprise" dinner. Even if the freezer items don't seem to match up, you may be able to pull off a smorgasbord. You can combine leftover chicken soup with some frozen chicken to make a potpie base, or use some cooked meats to make several sandwiches.

BUDGET TIP

These are the top budget ingredients to have in your freezer: stale bread, chicken and veggie trimmings, ground meat, leftover wine, rinds of Parmesan cheese, leftovers, fresh ginger, nuts, and frozen veggies.

Frozen pastas are a lifesaver. You can find frozen pasta that cooks in minutes, including stuffed pastas like tortellini and ravioli, frozen dumplings, and pierogies (large dumplings stuffed with potatoes and cheese).

Vegetables can be frozen too. Some vegetables, like potatoes, don't freeze well, so choose prefrozen potato products from the store. You can freeze tomatoes; blanch them as you would peaches. Then crush them or cut them into quarters and sprinkle with lemon juice. Place in plastic containers and freeze. Frozen vegetables have many virtues that canned veggies do not. They usually have better color and texture and less sodium. Unused portions can be returned to the freezer for later use, unlike canned veggies.

Be sure to organize like food items together in the freezer so they're easy to find. And always, always label the food! Use a permanent market or grease pencil to write the name of the food, the date it was frozen, and any preparation instructions.

PERISHABLES

Perishables are foods that must be refrigerated because otherwise they'll become dangerous to eat. Perishable ingredients can't be bought too far in advance or they will spoil. What's the solution? Make your perishable purchases count, and plan your meals so you'll use those foods promptly. Refrigerate these foods as soon as you get home from the grocery store. Buy perishable foods in small quantities and keep them at the front of the fridge so you'll remember to eat them.

Refrigerator Perishables

Berries. Strawberries and raspberries should be eaten within a day or two of purchase. Blueberries will keep a little longer, as will blackberries. Never, ever rinse berries until the minute before you eat them or they will mold.

Cheeses. Many soft cheeses only last a few days in the refrigerator. Follow use-by dates carefully. If a hard cheese develops mold, you can still eat it if you cut off the mold and 1 inch of the cheese next to the mold. If a soft cheese develops mold, it must be discarded.

Dairy products. Some dairy products, like milk, cream, cottage cheese, and soft cheeses last only a week or two in the refrigerator. And they must be returned to the fridge within two hours of being taken out, or they could develop bacteria.

Fish and Seafood. Fish and seafood are very perishable and should be used within a day or two. Unless you buy fish straight off a fishing boat, it's probably been frozen. Yes, even the fish in the "fresh" fish case! Do not refreeze fish you've bought from a fish case or butcher counter.

Fresh herbs. Store fresh herbs in a glass of water, with a paper bag placed loosely over them, and they will last for a few days. Basil is probably the most perishable, while thyme, parsley, and oregano will last a bit longer.

Meats. All raw meats must be refrigerated and used within a few days. Ground meats, especially, are quite perishable. Ground chicken and turkey should be used within two or three days. You may need to freeze ground meats if you do not use them quickly.

Salad greens. Delicate salad greens should always be refrigerated. Bagged salad mixes are clearly marked with expiration dates. Whole lettuces will last a little longer if stored in produce storage bags.

FRESH, CANNED, OR FROZEN?

Chefs and good cooks agree: the fresher the food, the better. Fresh foods are always a good option when cooking up a delicious meal. Fresh foods often taste more vibrant than canned options. And fresh foods are often grown locally, which supports small farms.

Proper storage of fresh foods in your kitchen is paramount for ensuring the quality of the food. Place items you want to ripen, such as avocados and melons, in a sunny window. If you want these items to ripen slowly, place them in a cool, dark area of your pantry or in the refrigerator. Most fresh foods are stored in the refrigerator. Even "winter" vegetables keep longer when refrigerated. Salad greens are the most delicate. Cabbage, escarole, chicory, kale, spinach, mustard greens, and collards will stay fresh longer if they're refrigerated.

Fresh fruits and vegetables are tastier than canned or frozen and can be eaten out of hand with no more preparation than a quick rinse. When buying fruits and veggies from the market, remember to dry them before storing. Most supermarkets "mist" their vegetables. This makes them glisten and look appealing, but the moisture rots the vegetables very quickly.

Frozen foods can sometimes be more nutritious than fresh. If the only fresh strawberries in the market were shipped to Washington State from Peru, those berries spent a long time in transit. And they lost nutritional value every second of that trip. Frozen fruits and vegetables are usually frozen right in the field, minutes after harvest. This

> **Helpful Tip**
>
> Some produce should not be refrigerated. Tomatoes become mushy and lose flavor when refrigerated. Melons such as cantaloupe and honeydew melons should be kept on the counter until they are ripe; refrigerate just to chill. Bananas can be refrigerated, but the skin will turn black; this doesn't affect the flesh.

preserves many of their nutrients. The taste of frozen fruits and vegetables is also very good, since they don't have to be picked unripe to survive transit. Since they are processed so quickly, the harvest can be delayed until they are the peak of ripeness.

How long should perishable foods be stored? All foods have different life spans and different expiration dates. For charts that tell you exactly how to store foods and for how long, see Chapter 5.

ORGANIZE YOUR KITCHEN

An organized kitchen is key to cooking. If you don't know where the balsamic vinegar is, you'll be spending a lot of time searching. And that makes cooking a chore. Your kitchen should be as organized as a professional kitchen.

Learn the phrase *"mise en place"* (rhymes with "peas on floss"). This is a French culinary term that means "everything in its place." With *mise en place,* the cook prepares each ingredient before cooking. The onions are chopped, garlic is minced, potatoes peeled and cubed, and chicken cut into strips.

Mise en place also means that your kitchen should have everything in its place. Every bit of food and each and every utensil should have a home that it is returned to after use. Then, when you need that balsamic vinegar or a wire whisk to blend the salad dressing, it's right there at your fingertips. You may not cook like a French chef, but you'll feel like one when you are gliding smoothly around the kitchen without a misstep. Store your favorite foods and utensils in a convenient place and keep them well organized to ease food preparation.

The Work Triangle

You may have heard a lot about the "work triangle" in kitchen design. In the traditional work triangle, the sink, stove, and fridge make up the three points of, well, a triangle. The distance between the points of the triangle should be 4 to 9 feet. Any closer, and there isn't enough counter space. Any longer, and you'll spend too much time walking from point to point. The work triangle is a good arrangement, but some larger kitchens may have two or even three work triangles. An island can break up several triangles so more than one cook can perform tasks in comfort.

If you can't design your kitchen from scratch (who can?), take heart. You can organize it to make it more efficient.

Be sure there is adequate counter space next to the refrigerator, stove, pantry, and sink. Food needs a "landing place" where you can set something down. Balancing a lot of food in your arms while you move it around the kitchen isn't safe, no matter how many times you see Rachael Ray do it on television.

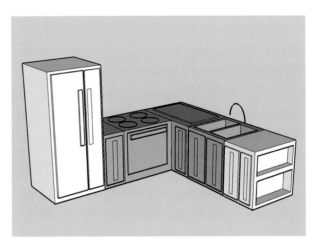

Clear off any unnecessary items from the counters. If you don't use an appliance every day, it should be stored in a drawer or cupboard. Try to keep artwork, bills, and other household paper off the kitchen counter. There are many organizing devices you can buy to keep paperwork in order.

Sort through your drawers and cupboards and organize them by type. Keep all your spoons in one drawer, spatulas in another drawer, and measuring tools in yet another. If you don't have that much space, use drawer dividers to keep things in order.

If your kitchen doesn't have enough counter space, think about bringing in a small butcher block table. It can create a work triangle, or can be used as a portable server or extra work space.

There are portable counter extenders you can buy that you can place over the kitchen sink or the stove to give you more work area. Only use these when you're not using the sink or stove.

The Pantry

The pantry can be a small- to medium-size room, a cupboard, or a closet; all you need are sturdy shelves to store food. Shelves along the basement stairwell or in a dry basement can serve as a pantry. Your pantry should be well stocked with all of the products that make cooking delicious and fun. To use space most efficiently, group like items together.

- Assemble all of your baking supplies in one area. Include containers of flour, sugar, and baking powder; large boxes of salt or salt substitute; and bottles of vanilla.
- Put your dry pastas in another area, with your canned tomatoes and tomato paste. Condiments that do not need refrigeration can also be stored in the pantry. Bottles of ketchup, Worcestershire sauce, hot sauce, and so forth, can be stored here.
- Keep condiments together, too. You may want to add a lazy Susan or other storage container for easy access. Just spin it to find the product you need.

- Herbs should be kept closer to the work space, typically near the stove. (Don't keep herbs and spices right next to the stove, since heat makes them lose their potency more quickly.)
- Cans of ground coffee, jars of instant coffee, and tea can be stored on shelves in airtight containers, such as jars.
- Keep your canned fruits and fruit juices together, arranging the smaller sizes at the front and the tall ones at the back. Keep any canned vegetables together. Broth in cans and dried legumes for making soup can all be put together.
- It's important to have plenty of plastic containers of various sizes on hand. You will also need tins for open packages of cookies and crackers. Mason jars are good for holding open boxes of tea, coffee, and so forth.

- Keep items you use most often front and center, and place the foods you reach for only occasionally toward the back or out of sight.
- Place heavier items on the bottom shelves to avoid tipping. You may have to rearrange some products to balance shelves, especially if you have pull-out shelves.
- Items that can spill or leave a sticky residue should be kept in spill-proof bins.
- Square containers stack together efficiently so you can get more items into the pantry. And ziplock bags take up less space than storage boxes for foods like chips, cereals, and open boxes of crackers.

Shelf organization is handy for keeping everything you need for one kitchen task together. If there is room to keep baking pans, pie pans, cookie sheets, and muffin tins together, then do so.

Just as with all other storage areas in your kitchen, the pantry needs to be emptied, cleaned, and reorganized periodically, perhaps two or three times a year. No matter how careful you are about putting things back where they belong, things will get out of place.

Setting Up Your Space

There are some easy ways to maximize your cooking abilities in a small space.

Space management is important, especially when space is at a premium in places like apartments or small houses. If you're not the only cook in the family, setting up your space to give everyone a better work environment is a great way to let everyone enjoy time in the kitchen. Food and cooking have an uncanny way of bringing people together, so capitalize on this opportunity.

Try to design your space with a few distinct sections:

A pantry for nonperishable food storage. This can be as small as a separate shelf, or can be as expansive as a separate room. Make sure that you keep your pantry well organized too.

A separate section for all your cooking utensils and food-storage containers. If you have to take down a lot of canned foods to get at your favorite saucepan, you'll waste valuable time in the kitchen.

A preparation area. This area should be a cleared counter space, as large as possible, where foods, utensils, and appliances are not stored. You need an uncluttered work space to keep track of ingredients as you cook.

A separate area for cleaning supplies. Always store any cleaning chemicals or detergents in a place where they cannot spill onto food or food-preparation areas.

You will also need **an area for fresh items,** such as fruit and bread, which should be stored at room temperature. A well-ventilated basket works well for fruits, and an airtight container keeps bread fresh. Organizing tools like paper towel holders and shelves with hooks for utensils can help keep your kitchen in order.

Storage options are limitless these days. Shelves in home centers, bed and bath stores, and big box stores are filled with all sizes of plastic tubs, stackable boxes, and snap-together shelving. Before heading out to the store to stock up, lay out the space in the kitchen and draw a basic diagram with measurements on it. Then when you go shopping, you won't have to guess if items fit where you hope they will.

Be creative and make use of all the spaces available to you. Vertical space can come in handy; you can find wire shelf units that can divide large shelf space into smaller sections. Look for stackable plastic drawers that you can pile up to the ceiling. Clear drawers and containers are better than opaque ones, just so you can see what's inside them at a glance.

Ordinary household items are safe to use and good for cleaning. Distilled vinegar and baking soda are safe cleaners and are inexpensive, too. A mixture of lemon juice and salt makes a good copper polish. Use paper towels to clean instead of dish towels, which can hold microbes.

Helpful Tip

Nesting mixing bowls and measuring cups take up minimal space and are easy to keep in order. You can find them on eBay or in antiques stores if they're not available in traditional stores.

HOW TO GROCERY SHOP

In an ideal world, Americans would shop like many Europeans still do, or Americans did in an earlier age: daily and develop relationships with farmers and dairy owners, butchers, and cheese mongers. But it is not realistic for most Americans to shop this way on a regular basis. Luckily, some of the modern shopping conveniences, such as online grocery stores that deliver food to the doorstep, have made it possible for many of us to cook more often.

Grocery Shopping Options

Neighborhood grocery stores While many "mom and pop" stores have disappeared from the landscape, there are still a few of these gems around. You can get personal service, order specialty items, and support the local economy. At the very least, most towns and cities have neighborhood bakeries that are a wonderful source for good breads and desserts.

Supermarkets. Also known as chain grocery stores, supermarkets are better than ever, partly because they're feeling the competition. Chains such as Whole Foods and Trader Joe's work hard to give consumers healthy options. Other large chains include Cub, Winn Dixie, Safeway, and Kroger.

Ethnic stores. You can't beat ethnic markets as a resource for exotic ingredients and cooking advice. These stores can be the best place to find fresh foods and meats, along with specialty flavorings and sauces.

Farmers' markets and farm stands. These are becoming increasingly popular and easy to find. This method of shopping supports local agribusiness and business and lets you buy the freshest produce, meat, and dairy products. Local seasonal vegetables travel shorter distances to reach the market and are in better overall shape. The produce also has higher nutritional content and is usually cheaper.

Online grocery services. Buying groceries online isn't perfect, but it is ridiculously convenient. If you can, use your online service for ordering staples and try to buy fresh local produce whenever you can. Explore your service's website carefully; some offer healthy prepared foods that might be good for busy work nights. Most sites will allow you to check previous orders, as most of us order the same things over and over. And if your family eats a lot of a certain food, you can buy in bulk so you're not putting the same nonperishable staples into your shopping cart every trip.

Big box stores. These stores certainly are a resource, so don't count them out for some of your regular food items. Nonperishable staples, such as olive oil, are much cheaper at big box stores, and good brands are available.

Cooperatives. Also known as co-ops, cooperatives are old-fashioned stores that are making a comeback. You pay a fee to join a co-op, then members band together to elect a board, which buys food and other items. These stores try to buy locally and offer many ethnic and health foods. They focus on sustainable agriculture and consumer education.

CSAs. Many cities now offer residents the opportunity to sign on with community farm organizations, known as Community Supported Agriculture (CSA), that will deliver a box of fresh food to our house every week throughout the year. These organizations are a great way to support farmers and enhance your family's diet.

But when all is said and done, most of us do our shopping at supermarkets. These large stores have come a long way since their inception decades ago. When shopping, it is important to remember that most supermarkets have been laid out with the refrigerated, most perishable, and healthier items at the perimeter. The best way to navigate the market is to shop first for all your nonperishable and nongrocery items (paper towels, toiletries, and so on) in the interior section of the store.

Then, after you have procured all your nonperishables, head toward the perimeter. Shop first for fruits and vegetables, then move to prepared items, such as deli meats and prepared meals. Then move on to the dairy section and finally to the fresh meat, seafood, and frozen items. This way the most perishable items spend minimal time out of refrigeration.

Shopping Efficiently Saves Money and Time

Make a list every time you go shopping. Make a master list of the items you buy regularly and copy it. Then plan out your meals for the week and note the foods you need. Add those foods to your master list and head to the store.

Stick to your list. This is the best way to save money and avoid waste. Grocery stores are very tempting places, but if you buy $20 worth of extra food every week, that adds up to more than $1,000 a year. Can you afford that?

Use coupons whenever possible. Many manufacturers and supermarket chains now offer coupons that will load directly onto your cell phone. But be sure you don't buy a product just because you have a coupon. Even with a coupon, if you throw away that product because you don't know how to use it or your family doesn't like it, you haven't saved any money.

Health Tip

Here's what it comes down to: Eat as many unprocessed foods as you can. You want to avoid processed foods because many of the nutrients have been stripped away, and unhealthy ingredients like food dyes, fake fats and sugars, and preservatives have been added. Eat until you're satisfied, then stop. Keep healthy foods around the house for snacking: carrot and celery sticks, fruit, yogurt, whole grain crackers, popcorn, and dark chocolate.

Helpful Tip

If you must drive half an hour or more to the grocery store, or plan to make stops on the way home, put perishables like meat and dairy products into an insulated cooler. These foods can't be held outside of the refrigerator longer than two hours, or they will spoil.

Shop during off-hours for the most efficient trip. Make sure you know the layout of the grocery store so you can shop quickly. This not only helps preserve perishables, it helps you avoid temptation.

Try not to take children with you when you shop. Grocery stores are laid out to be as tempting as possible to small children, with sugary cereals and bright products placed right at their eye level. If you must shop with children, try making a game out of the effort and give them tasks to complete. This will save your sanity and will teach them valuable skills.

Now that you know which items you need to start your cooking adventure, how to organize your kitchen and plan the pantry, and how to make a list and grocery shop, let's learn about the gear you'll need.

2

GEAR MUST-HAVES

Basic kitchen necessities belong in every home, but once you get beyond pots and pans and utensils, there are literally millions of products to make cooking easier and more fun. Buy the best quality preparation equipment you can afford.

A good knife set is essential to a good kitchen experience; and they must be kept sharp. Tools like basting brushes, graters, microplanes, and mandolines make food preparation easy. And when cooking is easy, you'll be encouraged to spend more time in the kitchen. You can find this equipment in grocery stores, in kitchenware shops, at hardware stores, online, at big box stores, and even at garage sales and antiques stores.

BASICS

The basics are the tools you need to cook most meals. With these basics you'll be able to fry an egg, cook pasta, make soups and stews, and even cook stove top and oven casseroles.

Pots and Pans

What type of cookware should you buy? It depends on what you cook. Glass cookware can break, but it goes from oven to microwave to table. Stainless is sturdy and dishwasher safe. Cast iron will last a lifetime, but it can be heavy. Anodized aluminum is sturdy but expensive. "Clad" pans, which have a combination of metals including copper, stainless, and aluminum, are excellent for all uses.

Nonstick cookware is a good choice, but you must be careful handling it. Always use wooden or silicone utensils to cook food in a nonstick pan; metal will scratch off the nonstick coating. Nonstick pans are perfect

Helpful Tip

Uncoated aluminum pots and pans are not suitable for cooking acidic liquids such as vinegar, citrus juices, most marinades, and tomatoes. The acids react with the aluminum and can cause discoloration and off-flavors in the foods. Use either nonaluminum pots and pans or aluminum cookware with a coated interior for acidic foods.

for cooking foods that are notorious for sticking: fish, eggs, potatoes, and pancakes.

Lift and examine the pots and pans before you buy to make sure they are comfortable. This is really a personal choice.

Look for pots and pans that are ovenproof. That means the handles can be placed in the oven or under the broiler without danger of melting. And make sure the handles are designed to stay cool on the stove top. Make sure that the pots and pans feel good in your hand; the weight should be evenly balanced and they shouldn't be too heavy for you to lift comfortably. Also, all pots should have sturdy, close-fitting lids.

Frying pans have sloped or flared sides and a large bottom. Several different frying pans are nice to have on hand. An 8-inch pan can double as an omelet pan. You'll probably use the 10-inch pan most often, and a 12-inch pan is useful for pan-frying large batches of food.

Saucepans are about 4 to 5 inches deep with straight sides. They are good for making, well, sauces! They may have one or two handles.

Sauté pans are sized in between skillets and saucepans, with sloping sides. They are made to keep the food in the pan while it's cooking. They're good for cooking rice and sautéing onions and garlic.

Skillets have low, straight sides and large bottoms. These pans usually have just one long handle. Their low sides allow for evaporation while cooking.

Stock pots are very large containers. They come in sizes that range from 8 quart to 16 quart and are used to boil pasta, make soups, and cook large quantities of liquid. Because most stockpots are deep and narrow, with straight sides and a well-fitting cove, they help soup to cook without losing too much liquid to evaporation.

Here are some other good pots to have in your kitchen:

Cast-iron pans are good for more than frying. Black and heavy, they are wonderful for all kinds of cooking. They hold the heat and distribute it evenly. Cast-iron pans are perfect for using in the broiler to brown food before serving. Always use a potholder when picking up a hot cast-iron pan, because the handles aren't heatproof. These pans must be seasoned before using. First, heat the pan; then remove it from the heat and add unflavored vegetable oil (not olive oil!). Let the oil soak in while the pan cools, and then wipe it off with paper towel. Repeat until the surface is nonstick. Once the pan is seasoned, don't wash it with detergent or you will have to go through the oiling process all over again. Just rinse the pan in hot water and wipe it dry with a paper towel after each use. You will have to reseason it occasionally.

Double boilers are wonderful for simmering sauces or soups over very low heat without burning them. They also are a great tool for cooking puddings and other delicate foods. Double boilers consist of two pieces: a bottom part that holds simmering water and a top part that holds the food. To use one, remember that the boiling water in the bottom pot should not touch the pot that sits on top.

Dutch ovens are made of heavy material and have a tall shape with a domed lid to hold a lot of food. Their shape makes them a very efficient cooking vessel. They're perfect for long-simmering dishes like braised meats, the Thanksgiving turkey, and soups and stews. Enamel-coated cast-iron dutch ovens let you cook acidic foods that would normally react with the uncoated iron. Use a dutch oven when cooking for a crowd, especially when you need to double or triple a recipe.

Roasting pans are large and heavy, with sides about 3 inches tall. They should come with sturdy attached handles. Look for roasting pans made of stainless steel, clad aluminum, or anodized aluminum. A wire rack that fits into the pan is a great way to cook large roasts and the Thanksgiving turkey.

Baking Dishes and Pans

Metal and most glass dishes and pans are excellent for baking, whether you're making a delectable dessert or a hearty entrée. Casseroles are baked in 2- to 3-quart ceramic or glass containers, whereas many pasta and cheese dishes are baked in rectangular glass pans measuring 9 x 13 inches. And a cookie sheet is an essential part of any kitchen.

Most baking dishes are multipurpose. When you acquire kitchen equipment, buy multipurpose pots, pans, muffin tins, and dishes. These can be purchased from manufacturer websites or at discount stores. Many upscale department stores and culinary stores offer this equipment, and they also have kitchen departments that offer cooking classes.

These are the basic baking dishes and pans you'll need:

Casserole dishes. Look for round and oval casserole dishes in 1-quart, 1½-quart, 2-quart, 3-quart, and 4-quart sizes. They should come with sturdy lids that fit the casseroles tightly. Casseroles can be made of ceramic or stainless steel. Bake egg dishes, one-dish meals, stratas, and casseroles in these pans.

Cookie sheets. Many foods can be cooked on cookie sheets, from pizzas to cookies. You should have cookie sheets both with and without sides. The sheets with sides, which are about 1 inch high, are called jelly roll pans, because the thin cake for jelly rolls is baked in them.

Glass baking dishes. These dishes are round, square, and rectangular. They usually have built-in handles on two sides. Some Pyrex will break if heated to 450°F. These dishes usually don't come with lids, but are perfect for making lasagna and other casseroles.

Specialty pans. Angel food pans, also known as tube pans, are round and tall with a cone that extends up the center. This cone helps hot air circulate around the center of the cake so it bakes evenly. Bundt pans are like tube pans but are scalloped for a pretty presentation when the cake is unmolded. These pans are made of aluminum or coated aluminum.

Measuring Tools

Measuring tools include measuring cups and spoons and a scale. Measuring is critical in baking; it's less critical in cooking. When you are adding broth to your stew, a half cup more or less doesn't make much difference. But when you are baking a cake, an ounce of flour, baking powder, or sugar, more or less, can mean failure. Learning how to measure ingredients properly is an important part of cooking.

Don't use coffee cups or regular tableware to measure ingredients because they're not accurate. Coffee cups or teacups are not measuring tools; they vary in size and there's no way to know if you're adding ½ or ⅔ cup to the recipe. Teacups can range from 5 to 6 ounces, while coffee cups range from 6 to 10 ounces.

Always have at least two sets of measuring cups and spoons on hand. Then you can drop them into soapy water or the dishwasher as you use them. You'll need measuring cups and spoons for dry and liquid measuring. For dry ingredients, the cups are straight sided with a handle. For wet ingredients, the cup is made of tempered glass with the measurements marked on the side. And there's a new type of glass measuring cup that lets you measure by looking straight down into the cup.

The measuring tools you'll need include the following:

Dry measuring cups are used to measure flour, chopped fruits and vegetables, granulated and brown sugar, cheese, shortening, peanut butter, pasta, rice, and grains. When measuring flour or sugar with dry measuring cups, spoon the ingredients into the cup, overfilling it. (The one exception to this rule is brown sugar; it must be firmly packed into the measuring cup.) Then use the back of a knife and level off the top so that the ingredient is perfectly even with the top of the cup. If the recipe calls for sifted flour, sift it first in a sieve or sifter, *then* measure. Be sure to use the knife again to scrape off the extra flour. You should have, at mini-

mum, ¼-, ⅓-, ½-, and 1-cup measuring cups. Look for nested measuring cups to save space. Stainless steel will last longer than plastic, and you can use the steel cups to melt small quantities of butter and shortening on the stove top.

Liquid measuring cups are specially formulated to measure, well, liquids. They are made of Pyrex glass, with cups, ounces, and milliliters marked on the side. To measure liquids, stoop down so your eye is level with the cup. Pour in liquid until the liquid reaches the desired level. These cups are available in 1-, 2-, and 4-cup sizes. You can also find 8-cup glass measuring cups.

Measuring spoons are made of plastic or metal. Plastic measuring spoons are kept together by a plastic ring. Metal spoons are kept nested by a metal ring. Many cooks detach them for easy use. If you keep them attached, you have to clean them all even if you only use one. So detach and store them in a ziplock bag. Measuring spoons will give you a more accurate measurement than flatware spoons. You need spoons that measure ⅛-, ¼-, ½-, and 1 tea-spoon, along with a tablespoon measure.

Scales, whether manual or digital, help in measuring and controlling portion sizes. When baking, measuring ingredients by weight is most accurate and will give you the best results. High-tech scales can have nutritional content of the food you are weighing programmed into them. You can add up to 1,000 foods to the programs in these dietary computer scales. You can also record food intake and keep track of total calories.

EXTRAS

You'll probably need some extra gear beyond the basics, depending on what you cook the most. Some machines are simple, perform their tasks well, and actually improve time management in the kitchen.

Many of the gadgets you see in gourmet cooking stores are not absolutely necessary, but they are fun. When looking for kitchen gadgets, think about the foods you like to eat every day. Do you eat a lot of salad? You'll probably need a colander and a salad spinner in your kitchen. Sieves and colanders are great for rinsing fruit and vegetables. Think about what you cook and look through a kitchenware catalog to see what's available to make preparing those foods easier.

These are some extras you may want in your kitchen:

Colanders. A large colander is excellent for washing spinach and lettuce. It's easy to put the colander in a large pot of cold water and swish lettuce around to remove the dirt. When you remove the colander from the water, the leaves will be clean. Colanders that can stand in the sink are ideal for draining cooked pasta, beans, and legumes. They are also used to drain frozen fruits and vegetables, and to wash produce like lettuce, tomatoes, and grapes.

Fat separator. This gadget is useful if you make a lot of soups, sauces, and pan gravies. You just pour the liquid left over after braising or stewing into the container. Let it stand for 10 to 15 minutes, then the fat will float to the surface so you can pour it

off. Some gadgets have a spout on the bottom to drain out the liquid, leaving the fat behind.

Multi-event timer. When more than one dish is being prepared at the same time, a multi-event timer can be very handy. It allows you to monitor separate cooking tasks of varying lengths at the same time. One dial can time a dish that takes a long time to cook, while another dial can be used to time another dish that doesn't take as long. Each timer has its own audible alert to let the cook know when time is up. Pick a timer that's small enough so you can slip it into an apron pocket. Some timers come with thermometers, so you can place food in the oven, set the final temperature, and the timer will beep when that temperature is reached.

Oil thermometer or candy thermometer. An oil thermometer is a precision instrument that helps ensure successful frying. Professional chefs have used instant-read thermometers for years, and now they are widely available. You might also try a chef's thermometer fork. Stick the fork into the cooked item and get an instant temperature reading on the handle. Manual oil thermometers clip to the rim of pots. They are calibrated to measure the wide range of heat required when cooking with oil. They measure temperatures from 100°F to 400°F. Candy thermometers are made for making candies and jellies. Any candy is made by concentrating sugar syrup so it will form a structure.

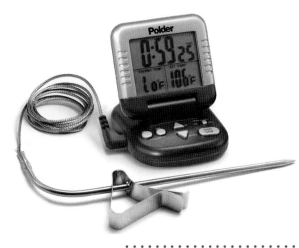

Panini press. A panini press literally presses a sandwich together as it grills, creating a magical transformation. It melds flavors, compressing them to the point of total flavor integration. If you love grilled sandwiches, get a panini press. All you do is put a sandwich in the press and close it. In a few minutes you'll have a beautifully browned sandwich with melted cheese and super crisp bread. Many cooks are now buying panini makers because they can make a huge grilled sandwich and then cut it into snack-size pieces. If you get serious about your panini making, get yourself a double-sided, folding electric panini grill.

Salad spinners. These clever inventions use centrifugal force to spin water off the leaves. After you wash your greens, spin them as dry as possible. Drain off the water in the bottom of the container and spin the greens again for good measure. If you are storing the greens, wrap them in paper towels and then place them in a plastic bag. Packaged this way, greens will stay crisp in the refrigerator for several days.

> ## Helpful Tip
>
> Clutter is the hallmark of an inefficient kitchen. Too many machines and tools choke the work space and hinder preparation. Try to keep counters as clear as you can. And learn how to use knives before you invest in a mandoline, garlic press, nut chopper, or food processor.

Strainers or sieves. Keep a long-handled fine-mesh strainer handy for removing solids from broths and clear sauces. You'll need a medium-mesh strainer, preferably one that can balance over a pot or sink, to drain water from noodles and for straining large bones and poultry carcasses from stock. And a fine sieve can be used for making a puree. Push berries or tomatoes through a sieve to remove seeds. For the longest wear, look for stainless steel, enamel-coated, or rust-resistant strainers. To keep particles from drying in the mesh, clean strainers with a brush or nylon scrubber immediately after use. Sieves also are excellent for sifting flour and dry ingredients.

Wok. Made of various materials, from cast iron to carbon steel and stainless steel, woks come in two different shapes: either with a round bottom or a flat bottom. The main advantage of a round bottom wok is in its "pooling" effect; liquids such as hot oils are not distributed across the entire cooking surface but remain in one small area. Foods can then be maneuvered into or out of the oil as needed. The same principle is at work when stir-frying—ingredients that are already cooked can be pushed aside, preventing overcooking. A flat bottom wok is a good compromise between a traditional wok and a frying pan—foods can still be distributed or pushed out of the way as needed.

UTENSIL KNOWLEDGE

Good utensils are like extensions of your hands. They have to be comfortable and easy to use and must be sturdy. Hold them in your hand before you buy. A good quality utensil will last for many years; you don't want to buy something flimsy. There's nothing more frustrating than stirring a thick frosting or batter and watching the handle snap off the spatula.

Take time to browse through a kitchenware store or a well-equipped grocery store. There are lots of specialty utensils that you may want to buy if it will make your cooking chores easier. Not everyone needs a shrimp deveiner or an egg slicer, but if you do, don't feel guilty about buying one.

These are the utensils you need:

General Utensils

Can openers are essential. The electric models take up valuable space and are difficult to clean. These days there are many can openers that have a "safe edge" or branded "safe-cut" can openers that do not leave behind a razor-sharp lid or can top for you to cut yourself on. Seek these out. Be sure your can opener and can top are clean before you open the can. Always clean your can opener with an abrasive sponge, dish soap, and hot water.

Cutting boards are essential, unless, of course, you want to ruin your counter (or your knives). Butcher-block cutting boards are beautiful. Prop them on the counter as kitchen art. Cutting boards in solid-surface countertop materials like Corian and Silestone have heft and are easy to clean. For lighter weight cutting boards, hard, molded synthetic materials can be found in decorative shapes and colors and washed in the dishwasher. Shop for a package of multicolored flexible silicone cutting mats that can be washed and rolled up for storage.

There has been a lot of back and forth about the sanitation of cutting boards over the last few years. Some say that plastic boards are much safer than wooden boards because they can't harbor bacteria, but others say the opposite is true. Here are the important considerations when buying a cutting board (or boards): Is the board large enough to hold what you need? Is it too large to store or so heavy that you need a helper to lift or clean it? Will it comfortably fit in the sink you use for cleanup? Discard any cutting boards that have large cracks, and always clean and sanitize your board between uses to kill all lingering bacteria.

Instant-read thermometers are essential tools to keep your food safe. This type of thermometer is inserted into meats (and breads and cakes, too, if you want to be very precise in your baking) and gives you an accurate temperature reading in a few seconds. Meat doneness tests are precise. Never serve underdone meat.

Spoons and ladles come in handy when cooking. Metal, wooden, and plastic spoons, some with long handles, are recommended. There are various types of spoons for baking. Sturdy stainless steel spoons with a wide bowl are the most basic. Slotted spoons are helpful for lifting marinating foods out of a liquid or cubed pineapple from a can. Wooden spoons are wonderful for stirring stiff batters and working with hot mixtures on the stove top. Teaspoons, coffee spoons, and iced tea spoons can all be used to garnish foods and for serving.

Ladles are different. The bowl is larger, deeper, and wider and attached to the handle at a perpendicular angle. One-piece ladles are sturdier than those with an attached handle. Metal and plastic ladles can be used to scoop up everything from pasta sauce to lobster bisque. A slotted ladle can be used to lift out food without any of the cooking liquid.

Spatulas and turners are useful when cooking fish, pancakes, chicken, beef, pork, vegetables—just about everything! Spatulas are used to move cookies and cakes, to scrape down the sides of a mixing bowl, and to frost cookies and cakes. Buy round and square spatulas for moving food, as well as a plastic one for working on nonstick equipment. Spatulas for scraping should be sturdy with a well-attached handle and firm bowl. And narrow, straight, and offset spatulas smooth frostings while keeping your fingers away from the surface. A small spatula is useful for turning crepes and omelets.

Plastic spatulas are more versatile than metal ones, as metal spatulas can't be used in nonstick pans. And buy some heatproof spatulas for making risotto and sauces. They can withstand heat

BUDGET TIP

When buying stainless steel utensils, look for those made of 18/10 or 18/8 steel. The numbers refer to the percentage of chromium and nickel used to make the metal. The first number is chromium, used for strength. The second is nickel, used for shine. If the utensil isn't marked, it's probably 18/0, which is a lower quality. Avoid these tools, since they may not stand up to repeated use.

up to 450°F. The extra-wide metal fish spatula, called the fish slice, is a handy tool. Because of its width, the fish slice can easily turn fish over to cook on the other side. When the fish is done, this tool can lift up the entire piece of fish without breaking it.

Tongs really are extensions of your hands. You can use them to toss pasta or a salad, to turn bacon as it's cooking on the griddle, or to rearrange kabobs on the grill. Look for spring-loaded tongs that automatically open when you close them. Otherwise, you'll need to pry the tongs open to use them.

Whisks are essential for beating egg whites and making smooth sauces, gravies, and puddings. They are made of wire, silicone, or nylon. Whenever you make a white sauce by stirring liquid into flour cooked in butter, you need a whisk to prevent lumps. There are several types of whisks: ball whisks, balloon whisks, and combination whisks. Balloon whisks are the bulbous type we all know. Ball whisks are made of long strands of metal with tiny balls at the end. And combination whisks are balloon whisks with loose balls inside, made to thoroughly mix heavy or thick mixtures. Wire whisks come in many sizes, from tiny to huge. Large whisks shouldn't be too big or they can become unwieldy. Look for whisks about 8 inches long. Small whisks can be very handy when making a small amount of sauce. If you have an old hand mixer that breaks, save the whisk beaters.

There are other general utensils, too, like nut choppers, swivel-bladed peelers, microplane graters, spice grinders, and specialty tools like cherry pitters, strawberry hullers, apple corers, and honey dippers. Choose the ones you need based on the types of food you handle most often.

Knives and Graters

Knives and graters are essential in any kitchen. With a knife, you can reduce nuts to powder, bone a chicken, and chop any produce from apples to zucchini. Good quality knives will last a long time with proper care. Always buy the best you can afford. Knife sets are often affordable and come with a knife block that will store the knives safely. Don't store knives in a drawer because their blades can become dull—and reaching into a drawer to get a knife is a safety hazard.

Full-tang knives are forged in one piece, with a metal strip that extends into the handle. The most important thing about a knife is that it's comfortable in your hand. If the handle is too thick or too round or the blade is too long or heavy, it won't be an effective tool. Go to the store and hold the knives in your hand. You can even bring a small cutting board to more realistically test the motions of cutting. You need a chef's knife, a serrated bread knife, several 4- to 6-inch paring knives, and an 8-inch utility knife. A steel or knife sharpener is necessary, too. It may seem contradictory, but a sharp knife is a safe knife. Dull knives can easily slip and cut you instead of the food. For more about knives and knife safety, see Chapter 5.

Apple corers are inexpensive tools that make working with apples easy. Place the tool over the peeled apple and simply press down to make nice slices. It works like a cookie cutter.

Box graters are essential if you don't have a food processor. And for many recipes, the box grater works just as well and is easier to control. Use it to grate cheese, carrots, onions, and potatoes. Each side has a function. One wide side grates; the other wide side slices; one small side scrapes; and the other is a mini grater.

Garlic presses can be a valuable tool if you use a lot of minced garlic. It can mince a head of garlic in seconds, and since the mince is so even and fine, the garlic flavor is spread evenly throughout the dish. Look for a self-cleaning garlic press, with little pins that clean out the tiny holes.

Mandolines have long been used in professional kitchens but are just recently gaining favor with some home cooks. While not a necessity, a mandoline makes slicing much easier. It makes julienning vegetables or making uniform slices simple and quick. It's great for making homemade french fries, potato chips, and waffle fries. If you are making potato chips, use a mandoline set at $\frac{1}{16}$ inch. If you are slicing for scalloped potatoes, use a mandoline set to cut potatoes $\frac{1}{8}$-inch thick. A mandoline is sharp and dangerous. Understand its functions thoroughly before you use it. Some have handles for safety. Look for a "food holder" that will protect your fingers from the blade.

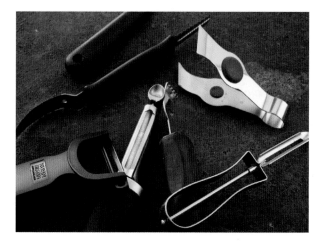

Vegetable peelers are specialty tools that easily remove the peel from potatoes, carrots, parsnips, and other root vegetables. Get a swivel-bladed peeler that will turn as you work with the food. The peeler makes an excellent cheese "shaver," too. Try it with Parmesan and peel some nice curls over pasta. Your peeler also does an excellent job shaving vegetables into thin strips. Try shaving carrots or apples into a salad.

Wisps of chocolate over a dessert are such an elegant way to present your sweet creations. Try using your peeler to shave chocolate, too.

Zesters, microplanes, or rasps make fine zesting of oranges or lemons easy. The "microplane" has been adapted from the woodworker's bench to the kitchen. Rasps are woodworker's tools; find them in hardware stores. Zesters have tiny holes that make very fine citrus zest. Constantly turn the fruit as it is rubbed against the tool. A small amount of zest is added to dishes at the end of the cooking process for a bright citrus flavor.

SMALL APPLIANCES

While not every appliance is needed for a gourmet kitchen, every kitchen does need some small appliances, which include food processors, blenders, and electric mixers. When you buy a new appliance, whether it's a dual contact indoor grill or an immersion blender, be sure that you read the manufacturer's instruction booklet from front to back before you use it. The booklet has lots of safety information, and there are usually some easy recipes that will get you started using that appliance.

Small appliances are those you can pick up by hand and move around the kitchen. You may want to store them in a cupboard if you don't use them every day, but if you have a lot of counter space, they can look really nice and make your kitchen look professional.

Mixers

You can, of course, mix any recipe by hand. My maternal grandmother made divinity, one of the most complicated candies, by beating the meringue with a wooden spoon! But a hand mixer, stand mixer, blender, and food processor make baking much easier. There are literally hundreds of types and styles of mixers and processors on the market, at every price point. You can find these appliances at big-box retailers, baking supply stores, grocery stores, and hardware stores.

Buy the best-quality appliances you can afford. The prices of many of these products have declined in recent years; it's possible to buy a good-quality hand mixer for $30 or less. It's always a good idea to check out reviews and ratings of appliances at online sites like www.ConsumerReports.org and www.Epinions.com. Professional testing is used as the standard at the former site, and regular users rate lots of products at the latter. These reviews and ratings will help you find the right small appliance for your kitchen.

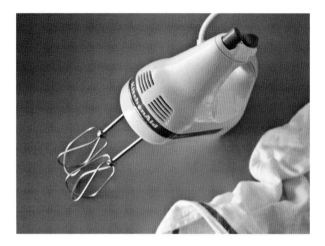

Handheld electric mixer. The handheld electric mixer can be used for many kitchen chores. Use it to mash potatoes, make fluffy frostings, and beat eggs for omelets. Handheld mixers can't knead dough, but they can easily mix cake and cookie batters. Hand mixers work well for almost every kitchen need and are much less expensive than stand mixers. Get a mixer with several sets of beaters: the whisk for egg whites, the sturdier mixer for cake batters. Extra beaters, whisks, and flat beaters for your hand mixer increase its usability and let you make multiple recipes without stopping to wash the beaters.

Stand electric mixer. If you make lots of breads and cookies, you may want to invest in a stand mixer. It lets you do something else while the mixer does the work. With a stand mixer and several bowls and mixing paddles, you can quickly make several batches of dough. These powerful machines come in many varieties. And because they are an investment, make sure you take good care of them. Buy more bowls and beaters for your stand mixer so you don't have to stop and clean a lot. Besides the obvious baking applications, many stand mixers have myriad attachments. Meat grinders, grain mills, and slicing and dicing blades are just a few of the possible options.

BUDGET TIP

Maintain appliances to extend their usable life. Always clean them thoroughly after each use. Never immerse them in water. Clean blenders and food processors by rinsing out the bowl, adding a drop of dishwashing soap and water, and whirling away. Wipe down appliances with a damp cloth and dry thoroughly so they're ready for the next use.

Food Processors, Blenders, and Grinders

Food processors knead bread, julienne vegetables, whip egg whites, and make pie crust. Just make sure you learn how to use the beast properly and keep those sharp blades away from your fingers. The first commercial food processor was made in France under the name Robot Coupe. This brand still exists today and is an industry leader in the commercial sector. There are many others brands for home cooks found in many retail shops.

Today's food processors come in many different shapes, colors, and sizes. Most have a slew of interchangeable blades and feeder tubes that let you perform a huge variety of kitchen tasks, which, in turn, let you have more fun in the kitchen. If you prepare large quantities of food, a full-size food processor is probably for you. But if you only make small quantities, think about buying a mini food processor. This smaller appliance can be very versatile.

Large food processors can make everything from pureed soup to chocolate mousse. The capacity of large food processors ranges from 8 to 14 cups. Some large food processors have mini bowls to chop and mince smaller amounts of food without dirtying the big bowl.

Slicing and dicing is the real "meat and potatoes" food processor chore. The slicing blades let you make perfect thin slices of any vegetable—great for making soups. The grater attachment makes short work of grating cheeses for nachos or mac and cheese. The julienne blade lets you cut thin strips (known as matchsticks) in a fraction of the time a knife would take. It saves fingertips, too!

Food processors are equipped with blades that have different uses. The basic grinding blade also chops, minces, and purees. It works well with carrots, onions, and nuts. It is an alternative to a blender for pureeing soups and smoothing out sauces. The grating blade works from the top down, while the basic blade works from the base up. It grates potatoes, carrots, cabbage, and cheese, among other things. The slicing blade works well on vegetables, such as carrots and cucumbers, for salads. It also slices potatoes very efficiently.

These machines can also whip sauces and vinaigrettes together (known as emulsifying). Make homemade mayonnaise for your sandwiches in the food processor that blows store-bought away. Dips such as hummus and vegetable purees come out silky smooth when made in a food processor.

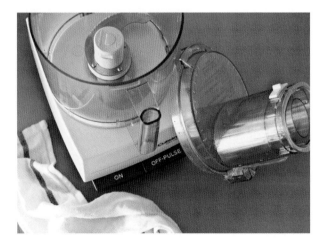

> ### BUDGET TIP
>
> The food processor is an amazing dough kneader. If you make a lot of bread, you don't need to buy a bread machine or a large stand mixer if you have a food processor. Pasta dough is a snap in the food processor well.

Mini food processors are much less expensive than larger food processors. They range from 2 to 4 cups. With a mini processor, you can chop an onion, mince garlic, puree beans, and chop carrots, bell peppers, and mushrooms. Even the mini processors have feed tubes and shredding and slicing discs.

In fact, you may wish to experiment first with a mini food processor before buying a big food processor, as the smaller appliance can perform the same basic functions at a fraction of the cost.

Blenders have many uses, from pureeing soups to making sauces and pesto. There are several types of blenders, including the most common variable-speed blender. These blenders have buttons for a wide variety of speeds, from puree to liquefy and everything in between. Many home blenders come with extra attachments, such as juicers, which can make the blender more versatile. There are new generation blenders with "dual wave action" that work much better than old-style blenders.

A bar blender is a souped-up yet simplified home blender and is the best tool for blending sturdy purees and ice for frozen drinks. Bar blenders have stronger motors and often utilize a stainless steel "pitcher" as opposed to the heavy tempered glass that most home blenders have. Bar blenders are available at restaurant-supply stores and retail shops and come in a variety of sizes and configurations. Look for one that will fit your storage and cooking needs.

Immersion blenders are a relative newcomer to the home kitchen. Professional cooks have been using them for decades. Known as Burr Mixers or burr sticks, immersion blenders are made by many different professional equipment suppliers. The beauty of an immersion blender is that it can be immersed into a pot of hot soup or sauce. This

Helpful Tip

Be very careful of food processor blades; they are razor sharp. Choose a processor that has dishwasher-safe blades and attachments. Be careful where you load the blades in the dishwasher too. If you don't have a dishwasher, wash the blade carefully with soapy water and dry well before returning it to the machine. Regularly clean the food processor casing and inspect the cord before each use.

Helpful Tip

Be careful when pureeing hot liquids in the blender. They will expand tremendously when blended. Only puree hot liquids with the blender half full. Use a dry towel to cover the top, and hold it down with your hand. Use a slow speed, pulsing to blend. For increased safety, let the liquid cool to room temperature before blending well before returning it to the machine.

minimizes the risk of burns from the splash back that can happen when you place hot liquid in a blender. The bottom part contains a blade that will puree soups and sauces in seconds.

Immersion blenders are best for pureeing hot items, such as soups and sauces, especially if you are going to serve the food right away. They can be dangerous, however; the blades are exposed and very sharp. Always be careful when using one. Some immersion blenders come with a micro–food processor attachment. This is handy for chopping small items like two or three garlic cloves. Clean your immersion blender in the dishwasher or by running the blade in soapy water.

Peppermills, coffee grinders, and spice grinders may become indispensible in your kitchen. A good peppermill is essential. Freshly ground pepper tastes nothing like

preground, store-bought pepper. Always use the real deal. Freshly ground coffee can be an amazing and everyday treat. An electric coffee grinder can do double duty as a spice grinder, but you may want separate appliances, since spices can flavor your coffee. Some manufacturers are now producing grinders made for both coffee and spices.

You can clean a grinder two ways. To remove any residual coffee grounds, simply wipe the grinder out with a dry cloth. To clean away any residual spices, add 1 tablespoon uncooked white rice and grind up. Throw away the ground rice. Any residual scent or flavor will be absorbed and taken away by the rice.

Specialized Cooking Equipment (Grills, Slow Cookers)

Some specialized cooking equipment does belong in most kitchens. The dual-contact grill or sandwich press has become one of the best-selling cooking gadgets of all time. George Foreman is one brand of this indoor grill. Slow cookers have transformed the way many people cook. Put food in this appliance, turn it on, and come back hours later to delicious stews, soups, and casseroles.

Dual-contact grills are modeled after Italian-style sandwich presses, and they can do a lot more than make grilled cheese sandwiches. Dual contact indoor grills are countertop appliances that cook food on both sides at the same time. They are effective for grilling thinner pieces of meat and fish with little mess and in a short time. The large versions of these grills can cook enough food for four to six people at once. Grease and fat drain off, so the food is healthy too. It also has a grilled flavor without the hassle of dealing with charcoal or gas in an outdoor grill. Follow the directions for use and cleaning of your particular grill. Watch the food carefully the first few times you use it, because you'll need to get used to the timing. And be sure to use the extra equipment used to hold the fat that drains off the food as it cooks.

Toaster ovens do more than just make toast. They are great for snacks, such as crostini; for making fast top-browned, toasted sandwiches; for melting cheese on omelets, and for toasting nuts. They are also great for reheating single-serving leftovers. Pick a toaster oven that is sturdy and heats evenly. Look at ratings on websites like www.ConsumerReports.org and www.epinions.com. Use your toaster oven for baking small quantities, browning, and, of course, toasting.

When you have several people at breakfast, most toaster ovens will hold four split English muffins at one time, or four to six pieces of bread.

Coffeemakers are considered by most cooks to be essential to life, let alone the kitchen. They can do more than just brew coffee. You can heat up punch or juices for winter parties. Put some spices in the basket that holds the ground coffee and fill the reservoir with juice. Turn it on for hot mulled cider. Electric teakettles are also a great appliance because of their speed and convenience. The water comes to a boil in an amazingly short time, and there is no need to discard excess water in the pot; simply use it later.

MIDSIZE APPLIANCES

While these kitchen items are more expensive than a mini food processor or toaster oven, they will help save you time in the kitchen. They take up space and need to be cared for just like large appliances, but they really can help make cooking easier.

Do your research before buying any appliance. Be sure to check ratings and read up on the advantages and disadvantages of each. Some appliances come with an Energy Star rating, which will not only save you money in utility charges but will also benefit the environment. With so many models out there, you have a lot of choices, so don't buy without first doing your homework.

Microwave ovens help with faster prep times. They range from simple counter appliances that basically pop popcorn, to over-the-range installed ovens with lights and vent fans. Microwave ovens cook by making molecules vibrate, creating heat in the food. The waves the oven uses are radio waves and are not radioactive. The microwave can cook vegetables in minutes. It melts butter, defrosts frozen foods, makes popcorn, and can rewarm foods beautifully.

Every microwave oven has hot spots and cold spots. That just means there are areas where the microwaves concentrate, and areas they miss. That's why all microwave recipes call for turning and stirring the food while it cooks.

Microwave recipes usually call for covering foods to avoid spills and the small "explosions" that can sometimes occur as food cooks. Always "vent" a corner of the plastic wrap you use to cover dishes so steam and pressure don't build up. And standing time, which lets the heat move evenly through the food, is important. Always let microwave-cooked food stand on a solid surface (*not* a rack) for the time specified in the recipe so the food finishes cooking. Follow cooking, covering, stirring, venting, and standing times to the letter for best results.

Pressure cookers have come a long way from the unwieldy old-fashioned appliances with a stopcock and tendency to explode. The newer pressure cookers have lots of built-in safety features and can make a complicated soup in minutes rather than hours. Electronic pressure cookers don't even need a stove top. Older pressure cookers had to be cooked over high or medium heat on a burner, so it was difficult to regulate temperature and pressure. The pressure that builds up inside a pressure cooker brings the liquid to a higher temperature than the boiling point of 212°F. This is what cooks the food more quickly, usually reducing cooking time by 60 to 70 percent.

The electronic pressure cooker is very easy to use. You just fill it up, choose the pressure (high, about 9 psi, or low, about 5 psi) and time and turn it on. These appliances have self-locking lids and automatic pressure release. The lid can't be opened until the pressure is reduced to a safe level through the release of steam.

Whichever type of pressure cooker you use, be sure to follow the manufacturer's instructions to the letter. Always use care around the pressure cooker, as steam can burn. And remember that timing is important when cooking in a pressure cooker. Vegetables can overcook in the time it takes some meats to cook, so follow recipes and instructions carefully.

One of the best things about making soup in a pressure cooker is how it cooks dried beans and peas quickly and evenly. Even after overnight soaking, sometimes these products don't get soft enough with regular cooking methods. The pressure cooker eliminates that problem.

Helpful Tip

Not all glass is microwave safe. To check if a container is microwave safe or not, fill it with water. Microwave on high power for one minute, then let stand for one minute. If the container is hot but the water isn't, don't use it to microwave food. Never use glass or ceramic dishes with metallic trim or decorations because they can cause arcing or sparks.

LARGE APPLIANCES

Every kitchen needs large appliances. The refrigerator and oven, with a stove top attached or a separate stove top, are the basics. You could also add a microwave with a built-in fan to help remove cooking odors from the kitchen. And a stand-alone freezer is a good choice if you plan to freeze lots of foods, or like to keep frozen foods on hand just in case.

Ovens are a kitchen necessity, and should be kept clean and well maintained. They also must be properly calibrated for best results. Over-baked and underbaked foods are usually a result of inaccurate oven temperature. To check, preheat your oven for 15 minutes, then check the thermometer temperature. If the temperature on the dial and the temperature on the thermometer don't match up, have the oven serviced.

You can usually calibrate some ovens yourself, with some small adjustments of the controls. Check your oven instructions for information. Do not try to service any oven components yourself. Recalibrate your oven every few months to guarantee that it's working properly. Even a few degrees' variation can affect recipes.

Most recipes are baked on the center rack of the oven, right in the middle, so heat circulates around the pan or cookie sheet. Unless you're using a convection oven, bake one cookie sheet or one pan at a time.

Gas ovens start by igniting a pilot light. The timing for gas ovens is the same as for electric. There is one difference: Gas ovens introduce water vapor into the oven cavity, which can reduce browning. Gas stove tops heat food more quickly and are easier to control than electric burners. When you turn them off, they go off. Gas ovens may bake less evenly than electric ovens, so you may need to rotate the food during baking.

Electric ovens are drier than gas ovens and bake more evenly. If you're designing a kitchen, you may want to choose electric wall ovens and a gas stove top. Since electric ovens are just plugged into the wall and vented, they're easier to install.

Induction burners use electromagnetic induction to heat certain metals. These burners can be used only with stainless steel cookware; they will not work with copper or aluminum. The heat is transferred only to the stainless cookware. The burners themselves do not become hot. This makes this type of stove top very safe! The heat transfers quickly, so a pot of water comes to a boil quickly.

Cleaning ovens doesn't have to be difficult. Newer ovens have self-cleaning features. Self-cleaning ovens work by heating to very high temperatures to burn off spills. Make sure to turn on the oven fan and crack a window when using this feature. Oven-cleaning products have improved in recent years, too. Look for organic or alternative products that use more gentle ingredients. Leave these products on overnight, then clean the next day for better results.

Helpful Tip

Don't buy pressure cookers at garage sales or consignment stores. There's no way to know if they can still be safely used. An accident can cause serious injuries. Everything about the pressure cooker must be in top condition, including the gaskets, vent tubes, seals, and stopcock.

Helpful Tip

Convection ovens are regular ovens with a fan. The fan moves hot air around the food so it cooks quickly and more evenly. If you bake a lot, a convection oven may be a good investment. Make sure that you reduce baking time if you use a convection oven, since foods cook more quickly. Some built-in microwave ovens are also convection ovens.

Refrigerators are also necessary in every kitchen and should be kept clean and be well functioning. Buy the largest refrigerator you can afford that fits your space. You may not need some of the bells and whistles like ice makers or cold water dispensers that are offered on many models. Do your research before you purchase this appliance.

Your refrigerator manual is your friend! It's important that you actually read the manual. Some refrigerators have drip pans that must be periodically emptied, and you must clean the refrigerator coils from time to time. Keep the manual in a cupboard near the refrigerator so you can refer to it as necessary.

Clean out the refrigerator once a week so you know what foods need to be used and replenished. Remove everything, check the use-by dates, throw away old food, and clean the shelves with soapy water. Clean your freezer every three to four months.

Stand-alone freezers are a real luxury but enable you to prepare quick and easy meals. Modern freezers are energy efficient and relatively modest in cost compared to other large appliances. But even if you have only the freezer attached to your refrigerator, you can stock a great selection of foods that will help you get food on the table in a flash.

If space is at a premium in your kitchen, you could put a stand-alone freezer in a spare room, a closet, the basement, or laundry room—as long as it's temperature-controlled.

Pick your freezer according to the size of your family and what you intend to freeze. If you raise your own meat or buy a side of beef, you'll need a large freezer regardless of your family size; you may even need two! Each cubic foot of freezer space stores about 35 pounds of food. For most families, 5 to 6 cubic feet of freezer space per person is recommended.

Remember the quality of food can only be as good as it was when you froze it. Freezing doesn't kill the microorganisms that cause food spoilage; it just stops their growth until the food is thawed. Freezing spoiled meat, for example, will not make it safe to eat.

To freeze food most efficiently, follow these rules:

- **Cool it!** Always cool food before placing it in the freezer. Putting hot food into the freezer will warm everything around it, which reduces the food's lifespan and can cause bacterial growth. It's also desirable to freeze food as rapidly as possible for best quality. Place packages to be frozen against the freezer walls or on shelves in the coldest part of the freezer. Don't try to freeze too much food at one time. You can add 2 to 3 pounds of food per cubic foot of freezer space over the course of 24 hours. Check your freezer manual for its specifications. Keep the temperature set at 0°F or below. An open container of baking soda will help absorb any odors.

Helpful Tip

Freezer burn occurs when frozen food is improperly covered. This isn't a food safety issue; it's a quality issue. The food literally becomes dehydrated and unpalatable. It can develop off-flavors due to oxidation. Wrap foods well in containers and wrapping labeled for freezer use to avoid freezer burn.

- **Keep it full** to help your freezer work most efficiently. But don't pack food tightly. There should be about an inch of airspace around each package so the cold air can circulate. Fill empty spots in the freezer with milk jugs or 2-liter pop bottles filled with clean water. In case of a power failure, these also help keep the freezer cold. The water in the containers can be used for emergency drinking or cooking water, but be sure to melt and boil it first. And defrost manual-defrost freezers when ¼ inch of frost has built up on the sides.
- **Organize it!** No packages of mystery meat are allowed! Wrap and label everything you put in the freezer and keep a notebook with a running list of what the appliance contains. When you use a food from the freezer, cross it out in the notebook. If it's a staple, make a note on your grocery list to replace it.
- **Wrap, label, and rotate!** Use freezer wrap, paper, or bags; ordinary wraps and foils aren't thick enough to protect the food from the harsh freezer environment. You must mark and label every item that goes into your freezer. Regular labels may not stick in the freezer, so use freezer labels or mark the package itself with a permanent marker or grease pencil that won't come off when the package thaws.

While food will be safe in the freezer for a long time, quality and flavor decline. Rotate older food to the front and top of the freezer, where it's easily seen and used first. Use your notebook to keep track of the date food was frozen and the use-by date. As a general rule, use frozen food within one year. For specific dates, see Chapter 5. You can refreeze some foods, like phyllo dough or food that has been thoroughly cooked.

No matter how you package them, some foods don't freeze well. Leafy greens and vegetables with a high water content usually don't freeze well. Other foods freeze well when specially treated. Each cell of a fruit or vegetable contains water. When that water freezes, it expands and bursts the cell wall. This changes the texture of frozen produce, making it softer when thawed. Foods that are mostly water, like tomatoes and spinach, are not good candidates for freezing.

Freezing supplies. There are some supplies you need to properly prepare and store food in the freezer. Use freezer bags, not ordinary storage bags, and certainly not the package the food came in (unless it starts out frozen from the store!) for freezing, and use food-grade plastic bags, not garbage bags or recycled bread bags.

Hard-sided containers are better for liquid foods. Butcher or freezer paper needs special freezer tape to seal it. Don't use regular waxed paper, parchment paper, newspaper, or other papers. And remember that several small packages freeze better than one large one.

> ## Health Tip
>
> Vacuum sealed bags that thaw and warm to above 40°F can develop botulism, which is the most deadly type of food poisoning. The vacuum removes oxygen. Botulism spores grow in anaerobic (without oxygen) environments. Always thaw frozen vacuum-sealed bags in the refrigerator, and use or cook as soon as it's thawed.

Vacuum sealing can increase the lifespan of frozen foods. There are several easy-to-use and inexpensive vacuum sealers on the market today. Vacuum sealers suck air out of the bag and then use heat to make a tight seal. They help prevent freezer burn. Buy freezer, not storage, bags for your type of sealer and follow instructions.

GENERAL COOKING METHODS

3

There are several cooking methods you must understand before you can start cooking. None of them need special equipment; if you have the basics listed in Chapter 2, you can start cooking.

There are two basic kinds of cooking: dry heat and wet heat. Dry heat includes frying, sautéing, stir-frying, deep-frying, roasting, grilling, broiling, and baking. Wet heat cooking methods include the slow cooker, braising, poaching, steaming, boiling, and stewing.

Cooking is applying heat to food to change its characteristics. Vegetables become tender, fruits become soft, the protein in meat denatures, bacteria are killed, eggs become hard, cheeses melt—well, you get the idea! Once you've mastered these basic cooking methods, you can cook just about anything.

But before you can cook the food, it usually needs to be manipulated in some way. Marinating, breading, and other coatings add flavor and texture to cooked foods.

MARINADES, GLAZES, AND BREADING

Three techniques you will use again and again are marinating, glazing, and breading. Marinating adds flavor before the food even starts to cook. Glazing puts the finishing touch on many recipes. And many foods are breaded or crusted, coated with everything from flour to special bread crumbs before cooking to add a crisp crust and seal in the juices and flavor.

Marinating is soaking a raw food in a mixture of oil, seasoning, and an acid such as wine, vinegar, or lemon juice. A simple marinade is just oil, lemon juice or white wine, and flavorings. Flavorings can be everything from scallions or garlic to root vegetables such as carrots and celery.

You must marinate ingredients in a glass container or plastic bag instead of a metal bowl. Acidic ingredients react with metal, creating off-flavors in the marinating food.

Just about any food can be marinated. Beef and chicken marinate the longest, up to 24 hours. Pork can also marinate for 8 to 24 hours. Fish should only be marinated for a few hours. Vegetables and fruits marinate for the shortest amount of time; they don't really absorb many flavors, but for stir-frying and kabobs, a marinade can add flavor. Always marinate foods in the refrigerator.

Glazing finishes meats and vegetables. To glaze, apply a thick liquid to the food being cooked, adding flavor and a beautiful sheen. Some glazes are reduced, highly concentrated stocks. Glazes can be a simple coating of mustard or a more exotic combination of ingredients. Meats can also be coated with a sweet glaze made with honey, sugar, or mirin (sweet sake). A popular glaze for many meats and vegetables is made by combining honey and mustard.

Crusting or breading coats food that is fried, grilled, or baked. Bread crumbs or cornmeal are the basis of the crumb coating, which creates a golden and crispy finished product. Different seasonings can change the dish completely. When crusting meats, first coat in flour, then in beaten egg, and finally in cornmeal or bread crumbs before frying. The coating can be plain or made exotic with the addition of shredded coconut, curry powder, coriander, cumin, or chili powder.

FRYING

Frying means to cook food quickly in oil until the food is browned and crisp. There are several different types of frying: panfrying, deep-frying, searing, sautéing, and stir-frying. Each uses a different method, a different amount of oil, and produces different results.

Panfrying is done in a large skillet with straight deep sides. A specialized frying thermometer will help you maintain an even temperature in non-electric frying pans. Foods qualify as panfried if the oil only covers them halfway. The food is turned during cooking. Always use a long-handled, sturdy spatula and handle the food with care so you don't splash oil as you turn. Any water or liquid will cause spattering, so stand back when you add food to hot oil. You can keep deep-fried or panfried food warm in a 200°F oven while you finish cooking all the food.

Electric skillets offer a temperature control for even panfrying. Cast-iron skillets can be used for panfrying, but they heat up and cool down slowly. The preferred fat for stir-frying and frying is peanut oil, which can withstand high heat without breaking down or burning. Peanut oil brings out the natural flavor of foods, rather than masking or adding to it. Good quality canola or vegetable oil are fine substitutes, especially if you're concerned about peanut allergies.

Deep-frying is when you cook foods in enough oil to cover them completely. Most deep-fried foods are cooked in 6 to 8 cups of oil or melted fat. Most deep-fried foods are done when they float and turn a deep golden brown.

A thermometer is an important tool for deep-frying. The temperature of the oil should be around 350°F to 375°F. Use a heavy, deep pot with two sturdy handles. A wire basket insert to hold the food is a good idea. If you do a lot of frying, you may want to purchase an electric deep-fryer, which is a deep electric pot with a wire frying basket. It has a temperature control, which helps you maintain an even frying temperature. Electric deep-fryers come in a variety of sizes for the home cook.

To deep-fry meats, doughnuts, and french fries, you'll need a very heavy pan with sides at least 3 inches deep. You can also use a deep-fryer. But never fry food in a pressure cooker; you're just asking for disaster. Add 4 to 6 cups of oil to the pan. Be sure that you leave at least 2 inches of headspace between the oil and the top of the pan to prevent spillover.

The best oils for frying and deep-frying have a high smoke point, such as canola, corn, peanut, and safflower oils. The smoke point is the temperature at which the oil starts to break down and develops off-flavors and toxins. It's also the point where the oil gets so hot it can burst into a flame. These are the smoke points for oils:

> ## Helpful Tip
>
> Deglazing the pan removes the natural glaze and browned bits that accumulate after panfrying and sautéing. Remove the food and add a liquid, such as wine or broth, to the hot pan. Scrape up any bits of food (called fond) as the liquid boils. This will produce a pan sauce.

- Butter: 350°F
- Canola oil: 400°F
- Corn oil: 450°F
- Lard: 400°F
- Olive oil: 400°F
- Peanut oil: 450°F
- Vegetable shortening: 350°F
- Sunflower oil: 450°F

The food you're going to fry must be completely dry before you add breading or battering. Pat it dry and roll it in flour or bread crumbs.

Remember that oil and water do not mix, so keep water away from the hot oil. When you remove food from the frying pan, place it on plenty of paper towels to drain off any excess fat. Keep the cooked food in a warm oven until all the food is done. This will keep the coating crispy.

Searing browns food quickly in a pan or under the broiler. This is done at the beginning of the cooking process to seal in the juices, add color to the finished dish, and develop the flavors in the food. Searing creates a caramelized exterior for great flavor and color. Be sure the pan is very hot before you add the oil. There should be only a thin film of oil in the pan, and it should be barely smoking. Do not crowd the pan when searing, or your product will steam instead of sear.

Sautéing is a versatile skill that every cook should learn. A sauté pan is made of tin or stainless steel–lined copper, heavy stainless steel, enamel-clad metal, or good-quality nonstick material. The sauté pan is not as deep as the frying pan. It can be substituted for a wok when stir-frying.

Aromatic vegetables are sautéed before adding them to soups, stews, and braises. Meats such as filet mignon and veal scallopine are sautéed or panfried. Delicate fish fillets and chicken breasts are cooked by sautéing.

Even when you use a nonstick pan, it's wise to add a bit of olive oil or nonstick spray when sautéing. The first step is to sear the food. Make sure the pan is hot and the oil is shimmering before you add the food.

To sauté, start by placing flour, salt, pepper, and herbs on a piece of waxed paper. Thoroughly dry the piece of meat, poultry, or fish to avoid making a gooey mess when you dip it in the flour mixture. Dip the food in the flour mixture, or layer it with flour, beaten egg, and bread crumbs. Heat the pan over medium-high heat. Add oil, butter, or nonstick spray and wait a few minutes to let it get hot. If you're using butter, wait until the butter has stopped foaming before adding the food, because then the butter will be at the correct temperature for sautéing.

Add the food, then leave it alone! Listen for the sizzle before lifting the food. When the meat releases easily from the pan, lift it for a peek. When you see that it's nicely golden on one side, turn it carefully with tongs or a spatula. At this point, turn the heat down to medium. Cooking time depends upon the type and thickness of the meat or fish.

Once you've finished sautéing and have removed the food, you'll see brown bits in the bottom of the pan. These nuggets of flavor are called fond and are the base for a sauce. To make sauce, add liquid to the pan. If you've cooked chicken, add ½ cup of chicken broth; if beef, add beef broth; if a lamb or veal chop, add chicken broth. With fish, add water or clam broth. Raise the heat to medium and simmer, stirring to incorporate the fond into the sauce. Season with pepper and your favorite herbs, pour over the food, and eat.

Stir-fry is the Asian cooking technique of frying small pieces of food quickly in very little fat in a wok over very high heat. You must constantly stir the ingredients for a proper stir-fry. The wok can steam, deep-fry, smoke, braise, and even bake—if an expert is at the helm.

Stir-frying requires high heat. A wok is the best pan to use, but a cast-iron pan or large skillet will work well too. The key is to not lose heat as the food cooks, ensuring a nice sear on meats and veggies that give stir-fried foods their smoky flavor.

Almost all stir-fries follow the same basic steps or stages. First, sauté onions and garlic in the oil; remove. Next, sear and briefly cook the meat. Take it out of the wok and set aside. Next, stir-fry the vegetables and add flavorings such as chile or black bean sauce .Then add the sauce components and put the meat back into the wok. Thicken the sauce for a few seconds—and that's it.

This order of steps has a purpose. Onions and garlic flavor the oil. The meat is cooked next, for pan drippings and more flavor. Then the meat is removed so it doesn't overcook. Vegetables are cooked last to pick up flavor. The sauce brings everything together at the end. Always stir the sauce before adding it to the other ingredients so the cornstarch is evenly distributed.

Make sure all the ingredients are ready and waiting for you before you start stir-frying. The cooking process is so quick that there is no time to stop and chop something you forgot. Cut all the ingredients about the same size so they cook evenly and keep all the food in bowls, lined up in the order you'll add them to the wok. With a sturdy spatula with a long handle, use a scooping motion to move the food around in the wok. Stir-frying only takes a few minutes.

BROILING

Broiling is a dry-heat cooking method. It cooks food quickly and adds wonderful flavor and color. Broiling is not the same as grilling. Broiling supplies flame from above, while grilling supplies it from below. Broiling employs gas or electricity; grilling uses gas, wood, or charcoal. Broiling can be a great cooking technique when you're trying to stick to a calorie-controlled diet, since much of the fat drains away. Keep your stove hood working constantly when you broil and be sure to follow the manufacturer's instructions at all times.

Oven broiling employs the use of high, direct heat placed close to the food. When broiling in the oven, use enamel or nonstick-coated metal pans. These pans should have racks to keep the meat off the bottom of the pan.

In most ovens, the broiler must be preheated to get the food cooked through, and the oven door must be left slightly ajar. The coils will stay bright red the entire time the broiler is on. Think of the broiler as an upside-down grill. Arrange the racks to the proper distance from the coils before turning on the broiler. For most purposes, the oven rack should be 6 to 8 inches from the hot coils. Watch food under the broiler carefully; it can go from beautifully browned to burned in seconds. Turn the rack around from side to side and from front to back so the food cooks evenly.

Use rubs, marinades, and dressings when preparing broiled foods. Salad dressings make excellent marinades. Vinaigrettes are fine with steak, shrimp, or fish. Lemon or lime juice and oil make a good basting sauce for fish and seafood.

Timing is of the essence when broiling. A meat thermometer is far more reliable than a timer. Timing varies according to how you like your food done. If the food browns too fast, lower the rack that holds the food. You may want to turn it more often. Be vigilant with the broiler. It's easy to burn the top of a dish and leave the inside raw.

OUTDOOR GRILLING

Grilling, the oldest form of cooking, is a method of quick cooking. Food that is grilled is cooked on a rack or pan over a heat source of charcoal, wood, propane, or natural gas. Barbecuing and smoking are not grilling. Barbecued food is cooked over low coal temperatures for hours. Smoked foods are cooked with smoke at low temperatures for days at a time.

Grill-frying and grill-roasting are two newer forms of grilling. The food takes about as long to cook as stir-frying on the stove or roasting in the oven. You can cook quickly on a grill wok, which is perforated to add smoky flavor to the food, or roast larger cuts of meat, like roasts, turkeys, and hams, in your outdoor grill.

Organizing your grill space is just as important as organizing your kitchen. You must have a clean and sturdy outdoor work space that's large enough to hold platters, food, and utensils without crowding. Everything has to be ready and waiting for you before you start grilling. Prepare all of the ingredients, collect the utensils and equipment you'll need, and review the recipe. Then you're ready to grill.

Follow safety rules and apply common sense whenever you use your grill. Keep kids and pets away from the grill area; they can distract you or get hurt coming into contact with the hot surfaces. And never leave the grill while it is lit. For a charcoal grill, dispose of coals carefully and according to fire safety standards. Never ever use an outdoor grill indoors. Even a covered porch or garage is a no-no, because carbon monoxide from the combustion process can build up rapidly. Place your grill on a heatproof surface. Keep an eye on your outdoor grill until it has completely cooled.

Tools for grilling

You do need some specialized tools for grilling. You may want to have a separate set of tools just for grilling that are more heavy-duty than standard kitchen tools. If you have a large grill, store these tools in cupboards attached to the grill so they're handy.

You need spring-loaded tongs, which open automatically; spatulas for turning food; brushes and mops to add glazes and sauces (think about purchasing new silicone brushes for easier care); instant-read thermometers to check the doneness of meats and fish; a grill mat to hold delicate foods like fish fillets; grill baskets to hold delicate foods and small foods; and skewers to make kabobs.

If you want to stir-fry on the grill, you have two choices: You can grill on a closed wok or on a wok pierced with holes. The closed wok will give you the same results as indoor cooking, while the pierced wok adds smoky grill flavor, but you'll have to forgo a sauce. Be sure to use a heat-resistant spatula when stir-frying food on the grill.

As with any activity that involves high heat and fire, you must have a safety kit on hand at all times. And be sure that you know how to use it. The kit should contain a well-stocked and up-to-date first aid kit. Be sure you include medicines and salves to treat burns. The kit should also include a fire extinguisher that you know how to use, along with boxes of salt and baking soda to put out fires. Access to a hose or running water is also important.

Building the Fire

Gas grills and charcoal grills use different methods to get the fire started. Charcoal grills are less expensive and offer fewer features, but creating and maintaining the fire is more challenging. Here's where you can satisfy your primitive urge to cook over flames. Building and maintaining a fire will take just as much or more time as grilling the food. Most charcoal aficionados love this part of outdoor cooking.

Charcoal grills are started manually, and you have to keep the fire going if you're cooking longer than 1 hour. You can use lump coal, briquettes, or dry seasoned wood to cook food on a charcoal grill.

Real charcoal is made of wood that has been burned in an oxygen-starved environment, removing everything but carbon and ash. Lump charcoal is an efficient source of heat that burns evenly. Lump charcoal is made from real solid wood—unlike briquettes, which are often made from sawdust and fillers—so you don't have to worry about additives or chemicals in your fire. Actual charcoal burns slightly hotter than briquettes and will be ready for food in about 20 minutes.

You can use hardwood logs in your charcoal grill for a true grilling experience. But never use treated woods or softwoods like pine, which contain resins that give food an off-flavor. Be sure the woods are not moldy. It takes more skill to cook over actual wood, since the temperature of the fire varies according to the moisture in the wood. Build a hardwood fire as you would a campfire, starting with kindling and stacking small logs on top.

To start lump charcoal or briquettes, use a chimney starter. This looks like a round metal can with a handle. Remove the grill rack and place the chimney in the grill pan, then fill the chimney with coals. Tip the chimney slightly and tuck newspaper or paraffin starters in the bottom. Light the paper through the holes at the bottom of the starter. Let the charcoal burn until covered with ash. Using a fireproof glove, tip the coals into the grill pan and arrange. Let the chimney cool completely before storing.

You can also place coals directly on the grill pan and light them without a chimney starter. You'll need about 100 coals to cook 4 to 6 steaks, and you'll need to add 20 to 40 coals per hour for each hour you cook to maintain a constant temperature. It's easy to gauge the temperature of a charcoal fire using your most sensitive cooking tool: your hands. If you can hold your hand 2 inches above the grate for:

- 2 seconds, the fire is high, about 500°F.
- 3 seconds, the fire is medium-high, about 400°F.
- 5 seconds, the fire is medium, about 350°F.
- 6 seconds, the fire is medium-low, about 300°F.
- 7 seconds, the fire is low, about 250°F.

Always leave a space in the grill pan empty of coals, even if you're making a direct fire and grilling only quick-cooking meats and vegetables. Control flare-ups by moving the food to the area with no coals. You can use a water bottle to spritz charcoal to stop flare-ups, but never use water to control flare-ups on a gas grill.

Charcoal briquettes should extend at least 2 inches beyond the foods you are cooking for best results. When you add more coals to the grill, move them around and mix them together so the newly lit and dying coals are combined, or light them in a chimney starter. A grill with a hinged rack makes this easier.

Health Tip

Never bring a charcoal or gas grill indoors. Ever. Don't even use a grill in a garage with the door open. It's just too easy for carbon monoxide, which is a deadly, odorless gas, to build up in any enclosed space.

Weather plays a part when cooking on a charcoal grill. Read your manufacturer's instructions to see if there are any special instructions for cooking in very cold, stormy, or windy weather. Charcoal grills cook faster on calm, warm days and slower on cold, windy days, so adjust recipes accordingly. To grill in winter or rainy weather, you'll need more charcoal to sustain a consistent fire. Position your charcoal grill so it faces away from wind and weather, which can affect how quickly the coals burn.

Clean the grill right after you finish grilling, then again before you start a new grilling session. A hot grill is easier to clean. Once you've lit the grill and it's hot, scrub the grate with a piece of crumpled foil held by long tongs or use a grate cleaner. Then lightly oil the grate using a clean cloth dampened with oil, held again with those long tongs. Then you're ready to cook!

A note about lighter fluid: It does burn off when used to start coals and logs, but be careful that it doesn't spill on the grill sides or grate. There, it will slowly evaporate, adding an unpleasant flavor to your food. Only use lighter fluid, never gasoline or kerosene, to start a fire. And never put lighter fluid on glowing coals.

Store used charcoal in a metal bucket, not in the paper bag it came in. A sturdy metal shovel and bucket to move and hold ash is necessary for safety.

Gas grills are more expensive because they are more complicated than charcoal grills. They're easier to use because there's no need to build a fire; you just flip a switch. The fuel is natural gas or propane, which is clean burning and quick to heat. You can start cooking much sooner with a gas grill, and you buy propane tank refills less often than you do charcoal and fire-starting equipment.

You must perform several safety steps before you start a gas grill. Check all equipment before you turn it on. Be sure the propane tank is free from rust and dents and that all of the hoses and knobs are secure, with no holes, worn areas, or kinks. You'll be able to smell most leaks. But others are subtle and, with the smell of cooking food, can go unnoticed. Brush soapy water over all the gas line connections. If you see bubbles, turn everything off and get the grill repaired by a qualified technician. If there are no bubbles, the grill is safe to use. Wipe off the soapy water with a dry cloth.

The tank for a propane grill is stored under or next to the grill. Some grills have a built-in shelf to hold it securely. A gas gauge is helpful to keep track of propane so you don't run out of fuel while cooking.

There are two different types of gas grills: those powered by propane and those permanently attached to a gas line through your house. Propane for a gas grill must be handled carefully. When you take a tank for refill or replacement, be sure that a qualified technician fills it. Have the tech inspect the tank to make sure there aren't any leaks or dents. Bring it directly home; don't make any stops on the way. And open the car windows and keep the tank propped in an upright position in the car.

Controlling Temperature

Did you know you can regulate the heat on a grill to create different cooking areas? You can adjust the temperature of a grill for perfect results, just as you can the stove top or oven. Control cooking temperatures by moving the coals around, opening and closing the vents, and moving food away from or closer to the coals.

Helpful Tip

Regularly clean your grill. You must scrape off the grill rack and keep the area under the coals or ceramic grates clean. Charcoal grills have deep pans to hold coals. This burns down to ash, which must be removed (in a *metal* bucket). Gas grills have grease traps or trays under the ceramic or stainless steel bars over the burners. Clean them regularly, according to the manufacturer's instructions.

There are two kinds of grilling: direct and indirect. To direct grill, place the food on the rack directly over hot coals. The indirect cooking method turns your grill into an oven. An empty space is created in the coals. A drip pan is usually placed in this spot to reduce flare-ups. Food cooked on the rack above the drip pan will take longer to cook because the heat circulates around the food, rather than cooking it directly. Set up indirect cooking on a gas grill by turning off one burner.

Before you light the coals, you can arrange hotter and cooler areas on the grill or set up for indirect grilling. You can create a two-level fire by piling coals thicker on one side of the grill than the other. You may want to build a graduated fire, where the coals gradually become thicker from one end to the other. Start with a single layer of coals on one end and build to four or five layers on the other. You can easily move the food around to the different temperatures while it's cooking.

To increase the heat on a charcoal grill, open the vents that ring the grill pan. To reduce the heat, close the vents. A thick stack of coals produces more heat. A single layer of coals produces lower heat. Move the grill rack away from coals for lower heat. Move the grill rack closer to the coals for higher heat.

You can control gas grills by turning the burners on and off and by choosing low, medium, and high heat. You can then move the food around to hotter and cooler parts of the grill.

Adding Flavor

Believe it or not, you can add more flavor to a grill than just the rich smokiness that comes from cooking over a fire. Marinades add great flavor to any grilled food.

Add wood chips, herbs, or vines to the coals, or place them on the gas heating element in a foil pan to add more flavor. Three types of wood are used in grilling: basic, fruity, and specialty. The basic woods are white and red oak, pecan, hickory, maple, and mesquite. Fruity woods include apple and cherry; they add sweetness to the food. Specialty woods are the woody stems of herbs (especially rosemary), lilac, olive, grapevine, and seaweed. Cherry and hickory have a heavy, assertive flavor. Maple smoke is mellow, warm, and slightly sweet, while

mesquite and oak are woodsy and earthy. Grapevines are rich and fruity, while pecan is sweet and nutty.

Smoke is key to grilling flavor. Some people say that food isn't on the grill long enough to impart true wood flavor, but there is a taste difference between food cooked over smoke and food that is simply broiled. Milder foods like vegetables or fish will pick up more smoke flavor than strongly flavored foods like ribs or beef steak.

Vines, herbs, wood chips, and wood chunks can be placed directly on charcoal. Chips and chunks must be soaked, but flavored wood pellets can be used dry. Any herb or spice, dried or fresh, can be added directly to a burning charcoal fire. Herb stalks can be used as kabob skewers. Soak wood chips and chunks in water for 15 minutes before adding to the fire.

Herbs, vines, and wood chips and chunks can't be placed directly on gas grill burners. They should be enclosed in foil packets, pans, or smoke boxes. To form a foil packet, use heavy-duty foil and wrap the items, using a double fold. Make several slits in the top of the packet so smoke can escape. A smoke box should be made from stainless steel. It has a cover with slits in it to release the fragrant smoke.

Cedar planks are a great way to grill delicate meats like salmon or other fish fillets. Buy untreated cedar from a hardware or kitchenware store only. Make sure the plank is made from untreated wood. Soak the plank in plain water for 24 hours. Prepare and preheat the grill. Place the plank on medium coals and cover; cook until the plank starts to pop. Turn the plank over and add the food. The plank does add flavor, but its main purpose is to shield delicate foods from the heat of the grill. The plank can be reused many times. Just sand it to remove the burned part and it will be ready to use.

How to Grill Different Foods

All foods have different cooking times and temperatures. Heavy-duty pots and pans can be used on the grill. You may want to designate them just for grill use, as they can become stained with smoke. Special pans let you stir-fry on the grill. And a cast-iron pan can let you precook root vegetables so they can be skewered. You can also cook breakfast foods on the grill; cook pancakes and bacon on a griddle and eggs in a heavy saucepan right over the coals for a wonderful smoky flavor.

Here are the best ways to grill the most common foods:

Burgers. For the best grilled burgers, follow a few rules. Make sure the coals are covered with

> ## Helpful Tip
>
> Foods that cook best over direct heat are those that cook quickly, like thin steaks and pork chops, boneless chicken breasts, kabobs, tender vegetables, and fruits. Indirect heat and two-layer cooking is best for bone-in chicken, burgers, and thicker steaks, chops, and roasts. Cook these foods with an initial sear, then finish them over cooler coals.

gray ash before you start, or preheat a gas grill for at least 10 minutes. Never press down on the burgers while they are grilling; that just removes the juice! Always cook burgers well-done, or to 165°F.

Boneless, skinless chicken breasts. Chicken can be flavored many ways, but is very easy to overcook on the grill. Watch your time carefully when grilling this simple meat. It must be cooked to an internal temperature of 165°F, but the temperature will rise about 5° after it's pulled from the grill. So cook the chicken to 160°F, then let it stand, covered, for 5 minutes.

Desserts. The grill is not just for the main course and side dishes. Desserts can be delicious on the grill, too. Everyone has heard of s'mores, of course—that tasty combination of grilled marshmallows, chocolate bars, and graham crackers. But you can also grill fruit to serve over ice cream or grill slices or cubes of pound cake or angel food cake to serve with fresh fruit sauce and whipped cream.

Fish fillets. You can grill everything from salmon fillets to trout or walleye. It's difficult to grill these boneless and delicate tender cuts of meat directly on the rack, because they tend to stick. To add flavor and prevent sticking, make a bed of lemons, onions, or herbs to put under the fish. Or you can use cedar planks or cedar paper. Because fish fillets cook so quickly, make them the last item on the menu that you prepare. Have everything else ready and waiting for the fish. Choose fillets that weigh 4 to 6 ounces; no smaller, or they'll overcook even in the brief grilling time.

Fruit. The grill and fruits are natural partners. The heat of the grill caramelizes the sugar in fruits. It also softens fruits that aren't quite ripe, so they become smooth and rich. Fruits have a relatively high water content. The heat of the grill evaporates the water as they cook, concentrating the flavor.

Packets. Filling packets of aluminum foil with delicious foods is a great way to feed a crowd, and because it is one-dish cooking on the grill, cleanup is a lot easier too. Fish and chicken cook very well in packets. Burgers and steaks, which require

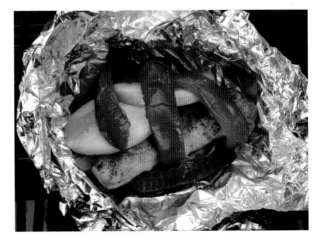

direct high heat to caramelize, don't work quite as well. Almost any combination of flavors will be delicious. A sauce helps flavor the food and keep it moist. Use only about ¼ cup of sauce for each packet; any more and the packets will leak.

Don't skimp on the foil for packets; use a full 18 x 12-inch piece and use heavy-duty foil or doubled plain foil. Spray the area where you'll place the food with nonstick cooking spray. Then stack the food. Drizzle with the sauce, then bring the 18-inch sides to the middle; fold once, then twice. One at a time, fold the 12-inch sides together, once, then twice. There should be air space around the food to leave room for expansion; don't fold the foil tight against the food.

For more control, use a two-level fire when cooking packets. Move them around on the grill. Start over direct heat, then move them to indirect heat. You can check doneness by sticking a meat thermometer probe through the foil into the chicken, or carefully unwrap one packet to check. The packets may finish cooking at different times; pull them off as they are finished and cover to keep warm.

Pasta. You can boil pasta in a sturdy pot on the grill or side burner. Cook just as you would on the stove top, stirring frequently so the pasta doesn't stick together.

Steaks and chops. These meats, whether made of pork, lamb, or beef, are delicious cooked on the grill. You may want to marinate tougher cuts, but many steaks are delicious just seasoned with salt and pepper. Remember to oil the grill rack before you add these meats and don't turn them until they release easily from the rack. Use an instant-read thermometer to check doneness. For food safety, all beef steaks should be cooked to a minimum of 140°F; pork, lamb, and veal chops, steaks, and roasts to 145°F.

Root vegetables. Potatoes, carrots, squash, and parsnips take on another dimension when grilled. The heat caramelizes the sugars in these vegetables, forming a delicious crisp crust, and the grill adds a wonderful smoky flavor. Because root vegetables take so long to cook, they must be precooked before grilling. You can precook them in boiling water, in the oven, or in the microwave.

Soft-skinned veggies. One of the most popular grilled vegetarian entree and sandwich options is soft-skinned vegetables. Tender vegetables contain more water and have thin skins. They are ideal for very quick grilling. When these vegetables are grilled, they become soft and slightly sweet. You can use them as a side dish or add them to a green or pasta salad. Be sure your grill is hot and clean and rubbed with a film of oil to prevent sticking. Toss the veggies in a bit of oil to coat and then season with salt and pepper. Grill immediately; leave some space between the veggies so you have room to turn them.

INDOOR GRILLING

Grilling aficionados can now grill their favorite foods year-round and in all kinds of weather, thanks to new indoor grills. There are three types of indoor grills. The open grill is a freestanding electric unit that looks a lot like a small outdoor grill. The countertop, or dual contact, grill is an electric press that grills food on both sides at the same time. A grill pan is placed on stove burners. All of these grills have ridges to mimic the grill marks created by outdoor grill racks.

Indoor grills require a cook's complete attention. If possible, keep your indoor grill near an open window or turn on your stove's exhaust hood. You also have to be aware of the fire risk. Always keep a fire extinguisher on hand. A list of the latest and best indoor grills can be found online. Simply search the phrase "indoor grills." The advantages of indoor grilling include convenience and safety. The disadvantages include a lack of wood smoke flavor.

MOIST-HEAT COOKING METHODS

Moist-heat cooking methods include blanching, boiling, braising, poaching, pressure cooking, steaming, and stewing. These gentle cooking methods are good for cooking tender vegetables and low-fat meats like fish and chicken breasts.

Blanching means submerging food briefly in boiling water, then plunging it into ice water. It is used as a precooking technique, to remove the peel from tomatoes and peaches, and to set the color of fruits and vegetables before preserving them. Blanching also denatures enzymes in fruits and vegetables before they are canned or frozen. To blanch, bring a large pot of water to a rolling boil. Immerse the food in the boiling water. Return to a boil and cook for 10 seconds (for tomatoes and peaches) to 4 to 5 minutes (for hard root vegetables), depending on the kind of food and level of doneness you want. Drain the food, then "shock" it—plunge it immediately into ice water—to keep it from cooking and to brighten the color.

Boiling is used for dried foods, like pasta, dried grains, polenta, and legumes. These foods are boiled because they must absorb moisture to be edible. Boiling occurs in three stages. The first is the scald or simmer stage; tiny bubbles appear around the side of the pot. The second stage is the slow boil, with gentle bubbles all over the surface of the liquid. The rolling boil is just what it sounds like—the water moves vigorously and constantly.

You need a good 2- to 4-quart pot for boiling dried foods. Use a pot that's big enough to handle the food and water without overflowing. The pot should have two handles for gripping, since you need to lift the pot to drain it. Pasta pots with a removable colander make lifting and draining the food easier.

Braising is an age-old technique that involves a continuous progression from sear and sauté to simmer. When braising, first you sear the meat in hot fat, then you add liquid and allow the meat to simmer long and slow on top of the stove, in the oven, or in a slow cooker. Braising produces comfort food, the stuff of cold winter nights and chilly days out-of-doors. Cheaper cuts of meat with more connective tissues such as beef shanks, brisket, roasts, legs, and thighs become very tender when braised. Chili, stew, fricassee, and pot roast all involve braising.

Remember: Too much heat at the wrong time makes meat tough. The only blast of heat you give a braised dish is at the very beginning. The sear is the one short exposure

to high heat. Never let a braising recipe boil. Add liquids as necessary, keeping an even level of wine, broth, or tomato sauce to almost cover the meat.

After browning the meat, sauté aromatic vegetables, which include garlic, onions, and parsnips, to add essential flavor to the braised dish and create deep, rich flavors. Other flavors can be added as you go along or toward the end of the cooking time.

Braising requires a heavy pot. A dutch oven, either all metal or ceramic-clad metal, works beautifully. The pot must have a tight lid to retain the steam.

Poaching is the gentlest method of cooking. Poached foods are cooked in a simmering liquid on the stove top or in the oven. It's important to watch the clock while poaching to prevent overcooking. Poaching is recommended for chicken; firm-fleshed fish such as salmon, tuna, and halibut; and eggs.

When poaching, the cooking liquid does not come to a boil or even a simmer. The French say the liquid is "smiling," that is, it moves gently without forming bubbles that break the surface. Sometimes the poaching liquid is transformed into a sauce by reducing or adding butter or both. Sometimes when poaching a food fully submerged, the food will poke out and float. You can use a clean dish towel to keep the food covered while poaching.

You can serve your poached food with the broth it was cooked in, or you can reduce the poaching liquid to a sauce-like consistency. Boil the liquid until the volume is reduced by at least half, then remove from heat and swirl in a tablespoon of cold butter to finish the sauce.

Pressure cooking works by trapping hot steam inside a pot, which builds up extreme pressure. This makes the temperature rise dramatically, and the food cooks quickly. Old pressure cookers used to be fraught with peril. They sometimes exploded on the stove. The new models are electronic, with many fail-safe features that make pressure cooking much easier. Cooking times are based on pounds of pressure per square inch. Always, always follow manufacturer's directions for using a pressure cooker. Avoid used pressure cookers from garage sales and antiques stores. Never open a pressure cooker under pressure. And follow cleaning and storage requirements carefully.

Steaming is a healthy and quick way to cook food. The food is put into one or more steamer baskets—metal or bamboo contraptions that have holes in the bottom to let steam through. The baskets are stacked on top of each other and placed over simmering water. The steam from the water moves through the openings in the baskets to cook the food. The steamer baskets should be tightly covered to keep the steam moving around the food. Make sure that the food is placed in a single layer in the baskets, unless the recipe specifies otherwise.

The baskets should be rearranged every 3 to 4 minutes when cooking so all of the food cooks evenly. Move the bottom basket to the top, then keep rearranging them so all of the food is exposed to steam for the same amount of time. Broths, fruit juices, and wine are good additions to the steaming water. You can also add aromatic ingredients such as chopped onion, gingerroot, and herbs.

Be sure to leave a bit of room around each piece of food so the steam can circulate and the food cooks evenly. Make sure the bottom of the steamer basket does not touch the simmering liquid. If it does, carefully remove some of the liquid, because you don't want the bottom layer of food to overcook. Use hot pads to protect your hands while you're rearranging the baskets, especially if they are made of metal. The same steam that gently cooks food can burn you in seconds.

Stewing is similar to braising, but more liquids are used and the meat is not always browned first. Braising and stewing are slow-cooking methods that tenderize the foods being cooked. With stewing, the ingredients are totally submerged and simmer for a long time.

Microwave ovens can do more than just pop popcorn, melt butter, and defrost foods; you can cook an entire meal in this appliance. It just takes a bit of attention and following a few rules.

There are several types of microwave ovens. You can buy very basic models that are low wattage, but remember that it can be difficult to cook in these appliances. High-end microwave ovens, which are usually mounted over an oven, can have 1200 watts, with lights and vent fans. Whichever type of oven you buy, be sure you understand how to use it before you start cooking.

Most microwave ovens have about 600 to 800 watts of power. That's the range that recipe developers use. If your microwave is more or less powerful, reduce or increase the cooking time by 30 to 40 percent, then write down the changes on the recipe. With some experimentation, you'll be able to accurately estimate cooking times.

> ## Helpful Tip
>
> To poach eggs, use the "whirlpool" method. Stir the liquid vigorously (being careful not to splash yourself). Then gently slip one egg into the hot liquid at a time, right in the center of the vortex. This helps keep the whites together so the egg looks neater. Or you can buy special egg poacher pans that keep the eggs in a nice shape. A bit of vinegar added to the water also will help the whites coagulate more quickly and neatly.

Microwave recipes are written with venting, stirring, rotating, and standing times included; follow all of them to the letter for best results.

Always use microwave-safe cooking dishes. The correct pots and pans are labeled as microwave safe. Also use microwave-safe plastic wrap and paper towels. If you cover a dish with plastic wrap, be sure to vent it by peeling back one corner. You can use small pieces of foil in the microwave to help prevent thinner pieces and edges of foods from overcooking. Wrap the foil around the area you want to protect. Be sure that you curve and mold the edges to the food. Any other metal, unless it's built into special cooking equipment, should not be placed in the microwave.

Dense foods like meat loaf, pork chops, or chicken breasts take some time to microwave. The energy needs a few minutes to move through the food. Check the final temperature with an instant-read meat thermometer after standing time. If it's not correct, microwave for 1 to 2 minutes longer, let it stand, then check again.

Foods don't brown in the microwave oven, but you can compensate for that shortcoming by searing food in a pan or under the broiler before microwaving or by using browning agents like colorings and spices.

SLOW COOKING

The slow cooker is a special appliance that cooks food with low heat. This appliance lets you walk away from the kitchen while your dinner cooks. A slow cooker is the next best thing to having a chef. You just add food, turn it on, and come back hours later to perfectly cooked food that fills your home with wonderful aromas. Better taste; time, energy, and money savings; ease of clean-up; and healthier food are all reasons for using the slow cooker.

Since the slow cooker uses wet heat, certain foods cook best in it. Tough meats become tender as the tendons and fibers gelatinize. Stews and soups are perfect for the slow cooker. Casseroles are also delicious in this appliance.

Rules of the Slow Cooker

To cook recipes in a slow cooker, follow these rules:

Adding layers. Meats are placed on top of vegetables because they cook more quickly. Root vegetables should always be placed on the bottom of the slow cooker. They will become tender and sweet, and all of the juices from meats and broths will infuse them with flavor.

Stirring it up. Some recipes need to be stirred during the cooking time. Do this quickly so not much heat escapes. Keep in mind that every time you lift the slow cooker lid, you need to add another 20 minutes to the cooking time.

Filling it up. Fill a slow cooker between one-half and three-quarters full. If you use less food, it may burn. And if you use more, the food may not cook through or the slow cooker could overflow as foods release juices.

Thickening recipes. To thicken soups, chilis, or stews, combine 2 tablespoons cornstarch with ⅓ cup liquid in a small bowl. Stir into the slow cooker at the end of cooking time; cook for 20 to 30 minutes on high until thickened. If the sauce isn't thick enough after cooking, you can add a cornstarch slurry or just turn the slow cooker to high and remove the cover for 20 to 30 minutes until some of the liquid has evaporated and the sauce is thicker.

And these tips for specific foods will come in handy:

Adding dairy products. Dairy products such as milk, cream, and cheese are added at the very end of the cooking time. Often, stabilizers like flour, cornstarch, or arrowroot are stirred in with dairy products to help prevent curdling.

Preparing meats. Meats can be browned before being added to the slow cooker to add color and improve appearance.

Adding rice and grains. Rice and grains should be placed on the bottom of the slow cooker. They have to be completely covered with liquid as they cook or they will never become tender. One way to make rice successfully in the slow cooker is to toast it in a dry pan or in butter or olive oil. This helps firm up the rice coating, which delays the absorption of liquid. Brown rice and wild rice cook better in a slow cooker than white rice.

Cooking seafood. With a few tricks you can cook seafood to perfection in a slow cooker. The low, moist heat is ideal for producing tender, melting fish and seafood. Cook a "base" for the fish first. Cook potatoes—or root vegetables—or wild rice or other grains first, then add the fish during the last hour or so of cooking time. The fish will be perfectly cooked and will pick up some of the other flavors in the dish.

Preparing vegetables. Chop or slice vegetables to the same size so they cook evenly. Tender vegetables should be cut larger than root vegetables. Greens that stand up to the slow cooker's environment include mustard greens, kale, turnip greens, and chard. These strong-flavored greens add a punch of flavor.

Even when vegetables like onion and garlic are cooked in the slow cooker, cook them in fat first for better texture. The onion and garlic flavor will permeate the fat, adding flavor to the whole recipe. You can cook the onion and garlic just until tender or cook them longer until they turn brown.

Helpful Tip

The slow cooker used to cook at 180°F on low and 200°F on high. But in the past few years, manufacturers have made them hotter. Now low is 200°F, and high can be as hot as 300°F. If you have a new slow cooker, you'll need to reduce cooking times for recipes or the recipe will overcook. Cut the time by a third, then check the food at the earliest time.

Caring for Your Slow Cooker

Slow cookers are easy to care for. The inserts are usually dishwasher safe (read the instructions!), but it's a good idea, after you remove the food, to fill the insert with hot soapy water and let it stand until you're ready to clean it. If you use a slow cooker liner, cleanup is a breeze; just throw away the liner after you've removed the food. Spray the insert with nonstick cooking spray to help make cleanup a wipe with a soapy sponge. Never add cold water to a hot insert; the ceramic could crack.

And speaking of cracks: If your insert develops cracks, even tiny hairline cracks, you shouldn't use it. Those cracks can harbor bacteria. And the insert could crack while the food is cooking. Many companies offer insert replacements; check their websites.

Adapting Recipes to the Slow cooker

Many recipes that you cook in the oven and on the stove top can be adapted to the slow cooker. There are just a few rules to follow. First, choose a recipe. If it's a soup or stew, reduce the liquid by about half and you're ready to go. You may want to add a browning step if the recipe calls for beef or pork. Ground meats must be cooked and drained before slow cooking. Any recipes that call for long cooking times, like braising or roasting, are adaptable. Just remember to place root vegetables in the bottom of the slow cooker and top with meats and tender produce.

When cooking meat, be sure to first trim off any visible fat, since that will affect the taste and texture of the final dish. Reduce liquids by two-thirds because of the slow cooker's moist environment. For timing, multiply the time of your recipe by 6 for low-heat cooking, by 3½ for cooking on high. In general, cook a 3-pound chunk of meat 4 hours on high or 7 hours on low. Chicken breasts take 5 hours and dark meat 6 to 7 hours on low. Always check the recipe at the shortest cooking time so foods don't over-cook or burn.

When adapting recipes, add milk, cream, sour cream, and cheeses at the end of cooking time. Some recipes are the exception: Cheesy dips cook for only a short period and you can add cheeses at the beginning. Add tender vegetables like peas at the end of the cooking time. Dried beans should be soaked before adding to a slow cooker recipe; don't add salt or acidic ingredients until the beans soften.

Other Slow-Cooking Tips

Foil is an essential slow cooker tool. Foil balls, made by crumpling the material in your fist, will help hold meat out of the liquid for roasting. Crossed foil strips fit neatly under a meat loaf so you can lift it out of the appliance when it's done. To make the foil strips, tear off two 24-inch-long strips of aluminum foil. Fold the foil in half lengthwise, then fold in half again to make two 24 x 3-inch-long strips. Cross the strips over each other and place in the bottom of the slow cooker. Let the ends extend beyond the lid. Add the meat loaf or roast and cover and cook as directed. Use the foil to lift the food carefully from the slow cooker.

Paper towels also have a place in your slow cooker collection. When baking, paper towels are placed under the lid to catch moisture so it doesn't drip onto the baked goods.

ROASTING

Roasting is a dry-heat cooking method, usually used on large cuts of meat or whole chickens, turkeys, ducks, or pheasants. To roast, start cooking at a high temperature and then reduce the heat to let the food cook through. However, the reverse is true of a large turkey. It should be covered and cooked slowly until it's almost done, and then uncovered to brown. Essential equipment for roasting includes an enamel-covered metal roasting pan with a rack, or a disposable aluminum one, and a meat thermometer.

The equipment needed for roasting is simple. If you can't afford a high-quality roaster, use an aluminum foil pan. A meat thermometer comes in handy, and some ovens even have them built in. Most meat thermometers connect to the meat with a long cord and sit on the top of the oven.

Even though roasting is a dry-heat method, you need to use some liquid. This helps the meat brown and adds flavor and moisture. Use a baster, a spoon, or a silicone brush to put drippings from the bottom of the pan on the meat. If you're roasting a large rib roast or turkey, you may need to "tent" it with aluminum foil to ensure it doesn't get too brown.

The roasted meat must rest for 10 to 20 minutes after it comes out of the oven. Use aluminum foil or heavy kitchen towels to cover the meat while it rests. This step is essential. During the resting time, the juice returns to the fibers in the meat. If the meat does not rest, the juices will run out onto your cutting board.

Roasting poultry is a bit different. Some recipes tell you to place turkeys, chickens, ducks, and geese breast side down on a bed of celery and carrots. This method helps protect the more delicate breast meat so it stays juicy. When roasting small birds such as ducks, game hens, or quail, wrap the drumsticks in foil to keep them from drying out.

> ### Helpful Tip
>
> Baste your roast with a tasty liquid to add flavor and keep the meat moist. The basting liquid along with the meat drippings create the gravy or sauce. Baste about every hour, using a baster to take liquid from the bottom of the pan and squirt it over the meat. You can use a variety of liquids and ingredients to baste, including wine, broths, herbs, soy sauce, or Worcestershire sauce.

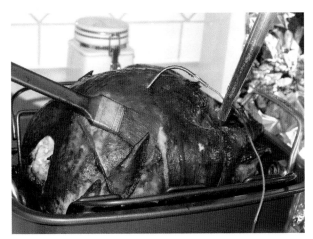

④

COOKING RULES

Cooking has rules. Cooking is different from baking, which requires precise measurements and no substitutions. It's good to learn how to cook before you learn how to bake simply because cooking recipes are more tolerant. That means you can substitute ingredients and you have a little leeway when measuring and combining ingredients.

Having said that, you still need to understand weights and measures, read a recipe, interpret recipe jargon, understand recipe punctuation (yes, really!), and measure ingredients, especially when you first start cooking. When you first try a recipe, make it the way the recipe writer instructs. When you've had a first success, then you can start fiddling with the ingredients, amounts, and proportions.

You also need to know the yield of produce and meats. If a recipe calls for 8 cups of chopped apples, do you know how many apples to buy? How many peaches are in a pound? Memorizing these numbers will make cooking easier. You don't really have to know them all, but you certainly should know where to find this information.

WEIGHTS AND MEASURES

Weights and measures are basic cooking tools. There are some easy ways to remember basic measurements. For instance, you can memorize this saying: 2 cups equal 1 pint; 4 cups equal 1 quart; 4 quarts equal 1 gallon. This can help you figure out the size of the slow cooker you need or the size of the casserole dish you need to make any recipe. Pots, pans, baking dishes, and slow cookers have their capacity printed right on them so you can choose the correct dish for the recipe.

Volume and Weight

Most recipes in American cookbooks are written in terms of teaspoons, tablespoons, cups, and quarts. Grams, cubic centimeters, and liters are prominent in European recipes.

But that's changing. More and more American cookbooks are using both measures by teaspoon and cup (which is volume) and measuring by grams and ounces (which is weight). Measuring by weight is much more accurate than measuring by volume.

That's where the numbers on the other side of the measuring cups come in. Liquid measuring cups usually have milliliters on one side, cups on the other. When you are using a European recipe or following a diet that's measured in grams rather than in ounces, you may need a recipe convertor. These are available at cooking supply stores and at www.Amazon.com. You can make close approximations for cooking recipes, once you understand the basics of weights and volume.

You may want to purchase a kitchen scale for the most accurate cooking (and baking). A scale is easy to use; just place the mixing bowl on the scale and zero it out (there's usually a button for this) to allow for the weight of the bowl. Then add the ingredients, carefully noting the ounce or gram amount of each. You can measure ingredients individually and place them in separate bowls to add to the recipe individually, or you can zero out the scale after each ingredient is added. When you're experienced, you can add the ingredients to a single bowl as you work. This takes a little bit of skill, but with practice you'll find that measuring by weight is actually faster than measuring by volume.

The weight of dry measures varies by product. For instance, different flours have different weights per cup. A cup of all-purpose white flour weighs about 125 grams. But a cup of rye flour weighs 102 grams. A pound of white sugar equals about 2 cups, while a pound of brown sugar equals 2⅔ cups. When substituting for flours, always substitute by weight, not volume. If a recipe calls for 100 grams of all-purpose flour, use 100 grams of whole wheat flour.

Temperature

To convert temperature from Fahrenheit to Celsius, subtract 32 from the Fahrenheit temperature, then multiply by 5, then divide by 9 (good grief!). Or you can go online and type the temperature you want to convert into Google using this method: "350 degrees F to C" or vice versa. Google will automatically calculate it for you.

Yields of Produce

Produce yields are the amount of the food that can be measured after it is peeled, cored, seeded, and minced, chopped, or diced. Produce yields depend on the size of the

3 teaspoons = 1 tablespoon

2 tablespoons = 1 fluid ounce

4 tablespoons = ¼ cup

5⅓ tablespoons = ⅓ cup

8 tablespoons = ½ cup

16 tablespoons = 1 cup

1 cup = 8 fluid ounces

2 cups = 1 pint

2 pints = 1 quart

4 quarts = 1 gallon

8 quarts produce = 1 peck

4 pecks produce = 1 bushel

Metric Equivalents

59.15 milliliters = 4 tablespoons

250 milliliters = 1.05 cups

1 liter = 1.06 quarts

28 grams = 1 ounce

454 grams = 1 pound

fruit or vegetable and how it is prepared. Be sure that you know the difference between minced, diced, and chopped; to learn more, see more information on this topic in the glossary in the back of this book. The smaller the size, the more of the food that can fit into the measuring cup.

These yields are for canned or frozen foods, not dried. Remember that yields can vary with the size of produce, amount of waste, and other factors. But these numbers are a good general guide.

Apples: 1 pound is 6 medium and yields about 3 cups chopped. 1 bushel will fill about 18 quart jars.

Apricots: 1 pound is about 8 to 10 apricots and yields about 2 cups chopped.

Beans (green): 1 pound yields about 3 cups cut; 1 bushel will fill about 18 quarts.

Beets: 1 pound beets is 4 to 6 medium and yields 3½ cups diced.

Blueberries: 1 pound yields about 3 cups.

Cabbage: 1 pound cabbage yields about 3½ cups sliced; 50 pounds fills about 20 quarts.

Carrots: 1 pound is about 4 large carrots and yields 2½ cups diced; 2 pounds are needed for each quart.

Cherries: 2½ pounds yield 4 cups whole and pitted.

Corn: 16 to 20 ears yield about 2 quarts kernels cut from the cob.

Cranberries: 1 pound yields 4 cups whole.

Cucumbers: 1 pound is about 2 large and yields 2½ cups sliced; 6 pounds yield about 1 gallon slices.

Grapes: 1 pound yields about 4 cups whole.

Onions: 1 pound is 3 large and yields about 2½ cups chopped.

Peaches: 1 pound is 3 to 5 peaches and yields about 2½ cups chopped or sliced.

Pears: 1 pound is 4 to 5 pears and yields 2½ cups chopped.

Peas: 1 pound peas in the pod yields about 1 cup shelled peas.

Peppers (hot): Depending on type, 1 pound raw yields about 1 cup cored and chopped.

Peppers (sweet-bell types): 1 pound is 4 large and yields about 2 cups chopped.

Plums: 1 pound is 12 to 20 plums and yields 2 cups sliced.

Potatoes (sweet): 3 pounds yield about 4 cups chopped.

Potatoes (white): 3 pounds yield about 4 cups sliced; 1 bushel fills about 20 quarts.

Pumpkin: 1 pound yields 2 cups chunks.

Raspberries, Blackberries: Each quart box weighs about 1½ pounds and yields about 3 cups whole berries.

Strawberries: A dry quart box yields 3 cups halved berries.

Tomatoes: 1 pound is 4 medium tomatoes and yields 3 cups sliced; 1 bushel slicing tomatoes yields about 18 quarts.

Zucchini: 1 pound yields about 2 cups diced.

Measuring

Most people measure many ingredients incorrectly. Measuring flour is the main culprit. Too much flour in a recipe will make a sauce too thick, breading on meats spongy and tough, and dumplings or the flour topping on a casserole heavy and tough. Too much flour in a baking recipe makes that recipe dry and crumbly. Too little flour means the food's structure will not hold up, sauces will be too thin, dumplings and flour toppings will fall apart, and cakes and bars will collapse or sag in the center.

When you're cooking soups, creating casseroles, or making salads, you can substitute some ingredients or change proportions slightly with little problem. The key word here, however, is *slightly*. You need to understand basic measuring techniques and measure accurately until you're an accomplished cook.

Each ingredient is measured in a different way. Good calibrated measuring cups and spoons are essential to baking success. Dry ingredients should be measured using nested measuring cup and spoons, not coffee cups or the spoons you use to eat. And liquid ingredients need liquid measuring cups, which must be used properly.

Dry ingredients should be measured with dry ingredient measuring tablespoons and cups.

To measure flour correctly, lightly spoon it into a measuring cup until it overflows. Keep adding flour until it heaps up over the top of the cup. Then level off the top with the back of a knife. Never scoop the cup or spoon into the flour or pack the flour down. You can also sift the flour and then scoop it up with a spoon and place it in the measuring cup. You may want to use a scale to measure flour, or to test your measurements. One cup of all-purpose flour should weigh 125 grams.

Brown sugar is measured by packing it into a cup or spoon.

Baking powder and baking soda are measured by scooping out a heaping measuring spoonful, then leveling it off with the back of a knife.

All other dry powder ingredients are like flour, spooned into the cup, then leveled off with the back of a knife.

Produce and meats are measured by adding them to the cup measure until level with the top.

Shortening or other solid but pliable ingredients such as peanut butter are measured by packing them into the measuring cup, then leveling off the top.

The size of eggs is specified in a recipe. Don't substitute jumbo eggs for large, and vice versa.

Wet ingredients are measured by pouring them into a glass measuring cup with a spout and markers on the side. You must bring the cup to eye level. The liquid should come up to the marker on the side of the cup. Don't use dry ingredient measuring utensils to measure wet ingredients. But take heart—there are new liquid measuring cups that let you measure by looking straight down into the cup! For small liquid amounts, use ordinary dry ingredient tablespoons and teaspoons.

READING A RECIPE

Before you can bake or cook you must understand what the terms in a recipe mean. Cooking and baking are like any other science. Before you can master the discipline, you need to learn the language. If this is your first time cooking, read through some simple recipes and make sure you understand all the terms and directions. Never assume that you know what a term means; if you're unsure, look it up. Start by making some very simple recipes with short ingredients lists, preferably those that just assemble food. Make a simple chicken salad or sandwich spread for your first attempt.

The language of cooking is very specific. And words can mean things that you don't expect. For instance, *cream* can mean the white liquid you whip into soft peaks, or it can mean combining sugar and fat to start a baking recipe. Read through the glossary at the end of this book before you start cooking!

Most recipes call for adding ingredients in certain steps and at certain stages. Don't think you can just throw everything in a bowl and mix it. Most foods must have their structure created in a certain way. All the steps in a recipe are critical to the recipe's success.

A recipe is really a scientific formula. Chemistry and physics rule the kitchen! That's why many beginning cooks have failures in the kitchen. You don't need a degree in food science to be a good cook, but you do need to understand a little bit about why recipes are put together.

Every recipe begins with an ingredients list, which should be arranged in the order the ingredients are used. The amount of the ingredient is placed in front of the food. The instructions follow the ingredients list and should be listed in the order they are performed. This tells you how to manipulate the food, combine it, heat it to finish cooking, and serve it. You may need to read the recipe more than once to fully understand all the instructions.

As you read the recipe, try to picture each individual step, how the food will look as it is manipulated and heated, and what the finished recipe will look like. Pictures of the finished recipe certainly will help you prepare it, but with practice you'll be able to visualize what the food will look like just by reading the recipe.

Recipe ingredients lists are very specific. If a recipe calls for "1 pound boneless, skinless chicken breasts, thawed if frozen," the recipe is not going to work if you substitute frozen bone-in, skin-on chicken thighs. The listed ingredients also include preparation directions. You may need to peel and chop an onion, cut a beef steak into 1-inch pieces, or cut corn kernels off the cob. Know what these instructions mean before you begin.

Then be sure you have all the necessary utensils, tools, and appliances on hand before you start cooking. Don't try to substitute utensils or pots and pans at this point. If a recipe calls for a large skillet, but you only have a medium saucepan, the food just won't turn out. Different pots and pans are needed to accomplish different things.

Breaded chicken cutlets, for instance, won't come out nice and crisp when piled on top of each other in a saucepan. The large surface area of the skillet is needed for evaporation and good contact between the food and the pan. And it's impossible to cook pasta properly in a shallow skillet or sauté pan. The pasta needs lots of roiling, boiling water to cook evenly.

Sometimes you'll need to perform several tasks at once when you're cooking. This doesn't mean you need four arms to accomplish six tasks! The term *meanwhile* is used in a recipe to let you know that while food is happily simmering or boiling by itself, there's a pocket of time to do other things.

When you're just starting out, you may find it helpful to put all of the ingredients on a large tray. As each one is used, take it off the tray. Then you'll be sure that you've used all of the ingredients the recipe calls for. This works well when you're using

> ## Helpful Tip
>
> Make sure you understand cooking terms before you start cooking. Look through the definition of terms in the glossary at the back of this book. Be familiar with each term in a recipe before you start cooking. Otherwise, how will you know the difference between *searing* and *sautéing*?

smaller quantities out of cans and jars, too. If a recipe calls for a teaspoon of soy sauce, put the bottle of soy sauce on the tray. Then when you add the soy sauce, take the bottle off the tray. You won't have to remember if you already used it.

Recipe Mistakes

Be sure to follow all of the recipe instructions. If a recipe tells you to brown cubes of meat in fat and then remove and set them aside before cooking other ingredients, don't leave the meat in the pan. It will overcook and be dry and tough. If you're told to strain broth or a sauce, do so unless you like lumps of starch in your food.

The largest variable in cooking and baking is the cook. Using improper measuring equipment, not following the steps of the recipe, not beating mixtures as long as the recipe directs, substituting improper ingredients, and using the wrong pots and pans are common mistakes beginning cooks make. Learn good practices and habits to become the best cook.

These are some common recipe mistakes:

Substituting nonfat products. Many recipes will not work with nonfat products, unless the instructions specifically tell you it's okay. Fat is essential in many recipes, even cooked recipes, to add flavor and moisture. In fact, until you're experienced in the kitchen, don't substitute ingredients, period.

Using the incorrect pan size. If the pan size you use is too small, the food won't fit, may overflow in the oven, and probably won't cook through to a safe temperature. A pan that's too big means the food will overcook and may burn or dry out.

Using dull knives. A dull knife is not only frustrating to work with, it can be dangerous. Dull knives can slip and cut you. Keep your knives sharp and in good condition. A dull knife can ruin the food. It can rip meat instead of cutting it, and mash tomatoes so the juice ends up on the cutting board instead of in your recipe. See Chapter 5 for more information on this topic.

Sautéing wet foods. If a recipe tells you to dry a food before cooking, blot it with paper towels until it is dry. Wet foods won't brown, even in a hot pan; they steam. And that changes the texture, appearance, and cooking time of the food.

Frying in oil that isn't heated properly. If you fry foods in oil that's too cold, the food will absorb the oil, becoming heavy and greasy. And the food won't cook through in the middle. If you fry foods in oil that's too hot, the foods can burn and the outside can get too brown before the inside cooks through. Always use a thermometer to test the temperature of cooking oil. And follow instructions about the oil temperature, such as "heat until a drop of water skitters in the oil" or "heat until a small cube of bread browns in thirty seconds."

Not preheating the pan. If a recipe tells you to preheat a pan, do it. A hot pan sears the food, starts the cooking process, and adds flavor and color to the finished dish. If you add food to a cold pan (unless the recipe says to) something will go wrong.

Using old herbs and spices. Dried herbs and spices keep their potency for about a year. Mark the purchase date on all of these products. And before you use them, smell them! Herbs and spices should have a very intense aroma. If that jar of dried marjoram smells of nothing or only faintly of marjoram, throw it away and buy a new jar.

Overhandling food. Foods like meat loaf need gentle handling, as do soufflés, many doughs, and other recipes. Only handle food as much as the recipe directs. If you turn food too often as it's panfrying, you can tear the food. Moving food that's frying before it's ready can also remove breading and reduce caramelization, which is crucial to taste and appearance.

Using lower-quality ingredients. Always use the best ingredients you can afford. Don't try to use wilted produce in a salad. For a salad dressing, choose extra-virgin olive oil over lesser grades. Choose good quality meats and seafood, the freshest produce, and high-quality dairy products. You can skimp on some items. Generic products are fine if they're used in a recipe that has many ingredients, such as a stew. And there's one food you can buy in a lower grade: maple syrup! Grade B maple syrup has more flavor and color than Grade A.

Rushing the cooking process. Don't remove food from the heat before it's done. Let onions cook until they turn brown if you want to caramelize them. Let the flour cook in the fat for a few minutes before you add liquid for a smooth, thick sauce. Heat pans for a few minutes before you add the food, and preheat your oven for at least 10 minutes. Let meat stand after cooking so the juices redistribute.

Overcooking or undercooking. Overcooked food is dry, may be burned, and is unpalatable. It's difficult to rescue overbaked foods, so always check doneness a few minutes before the minimum cooking time. Undercooked food can be dangerous. Undercooked eggs, meats, and seafood can make you sick. Always use a meat thermometer to check doneness.

Not watching or listening to your food. Foods tell you when they're done or when something is going wrong. Food should sizzle loudly as it's put into a hot pan or onto a hot grill. As it cooks, the sounds reduce. Foods brown when they're done; if they're burned, they were cooked, grilled, or baked too long. Fish flakes when it's done, chicken juices run clear, and vegetables turn a bright color and are tender yet still have some texture. Pay attention to your food while you're cooking.

Not seasoning food to taste. Taste is subjective. As food cooks, taste it (never taste uncooked foods like meats, chicken, or fish!). If it's too salty in an early step, don't add more until the recipe is complete. If it tastes bland toward the end of cooking, add more salt or other seasonings. And always, always taste food before it's served.

DISASTER FIXES

When you're cooking and baking, disasters are bound to happen. Some disasters are easier to fix than others! Here's a list of common kitchen disasters and how to fix them.

Curdled soup, sauces, and custards. Immediately pour the mixture and 2 tablespoons boiling water into the blender and whirl until the curds are gone.

Bread doesn't rise. The most common culprit in this problem is that the yeast is dead. Either you used yeast that was past its expiration date or the liquid used to dissolve the yeast was too hot. You can try dissolving more yeast in lukewarm water and kneading it into the bread. Let it rise again. The bread will have a different taste and texture, though.

Overcooked seafood. If you overcook fin fish, it will disintegrate into tiny flakes. Broiled, overcooked fish will dry out. Tuna hardens and salmon loses flavor and moisture when overcooked. Mince the seafood and use it in a sandwich spread.

Overcooked meat. You can add more moisture to overcooked meat by slicing it, putting it into a saucepan, and adding stock. Heat everything up, then remove from the heat, cover, and let stand 5 minutes. Serve the meat immediately.

Overcooked pasta. If you overcook your pasta so it's mushy, you can briefly panfry it in some butter or olive oil to firm it up.

Lumpy mashed potatoes. You can force the mashed potatoes through a ricer, which will remove all lumps. Don't try to process mashed potatoes in a food processor or they will become gluey.

Overcooked vegetables. Turn these into a puree or a soup. Just put them into a blender or food processor with a little bit of liquid for a puree or a lot of liquid for a soup.

Food that's oversalted. You can add some sugar or vinegar to the food to take away the salty flavor, but that just changes the flavor. If the problem food is a soup or stew, add more (unsalted) liquid.

Food that's too spicy. You can try to add some sugar to a recipe that has too many chiles or seasoning, but again, this changes the flavor. The only true solution is to add more of all of the nonspicy ingredients. This will increase the volume of the food; freeze part of it so it doesn't go to waste.

Food that's too acidic. Add a tiny pinch of baking soda to food that tastes too sharp or vinegary. It will balance out the pH of the food without affecting the flavor.

Scorched food. If the food you're cooking on the stove top scorches on the bottom, move quickly. Take the pan off the heat, trying not to move it around too much. Gently remove the top portion of the food with a ladle, leaving the scorched part behind.

READING LABELS

If you are going to buy processed foods (and who doesn't?), take the time to read labels so you can make informed food decisions. Nearly every packaged food sold has a label outlining its nutritional info. Some fresh foods now have labels, but they are mainly used to point out health benefits. The Nutrition Facts information tells you how much fat, cholesterol, sodium, carbohydrates, protein, vitamins, and minerals are in an average serving of that food.

What's On a Label

A food label will tell you everything you need to know about a food. It's important that you understand what terms appear on food labels, what they mean, and how to interpret them.

Serving size. The first thing to note is the serving size. Some serving sizes are surprisingly small, and some foods may appear to be packaged as a single serving, but actually contain more than one. If a package of food contains 2½ servings and you eat the whole thing, you've eaten 2½ times the amount recommended and consumed 2½ times the calories, fat, protein, carbohydrates, sodium, and so forth indicated on the label.

Recommended daily intake. The nutrition information is designed to tell you how much of the recommended daily intake of vitamins and minerals a serving of a food item contains. The label's information is usually calculated for a 2,000- or 2,500-calorie-per-day diet. If you are on a 1,600- or 1,800-calorie-per-day diet, you will have to adjust the Daily Value information by aiming to consume 80 to 90 percent of the Daily Value figure given.

Ingredients list. The ingredients on a label are listed in the order of the largest amount to the smallest. Many ingredients in packaged processed foods are long words that are unfamiliar to us. Some are simply technical terms for ingredients we know, while others are compounds created using industrial processes. When reading labels, avoid foods that contain partially hydrogenated oils (trans fats); list sugar, high-fructose corn syrup, or white flour as one of the first ingredients; and contain ingredients you can't pronounce.

Organic claims. The "organic" label is important for consumers looking to purchase and consume foods produced without chemicals or artificial agents. A food can't be labeled "organic" unless the ingredients used to make it are grown or produced without pesticides, herbicides, hormones, or antibiotics. Make sure that foods labeled "organic" are healthy in other ways; you can buy organic cheese puffs, for example, but are any cheese puffs really all that healthy? Some foods, when not grown organically, are loaded with pesticides. Although organic produce can be more expensive, prices will go down as more consumers buy organic.

Aliases. Food manufacturers sometimes try to hide certain ingredients, such as sugars, by listed them under different names. Sugar, for example, can be listed as fructose, sucrose, and dextrose. To avoid the food preservative known as MSG, look for terms such as *gelatin, yeast extract,* and *sodium caseinate.*

"Healthy" labels. Also watch out for the "healthy" claim on labels. The Food and Drug Administration (FDA) allows food manufacturers to use this claim on foods that contain at least 10 percent of the daily intake of vitamin A, vitamin C, protein, iron, calcium, and fiber. Raw produce can be labeled "healthy." Canned fruits and vegetables can carry the "healthy" designation. Frozen fruits and vegetables can as well. But you can't just load up your grocery cart with foods labeled "healthy" and assume you have all healthy foods. You must read labels and calculate how much of the required nutrients you're eating.

Sodium. The sodium content of processed foods is also important. Most nutritionists say Americans eat two to three times the amount of sodium our bodies need. Adults shouldn't consume more than 2,400 milligrams of sodium a day.

The FDA is always updating and revising its labeling rules, so you must read labels on all processed foods each and every time you buy them. The ingredients in any processed food can change at any time, so a food you thought fit into your diet may not next week.

UNDERSTANDING DONENESS TESTS

When you cook something, you have to understand when it's "done." Meat, poultry, and vegetables all have different doneness tests. There are three forms of doneness tests: internal temperature, observation, and physical tests.

Internal temperature test. This test is the most accurate of the three. Use a meat thermometer or instant-read thermometer to literally "take the temperature" of the food.

Observation test. Just look at the food! Cookies are done when they look browned. Fish is done when the flesh flakes after inserting a fork and twisting. Chicken is done when the juices run clear instead of pink. Brownies are done when the crust is shiny and the batter doesn't jiggle when the pan is moved. And quick breads are done when a toothpick inserted in the center comes out clean or has only a few crumbs clinging to it.

Physical test. These tests are less accurate. Chicken is done when it feels firm. You can check for the doneness of steak by pressing your finger onto the meat; different stages of doneness (rare, medium, well) feel different. Cakes and quick breads are done when they spring back when lightly touched with a finger.

Doneness Tests for Specific Foods

Listed here are the doneness tests for specific types of food. It's important to learn them before you start cooking. After all, if you don't know when hamburger is fully cooked or when a steak is medium, you can't serve a good meal. For more specific information about the doneness of each of these groups, see the chapter for each type of food.

Beef. Steaks can be cooked anywhere from rare to well-done. Bacteria on meat are present on the outside of the steak; the flesh is dense enough so most bacteria can't penetrate through to the center of the cut. You need to watch steaks carefully as they cook to be sure they don't overcook.

Roast beef (standing rib roast, rib eye roast, tenderloin roast) is cooked to the same finished temperatures as steaks. These meats cook anywhere from 20 to 40 minutes per pound, depending on the cut.

Pot roast (chuck, brisket, rump, and bottom round) is different from roast beef or steaks. These cuts of meat must be cooked with moist heat to 210°F. This temperature seems high, but there's a reason for it. The heat starts melting tough collagen present in these cuts at 150°F. At 170°F, the collagen starts to moisten the meat. Collagen doesn't become completely soft and gelatin-like until it reaches 200°F. At 210°F, the meat absorbs the cooking liquid, the collagen is very soft and flavorful, and the meat is moist and tender.

Ground beef must be handled carefully. Because the bacteria on the surface of the cut is spread throughout the meat when it's ground, the meat needs to be cooked to well-done, which is 165°F. You can't depend on the color of ground beef to tell the

Health Tip

The USDA recently changed the safe cooking temperatures for steaks. Rare is no longer considered safe for those in high-risk groups. The lowest internal temperature of a cooked steak should be 140°F before it is taken off the heat. After resting, the temperature should rise to 145°F, which is medium.

temperature; you need to use a meat thermometer. Hamburgers and any ground meat must be cooked to well-done.

Chicken. Chicken must always be cooked well-done. Chicken flesh is more porous than beef, pork, or lamb flesh, so bacteria from the surface of the meat can easily spread into the interior. And the way chicken is processed forces bacteria deep into the meat. Never serve chicken rare, medium-rare, medium, or medium-well.

You can test for doneness by pricking the chicken with a knife. If the juices run clear, with no tinge of pink, the chicken may be thoroughly cooked. When roasting a whole chicken, if the drumstick is loose in the joint when rotated, the chicken is ready to be tested. But these are just tests. For true safety, check the internal temperature of the bird with a thermometer. Cook until the chicken breast registers 165°F. The thigh temperature should register 170°F. The whole bird should register 180°F.

Ground chicken, like all ground meat, must be fully cooked to a temperature of 165°F. Chicken sausages should also be cooked to well-done.

Eggs. In the 1990s the FDA changed its recommendation for egg doneness. Eggs cooked "easy," or with the yolk still runny, were considered unsafe because of salmonella bacteria contamination. The recommendation was, and still is, that all eggs be cooked well-done. The soft-cooked egg for breakfast is no longer considered safe.

In recent years, many cookbooks have chosen to ignore this safety standard. If you want to serve eggs with a runny yolk, look for pasteurized eggs. They have been heat-treated with a proprietary process you can't duplicate at home. You can certainly serve eggs with runny yolks if you want to; but be aware that there are food poisoning risks.

Fish and seafood. Some fish are best served well-done, when the flesh flakes when a fork is inserted into it and twisted. Other fish are more popularly served rare or medium-rare. For instance, tuna is routinely cooked to rare. And salmon fillets and steaks are cooked to medium. The choice is yours. If you have a person with a compromised immune system in your family, it's a good idea to cook fish to well-done.

Fish fillets and steaks are cooked for about 10 minutes per inch of thickness. A whole fish is cooked until the temperature probe inserted into the thickest part of the flesh reads 140°F.

Shrimp are done when they curl and turn pink. There really is no other doneness test for shrimp, other than cutting open very large shrimp to make sure the center is opaque.

Clams, oysters, and mussels are done when their shells open. These shellfish are cooked while still alive. Before cooking, make sure that the shells are tightly closed. If any are open slightly, tap the shell. If the shells don't close, discard that shellfish. After cooking, be sure to discard any shellfish that aren't open. Never pry open a cooked bivalve to eat it.

Lamb. Lamb, like beef, can be cooked medium-rare to well-done. The doneness temperatures are a little lower than beef temperatures. Cuts like chops, shank, and roasts can be cooked to 145°F. Most people prefer lamb to be cooked to medium doneness. But just like all ground meats, ground lamb must be cooked to 165°F.

Pork. Pork no longer has to be cooked to well-done. That rule was instituted years ago because pigs used to eat food that could contain a parasite called trichinosis. Only five people were diagnosed with this disease in 2004, and they got it from eating wild pork that foraged for its food. Pork producers monitor their product for this parasite. Trichinosis is killed at 140°F.

Cook pork to medium, which is 145°F. Pork can contain bacteria, just like beef, that can make you sick, so don't serve rare or medium-rare pork. The juices should run slightly pink, and the meat should feel springy and almost firm.

Turkey. Turkeys, like all other poultry, must be cooked to well-done. A whole turkey is done when the temperature in the thigh is 180°F. The temperature at the center of the stuffing inside the cavity should be 165°F. The juices from the bird should run clear when the turkey is cut or pricked.

Vegetables. Vegetables are usually cooked to a crisp-tender texture. Vegetables that are going to be mashed or pureed, such as potatoes or parsnips, are cooked until soft. A knife inserted into the potato should go in and out without resistance. Overcooked vegetables can be pureed so they are palatable to eat.

Health Tip

Any fish eaten raw should be sushi-grade—that is, impeccably fresh and clean—and bought from a reliable fishmonger. Ceviche, which is raw fish "cooked" with acidic ingredients such as lime or lemon juice, is not safe for people in high-risk groups.

Health Tip

There is a caveat to pork safety. Many people are choosing free-range pork because of, well, unpleasant stories about intensive pig farming. These animals can carry trichinosis because they're allowed to roam and root in the ground. The meat also has higher amounts of bacteria. If you buy free-range pork, cook it to a higher temperature just to be safe.

5

KITCHEN SAFETY

If your food isn't wholesome and safe, it doesn't matter how good it tastes or how perfectly it's cooked. If someone gets sick from food you cooked, your work, time, and money are lost and there can be serious consequences. More than 75 million Americans get food poisoning every year, and 6,000 of those people die. Food poisoning can make you very ill. That's why you must follow food safety rules.

Physical safety is another important aspect of cooking. The kitchen is a hazardous place. It's very easy to hurt yourself with superhot appliances, hot food, knives, and food processors. You must learn how to use a knife and how to handle hot foods.

FOOD SAFETY

The topic of food safety has been in the forefront of the American consciousness in the last few years. With huge recalls of everyday items such as peanut butter and spinach in the headlines, and countless people getting sick, it is important to understand what we can do in our own kitchens to prevent food-borne illnesses.

Refrigeration's main purpose is to prevent bacteria from growing on foods. The problem with many so-called spoiled foods is that you cannot see or smell anything wrong. The most deadly bacteria, botulism, has no taste or aroma. It doesn't discolor the food, and you can't see it. But a tiny amount of botulism can kill.

Here are the basic food safety rules:

Wash your hands. Always wash your hands before and after handling food. Wash your hands in the middle of cooking, too. It's too easy to drop food or slip using a knife if your fingers are slippery or greasy. And wash your hands again with hot soapy water after you've handled perishable foods that need to be cooked before serving: raw beef, pork, chicken, seafood, and eggs.

Watch those temps. The "danger zone" temperature range for food is between 40°F and 140°F. Perishable foods left at room temperature for more than 2 hours can quickly reach this zone. Keep hot foods hot and cold foods cold. Cool hot foods as quickly as possible, and heat up cold foods quickly.

Never partially cook meat and then refrigerate or freeze it. This will put it through the "danger zone," where bacteria can grow and produce toxins, too many times. Always completely cook meat if you plan on holding it for later consumption or freezing it for later use.

Meats and eggs must be cooked to specific internal temperatures. Cook steak to 140°F, pork to 145°F, ground meat to 165°F, chicken breasts to 165°F, chicken drumsticks and thighs to 170°F, and whole turkeys to 180°F. Fish and seafood should be cooked until opaque, or until the flesh flakes with a fork. Eggs should be cooked until the yolk is firm and set. You can use pasteurized eggs to make eggs with runny yolks, but still, the white must be cooked until it's firm.

Don't leave food on the counter for several hours to cool before putting it in the fridge. The latest research advises cooks to let hot foods cool at room temperature for an hour before refrigerating or to place them in an ice-water bath so they cool quickly. If you place very hot foods in the fridge, the outside edges will cool long before the center does. This keeps the center of the food in the danger zone too long.

Buy yourself a food thermometer. It is a handy tool for measuring how hot or cold your foods are and how long it takes them to effectively chill or heat. Four hours is the absolute maximum time cold food should take to heat to 140°F or above and for hot food to chill to 40°F or below.

Defrosting and cooking food is a tricky business. Never thaw frozen meats at room temperature. Allow enough time to let them defrost in the refrigerator. This can take a few days with a frozen turkey or roast.

Sanitize work spaces. There is a big difference between clean and sanitized. Something may look, smell, and seem clean but still be dangerous. Make a sanitizing solution with one teaspoon bleach per one quart cold water. Or, sanitize using boiling water.

Avoid cross-contamination. A major source of food poisoning is contamination from other foods. Always cut raw meat, fish, or poultry last. Buy three separate cutting boards: one for fresh

Helpful Tip

Cool soups quickly by making an "ice wand." Fill a clean 20-ounce plastic soda bottle with water and freeze. Insert the wand into the soup and place the pot in the fridge uncovered; stir frequently. Use a shallow container to get more surface area to help cool foods quickly. Make an "ice bath" by placing ice and cold water in a large bowl and nesting a smaller bowl inside it with the item you want to chill.

veggies, one for raw meats and poultry, and one for seafood. If using the same board for multiple tasks, always sanitize between uses. Store raw meat, fish, poultry, and eggs in the bottom of the fridge so juices don't drip onto other foods.

Keep cooked and uncooked foods separate. Never place cooked meat on the same platter used to hold uncooked food. Be sure to wrap raw meats well, and don't let their

juices drip onto foods that will be eaten raw, like fruits or vegetables.

When raw meat is marinated in a dressing mixture, it must be handled carefully. Always marinate meat in the refrigerator, *never* on the counter. Don't let the marinade come in contact with already cooked food until the marinade has been boiled for at least 2 minutes. Place the container holding the marinating meat on the lowest refrigerator shelf so it doesn't drip onto other food.

Inspect cans carefully. When using canned foods, always make sure that cans are free of rust, are not bloated, and have no dents. Discard any cans that have any of these traits. Food in cans has been cooked to a safe temperature. It is theoretically safe to eat any canned food without heating it.

All these rules sound intimidating, don't they? But once you study and understand them, they will become second nature. Soon you'll be arranging your refrigerator to keep raw meats away from the strawberries and cooking meat to the proper temperature without a second thought.

THE LIFETIME OF FOOD

Handling and cooking food improperly can compromise its safety. But how you store food also plays an important role in keeping it safe and wholesome and at peak quality. No food, no matter how well prepared or how many preservatives it contains, lasts forever. It's crucial that you keep track of foods: the day you buy them, their expiration date, and where they are stored.

Some foods will last only one day in the refrigerator; others will last for weeks. Some foods last only a month or two in the freezer; others will last for a year. You must know how long food lasts to avoid throwing away perfectly good food (which is just like throwing away money).

BUDGET TIP

Many expiration dates on foods don't mean the food will be unsafe to eat after that point. By law, most of the dates just mean that's the day the food will lose quality or some nutritional value. Still, it's best to respect those dates. You really don't want to eat pasta that's dried on the edges or some breadsticks that won't rise because the expiration date has passed.

Produce Lifespan

Produce	Pantry or Counter	Refrigerator	Freezer
Apples	1–2 weeks	3 weeks	Cooked only; 6–7 months
Berries	Do not store	1–2 days	3–4 months
Citrus fruits	4–6 days	1–2 weeks	2–3 months
Fragile skinned vegetables: mushrooms, cucumbers, peppers	Do not store	2–5 days	10 months
Grapes and soft fruits	1–2 days	4–6 days	1 month
Lettuce	Do not store	2–4 days	Do not store
Melons	2–3 days	3–5 days	Peeled and cubed: 6 months
Onions and garlic	2–3 weeks	Do not store	9–10 months
Potatoes	1 month	Do not store	Do not store
Root vegetables: carrots, parsnips	1 week	2–3 weeks	2–3 months
Tomatoes	2–6 days	Do not store	Only after processing: 2–3 months

Meat Lifespan

Produce	Pantry or Counter	Refrigerator	Freezer
Cuts of beef	Do not store	3–5 days	4–6 months
Chicken	Do not store	3–4 days	9 months
Fish	Do not store	1–2 days	3–5 months
Canned meat	3–4 months	1 week after can has been opened	Do not store
Ground meat	Do not store	1–2 days	3–4 months
Processed meats	Do not store	2 weeks	2 months
Fresh pork	Do not store	3–4 days	4–6 months
Shellfish	Do not store	1–2 days	3–4 months

Dairy Products Lifespan

Produce	Pantry or Counter	Refrigerator	Freezer
Butter	Do not store	1–2 months	6–8 months
Hard cheese	Do not store	2–4 months unopened; per expiration date	6 months
Soft cheese	Do not store	1–2 weeks	4 months
Eggs	Do not store	3–4 weeks	Only store beaten eggs: 2–3 months
Milk and cream	Do not store	1–2 weeks; per expiration date	Do not store
Shelf stable milk	1–2 weeks	1–2 weeks	Do not store
Sour cream	Do not store	2 weeks	Do not store

Bakery Items Lifespan

Item	Pantry or Counter	Refrigerator	Freezer
Sliced bread	3–6 days	2–3 weeks: Check label; some breads should be stored in the fridge	4 months
Unsliced bread	4–6 days	1 week	4 months
Cake	2–5 days	1 week	2 months
Cookies	1–2 weeks	1 month	1 year
Muffins	2–3 days	3–6 days	2–3 months
Pies	1–2 days; store cream pies in fridge	3–4 days	2 months

Baking Supply Lifespan			
Item	Pantry or Counter	Refrigerator	Freezer
Baking powder and soda	3–6 months	3–6 months	3–6 months
Chocolate	4–6 months	Do not store	1 year
Cocoa powder	6–8 months	1 year	1 year
Dough	Do not store	Use by date: 2–3 months	2 months (do not freeze tube cans)
Flour	6–12 months	Do not store	Whole wheat flour: 6 months
Herbs and spices	6 months	6 months	1 year
Nuts and coconut	2–3 months	3–4 months	1 year
Sugar	1–2 years	1–2 years	1–2 years

For proper storage, make sure your refrigerator and freezer are in good working order. Keep a thermometer in your refrigerator and freezer and check it frequently. The refrigerator temperature should be between 35°F and 40°F. The freezer temperature should be below 0°F. Your pantry should be dry, dark, and cool, below 80°F.

FOOD SAFETY AND APPLIANCES

Appliances can help you keep your food safe, if you use them properly. As long as you keep your appliances in good working order; follow the manufacturer's directions for use, cleaning, and repair; and obey food safety rules, you can use these machines without worry.

Freezers. The freezer can be used to safely store food for long periods of time. It's inherently safe, but there are some rules you need to follow.

■ Be sure that the freezer is set to 0°F or below. The freezing point of water is 32°F, but sugar and salt content in food lowers the freezing point.
■ If you lose power, don't open the freezer. The food should stay frozen for 24 hours. After that point, check the food carefully. If it still has ice crystals, it's safe to refreeze or use immediately.
■ Make sure that the freezer door closes tightly and completely. Even a small gap can let the cold air out, which will increase the temperature inside the freezer.
■ Regularly defrost your freezer to keep it working well.

- Freezing doesn't kill bacteria or mold. It inactivates them, but when the food is thawed they will start growing again.
- Part of cooking ahead is knowing how long your leftovers can last. Always label frozen food with the date it was prepared and frozen. Most frozen foods retain quality for about three to four months.
- When you add homemade foods to the freezer, they should already be cool. You want foods to get quickly out of the danger zone of 40°F to 140°F.
- Use freezer wrap and containers to wrap the food to avoid freezer burn. Freezer burn isn't harmful, but it affects the texture and flavor of the food.

Microwaves. Microwave ovens do not make food radioactive. Instead, they emit radio waves, which are absorbed by sugar, fat, and water molecules in food. These molecules start to vibrate, which creates heat. This heat cooks the food. Like other appliances, microwaves have safety rules:

- Be careful when cooking meats in the microwave and always use a thermometer to check meat and poultry doneness. Read the owner's manual carefully and always follow cleaning and operating instructions.
- Foods cooked in the microwave must be rotated and stirred often. All microwaves have "hot spots," where more energy is concentrated, and "cold spots," which have less energy. If a piece of raw meat or fish is left in a "cold spot," it will be undercooked. That's why food is rearranged, turned, stirred, and rotated in the microwave oven.
- Standing time is also crucial in microwave cooking. The food must stand on a solid surface, not on a wire rack or trivet. The heat is moving through the food during this standing time, and the hot spots begin to cool. If you eat food directly out of a microwave oven without letting it stand for a few minutes first, you run the risk of mouth burns.
- Never operate a microwave oven that is broken in any way. Get it repaired by a qualified technician.
- Steam from microwaved foods can billow out when you uncover the food. Be careful to avoid burns.
- When boiling plain water for coffee or tea, first nudge the cup or bowl with a knife before you pick it up. Plain water can sometimes be heated past the boiling point, then violently erupt when it's first moved. Wait a minute before you remove the cup from the microwave oven.

Refrigerators. Your refrigerator is where you store perishable foods. It, too, must be kept clean and in good working condition. Regularly vacuum the condenser coils that are either underneath or behind the fridge; read the owner's manual for complete instructions. For the safest food, follow these rules.

- The temperature of your refrigerator must stay between 32°F and 40°F. This is the cut-off point where bacteria start to grow. To be sure your refrigerator is safe, purchase a refrigerator thermometer. Hang it on the front of the middle shelf so you can see it every time you open the fridge.
- Organize your refrigerator by using the shelves to group the food. Read the owner's manual to discover the coldest part of the appliance, then store fresh meats there. Keep all dairy products on the top shelf, use the second shelf for salad dressings and cheeses, and the third and fourth shelves for the perishable products you buy and use frequently. The door is a good place to store ketchup, mustard, pickles, and olives. Oddly enough, the door, which usually has those cute little indentations to hold eggs, is not the place to store them; it's too warm. Keep eggs in their original carton in the body of the fridge.
- Cooked refrigerated leftovers are fine for three days. Don't store leftovers longer than that.
- Since the refrigerator is very dry, unwrapped fresh foods will quickly dry out, shrivel, or otherwise spoil. More delicate foods can also absorb flavors of other foods. It's a good idea to keep everything in your fridge wrapped in good quality bags or wrap.

Slow cookers. Some have questioned the safety of slow cookers because they cook at low temperatures. There's no need to be concerned. Older slow cookers low setting cooks at 180°F and high setting cooks at 200°F. Newer slow cookers have been made to cook hotter: low is 200°F and high is 300°F, well above the "danger zone" of 40°F to 140°F. But there are some food safety rules you need to follow when using a slow cooker.

- Don't cook frozen meats in the slow cooker. The cold temperature of the meats can keep the entire temperature of the dish in the danger zone too long.
- Slow cookers can damage laminate countertops, so look for large ceramic tiles at outlet stores to place under them.
- Don't cook a whole chicken or whole turkey in this appliance; the slow cooker just can't heat these birds fast enough to prevent bacterial growth.
- Don't cool food in the slow cooker. The thick ceramic insert is designed to hold heat for a long time. If you place food in the insert into the refrigerator, it will take too long to cool below 40°F. Always remove cooked food from the insert and store in food-safe, well-sealed containers.
- Many of the newer slow cookers have built-in timers and keep-warm features that can turn a 6-hour recipe into a 10-hour recipe, giving you

Health Tip

Lunchboxes and coolers are used to keep food safe until it's time to eat. But these products can't cool food down. Pack hot foods to keep them hot and cold food to keep them cold. Never return food to a lunchbox or cooler and plan on eating it again. They can only hold temperature; they can't change it.

more time away from the kitchen. But you must follow the 2-hour rule. Never let perishable food (meat, eggs, dairy products) sit out at room temperature longer than 2 hours (one hour when the ambient air temperature is 80°F or higher).

- Attaching a timing device to the slow cooker can be risky. Some people have used devices that will automatically turn on lights to delay the start of their slow cooker, but it's not wise to gamble with your food.
- If the power goes out while your food is cooking, and you don't know exactly how long it was out, you must throw the food away. An outage of 2 hours or less is safe. If you're at home during the outage, monitor the time.
- Locking lids are a great feature that make it easy to safely transport food in your slow cooker. Be sure the locks really are fastened securely. It's still a good idea to place a hot slow cooker filled with food in an insulated case.
- Do not reuse heat-resistant cooking bags, foil, or paper towels. These materials are intended as one-use products and can't be sufficiently cleaned to make them safe for reuse. Regular plastic bags should not be used in the slow cooker. They can melt and ruin your food. And these products, which are not designed for the slow cooker, can emit chemicals into your food that can be harmful.
- A hinged lid is a great safety feature for slow cookers. Lids drip hot water when lifted, and steam will rush up from the food. Steam burns, and hot water can drip on your hands or arms.
- Even if you have an insulated carrier that will keep the food in the slow cooker warm, you still have to follow food safety rules. Don't let the food sit in the slow cooker without cooking for more than 2 hours.

SAFETY RULES FOR SPECIFIC FOODS

There are a few foods that have special food safety rules. These must be followed to the letter to prevent food poisoning. The most important rules for perishable foods is to store them and serve them at the correct temperatures.

Food Thermometers

If you don't have a food thermometer, go get one! It's that important to safe cooking. Use a thermometer to check the temperature of beef, pork, and chicken before you serve them. And remember that placement of the thermometer in the food is crucial. When you're checking the temperature of meat, the probe has to be in meat, not in fat or touching bone.

Before you use a thermometer to check foods, make sure it's properly calibrated. Bring some water to a boil and place the tip into the water. It should read 212°F, or 100°C. If it doesn't, return the thermometer to the store or add or subtract the amount it's off to your readings.

There are several types of food thermometers. The two most popular are permanent and single use. Permanent models come with a dial or electronic reading and can be used many times. Single-use thermometers can be used only once and are made of temperature-sensitive material. These thermometers can't remain in the food as it is cooking because the controls aren't heatproof.

The least complicated thermometer, a dial thermometer, should be placed about 2 inches into the food for an accurate reading. It can take a minute or so for this type of thermometer to register the temperature, so you have to be patient while you hold it in the food. Keep the thermometer in the food until the register stops moving.

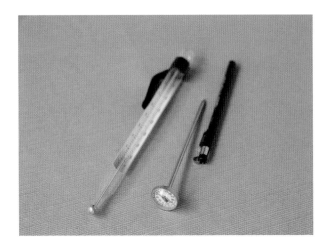

More sophisticated thermometers have digital readouts. These thermometers take the temperature of the food more quickly. And digital, instant-read, and thermometer forks can take a reading with just a 1-inch insertion, making them useful for thin foods.

Thermometers that stay in the food while it's cooking can be programmed to alert you with a beep at certain times in the cooking process, such as when the meat reaches a certain temperature. This type of thermometer is more expensive, but it's worth it if you cook a lot of meat.

Chicken can be a prime source of food poisoning. An accurate food thermometer is an important tool when working with chicken. Always wash your hands, utensils, and work surface before and after working with raw chicken or poultry. Stuffing poultry can be risky. The temperature inside the stuffing in the center of the bird must reach 165°F.

Never stuff a chicken or turkey ahead of time; stuff it only when you are ready to put it in the oven. And don't grill a stuffed chicken or turkey, because the center of the stuffing won't get hot enough.

Helpful Tip

When you use a thermometer, and find that the food isn't at the correct temperature, always wash the probe in hot soapy water and dry it before using it again. It's possible to transfer bacteria back into the food when you recheck the temperature.

Most cases of salmonella, the bacteria present in chicken, come from cross-contamination, when people eat foods tainted with raw chicken. When you're cutting raw chicken or handling it, make sure you do it on a surface (like a thin plastic cutting board) that can easily be whisked to the sink and washed with soap and hot water. Clean each utensil (and the sink!) before moving on to the next ingredient or preparing another dish.

Eggs. If you choose a recipe that uses raw eggs, use pasteurized eggs—eggs that have been heated to 140°F. Unpasteurized eggs must be cooked to 160°F.

Ground beef. Ground beef can contain one of the most dangerous pathogens in food: *E. coli.* These bacteria live in the intestinal tract of cattle and are transferred to ground beef by butchering and cross-contamination at the plant. If you want to eat rare burgers, grind your own hamburger; but, really, no ground meat cooked to less than 165°F is safe. Make sure to immediately clean any surfaces and equipment you use to make ground meat. Wash your hands frequently. Keep the meat below 40°F in storage and work with small amounts. Freeze or use ground meat within two days.

Meat marinades. Any meat marinade should be handled with care. After marinating the meat (in the fridge!), discard the marinade or brush it on the food as it cooks. Be sure to "cook off" the marinade. This means you turn the marinade-brushed side to the heat for a minute or two.

If you want to serve marinade as a sauce with the cooked meat, you must boil it before serving. Bring the marinade to a full boil for 2 minutes to kill bacteria, then serve. Never reuse marinade that has not been thoroughly cooked.

Shellfish. There's a strict rule about shellfish and food safety. When raw, clams and mussels should be tightly closed. Tap on an open shell; if it doesn't close, discard it along with any shellfish with cracks or chips. After cooking, the clams and mussels must be open. Discard any that are closed.

Canned tuna. Mercury levels in tuna are a concern. Mercury is a poisonous heavy metal found naturally in the environment. It moves to the top of the ocean food chain. Since tuna are an apex predator that eat other fish, they can have high levels of this metal. Pregnant women and small children shouldn't eat tuna more than once a week. Check sites like www.healthytuna.com for the latest government updates.

> ## Helpful Tip
>
> Did you know that rubs and marinades do more than just add flavor? When you grill, two kinds of carcinogens are created. Poly-cyclic aromatic hydrocarbons occur when food burns. And heterocyclic amines, or HCAs, are created from the high heat of the fire. Marinades reduce the amount of HCAs on food by acting as a barrier, or the acids and herbs themselves may be preventive.

PHYSICAL SAFETY

Now that you understand food safety, which is all about avoiding contamination of food, let's learn about physical safety. The kitchen is a dangerous place. Look at the arms and hands of an experienced chef. They often are crisscrossed with scars from knives and hot foods. You can cut yourself with a knife, box grater, mandoline, or food processor. You can be burned with boiling water or hot grease. Steam can burn.

These rules will protect your physical safety in the kitchen:

- Always wear shoes in the kitchen. It's too easy to drop a knife or splash some hot water out of a pot onto bare toes. Shoes protect your feet and stabilize your balance.
- Keep kids and pets away from the cooking area. They can distract you when you're stirring something hot on the stove. It's too easy for a child to grab a hot pan that's tantalizingly within reach.
- Always turn the handles of pots and pans on the stove inward. Not only can kids grab them, but clothing can catch on them and pull the pan off the stove.
- Never use wet potholders because they'll transmit heat easily to your hands. Hot pots can turn moisture in the potholders to steam, which burns.
- Never combine water and hot fat. The water will spatter and steam, releasing little fat bullets that fly everywhere.
- Don't wear loose clothing or flowing sleeves. These items can catch on pot handles or even catch fire if they come in contact with a hot surface, hot pot, or gas flame.
- Be careful when stirring pots of boiling liquid. And put foods gently into boiling liquids; don't throw them in, because they will splash.
- Lift lids off boiling foods carefully. The hot steam that billows out will burn.
- Never leave a hot stove top, broiler, or grill unattended.

KNIFE SAFETY

Well-balanced, sharp knives will make chopping, mincing, and dicing much easier. Keep your knives sharp and in good condition, and you will be able to slice, chop, and cut foods more easily and efficiently. What's more: Sharp knives are safer!

The Knives You Need

You don't have to spend a fortune on good knives. The truth is, there are a few essentials that will cover your entire cutting and chopping needs. Be sure that any knife set you buy is heavy-duty, with a full tang, or steel blade, running the length of the knife. The basic design for cooking knives has remained unchanged for a long, long time for good reason. Knives are made in two ways: forged or stamped. Forged blades last longer than stamped blades.

Whether you buy knives individually or in sets, there are certain basic knives every kitchen needs.

Chef's knife. This large knife is used to mince and finely dice foods. The blade should slope toward the handle and the tip. This allows the knife to effectively rock back and forth on a fulcrum. The blade length should be between 6 and 10 inches, depending on your hand size.

Paring knives. These small knives, with blades about 3 to 4 inches long, are used to pare (peel) the skin from fruits and vegetables. A well-equipped kitchen should have two paring knives of different sizes.

Scissors. A pair of scissors is used to open packages, to cut apart chickens, and for general kitchen tasks.

Serrated bread knife. This knife is a real workhorse in the kitchen. It can cut bread, tomatoes, and tough root vegetables. An offset serrated knife can help protect your hands as you work.

Sharpening steel. Learn how to use a sharpening steel to keep your knives sharp and in good condition. It's used not for sharpening an edge but rather to perfect the edge and keep the knife sharp during use.

Utility knife. At 6 inches in length, a utility knife is used for boning meats and filleting fish. The narrow, pointed blade is also good for cutting and chopping fruits and vegetables.

Purchase other knives, like boning knives, as you need them. A knife block keeps knives stored safely and looks nice in your kitchen. Don't store knives in a drawer. They will get knocked around, which dulls the blades. And it's too easy to cut yourself on a sharp knife blade when you're reaching into the drawer.

Knives are made from two metals: stainless steel and carbon steel. Stainless steel knives do not rust. The downside is they are difficult to keep sharp. That's why you see chefs on television constantly sharpening their blades. Carbon steel knives hold a razor edge, but they can discolor, are very brittle, and can break if dropped or mishandled. High-carbon stainless knives combine the best of both carbon and stainless steel and, as a result, are more expensive.

Sharpening Knives

Dull knives can slip and cut you while you work. To sharpen a knife, hold the blade at a constant 20-degree angle to the steel. Make light strokes, first on one side of the blade and then on the other. Do not use more than five or six strokes on each side, as more strokes will actually dull your knife.

A sharpening stone is the best way to sharpen your knives. Hold the blade at a 20-degree angle to the stone. Make light, even strokes, the same number on both sides of the blade. Sharpen in one direction only, to obtain a regular even edge. Don't over-sharpen. When finished sharpening, wipe the knife clean.

Using Knives

How you hold your knife will make the difference between working quickly and safely or getting hurt. Until you're experienced with knife use, work carefully and slowly. There's no need to rush.

Hold the food with your nondominant hand, with the fingers curled under like a claw. Move your curled fingers away from the knife as you move through the food.

Hold the knife with your dominant hand. Grip both sides of the blade with your thumb and forefinger, right at the very top of the knife blade, just forward of the handle (this gives you the most control over the blade). Curl the rest of your fingertips underneath the handle. Angle the tip down while cutting down to the cutting board with the back of the blade (don't use it like a cleaver!). The tip of the knife shouldn't leave the work surface as you cut.

When cutting with a chef's knife, the blade should touch the knuckles of the hand holding the food. Tuck your fingertips underneath to keep them out of the way. The knife should rock on its fulcrum, not guillotine straight up and down. The knife is meant to move through food by sliding across it, not cutting straight down.

When cutting with paring or utility knives, use the knife as an extension of your hand. When paring, hold the knife with your fingers, and use your thumb to guide the knife along the food. For chopping, slicing, and mincing, hold the knife like you hold a chef's knife.

6

HERBS, SPICES, AND SEASONINGS

Herbs, spices, and other seasonings add flavor, aroma, and interest to your food. There are dozens of herbs and spices you can use in your cooking, as well as hundreds of condiments and flavor enhancers. What spices and herbs pair the best with foods? Is there a difference between dried and fresh? And what's the best way to handle, store, and use these aromatic ingredients?

HERBS

Herbs are the edible leaves of plants. These herbs are available fresh or dried. Be generous when adding fresh herbs to foods—they add color, taste, and nutrients to your meals.

Herbs, since they are leaves of a plant, add phytonutrients, also known as antioxidants, to your diet. These compounds help prevent the risk of cancer and heart disease and protect your body against inflammation and oxidation, two causes of disease. And scientists are discovering that the essential oils found in herbs can improve your immune system and help prevent other diseases, such as diabetes and asthma. For instance, fresh basil is a good source of vitamin A.

Popular Herbs

These are the fresh herbs most often found in supermarkets, farmers' markets, and backyard gardens. The best way to learn about herbs is to work with them. Browse through a farmers' market and smell and ask to taste all of the fresh herbs you can. You can even bring along a notebook and make a note of the herbs you really like. When you're sampling, ask the grower what food he or she thinks pairs well with that particular herb or about his or her favorite herb combinations. With experience you'll learn to use the herbs you like best in wonderful ways.

These are the most common herbs:

Basil. This popular herb has a unique inherent sweetness and tastes lemony and peppery. It is a classic component in Italian cooking. Basil is a member of the mint family. It has natural antibacterial properties and anti-inflammatory effects. Sweet basil is by far the most common variety found in North American grocery stores. The leaves of sweet basil are bright, light green and broad compared to those of Thai basil. Sweet basil works well for Mediterranean fare and may be used in Thai cooking, especially if you prefer sweet over bitter tastes. However, be sure to use a generous amount; you will need much more sweet basil (than Thai basil) to make its presence known.

> ## BUDGET TIP
>
> To save money, grow your own herbs! Herbs are very easy to grow, and most (except mint) aren't invasive but will readily reseed. Grow herbs on a sunny windowsill, using kits you purchase from hardware stores. Or just assemble some small pots, fill them with a good sandy potting mix, and add herb seeds. As long as you continue to harvest the herbs by cutting them, the plants will keep producing. To get them at the peak of flavor, harvest your herbs before they flower. If flowers emerge, "dead head" them by lopping the flowers off.

Bay leaves. Many recipes for hearty soups and stews call for a bay leaf. It is literally the leaf of the bay plant. It contributes a warm, slightly bitter flavor to food. But bay leaves can be a health hazard. The leaves have a very sharp center spine that can hurt you if you eat it. Both dried and fresh bay leaves can actually cut the esophagus and the lining of the stomach. Always remove bay leaves from a dish before serving. If you want to use bay leaves in a blend, remove the center spine and grind it to a powder. You can easily grow a small bay tree on a sunny windowsill.

Chervil. This unusual herb is not often found in many spice cabinets. It's related to parsley but has a more delicate fragrance and flavor with a slight anise undertone. It's used in mild foods like eggs, fish, and chicken and in salads.

Chives. Part of the onion family, these narrow, hollow green stems have a mild onion flavor and are used as a garnish or stirred into fresh, uncooked recipes.

Cilantro or coriander. An Asian native herb plant produces fresh cilantro leaves, as well as coriander seeds. The dried seeds and fresh leaves have very different flavors. Cilantro wilts quickly and loses flavor when cooked for long periods. Fresh cilantro is usually sold in a bundle—look for it in the fresh herbs section of your local supermarket. Buying cilantro with roots still attached helps the leaves withstand a few days in the refrigerator.

Dill. Dill weed, the herb, is a feathery top of the dill plant. It's used in pickles and has a flavor that is spicy, sweet, and soft. The seeds are also used in cooking (see "Seeds" section later in this chapter). It's a good source of iron and manganese. You can often find fresh dill weed and dried dill weed in the supermarket.

Marjoram. This herb is related to oregano, but it has a milder taste and aroma and is a bit sweeter. The flavor is a bit like citrus with mint undertones. It's delicious paired with beef and vegetables. Marjoram is very easy to grow in the garden, either right in the soil or in pots.

Mint. This amazing herb has been cultivated for over one thousand years and has many uses, mostly sweet and in desserts. Some cultures dry the leaves and make tea from them. Others use mint as they would basil, adding it to salads of tomatoes and vegetables. To slice mint leaves, stack and chiffonade them by cutting thin ribbons with a sharp knife. Or tear the leaves into uneven slices. Mint can settle an upset stomach and help ease headaches.

Oregano. This strong and spicy herb is often paired with basil in Italian cooking. It's sometimes called "wild marjoram." It's most often used dried, but fresh oregano adds a wonderful flavor and aroma to foods. Oregano is very aromatic, with a warm taste and slight bitter flavor. Remove the leaves and use them only; the stem is too tough to eat.

Parsley. The most popular herb in the world, parsley is packed with nutrients! It is high in iron and vitamin C, which help fight anemia. It contains folic acid, which, among other things, is important for vascular health. It has a mild and fresh flavor. There are two kinds of parsley: flat leaf and curly. Curly parsley is used more as a garnish and has less flavor than flat-leaf parsley. Use flat-leaf parsley to add a fresh flavor and brightness to foods as a finish.

Rosemary. This strongly flavored herb is best used in soups, stews, and meat dishes. Rosemary is very pungent and penetrating since it contains so many aromatic

oils. This perennial herb is very easy to grow. Strip the leaves off the tough stem and chop very finely to use. Studies have shown that rosemary can improve liver function and is good for the skin.

Sage. Most commonly used in poultry stuffings, sage has a deep, rich, and earthy taste that can overwhelm foods, so it should be used in moderation. Fresh sage leaves make a beautiful garnish.

Summer savory. This is another member of the mint family. It has a pepper flavor and smells a little piney. It's mostly sold as a dried herb. Summer savory is a common ingredient in salt-substitute blends.

Tarragon. This delicate herb is paired with fish, eggs, and chicken. It has a licorice flavor. Its long, thin leaves are very tender. Tarragon is considered one of the four herbs of French cooking along with parsley, chives, and chervil. It is the flavoring in béarnaise sauce and is used in other sauces, too.

Thyme. This herb has a minty and lemony flavor. The tiny leaves must be stripped off the tough stem before using. Fresh, dried, and powdered thyme are all readily available.

SPICES

Spices are the dried root, bark, leaf, seed, or fruit of a plant. Spices are a fabulous way to add lots of delicious flavor to your recipes. You can grate or grind whole spices yourself or buy them already ground in small packages. Unfortunately, many of us cook with stale spices that we purchased months or even years ago. Be sure to smell ground spices before using them. They should smell very strong. If the aroma is weak, discard them and buy a new bottle.

Adding a teaspoon or so of dried spice to a dish does very little to affect its caloric value, but it can significantly boost its nutritional value. Many spices that have been used in traditional medicine have scientifically proven medical benefits. Paprika, for example, which is made from dried bell peppers, has about nine times the vitamin C content of tomatoes, because drying concentrates the vitamin.

When buying dried spices, opt for buying them whole rather than already ground, as the flavors and aromas of the spices last longer in their whole form. For example, a small bottle of ground cinnamon lasts only about a year before losing potency. But whole cinnamon sticks will keep their flavor for up to three years.

Spices can be purchased in tiny bottles, which are great for experimentation. Because they do lose their flavor after a few months, buy the smallest quantities you can, unless you use a lot of that particular spice. Add spices judiciously to your recipes, especially if you're trying one for the first time. You can always add more, but too much cinnamon or chili powder, for example, can ruin a recipe, and there's just no way to fix that mistake.

These are the most common spices you should have in your spice cabinet:

Allspice. This spice is not a combination of spices, as its name suggests, but the unripe, dried fruit of a tropical plant. The fruits look like little peppercorns. It is used in Caribbean and English cooking. Allspice has a warm, slightly sweet flavor and aroma.

Cardamom. This spice is expensive. It's mostly used in Scandinavian cooking, as an addition to breads and desserts. It's very aromatic, with a resiny taste and slightly smoky aftertaste. It's also commonly used in Indian cooking. You can buy the whole pods and crush them yourself or purchase it ground.

Chili powder. Like curry powder, chili powder is a combination of spices, not a single spice. Chili powder is a combination of ground chiles, cayenne pepper, cumin, paprika, and oregano or garlic powder. Ground chili powder is made of just the dried chile, finely ground. All of these powders are hot, but their flavors do vary. To make your own, in small bowl combine 2 tablespoons each paprika, ground chiles, and dried oregano; 1 tablespoon each ground cumin, garlic powder, and onion powder; 2 teaspoons cayenne pepper; and ½ teaspoon black pepper. Blend well; store in an airtight container.

Cinnamon. One of the oldest spices, cinnamon can be used in both savory and sweet dishes. It has a warm and powerful aroma and slightly peppery flavor. High in calcium, fiber, and iron, cinnamon can help prevent certain cancers. It also has an anti-clotting effect on the blood. Antibacterial properties make it a natural preservative for foods, too. There are two types of cinnamon: from the bark of the cinnamon tree (native to Sri Lanka) and from the bark of the cassia shrub. The latter is the most common cinnamon in use throughout North America.

Cloves. This spice is available whole or ground. Whole cloves look like tiny nails and are usually used for a garnish, as they are unpleasant to bite into. If a recipe calls for whole cloves, tie them into cheesecloth so they can be fished out and discarded before you serve the dish. Cloves have a warm and spicy taste and aroma.

Cumin. This spice has a very bold and strong smoky flavor. You can purchase dried ground cumin and cumin seeds. Dried cumin, which comes from the seeds of a flowering herb in the parsley family, is soothing to the digestive system and may lower the risk of certain types of cancer. The spice is used in Mexican, Indian, and Middle Eastern cooking.

Curry powder or garam masala. Garam masala is just a fancy name for curry powder. You can find it in the spice aisle of the supermarket, or you can make your own. It's made from cumin, turmeric, mustard, red and black pepper, mace, cardamom, cinnamon, and nutmeg. For a basic curry powder, combine one tablespoon each ground coriander seeds, ground cumin seeds, and turmeric; one teaspoon each dry mustard, ground ginger, salt, and pepper; and half a teaspoon each ground cloves, cardamom, and cayenne pepper. Blend well and store in airtight container.

Five spice powder. Five spice powder is a combination of cinnamon, star anise, gingerroot, cloves, and fennel. If you can't find it, combine an equal amount of these ingredients and mix well. Store in an airtight container and use in Chinese and Asian recipes.

Ginger. This spice is made from dried and ground gingerroot, a root vegetable. Ginger is a potent spice used in baked goods and curry powder. Ginger can help reduce pain and inflammation, and it is used as a natural remedy for heartburn, nausea, motion sickness, and migraine headaches.

Mace. Mace is actually made from the webbed, lacy covering of the nutmeg seed. And yes, it's the same thing used for self-defense, as pepper spray. It is very hot and spicy.

Dry mustard. This spice is made from the seeds of the mustard plant. It's used to make mustard and is very potent and hot. There are several types of dry mustard. English mustard is probably the most potent. Dry mustard has no scent until it's mixed with liquid.

Nutmeg. This spice is actually classified as a seed, but it's used as a spice because the seed itself is so large, usually about 1½ inches long. You can buy nutmeg as the whole seed or as ground nutmeg. If you buy it whole, store it with a tiny rasp to grate it fresh over recipes. It is used in both sweet and savory dishes. It brings a warm, slightly cinnamony aroma to recipes.

Paprika. This spice comes in mild, sweet, hot, and even smoked varieties. In addition to being high in vitamin C, paprika has been shown to improve circulation and normalize blood pressure. It is made from dried sweet or mildly spicy bell peppers that are ground until a fine powder is produced. It is used in Eastern European cuisine in Paprikash, as well as in goulash and other stews. Smoked paprika is made from smoked dried peppers.

Pepper. There are many different colors and varieties of peppers. Green pepper, pink pepper, white pepper, black pepper, and red pepper are the most common, listed in order from mildest to spiciest.

Saffron. Saffron is the most expensive spice in the world because the saffron threads are actually stigmas from the saffron crocus flower. It takes roughly 80,000 flowers to make one pound of saffron. It has a distinctive aroma and a penetrating, bitter, and highly aromatic taste. Saffron threads are red orange in color and sometimes yellow. The more vibrant the color, the higher the quality. Saffron is a key ingredient in the fish and rice dishes of Spain, France, and Italy. Before using this spice, crush the threads in a mortar and pestle and infuse in a little warm water to release the flavor. Turmeric is a substitute for saffron because it colors foods yellow.

Star anise. Although not related to anise, which is a sweeter, milder, fennel-like herb, star anise does have a similar taste profile. It adds a bold licorice flavor to Chinese dishes. The hard, star-shaped seedpods come from Asian evergreen shrubs. Whole star anise may be added to slow-simmered soups and stews, while ground star anise may be sprinkled into quick-cooking dishes or stirred into spice mixtures.

Turmeric. Turmeric adds a distinctive aromatic dimension and golden hue to a dish. It's a natural antiseptic and has been shown to prevent cancer in several studies. If you are on a gluten-free diet, note that many of the less expensive turmeric powders contain wheat (as a bulking agent). The same holds true for many curry powders.

SEEDS

Seeds used in cooking have wonderful flavors. They can be added to recipes whole or ground. Toasting seeds helps bring out their aromatic oils and enhances the flavor so you can use less. Don't let the seeds burn, however. If they do, you have to wash the pan and start all over again, because they will ruin the dish with their bitter, acrid flavor.

Buy seeds in small quantities. Because they are high in oils, they can become rancid. Always taste one seed before using to make sure they're fresh. You can grind seeds and spices in a spice grinder or coffee grinder or with a mortar and pestle.

These are the most common seeds you'll need in your pantry:

Anise. Anise is one of the oldest-known seeds. You should buy whole seeds and grind them yourself rather than relying on ground anise. This seed, with its licorice flavor, aids digestion.

Caraway. Caraway is the fruit of an herb plant, but it is classified as a seed. It's used to flavor rye bread, many soups, cheeses, and sausages. It's also very good in potato salad or, when ground, in spice cakes.

Coriander. The dried part of the coriander plant is the seed. While ground coriander is available in most supermarkets, you may want to buy the whole seed and grind it yourself for the freshest taste. Simply place whole coriander seeds in a coffee grinder and grind or use a pestle and mortar to pulverize the seeds into a powder.

Cumin. Cumin seeds are toasted to help bring out their flavors and release essential oils. Add the seeds to the hot oil and cook just a few seconds, until fragrant.

Dill. Dill is also available as a seed, which is the fruit of the plant. It has a stronger flavor than dill weed and is slightly bitter. Dill seed is used in bread and fish recipes. Its flavor is close to caraway seeds but is more mild.

Fennel. This seed of the fennel plant is most often used to make sausages and in Italian cooking. Fennel seed has a licorice taste and pairs well with rye breads, risottos, and vegetables.

Poppy seeds. Yes, this seed is from the opium poppy, and it can cause a positive drug test if eaten too soon before the test. But the seeds have a very low level of the opiate found in the unripe seed pod. They are mostly used for decoration and add crunch to foods. Poppy seed cakes and breads are popular. The paste is used as a filling for breads and cakes.

Sesame seeds. These little seeds taste nutty and are used to provide flavor and as a garnish. They are very high in copper, manganese, tryptophan, and calcium and are a great source of fiber. Tahini, the paste used in Greek hummus, is made from sesame seed paste. You can find white, black, yellow, and red sesame seeds.

Vanilla pod. Vanilla, that ubiquitous flavoring without which cookies and cakes would taste bland, comes from the seeds of the vanilla pod. For the most intense vanilla flavor, split the pod and scrape the tiny seeds off with your knife. Add to any cookie or cake batter. Vanilla is also available as an extract. Bury the leftover vanilla pod (after the seeds are scraped out) in a jar of sugar to make vanilla sugar, which is used in baking.

DRIED VS. FRESH

Most herbs come in two forms: dried and fresh. And most spices come in two forms: whole and ground. The type you choose depends on the recipe you're making. Generally, fresh herbs and whole spices are more expensive and potent than dried herbs or ground spices.

When substituting dried herbs for fresh, or vice versa, remember that 1 tablespoon of fresh chopped or minced herbs is equal to 1 teaspoon dried herbs. That's a 3-to-1 ratio. If a recipe calls for 1 tablespoon of fresh basil, but you only have dried, use 1 teaspoon of dried basil. Crush dried herbs between your fingers before stirring them into food to release more flavor. Or chop dried herbs together with fresh herbs like parsley.

Dried herbs have a different flavor and aroma than fresh. For instance, dried basil has more of a smoky, deep flavor, while fresh basil is more minty and lemony. Fresh oregano has a softer, herbaceous flavor, while dried is strong and intense. The essential oils become more concentrated as the leaves dehydrate.

BUDGET TIP

Growing your own herbs to dry for the cooler months is a great way to keep freshly dried herbs on hand year-round. Dry herbs very slowly to maintain the best flavors. Drying in an oven set to very low also works well. Then crumble the herbs and store in an airtight container. Make sure the herbs are completely dry, or they may mold in storage.

Really, the only way to learn the difference between fresh and dried herbs is to taste them and use them in recipes. Have fun experimenting as you learn more about these natural and healthy seasonings.

MATCHING HERBS, SPICES, AND SEEDS WITH FOODS

Matching herbs, spices, and the foods they taste best with is definitely an art. You need to experiment to find out which herbs, spices, and seeds taste best to you in combination with different foods.

Herbs	
Herb	**Foods**
Basil	Vegetables and spaghetti sauce and other Italian recipes. Pairs well with tomatoes, bell peppers, pesto, and chicken.
Bay Leaf	Soups, sauces, and stews. Good seasoning for meat, fish, and poultry.
Chervil	Fish, chicken, light sauces, and eggs. Used in French cooking. Add at the end of cooking.
Chives	Vegetables, fish, potatoes, salads, and soups. Excellent as a garnish for most savory dishes.
Cilantro	Coleslaw, marinades, and salsa. Used in Mexican cooking. Pairs well with vegetables. Too much can cause a soapy taste.
Dill	Vegetables, fish, omelets and other egg dishes, egg salad, potato salad, and pickles.
Marjoram	Vegetables, beef dishes, and seafood, especially tuna. Blends well with other herbs.
Mint	Desserts, mushrooms, salads, vegetables, chicken, and fish.
Oregano	Vegetables, fish, meat, spaghetti sauce and other Italian recipes, and pizza. Pairs well with onions, eggplant, tomatoes, beans, and meat.
Parsley	Vegetables and garnish for any main dish. Pairs well with fish and flavored butters.
Rosemary	Chicken, lamb, vegetables, tomato sauces, soups, and stews. Great with egg dishes.
Sage	Turkey stuffing and dressing, ham, liver, sausages, and veal. Pairs well with beans, peas, and kebabs.

Herb	Foods
Summer savory	Meat and vegetables. Pairs well with bean dishes. Try it in recipes that use thyme or sage.
Tarragon	Soups, stews, flavored vinegars, dips, egg and cheese dishes, chicken, fish, and seafood.
Thyme	Vegetables, stews, and fish. Combines well with garlic, onion, and red wine. Delicious in marinades.

Spices	
Spice	**Foods**
Allspice	Good in soups and stews and with beef, game, and chicken. Used in casseroles and fruit pies.
Cardamom	Used in Scandinavian baking and Indian food. Delicious with chicken and other meats, in curries, and with lentils and rice.
Chili powder	Essential for Tex-Mex cooking. Pairs well with beans, vegetables, beef, chicken, and fish.
Cinnamon	Used in savory and sweet dishes. Ingredient in curry powder. Blends well with chicken, lamb, fruit, and chocolate.
Cloves	Good with game, ham, and lamb and in sausages. Can be stuck into an orange to make a pomander.
Cumin	Pairs well with ground beef and chicken and is used in soups and stews. Essential to Mexican cooking.
Curry powder	Use in Indian recipes with chicken and fish and in pasta salads.
Five spice powder	Used in Asian cooking. Good in stir-fries and with chicken, fish, and beef.
Ginger	Used in savory and sweet dishes. Good in cookies and Indian cooking and with vegetables. Delicious with ham and pork.
Mace	Used as a hot spice in Mexican and Tex-Mex cooking and as a spice in baking.
Mustard	Use to make your own mustard by combining with water and vinegar. Pairs well with meats, vegetables, and potato salads.
Nutmeg	Used in savory and sweet dishes, especially baked goods. Pairs well with potato dishes, egg dishes, white sauces, pasta, veal, and lamb.
Paprika	Used as a garnish. Pairs well with chicken, fish, lamb, rice, and shellfish. Good with vegetables.

Herb	Foods
Pepper	Peppers of all kinds pair well with beef, chicken, fish, and vegetables. Good on the table as a condiment.
Saffron	Pairs well with chicken, fish, lamb, and seafood. Used in curries and risotto.
Star anise	Used in Chinese cooking and as an ingredient in five spice powder. Good with eggs, fish, pork, and poultry.
Turmeric	Inexpensive substitute for saffron. Delicious with fish, chicken, and vegetables.

Seeds

Seed	Foods
Anise	Licorice flavor used in baking and cooking. Pairs well with vegetables, fish, and seafood.
Annatto	Seeds are not eaten but steeped in hot water or simmered in oil, then strained. Substitute for saffron. Good with chicken and fish.
Caraway	Used in German cuisine, especially rye breads and baking. Pairs well with pork, sausages, cabbage, and cheese.
Coriander	Pairs well with fish, lamb, pork, and turkey. Used in curries and stuffing.
Cumin	Good with chicken, fish, lamb, pork, and sausages. Pairs well with eggs, lentils, and potatoes.
Dill	Good with vegetables like cabbages, carrots, and cucumbers. Used with chicken, fish, salmon, and veal.
Fennel	Licorice flavor is good with vegetables, fish, sausages, seafood, and tomatoes. Used in Pernod, a liqueur.
Poppy seeds	Used in baking, as a garnish, and as a pie filling. Delicious with fruit and rice and in curries.
Sesame seeds	Often toasted to bring out flavor. Good with chicken, lamb, fish, and shellfish. Used in baking.
Vanilla pods	Used mostly in sweet dishes but also in savory foods. Good with fruits and in pies, cookies, and cakes. Also used with fish.

Keep in mind that the point at which you add herbs, spices, and seeds in a recipe affects their flavor. Fresh herbs are best added toward the end of the cooking time or as a finish. Dried herbs are good in long-cooking recipes, but their flavor can fade and may need to be replenished before serving. And seeds are usually toasted before used in cooking.

To learn more about herbs, make your own blends. Herb blends add lots of flavor to foods. Think about your favorite herbs and how they complement foods. These are some common and easy-to-make herb and spice blends:

Bouquet garni is a combination of rosemary, thyme, sage, bay leaves, and peppercorns tied in a cheesecloth bundle. Use it in soups and stews.

Fines herbes is a mixture of thyme, tarragon, chervil, and parsley. Use this blend in egg dishes and sauces.

Herbes de Provence is made from basil, marjoram, thyme, summer savory, bay leaves, fennel, and white pepper.

Italian seasoning is a combination of dried basil, thyme, oregano, and bay leaves. Use in pasta sauces, marinara sauce, and pizza.

Seafood blend is a combination of crushed fennel seed, dried basil, dried parsley, and dried lemon peel.

When you cook with dried herbs and herb blends, start out using just a little bit. It's easy to add more, but you can't take it out if you've used too much. When you mix herbs, don't combine several very strong flavors. For instance, thyme is a mild herb with a minty lemon scent, while rosemary is very sharp, strong, and piney. Basil is warm and slightly spicy, and oregano is strong and pungent. Combine thyme with oregano, or basil with rosemary.

PREPARATION AND STORAGE

When cooking with herbs, spices, and seeds, you must know how to prepare them, how much to use, and how to add them to your food. You also want to know how to properly store them for maximum flavor. After all, these flavoring ingredients can be quite expensive, so using and storing them properly will help protect your investment.

Herbs

When you harvest fresh herbs or get them home from the supermarket, rinse them off, shake off the excess water, then wrap them in a paper towel and place in a plastic bag. They will stay fresh for days. Just pull off the leaves or slice them off the stems using a chopping motion. Parsley, basil, and sage should be cut from the stem, while rosemary, oregano, and thyme leaves are pulled off by hand. Tear, chop, or mince the leaves and then add to food.

For leafier herbs, use a sharp chef's knife to finely chop up the leaves. It's easy to chop fresh herbs using a chef's knife. Gather the leaves in a tight bundle and cut, rocking the blade across. Then fluff up the pile and continue cutting with the knife, changing direction to produce even, small pieces.

"Bruising" herbs is a common technique designed to release as much flavor as possible. Just rub the fresh or dried herbs between your fingers. You can also bend them, crush the leaves in your hand, or thwack them with the side of a knife.

Delicate herbs, such as basil, parsley, chives, and dill, should be added near the end of cooking time. Heartier herbs, such as thyme, oregano, and rosemary, can be added earlier on, as the heat from cooking will help spread their flavors throughout the dish. Always taste a dish seasoned with herbs before you serve it. It may need a little bit more of the herb, whether dried or fresh.

Spices

Whether you buy whole spices or ground spices, store them in airtight containers in a dry, cool place. Moisture, light, and heat rob spices of their flavor. A coffee grinder works well for grinding some spices, like cinnamon, allspice, cloves, star anise, and pepper. Buy a coffee or spice grinder just for that purpose, because the oils in the spices will "flavor" the grinder forever. There are new two-in-one grinders designed for both coffee and spices. A mortar and pestle work well to grind spices. Or place the spices in a heavy-duty plastic bag and crush them with a rolling pin, mallet, or heavy pan.

Seeds

Seeds should be stored in a cool, dry place in airtight containers. Because they have a high oil content, they can go rancid fairly quickly. If you don't

use seeds often, store them, tightly covered, in the freezer. And buy just small quantities of seeds at a time.

Most seeds are toasted before using. Place them in a dry pan over low heat and toast, shaking the pan frequently, until the seeds smell fragrant. You can also toast them in the oven. Heat the oven to 300°F and place the seeds in a shallow pan. Bake for 12 to 14 minutes, checking the pan frequently, until light golden brown. Or use the microwave to toast seeds. Microwave the seeds in a single layer on high power for one minute. Repeat until the seeds smell fragrant.

OTHER SEASONINGS

To maximize the flavor of food, it is important to have a variety of seasonings readily available. First and foremost is salt, which can be simple table salt or, even better, flaky kosher salt (for texture) or briny sea salt (for flavor).

Salt

Salt is a ubiquitous seasoning that has been used since the beginning of time to flavor and preserve food. Table salt, which we all have in our kitchens, is processed salt that can be used in any cooking or baking recipe. Sea salt comes in both a fine and coarse grain. Fine salt is good for cooking and seasoning, while coarse grain is used in a salt grinder, which produces a ground salt with a beautiful, crystalline texture. Sea salt is considered higher quality than table salt, which is usually made from rock salt.

Salt can be harvested from a mine or from the sea. *Fleur de sel* is literally raked from the surface of the sea in shallow-water areas of the Mediterranean. This mixture is then washed with more seawater and dried again. The salt has a very rich taste and is worth seeking out. There are many types of salts from different parts of the world. Since these salts are unrefined, they have more flavor and character.

Salt comes in almost all the colors of the rainbow. Hawaiian sea salt is red because of the volcanic clay found in the area it's harvested. Black salt, which is more gray than black, is used often in Indian cooking. It's also called *sanchal* and *kala namak*. Himalayan pink salt has lots of minerals like calcium, copper, and iron that color it. And smoked salt has literally been smoked to add a rich flavor and deepen the color.

A dash of salt will draw the moisture out of food, helping it evaporate quickly so food can brown. Salt brings out the flavors of food, too; just enough will intensify the flavors already in a dish, too much will make it just taste salty. Sprinkle a bit of salt over your salad just before serving to bring out the flavor of the lettuce and dressing and to give it a pleasing crunch.

Pepper

After salt, a good peppermill filled with whole peppercorns is a kitchen necessity; powdery preground pepper is a poor substitute. Buy whole peppercorns in bulk to save money.

You can find peppercorns in several colors. Black peppercorns are the most common, with a reliable heat. White peppercorns are slightly hotter and are good for light-colored dishes. Green peppercorns have a fruity and fresh taste. And pink peppercorns are tart and spicy.

Szechwan peppercorns aren't really peppercorns. They are dried flower buds from a type of ash tree that grows in Asia. Cooks toast and grind the husks of the tiny reddish brown buds to use directly in spicy dishes and as part of spice mixes.

Devotees note that Szechwan pepper isn't so much fiery as it is numbing.

Other Flavorings

With a collection of these ingredients in your pantry, you will never tire of the food you make, which often happens when you reach for the same seasoning dish after dish. Browse through the supermarket and pick up a small jar or two of one of these ingredients on your next shopping trip.

Capers belong in almost any fish dish; their salty flavor complements the briny flavor and perks up milder tasting fish like cod and sole. They're the tiny unopened flower buds of a bush that grows in the Mediterranean. Capers are preserved in a brine solution, marinated in vinegar, or packed in salt. A few added to a salad, tomato sauce, vegetables, or a fish dish can make all the difference. Rinse them before serving.

Chiles and peppers are very popular, as evidenced by the increase in Tex-Mex and Mexican food. If you enjoy hot and spicy foods, add chiles and peppers to your cooking and at the table. But chiles aren't just about heat. They have complex flavors, especially when roasted. Fresh chiles have a sweet undertone, and roasted chiles taste smoky and rich. Dried chiles taste smoky, too, with a slightly spicy flavor.

Chiles are "rated" according to the Scoville scale, developed by Wilbur Scoville in 1912. He measured how much sugar it takes to dilute the heat of peppers; that heat comes from capsaicin, an oil in the peppers' seeds, membranes, and flesh.

The mildest peppers are sweet bell peppers, with no capsaicin. As the peppers get hotter, the Scoville number increases, going up to 300,000. The heat is detected by pain receptors in your tongue, located slightly under the surface. This is why it takes a few seconds for a chile's heat to register when you take a bite of spicy food.

The chile's heat is concentrated in its inner membranes and seeds. For the most heat, leave those in when you cook. To make the chile milder, remove the membrane and seeds before using.

When you buy dried chiles, look for a deep color and firm texture. The chiles should be firm but not brittle or hard. If they are slightly pliable, that's just fine. You can grind dried chiles to make your own chili powder or paste (be careful to protect your eyes!). Or soak them in hot water for 10 to 15 minutes. Remove the stem and mince or chop the chiles before use.

There are so many dried chiles on the market, and each has its own unique flavor. Chiles are available fresh (like jalapeños and poblanos), dried whole (like anchos and guajillos), and dried ground (cayenne). Some, like chipotles, are smoked before they are dried.

Citrus juices and zest. These ingredients are wonderful to use to add flavor to your food. Lemon juice can actually make food taste a bit salty. Lime juice and zest perk up a marinade for ribs. The sweetness of orange juice adds wonderful flavor to chicken, fish, and pork dishes, and grapefruit juice sparks up a vinaigrette for your green salad. Citrus zest—from lemons, limes, oranges, tangerines, or grapefruits—is an easy way to add bright sophisticated flavor to your dishes. If you don't own a zester, you can use a microplane or fine hole grater to remove just the very top, colored layer of the peel where the essential oils reside. Take care not to grate into the white pith, which is usually bitter.

Fresh ginger is an excellent culinary ingredient and has been used in Asia for thousands of years. Look for gingerroot with smooth and shiny skin free of wrinkles. A large piece of ginger is called a "hand."

To prepare gingerroot, cut off about a 1-inch portion from the larger root. Then peel it using a swivel-bladed vegetable peeler. Or you can use a spoon to scrape off the papery skin. Grate on a grater or use a chef's knife to chop it fine.

International seasonings. Today's supermarkets have an array of international choices for adding heat to your food: *harissa* is a spiced chile paste favored in North Africa, *sambal* is a crushed chile sauce used throughout Southeast Asia, and smoky chipotle peppers in adobo (a rich tomato sauce) hail from Mexico. The Chinese have a hot chili paste that is used as a condiment as well as a sauce. All of these seasonings have a long shelf life and provide an inexpensive way to add dynamic flavor and spice to many dishes.

Lemongrass is associated with Thai and other Southeast Asian cuisines. A very fibrous herb, it therefore requires preparation before use. Sometimes whole pieces of lemongrass are added for a touch of flavor to soups and curries, while at other times only finely minced lemongrass is used. Lemongrass is sold both fresh and frozen—look for it at your local Asian food store. Frozen lemongrass comes as stalks chopped down to half their size or already minced and ready for cooking.

To prepare fresh lemongrass for cooking, first remove the bulb and upper stem. Cut the remaining stalk into thin slices. Then either pound the slices with a pestle and

mortar or process them with a mini chopper or food processor. You will end up with small, softened bits of lemongrass, which can be cooked and consumed. It can also be pounded into a paste with other ingredients and added to stews.

You can also cut off all but the bottom 5 inches of the stalk and discard the rest. Remove the tough outer leaves until you get to the tender, purplish inner stalk. Very finely mince this inner core and use it to season food.

Pesto. Pesto is an Italian uncooked sauce that is made with fresh basil, garlic, Parmesan cheese, pine nuts, and olive oil. The ingredients are whirled in a blender or food processor until a thick sauce forms. Pesto can be used in so many ways. Add it to pasta salads, combine it with sour cream for an appetizer dip, or use it as a sandwich spread. Spread pesto on pita pockets or naan and broil for a quick snack. It will last in the refrigerator about four days and in the freezer up to four months. If you grow your own basil in your garden, pesto can also be very inexpensive.

Pesto made with basil is traditional, but it is not the only choice. Arugula makes an unusual pesto with a bit of a bite. You can use parsley, mint, or any green herb. Avoid making pesto out of really strong herbs like oregano or rosemary, however. Instead, you can add these in small amounts as part of a pesto recipe. Pine nuts are also traditional, but walnuts or pecans are delicious options. You can leave out the cheese altogether if you plan on using the pesto as part of a creamy spread or dip.

Vanilla sugar. To make this sweet flavoring, place 5 cups of sugar in large sealed container. Place 1 vanilla bean in the sugar. Cut another vanilla bean in half lengthwise and scrape out seeds. Add the seeds and empty pod to the sugar as well. Stir well. Cover and let stand for 1 to 2 weeks before using in recipes. You can use this in any recipe calling for granulated sugar where you want a strong vanilla presence.

Sun-dried tomatoes can be soaked in hot water until soft, then chopped and added to soups, stews, and sauces. Some varieties come packed in oil. These don't need to be reconstituted before use. You can use the oil from these tomatoes in salad dressings or as the oil to sauté vegetables and meats.

Condiments

Condiments are a versatile way to add lots of flavor to foods. We're all familiar with ketchup and mustard, but other foods like horseradish, flavored vinegars, flavored oils, Worcestershire sauce, barbecue sauce, chutneys, mayonnaise, hot sauce, chili oil, hoisin sauce, plum sauce, mint jelly, and steak sauce should be in your pantry, too.

Chutney is a cooked sauce used in Indian cooking; it is sweet, tart, and thick. To make your own chutney, combine 1 cup sugar, ½ cup vinegar, and 2 peeled and diced mangos in a saucepan. Add ½ cup finely chopped onion, 2 minced garlic cloves, and 1 tablespoon grated ginger root. Simmer 1 hour, stirring frequently. Add ½ cup dried currants, ¼ teaspoon cayenne pepper, and 1 tablespoon Dijon mustard.

Mustard is a popular condiment, used on everything from hot dogs to potato salad. It's made from mustard seeds, some seasonings, and white wine or vinegar. To make your own, combine 2 tablespoons each yellow and brown mustard seeds with ¼ cup white wine vinegar or white wine. Add 1 minced garlic clove and ¼ teaspoon white pepper; mix and refrigerate overnight. Then blend the mixture in a food

processor; store in the fridge at least 3 days, stirring once a day, before using to release some of the volatile oils.

Dijon mustard is a strong mustard, made with white wine. Coarse mustard has lots of mustard seeds mixed in. Honey mustard is a combination of honey and mustard. You can make it yourself by mixing equal parts of honey and Dijon or coarse brown mustard.

Teriyaki sauce is made from soy sauce, ginger, garlic, and a sweetener like brown sugar or honey. You can find low-sodium versions of the sauce. Hoisin sauce makes a good substitute, for a slightly more complex flavor.

Vinegar comes in a variety of flavors that you can use to change the flavor of your mustard at will. Try substituting ¼ cup sherry or raspberry vinegar for the white. Or, substitute ¼ cup orange juice for the water. To make your own flavored vinegars, place herbs in a clean bottle with a cork top. Heat good quality vinegar to steaming, then add. Let stand 2 weeks, then use. Try using garlic, chives, tarragon, or rosemary for your flavored vinegar, or a combination of these ingredients. Store in a cool, dark place for up to 3 months.

Balsamic vinegar is a special type of vinegar that is sweet, dark, and thick. It's used in salad dressings and in marinades. The real stuff, which is aged for years, is so sweet it can be used as a dessert sauce.

Worcestershire sauce. No matter how you spell it or pronounce it, Worcestershire sauce has a unique "meaty" flavor and soy sauce–like character that make it indispensable. Add it to almost any soup at the last minute instead of salt for a deeper flavor. Add it to marinades, barbecue sauces, and bloody Marys and other cocktails. It is excellent with beef and pork, too.

LEGUMES, RICE, GRAINS, AND PASTA

7

Legumes, rice, grains, and pasta are an essential part of any pantry. With these ingredients on hand, you can whip up a dish in very little time. These foods all have different methods of preparation and different nutritional values. Legumes and grains are an important source of fiber, minerals, phytonutrients, and vitamins. If you choose whole grain pastas and brown and wild rice, your diet will be healthier.

Let's learn some more about each of these foods so you'll be comfortable buying them, storing them, and cooking them.

LEGUMES

Legumes are literally the fruit of plants. They include beans, peas, and lentils. These foods have been used by populations as a diet staple for thousands of years. Beans and lentils must be cooked before use. Some peas can be eaten raw, but many must be cooked.

Beans are one of the most nutritious foods. Their high protein and fiber content make them an excellent addition to your pantry. Beans are good for your heart. They are an excellent source of soluble fiber, which can help lower cholesterol. Beans are also a great source of B vitamins, iron, and potassium. A diet rich in beans can help stabilize blood sugar. In particular, black beans, cannellini beans, and chickpeas (garbanzo beans) each contain a trace mineral that can help detoxify sulfites. Most beans have twice the iron of beef, and beans are also rich in magnesium, an important mineral.

There are many bean varieties. They are all delicious, with a meaty and nutty taste and creamy texture. Different types of beans are used in different cultures and ethnic cuisines. These are the most common bean types:

Adzuki beans. These beans are small, oval shaped, and dark red. They're also called the field pea and red oriental bean. Adzuki beans are a staple of Chinese and Japanese cuisine, where they are made into a paste and used in candies and baked goods. They are a popular ingredient in the macrobiotic diet.

Black beans. Black beans are also called turtle beans, because they look like a turtle's back. They are black on the outside but light red or creamy white inside. Black beans are one of the healthiest foods you can eat. They are full of fiber, protein, and B vitamins like folate and thiamin. These beans are fat free and delicious, with a rich and nutty flavor. They are usually left whole when cooking and are often served in the cooking liquid.

Black-eyed peas. These are white dried beans with a small black dot centered with a white spot near the middle of the pea. The spot does look like an eye! Black-eyed peas are used in Southern cooking and soul food. They pair well with bacon, ham, and greens. Black-eyed peas are an inexpensive source of protein, B vitamins, and calcium. The tradition of eating black-eyed peas for good luck dates back to the Civil War. Northern troops considered black-eyed peas and corn unsuitable for human consumption, so left them in the fields for Southerners to eat.

Cannellini beans. Also known as the white kidney bean, these beans are a favorite in Italian cooking. They are very soft and tender when cooked. Their flesh is very creamy and the skin is thin and tender. They're used in salads, soups, and purees and are often paired with tuna in a main dish salad. Always rinse dried cannellini beans before sorting, soaking, and cooking.

Chickpeas or garbanzo beans. The main ingredient in hummus, a Middle Eastern appetizer dip. These legumes are nutty with a smooth texture. Since they take a long time to cook, most cooks used canned chickpeas. Just drain and rinse them before use. Chickpeas also are often used in stews and soups as a hearty winter dish.

Cranberry beans. Cranberry beans—also called roman or borlotti beans—were first cultivated by the Incas and Aztecs. When fresh, these beans are very large, about the width of a thumbnail. Cranberry beans are usually found at farmers' markets in the summer. They also can be bought dried or frozen. Many Chilean cooks freeze them fresh for use during the winter months.

Fava beans. These beans, used in Italian cooking, are also called broad beans, pigeon beans, and English beans. They take quite a bit of preparation. They must be shelled and parboiled, and then the outer skin is pinched off each individual bean. Fava beans are rich and buttery, but they have a bitter undertone.

Great northern beans. These beans are a bit smaller than cannellini beans and have a slightly grainy texture. They are a good substitute for cannellini beans. They have less flavor than cannellini beans or navy beans, but they do absorb the flavors of other foods very well. They're used in bean and bacon soup, baked beans, and the French cassoulet.

Kidney beans. These beans are kidney shaped, hence their name. Kidney beans, which are commonly used in chili recipes, are a great source of folate, potassium, and iron. Kidney beans must be cooked before you eat them, because raw kidney beans contain a toxin that can damage the liver. For this reason, always soak kidney beans and discard the soaking liquid before you cook them. And don't cook dried kidney beans in the slow cooker, since the toxin will remain in the food. Most people use canned kidney beans.

Lima beans. It seems that people either love or loathe lima beans. Laurie Colwin, author of "Home Cooking," may have said it best: "Lima beans are pillowy and soft and people should stop saying mean things about them." These beans are almost always sold dried; a fresh lima bean is rare. They pair beautifully with almost any ingredient and along with corn are a main ingredient in succotash.

Navy beans. Small and white, navy beans are most famous for their use in Senate Bean Soup, a hearty soup served in the United States Senate cafeteria. These pea-size beans are usually sold dried. Navy beans are a great addition to any soup or stew recipe, especially white chili, which is made with green chiles and chicken or pork. They're also used in baked bean recipes.

Pinto beans. These medium-size beans are light brown with darker brown speckles. They become a more solid brown when cooked. Pinto beans are the bean of choice for a common side dish called refried beans.

Soybeans. These beans are the only legume that provides complete protein. In fact, they're one of only a few plant foods that provide complete protein! They contain all the essential amino acids human beings need in their diet. They're also called edamame, which is their Japanese name. Soybeans are used to make tofu, soy flour, miso, tempeh, soy sauce, and soy milk. Studies show that consuming soy can help lower low-density lipoprotein (LDL)—the so-called "bad" cholesterol—and blood pressure.

Beans are available in dried and canned form. Dried beans are preferable in many dishes so they can absorb some of the flavors of the recipe. But they can take 6 to 8 hours to cook. Canned beans are a quicker alternative, but they don't taste as good and have a softer texture.

Canned Beans

Canned beans are especially helpful to busy cooks. The beauty of the canned bean is that it is perfect every time. And in a recipe like chili or a bean and vegetable salad, you won't notice that the canned bean texture and taste aren't quite as good as those of cooked dried beans. Always drain and rinse canned beans to remove the thick, sweet liquid they're packed in, unless the recipe calls for the liquid.

Canned beans are low in fat and high in protein and fiber, and they last practically forever on pantry shelves. Black, kidney, and pinto beans are the mainstay of a good chili, while creamy cannellini and cranberry beans are terrific tossed with braised bitter greens, like broccoli rabe, escarole, or mustard greens.

Dried Beans

Dried beans are inexpensive and nutritious. There are dozens of varieties of dried beans. Dried beans and peas come in all the colors of the rainbow. In fact, you can make very beautiful soups just by varying the types of dried beans and peas you use.

Dried beans are produce, so, like any vegetable or fruit, you must look them over and wash them before you use them. Sort to remove shriveled beans, bits of dirt, stones, or twigs. Rinse the beans well and proceed with the recipe. Most beans should be soaked before they are cooked. This makes for a better texture and removes the sugars that can cause, well, digestive upset.

There are several methods for soaking beans and legumes. With the slow soak, beans are soaked overnight for 6 to 10 hours. To hot soak beans, boil 2½ quarts water and add 3 cups beans. Bring to a boil, then shut off heat and let soak for 1 hour. To cold soak, simply cover the sorted and rinsed beans with cool water, cover, and let stand overnight. Soak different kinds of beans separately.

Cooking dried beans so they are evenly tender and soft can be a challenge. Here's the trick: Don't add any salt or acidic ingredients (tomatoes, vinegar, wine, olives, capers, fermented black beans, bacon and smoked sausages, citrus juices, sour cream, buttermilk) to the liquid they are cooking in, because acid toughens the skins. A pinch of baking soda added to the cooking water will make beans soft and tender.

To check for doneness, pick one up on a spoon and blow lightly on it. If its skin ripples and pulls away from the bean, the bean is done. Dried beans will triple in volume when cooked.

Some varieties of beans are less than a dollar a pound, which can make enough food to feed six people. When buying in bulk, be vigilant

> ## Helpful Tip
>
> Legumes have incomplete protein. That means they don't have all of the amino acids (the building blocks of protein) your body needs. Pair legumes with grains, nuts, or seeds to make complete protein. Scientists used to think legumes and grains or nuts and seeds had to be consumed at the same meal; this isn't true. Just eat a good variety of legumes, grains, nuts, and seeds every week.

> ## Helpful Tip
>
> Dried beans need to be soaked for at least 6 hours before cooking, but you can use this quick-soaking method: Put the beans in a large pot and cover with cold water. Bring to a boil, immediately cover the pot, and remove from the burner. Let stand for one hour. Drain the beans, and they are ready to use in the recipe.

about checking for small stones and other field debris. Rinse the beans in a colander and work through them with your hands. This will make the small stones more visible.

Watch dried beans when they're cooking and make sure they don't dry out. Add more beer, broth, or water as needed to keep them nice and saucy. When you are checking your beans for doneness, also check the flavoring. Season to taste and add spices if necessary.

Lentils

Lentils are an important food staple in many parts of the world. In India, where there is a huge vegetarian population, lentils form the bulk of the diet. Lentils are also called daal or dal. Dried lentils cook much faster than dried beans, so they're a good option when you want a hearty dinner on the table in under 30 minutes.

The lentil contains 25 percent protein, which is one of the highest in the vegetable world. Lentils are the seed of a plant family called pulses. Lentils must be sorted before cooking, just like dried beans. Unlike beans, though, lentils don't need to be soaked before cooking.

You can cook lentils al dente or until they fall apart and practically dissolve in soup; it's up to you. Lentils need at least 30 minutes of cooking time to become tender. Interestingly, lentils are never available fresh, only dried.

Lentils come in several colors and types:

Black lentils, also called beluga lentils, are very dark colored and keep their shape when cooked.

Brown lentils are the most common and the easiest to find. They have a mild, slightly earthy flavor and hold their shape when cooked.

French lentils, also known as Puy, are a dark blue green in color. The most expensive lentils, they keep their shape and texture when cooked.

Green lentils are very common. They take the longest to cook, but they retain their shape and texture after cooking. They're good to use in salads and side dishes.

BUDGET TIP

If you are watching your budget, beans are an excellent source of nutrition and a fine way to stretch a dollar. They can serve as a meat substitute. But beans by themselves are bland; they need plenty of aromatic vegetables and seasonings.

Red lentils are sweet and nutty tasting. They become very soft when cooked, so are often used to thicken soup. Red lentils are beautiful in appearance and have a lighter, sweeter taste than brown or green lentils. They cook in about half the time, too.

Always use 1½ cups liquid for each cup of lentils, whether you're cooking them for a salad or in a soup. Lentils should not be overcooked if they're being used in a salad or for a main dish. But if you're cooking lentils in soup, you can cook them until they fall apart. This will thicken the soup without any flour or cornstarch. For an interesting soup, add some lentils at the beginning of the recipe. Then add some more 30 to 45 minutes before the soup is done for some whole-lentil texture.

When cooking lentils, don't add salt at the beginning, because it makes them tough. Add salt just before serving.

Split peas

Split peas are dried peas that cook more quickly than dried beans because they are split by a machine. Because the liquid doesn't have to penetrate through the peas' skin, the peas soften easily, even in the presence of salty or acidic ingredients.

You can find yellow and green split peas in the supermarket. It doesn't matter which one you choose; they are both delicious and nutritious. Sort over the peas to make sure there are no small stones or dirt hidden among them. Then rinse the peas, drain them well, and proceed with the recipe.

Tofu

Tofu, or bean curd, is the original health food. Many people shy away from it, thinking it's just too New Age, but it can be very delicious when prepared with spices and aromatic vegetables. Tofu is fairly bland on its own but can be the basis of an infinite number of snacks, both hearty and delicate.

Tofu is high in iron and protein, although the protein is incomplete. There are dozens of kinds of tofu, from soft, medium, and firm blocks, to fresh tofu with the consistency of ricotta cheese. Tofu can be pressed into bars and used like pasta or meat in various dishes, such as Asian stir-fries.

Firm and extra-firm tofu are solid enough to stir-fry and grill. Real labels carefully to make sure that's what you're buying. Tofu must be drained before it's marinated or stir-fried because it contains a lot of water. Place the tofu in a strainer or colander and let it drain for a few minutes. Then press the tofu between kitchen or paper towels. When you press out the excess liquid, the firm varieties of tofu take on the texture of meat.

Tofu should be marinated for only a few minutes. To give firm or extra-firm tofu a meatier texture, freeze it and defrost before flavoring with a dry rub or marinade and grilling.

RICE

Rice has been cultivated in Asia for 5,000 years and has been nourishing populations for generations. It's a staple food in Asian countries and used in every cuisine in the world.

There are two forms of rice: brown and white. And there are several types of rice within those categories, depending on the type of starch it contains: amylopectin (highly branched) or amylose (straight line). Rice with more amylopectin is sticky when cooked, because the starch traps and holds water. There are more than 40,000 varieties cultivated in the world. Each has a distinct texture, color, and flavor.

Brown rice. Brown rice is unprocessed, unpolished, unhulled rice. It has more fiber, texture, vitamins, and minerals than white rice. To make rice white, the nutritious outer hull is removed using chemicals or polishing. The rice bran, the best part nutritionally, is used to make bran muffins and bran-based cereals.

Flavorful rice. Specialized rice types include basmati, jasmine, and wehani. They are all varieties of long grain rice with lots of amylose. These types of rice have very distinct flavors.

Glutinous rice. This rice is used in Asian cooking. It sticks together so much it's easy to use with chopsticks. It has tons of amylopectin and no amylose.

Long grain rice. This rice has more amylose than amylopectin, so the rice grains become separate and fluffy when cooked.

Medium grain rice. This rice has a bit more amylopectin than amylose starch. It also has a softer outer shell, so the finished dish is creamy.

Helpful Tip

Tofu is a flavor sponge. It will absorb the flavors of any food you cook it with. Build layers of flavor on bland tofu with a rub and a marinade. Be sure to taste your tofu dishes before you serve them and add more seasoning as needed.

Short grain rice. This rice has more amylopectin, so it cooks up sticky. Arborio rice, used in risotto, is a short grain rice.

When you boil rice on the stove top, watch it closely, as it burns easily. This can leave a sticky mess on the bottom of the pan. Use a nonstick pan and first sauté the rice with olive oil or butter. And you may need to add more liquid while rice is cooking.

Rice should not be cooked al dente. The easiest way to check rice doneness is to taste it. Rice actually "blooms," which means it absorbs the flavors in the broth and seasonings.

There is an unusual way to cook rice—actually, it's exactly the way you normally cook pasta. Bring a large pot of salted water to a boil, add the rice, and cook, stirring frequently, until tender. Keep tasting the rice until it's tender all the way through. Drain and toss with 1 tablespoon of butter.

Pilaf, also known as *pilau* or *pulao,* starts with toasting rice in fat, then adding broth or stock. This dish is served often in Middle Eastern, Latin American, and Caribbean cuisines. It was invented in the Persian Empire hundreds of years ago.

Risotto

The right ingredients and proper cooking turn plain rice into the gourmet dish known as risotto. Despite its finicky reputation, risotto is surprisingly easy to make. And since practically all its ingredients are pantry staples (rice, chicken broth, and Parmesan cheese), it's inexpensive, too.

In a well-cooked risotto, each grain should be slightly al dente, but the overall texture of the dish is creamy and smooth. Look for Arborio or *carnaroli* rice in the supermarket. Arborio rice has a small chalky white "pearl" in the center that keeps the rice al dente and prevents it from becoming mushy.

The finished consistency of risotto is very important. It can be loose and creamy, or it can be dry enough to hold its shape when stirred. As the cook, you get to choose the consistency! With that in mind, there are two secrets to risotto. First, use the correct rice. Short grain varieties, which have a very high starch content, make the best risotto. It's the starch that creates the creaminess of the resulting sauce, if it's cooked properly. Second, add hot stock to the rice in batches and stir constantly. Cold or room temperature broth will interrupt the cooking process.

Many rice recipes tell you to coat rice in fat before adding liquid. When cooking dishes like risotto, this step keeps the grains separate as they cook.

Wild Rice

Wild rice is actually not rice at all. It's the seed of a wild grass native to the northern part of the United States. It grows in shallow lakes and slow-moving streams near the Great Lakes. Native Americans harvest this rice by paddling a canoe through the shallow waters where the rice grows, beating the grass with sticks. Much of the nation's wild rice is grown on farms, but nothing compares to the flavor and texture of "wild" wild rice harvested by hand. Wild rice is an excellent source of dietary fiber and contains many essential vitamins and minerals.

Rinse wild rice before cooking it to remove any dust from processing. Don't boil the rice; just simmer it so it cooks evenly. It will "pop" if it's cooked longer than 45 to 50 minutes. Popped wild rice will curl and become thicker. If you cook the rice for 30 to 35 minutes, it won't pop, but will retain a firm texture.

GRAINS

Grains are the fruit of grasses. You can buy whole grains like quinoa and wheat berries, or processed grains like cracked wheat and oatmeal. Grains are very high in fiber, B vitamins, vitamin E, magnesium, zinc, and iron. Choose whole grains whenever possible for the best nutrition. Look for terms such as *whole grain, whole wheat,* or *whole oats* as some of the first ingredients on a food label.

Helpful Tip

Don't tell risotto purists, but you can make risotto without using Arborio rice or even short grain rice. Long grain or medium rice will make a creamy and delicious dish that's perfectly acceptable to everyone but the purist. Cook the recipe just as you would cook Arborio rice; you may just need a little more broth.

Barley

Barley is a delicious and healthy whole grain. It has a wonderful nutty taste and chewy texture that pair beautifully with tender vegetables. Barley is full of soluble fiber, which lowers cholesterol and reduces the risk of diabetes. And it tastes absolutely delicious, especially when cooked in a soup with vegetables. Barley's texture stays chewy and tender no matter how long it's cooked, and it adds a wonderful nutty and meaty flavor to many recipes.

This wholesome grain can be consumed hot or cold in soups, stews, and salads; as a breakfast cereal; combined with beans; or as a hearty stuffing. There are several types of barley available in the supermarket.

Hulled barley has the outer layer, or hull, removed so the grain will absorb liquid and be edible. This is called hulled or pot barley or groats.

Pearl barley has been polished to remove the bran layer. This makes it a little less nutritious than hulled barley.

Pot barley, also known as Scotch barley, has the endosperm layer left on, which makes it more nutritious than pearl barley.

Pressed barley, also called Job's tears, looks like oatmeal. It takes less time to cook than pearl barley.

Quick-cooking barley takes only about 10 minutes to cook. It's been precooked with steam, so is a great choice when you want a grain to serve in a hurry.

Toast barley before adding liquid for a better taste and texture. Place the barley in a dry pan and cook it until it smells slightly toasted. Then add vegetables and the broth and continue cooking.

Bulgur or Cracked Wheat

Bulgur, also known as cracked wheat, is a wheat kernel that has been cleaned, parboiled, dried, and then broken into pieces. There are several sizes of bulgur, ranging from fine grind to coarse grind to half cuts and whole-kernel bulgur. Bulgur contains more nutrients than rice or couscous—specifically, it has twice the fiber of brown rice, not to mention fewer calories and less fat.

To cook bulgur, bring 2 cups water to a boil in a small pot over high heat. Pour in 1 cup bulgur and turn off the heat. Let the bulgur stand until all the water is absorbed, 30 minutes to an hour. Drain any excess liquid, fluff, and serve. Of course, be sure to read package directions. Some types of bulgur cook (actually, rehydrate) more quickly than others.

Use bulgur in salads (particularly the flavorful recipe Tabbouleh), add to soups and stews, add to quiches in place of meat, or combine with cooked vegetables to make a pilaf.

Oats

Oatmeal is a whole grain cereal. There are four basic types of oatmeal: instant, quick cooking, rolled oats, and steel-cut oats, proceeding in order from most to least processed. Oatmeal is used as a breakfast cereal and as an ingredient in breads and cookies.

Oats, like all whole grains, have aromatic fats. Toasting brings out the flavor of these fats and enhances the nutty taste of the grain. Quick-cooking oats cook, well, quickly. If you want a sturdier oatmeal, use rolled oats. And for even more texture, steel-cut oats are very hearty. They are made of oat grains cut into slices. Follow package directions for cooking rolled or steel-cut oats; cook until just tender.

Polenta

Polenta is cooked cornmeal, a staple of the Native American diet and a key ingredient in Italian cooking. Polenta can be served soft and warm or chilled and then grilled or sautéed until crisp. Liven up basic polenta with the addition of various ingredients such as tomato sauce, meat gravies, or grilled vegetables.

When you cook polenta, add it to boiling liquid very slowly, stirring constantly as the cornmeal cooks for a lovely, smooth texture. Sift it through your fingers as you stir it in. If you add the cornmeal all at once, you will end up with a gummy clump. For a thicker consistency, increase the cooking time by a minute or two.

Polenta can be formed into squares or circles for sautéing after it's chilled. Serve sautéed polenta dressed with onions and black beans for lunch. Or top polenta squares or circles with a hearty tomato sauce, sliced black olives, and a sprinkling of Parmesan cheese for a light supper. Polenta can be made spicy with the addition of red pepper flakes or chopped, canned chipotle peppers. Make mini cakes and load salsa or guacamole on top for a fabulous football party snack.

> ### Helpful Tip
>
> Polenta, or cornmeal, is available in regular medium-grain or instant (precooked cornmeal). Choose the variety based on the time you have. The longer you cook cornmeal, the richer the flavor will be. While many Italian cooks claim that you should stir polenta in one direction only while it's cooking, this isn't really necessary. Just keep stirring!

Quinoa

Quinoa is often included with other grains like couscous and millet, but it is not a grain at all. Quinoa is a grainlike plant grown for its seeds. It's one of the few plant foods that offer complete protein; it contains all nine essential amino acids necessary to build muscle in the body. Quinoa is also an excellent source of fiber, magnesium, copper, and iron. It is grown in Bolivia, Ecuador, and Peru. Cooks love its versatility: It's good for breakfast, lunch, and dinner, as part of a main course, or as a side dish.

You can cook the quinoa until it's just tender, or cook it longer so it breaks down to thicken casseroles, soups, and stews. Quinoa cooks like rice, with a two-to-one water-to-grain ratio. As it cooks, it releases a thin spiral tail attached to the kernel and takes on a texture similar to couscous.

Although it's neither Mexican nor Spanish, quinoa is beginning to appear in the Spanish-Mexican sections of supermarkets. It is available in many health food/natural food chains and is easy to order on the Internet.

Wheat Berries

Wheat berries are actually the entire kernel of wheat. The hull has been removed so it can be cooked. Wheat berries are very high in fiber and B vitamins. They're easy to prepare; just rinse and add to a recipe. Their texture will soften but retain some crunch.

You can find wheat berries in health food stores and co-ops and in bulk bins in supermarkets. Store the berries in an airtight container in a cool dark place; a glass jar is ideal. Label with the date of purchase.

Wheat berries, because they are a whole grain and minimally processed, should be rinsed before using to remove the dust left over from processing, plus any dirt or sand.

Wheat berries work great in slow cookers. Put 2 cups of wheat berries in a Crock-Pot in the morning with 6 cups water, but no salt. Set it on low, cover it, and come home to perfectly cooked wheat berries you can use in salads, soups, or casseroles.

PASTA

What would Italian cooking be without pasta? Pasta making and cooking has become an art form. Sometimes it's hard to believe that pasta consists of just two ingredients: flour and water (and sometimes oil).

Although cooking pasta is easy, there are some rules you need to learn for best results. It helps to learn a bit about some of the different shapes and sizes of pasta and the types of sauces they pair with.

Helpful Tip

Quinoa must be thoroughly rinsed before use. The round seeds are coated with a sticky, very bitter substance called saponin. This coating protects the quinoa from animals and birds. Saponin creates suds in water, so rinse the quinoa until there are no more suds, and the seeds will be ready to use.

BUDGET TIP

To avoid the occasional pantry or grain moth outbreak, which can infiltrate your pantry from a poorly packaged bag of flour or the bulk grain bin at the health food store, store all your grains in glass containers.

Couscous is a type of pasta, even though many people think it's a grain. This quick-cooking pasta is fabulous for side dishes, main dishes, and as an ingredient in soups and salads.

Pasta Types and Shapes

Pasta is usually made from wheat flour, oil, and water. But it can also be made from rice flour or other flours for people sensitive to gluten. Pasta can be made with egg and with whole grain flour, and it can be flavored with everything from spinach to red bell peppers. Dry pasta (pasta secca) does not have much flavor by itself; it needs sauces to shine. Pasta made from durum semolina is best in pasta salads, because it stays firm, even when left in dressing for long periods of time.

There are so many types and shapes of pasta, it's difficult to list them all. Here are just a few:

Angel hair is an extremely thin and delicate pasta that cooks in a minute or two. It's used with very delicate sauces.

Campanelle looks like a small cone. In fact it looks just like the bell flower it's named for. It really holds onto a sauce and is excellent in pasta salads because of its beautiful shape.

Cannelloni and Manicotti are large round tubes of pasta that are filled with savory mixtures then baked in pasta sauce. Cannelloni shells can be filled cooked or uncooked. They are a bit easier to stuff when uncooked because they hold their shape. If you choose to stuff them uncooked, you must add more water to the sauce and cover the pan while baking so the pasta steams.

Ditalini means "little thimbles" in Italian. It's a small pasta that looks like a tiny O. Ditalini is about ¼ inch long and hollow, so it's great in soups and stews.

Egg noodles are flat, wavy noodles that range in width from ½ inch to about 1 inch. They are usually only about 1 to 2 inches in length. They're used to soak up a sauce, traditionally served with recipes like beef stroganoff.

Farfalle is Italian for "butterfly." The name for this particular type of pasta is derived from its shape; it resembles a butterfly or a bowtie. It's perfect paired with most sauces because it holds onto them well. Kids love it because of its shape.

Fettuccine is similar to linguine but wider. The word means "little ribbons" in Italian. It's perfect

for just about any sauce and is used in the classic Italian dish fettuccine alfredo.

Fusilli is a twisted pasta shape that looks like a long spiral. Its grooves really hold onto thick sauces. It's excellent in casseroles.

Gemelli literally means "twins." It's made of two thinner round strands of pasta that are twisted together. The pasta stays twisted even when it's cooked. It's ideal for pasta salads because it's sturdy enough to stand up to heavy dressings and it also traps the dressings.

Linguine is a thicker, longer version of spaghetti. Its name means "little tongues." It works very well with thick and creamy sauces.

Orzo looks like little grains of rice. It's a good substitute for rice in just about any dish. It makes a delicious pilaf and is good in soups and stews.

Penne is the Italian name for "quills." It is a tube of pasta about 3 inches long that is usually ridged to hold sauce. Similarly shaped pastas include mostaccioli and ziti. All three are delicious in salads and casseroles.

Rigatoni absorbs and supports strong sauces. Rigatoni, ziti, and penne adapt well to baked pasta dishes and remain evenly distributed throughout the sauce while baking. These pasta shapes are often made with ridges that hold onto sauce.

Rotelle or rotini is a tightly twisted pasta about 2½ inches long. It really holds onto small bits of meat and vegetables in thick pasta sauces.

Shells are exactly what they sound like. Shells come in many sizes, from tiny shells about ½ inch long to large shells for stuffing that are about 3 inches long.

Spaghetti is comfort food. Spaghetti's long strands work perfectly with any creamy or thick sauce.

Tortellini can be filled with myriad mouthwatering stuffings including cheese and meat mixtures. This pasta looks like little three-cornered hats. Most tortellini is frozen and cooks just a few minutes in simmering water.

You can substitute many pastas for each other. Just make sure they're about the same shape and the same size. And carefully follow package directions for cooking each type of pasta.

How to Cook Pasta

Cooking pasta to the al dente or "to the tooth" stage is critical for truly enjoying the dish. Pasta must be cooked in a large pot with lots of water so the pasta can absorb water evenly. While there are new types of pasta cookers that work in the microwave—the pasta just absorbs the hot water—the classic method of cooking pasta on the stove top really works best.

Dry pasta is made from durum semolina flour, a "strong flour" that results in a chewy bite. Look for good-quality pasta so you don't have to worry about limp pasta even when you overcook

> **Helpful Tip**
>
> Italian cooks know that pasta water is a fabulous free cooking dividend. Instead of dumping it down the drain, reserve a small portion. Reserved pasta water helps distribute and meld flavors in a sauce so you get the most out of your ingredients. Pasta cooking water is full of starches that help add body and creaminess to sauce. Use a little to warm the serving dish before you add the cooked pasta.

it. There really is a difference in quality among brands. Try different brands to find your favorite. Most cooks think De Cecco and Barilla pasta brands are the best.

Start with plenty of water—5 or 6 quarts for a pound of pasta. Salt the water until you can taste it. Italians say that pasta cooking water should be as salty as the ocean. This is the only chance you have to season the pasta. You may not think it makes a difference, but try a taste test some day! Pasta cooked in salted water is much more flavorful.

Bring the water to a rolling boil before adding the pasta. After you've added the pasta, the water should come to a boil again quickly. The pasta may foam as it's cooking. If this happens, reduce the heat a bit or stir the pot.

Set a timer for a minute or two less than the recommended cooking time. The only way to test for doneness is to taste the pasta. Pasta is done when it's tender but still chewy, with a small translucent area at the center. Pull out one piece and bite into it. Does it taste cooked, or is it a bit floury? Is it pleasantly resistant to the bite, or does it stick to your teeth? (By the way, there's no truth that pasta is done when it sticks to the wall. Pasta that sticks to any surface has been overcooked.)

To drain, place a colander in the sink. Pour the pasta from the pot into the colander, then shake the colander to remove excess water. Use the pasta immediately. Add it to the sauce and toss gently using tongs or two spoons. With delicate filled pasta, use a pasta scoop or slotted spoon to gently remove the pieces from the water.

Pasta should not be rinsed after it's cooked (except when used for pasta salad; and even then, if you want the pasta to absorb the dressing, don't rinse it). Rinsing removes the surface starch that melds pasta and sauce together.

When you're cooking pasta to use in a baked dish, cook it slightly less than al dente. The pasta will absorb liquid from the sauce as it bakes. If you cook the pasta to al dente in the first step, it will be mushy in the finished dish.

Couscous

If you haven't eaten couscous, you are missing out. Couscous can be eaten cold as a salad, mixed with oil and vinegar and garnished with dried fruits and nuts, or used as a base for stews and sauces. Many people think that couscous is a grain, but it's actually a form of pasta. Because couscous is very mild, like pasta, rehydrate it in broths and flavored liquids.

The large grains of couscous traditionally used in Moroccan cooking, called Israeli couscous, looks like white peas. This type of couscous takes a long time to prepare and cook. Some chefs cook Israeli couscous like risotto, slowly adding boiling stock and finishing with butter and Parmesan.

The most common type of couscous looks like a very small grain. This type of couscous is precooked. To prepare it, mix the couscous with boiling liquid, then cover it for 10 to 15 minutes to steam. Fluff the couscous with a fork and it's ready to eat. Then add a dressing, top it with a sauce, or use it in casseroles.

8

VEGETABLES

The inimitable Will Rogers observed that "An onion can make people cry, but there has never been a vegetable invented to make them laugh." Actually, properly cooked and seasoned vegetables can be the highlight of a meal. Everyone should eat three to five servings of vegetables every day. Once you know how to buy, store, and cook vegetables, you'll have no problem meeting this quota and enjoying every bite.

BUYING VEGETABLES

When vegetable shopping, follow the Fresh Vegetable Golden Rule: If it smells good and looks good, it will taste good. For top quality and price, buy vegetables at the peak of their season. And don't overload your shopping cart just because something looks like a good buy. If you buy more vegetables than you can store or use before they spoil you haven't saved a penny.

Look for bright, natural color and firm, healthy skin with no soft or wet spots. An overripe vegetable will be darker and softer than it should be. If a vegetable has bruises, cuts, holes, or spotting, avoid it; all of these are breeding grounds for rot and mold. Underripe vegetables,

Helpful Tip

Did you know that most produce in the United States is picked four to seven days before it gets to the market? And that it's shipped an average of 1,500 miles? When you buy from local growers, you're eating vegetables in season—at their peak in freshness and at their best price. These vegetables will not only taste better, they'll have more nutritional value too.

on the other hand, will be too tough and green or pale (if that isn't their natural color). Vegetables should feel heavy and solid. Some, especially root veggies such as rutabagas and parsnips, will look "rough"; that's okay. Peel them until you get to the white moist interior. Discard the peel or use it in your compost pile.

VEGETABLE CATEGORIES

Vegetables are loosely categorized according to their origin or how they're prepared. Some vegetables fall into more than one category. These categories aren't meant to be set in stone; they're just another way to get you to think about vegetables.

Aromatic Vegetables

Aromatic vegetables include carrots, parsnips, celery, onions, garlic, and turnips. They add flavor, fiber, and minerals to your recipe repertoire. Aromatic veggies are fragrant when cooked and many of them, in combination, are the basis of some ethic cuisines and recipes.

Battuto. This Italian combination includes celery, onions, celery greens, and red bell peppers finely chopped to a paste. They can be cooked just until tender or cooked until they're caramelized.

Holy trinity. This combination of vegetables, used in Cajun and Creole cooking, is made of onions, celery, and bell peppers.

Mirepoix. This combination of chopped onions, carrots, and celery is used to begin many soup and stew recipes. Some mirepoix combinations include garlic.

Root Vegetables

Root vegetables are literally the root of the plant. They are full of nutrients because they are storage systems for the plant, storing the plant's energy as sugar. Root veg-

etables were made for roasting; their tough interiors turn creamy and soft, while their skins crisp up to a golden brown. Any root vegetable, cut into bite-size pieces and tossed with oil, can be cooked—carrots, beets, celery root, parsnips, turnips, rutabaga. As the vegetables cook, the sugars become more prominent, concentrate, and develop.

There are many root vegetables that people just don't use anymore. But rutabagas, parsnips, and turnips are all delicious and sweet and tender when properly prepared. They are also quite inexpensive. You can find them by the potatoes and onions, usually stacked in bins. These big knobby roots look inedible, but when peeled and cooked, they are delicious.

Root vegetables are high in fiber, low in calories, and free from fat. They have lots of beta-carotene and vitamin E. They are filling, hearty, and easy to store and use, and they combine into sublime stews and soups. Prepare them by peeling them, cutting out any rough spots or eyes, then cutting them into slices or chopping them into cubes.

Tender Vegetables

Tender vegetables include fruits like tomatoes and bell peppers, lettuces, some leafy greens, cucumbers, summer squashes, beans, and peas. These vegetables have a tender skin. Handle them carefully and eat them both raw and cooked.

ALL ABOUT VEGETABLES

Let's learn about the vegetables you're most likely to see at the supermarket or farmers' market. Each has different preparation, storage, and cooking needs. And although you will get the best vegetables if you look for bright color, smooth skin, and relative heft to the size, there are some special things to look for when buying each vegetable.

Artichokes are the largest member of the thistle family. Artichokes have prickly, thick outer leaves. But once you get through to the artichoke's heart, the reward is worth the effort. Artichoke hearts are tender and meaty. They can be steamed, sautéed, or used as pizza toppings.

But artichokes aren't just delicious; they're good for you, too. One artichoke contains about a quarter of the recommended daily intake of fiber for adults, and artichokes are also rich in potassium, folic acid, magnesium, vitamins E and C, and phytochemicals. Choose artichokes that are wide and heavy and brightly green. The pointy tips should be fresh and not at all shriveled, which is just a sign of age.

The edible parts of the plant are the stem, bottom, and heart. The "choke" and the leaves are inedible. To prepare an artichoke, rinse it and then cut off the stem about an inch from the base. Snip off the spiny leaf tips with kitchen shears. Cut off the top ½ inch of the artichoke and scoop out the inner leaves and the fuzzy core to expose the smooth heart. Drop the artichoke into water mixed with a bit of lemon juice until you're ready to cook it.

Then simmer or steam the artichokes for about 30 minutes, until a leaf pulls off easily. Remove the artichokes from the water or steaming insert and drain upside down for a couple of minutes. Then serve. You don't need utensils to eat artichokes. Just pull the leaves off with your fingers, dip the tender ends in sauce, and scrape off the flesh with your teeth. After all leaves are removed, the heart will be visible. Scrape off any remaining choke that is still attached, then eat the heart with a knife and fork.

Asparagus is the vegetable of spring. These green stems appear in markets February through June. There's quite a controversy about whether thick or thin asparagus is more tender. Thin asparagus has less fibrous material. Choose thin asparagus when you want to make asparagus soup or puree or want to just quickly sauté the vegetable. Choose thick asparagus when you want to steam or grill it.

Look for firm stalks with tightly closed tips. If the tips have started to separate or flower, the asparagus is past its prime. Sometimes you can find white asparagus. This type has been specially grown in the dark so it doesn't develop chlorophyll, that green chemical all plants produce. White asparagus has a very delicate flavor, but it's much more expensive than green.

To prepare asparagus for cooking, remove the tough, woody ends from the stalks. Bend one spear between your fingers. It will snap when the asparagus becomes tough. Using that spear as a guide, cut the rest of the stems with a knife. Then peel the asparagus, using a swivel-bladed peeler, where the asparagus gets thick but is still green. You don't need to peel thin asparagus.

Avocados are a rich treat. They are high in fat, but that fat is monounsaturated, a good fat that helps lower cholesterol. Avocados are an excellent source of potassium, which helps regulate blood pressure.

The most common type of avocado grown in the United States is the Hass variety, which has a pebbly dark green or black skin. Haas avocados have a smooth, creamy, buttery texture. They are available in most markets year-round. Bacon avocados are large, smooth and green and have a more watery flesh.

Select avocados that are slightly soft under light finger pressure, but not overly mushy. Look for avocados that are even in tone without any dark spots or tears in the skin. When you cut the avocado open, it should be a uniform light green color without any brown spots. Remove and discard any discolored areas.

To prepare an avocado, use a sharp chef's knife. Slice the avocado in half lengthwise, cutting around the pit. Separate the two halves and take the side containing the pit. With your knife, carefully but firmly strike the pit of the avocado, hard enough for the knife to become stuck in the pit. Hold the avocado as you twist the pit using the knife as a handle. It should pop right out. Peel each half and slice or chop.

Beans. The kind of beans we're discussing here are green beans, also known as string beans. Choose tender, thin young beans. "Stringless" varieties are popular in home gardens, but older "string" beans may have a richer bean flavor. The strings should be pulled off the pod before cutting the beans.

Go through beans and discard those that look discolored or moldy or have soft or brown spots. Wash beans and trim off both ends. Cut or "snap" beans if desired. Then break or cut them into pieces.

Green beans are low in calories and high in vitamins A, C, and K. They are a good source of fiber, potassium, folate, iron, and magnesium. Green beans are also a good source of riboflavin.

Green beans store well in the refrigerator and can also be frozen for future use. If freezing, wash them first and then dry thoroughly. Prepare a cookie sheet with non-stick spray. Place the beans on the cookie sheet in a single layer and freeze about 45 minutes. Quickly place handfuls of beans in storage bags, seal tightly, and put right back into the freezer.

Beets are a vegetable people either love or hate. There are three kinds of beets: sugar beets, used to make granulated sugar; fodder beets, used as animal food; and the red beets we eat. Roasted beets pair well with oranges, arugula, goat cheese, walnuts, red onions, and balsamic vinegar. They are high in folic acid, fiber, calcium, copper, and iodine.

The smaller the beet, the sweeter it will taste. Large beets take longer to cook and always need to be peeled before use. Baby beets are tender with a thinner skin, so they are just scrubbed before using. There are all kinds of beets! Candy cane beets are striped with color, white beets are very mild, and golden beets are a beautiful gold color and are mildly sweet.

To prepare fresh beets, scrub them using a vegetable brush. Cut off the tops; you can wash, chop, and cook them—they're full of vitamins, minerals, and fiber. Beets will bleed during cooking. You can minimize this if you leave 1 inch of the long taproot and 1 inch of the top on during cooking. Carefully look at the beets; if there are any soft spots or bruises, cut them out.

Don't boil beets! This preparation method removes their sweet flavor and bright color. Roast them instead. Tightly wrap them in aluminum foil and place them on a cookie sheet in a single layer. Roast at 375°F until very tender, about 1 hour. Cool and rub off skins while still warm.

Helpful Tip

Do beets stain your fingers? Beets are used as a dye, so it's no wonder this is an issue. To prevent red fingers, just wear thin rubber gloves when preparing beets.

Bell peppers are a sweet and colorful fruit classified as a vegetable. Bell peppers are the sweetest member of the chili family. Red, yellow, orange, and purple peppers all have the same flavor. Green peppers are the unripened version of the vegetable, so they have a sharper taste.

To prepare bell peppers, cut them in half and pull off the stem. Cut off the membranes and rinse off all of the seeds. Place the bell pepper on your work surface, skin side down. Cut into strips, then cut those strips into cubes.

Roasted red peppers are sensational in salads and soups and as garnishes and hors d'oeuvres. If you have a gas stove, put a pepper on a long-handled metal fork and hold it over the flame, turning until evenly charred. Or, cut peppers in half and remove the seeds and cores. Place on aluminum foil and lightly brush both sides with olive oil. Roast in preheated 425°F oven about 45 minutes until the skins are blistered and burnt.

Immediately place the peppers in a paper bag to steam. When cool, the skins will slip right off. Whatever you do, don't rinse the roasted peppers; you'll rinse away a lot of the flavor.

Bok choy is a member of the cabbage family. It makes a perfect stir-fried vegetable, as it cooks in just minutes. To prepare bok choy, rinse it thoroughly, cut off the ends, then chop it into rough pieces.

Broccoli is part of the cruciferous family. Cruciferous vegetables are rich in nutrients, including fiber, beta-carotene, and vitamin C. Broccoli also has phytochemicals called indoles, which help prevent cancer. Broccoli is a strongly flavored vegetable that can be bitter when cooked in a small amount of liquid. When cooked in a lot of liquid, broccoli becomes tender, nutty, and slightly sweet.

To prepare florets, wash the broccoli head and strip off the leaves. Then cut the florets off one at a time, until you are left with stalk and stem. Peel and slice the stalk and stem into 1-inch pieces or smaller and add to the pile of florets.

There are a few ways to cook broccoli:

For quick steamed broccoli: Heat 1 inch water with ½ teaspoon salt. Bring to a boil, add bite-size florets, cover, and cook for 4 minutes. Drain and toss with melted butter (the water will already have salted the broccoli) or enjoy plain.

Boiling broccoli can be a good way to cook it because the large amount of water dilutes the unpleasant sulfur compounds. Boil the broccoli for just a few minutes until it's bright green, then immediately remove it from the water.

Broccoli roasts very well. Cut it into florets, cut the stems into 1-inch pieces, then place on a cookie sheet. Toss with olive oil and sprinkle with salt and pepper. Roast at 400°F for 10 to 14 minutes until tender.

Broccoli rabe, or rapini, is also known as "rape" and is beloved by the Italians, Spanish, and Portuguese. They prepare it by blanching it, then sautéing it in olive oil or butter.

Broccoli rabe looks a lot like broccoli; however, you do eat the stems and leaves. It has a slightly bitter or pungent flavor. It's very popular in Italian restaurants as a side dish or as a main course with sweet or hot sausage.

Unless your taste buds are very well conditioned to bitter tastes, always blanch broccoli rabe for a couple of minutes in boiling water to remove the bitterness. After blanching, cut it into 1- to 2-inch segments. Then simply sauté it with garlic and olive oil, cook it with lemon and other veggies for a side dish, mix it with other ingredients in a casserole, or use it as a pizza topping.

Broccolini is not, as most people think, young broccoli. This vegetable is a hybrid, a cross between broccoli and a Chinese cabbage called *kai lan*. It was developed in Japan and has become very popular worldwide because of its pleasant flavor and high nutritional content. Broccolini is long and leafy, with thick stems and a flower head that looks like a broccoli floret. Chinese cooks serve it lightly stir-fried alone or with other ingredients.

You can cook broccolini exactly the way you would cook broccoli. Because it's smaller, it cooks in less time. Broccolini is tender and delicious and is high in vitamin A, calcium, and iron.

Brussels sprouts are cute little cabbages that children usually hate. Brussels sprouts, like other cruciferous vegetables, contain special sulfur-releasing phytonutrients that can help prevent cancer. They're high in fiber and vitamin C.

To make them irresistible, roast them! Brussels sprouts become browned and crisped on the outside and tender on the inside when roasted, and their bitter flavor is minimized. Just rinse them, pull off any tough or flawed outer leaves, and trim off the bottom of each little cabbage. Then toss with olive oil, sprinkle with salt and pepper, and roast in a 400°F oven for 35 to 45 minutes, shaking the pan every 10 minutes, until they're dark golden brown and crisp.

Cabbage is an expensive and delicious vegetable that can be used in stir-fries, in salads, cut up for coleslaw, and stuffed with meats. Cabbage comes in several forms and colors. Red cabbage is actually purple. It's sweeter than the green cabbage you see in every grocery store.

Cabbages are very good for you. As a member of the cruciferous family, they have phytochemicals that are powerful cancer fighters. They also have anti-inflammatory properties that make them an important ally in the fight against heart disease.

To prepare cabbage, first wash it thoroughly. Then cut it in half from pole to pole. Cut out the core with a sharp knife. Then use a food processor to shred the cabbage, or cut it into strips and then into small pieces.

Napa cabbage originated in Asia and is now grown throughout the world. The long, slender heads have either slightly crinkled or very crinkled leaves and a pale green color. The leaves have a mild flavor, making them a favored vegetable for salads, stir-fries, soups, and dumpling or egg roll fillings. The leaves are flexible enough to be used as wraps. Napa cabbage is prepared just like romaine lettuce. Rinse the leaves and chop them into pieces.

Carrots are one of those vegetables that everyone loves. They're delicious eaten raw or cooked. Carrots belong to the same family as dill, cumin, fennel, and parsnips. They're actually root vegetables that are supersweet because they store and hold sugar for the plant.

Carrots have tons of beta-carotene, which your body converts into vitamin A. This is a powerful antioxidant that helps fight heart disease, cancer, and macular degeneration. The nutrients in carrots become more available when they're cooked, and are more easily absorbed when eaten with a bit of fat. So steam some carrots and toss them with butter for a nutritious side dish.

To prepare carrots, wash them, then peel if necessary. Cut into rounds or coins or sticks. Carrots are delicious served raw with a dip made from sour cream, mayonnaise, garlic, and dill.

Baby carrots are more tender than regular carrots. They are actually large carrots developed to be especially sweet with a small center core, trimmed down to a small size. They're delicious eaten raw or simmered in water or broth until tender.

Cauliflower is a cruciferous vegetable that is often ignored. Many people have memories of mushy, overcooked cauliflower served for school lunches. But this vegetable, with a delicate, nutty flavor, is delicious eaten raw. Cauliflower is exceptionally good for you, with lots of vitamin C and fiber.

To prepare cauliflower, tear the green leaves off the base. Use a paring knife to cut around the underside to remove the stem. Cut a cone shape into the underside to remove most of the core. Detach the florets. Cut florets into quarters or halves, depending on their size, to make them uniform so the pieces cook evenly.

Roast cauliflower to bring out its sweetness. Toss bite-size florets with olive oil and place in an even layer on a baking sheet. Sprinkle with salt; roast at 375°F until tender and golden, 25 minutes.

Celery is a versatile vegetable with a neutral taste and crunchy texture. When purchasing celery, look for solid, rigid stalks with a glossy surface of light to medium green. With a sharp knife, remove the base end of the celery and trim the leaves from each stalk. Remove strings of celery, if necessary, by hand. Then slice, dice, or julienne the celery as directed in the recipe. Store the prepped celery in water for a few days. But don't throw away the celery leaves! They are tender and full of flavor. Coarsely chop the leaves and add them to salads and soups.

You can serve celery raw or cook it to use in casseroles, soups, and stews. Celery is part of the holy trinity of vegetables in Cajun cooking and in the mirepoix of French cooking.

Celery root or celeriac is a root vegetable that's related to celery. It's big, knobby, and very unattractive, but it has a delicate celery-like taste and crunchy texture. It's usually used peeled and shredded to be used raw in salads, but can also be roasted like a potato.

Corn is one of those vegetables everyone loves. The sweet kernels are a great source of vitamin A. And it's such fun to eat corn on the cob in the summer. When you're purchasing corn on the cob, look for firm cobs with bright green leaves and silk (the white threadlike substance under the husk) that isn't brown or wet. Cook fresh corn as soon as possible. Its sugars start turning to starch as soon as it's picked, although new varieties do hold onto their sugar content longer.

To prepare corn on the cob, firmly grasp the leaves and pull them off the cob. Peel the husk back and pull off as much silk as you can by hand. Then dampen a rough washcloth or dish towel and run it down the ear to remove the rest of the silk. Trim off the end of the cob where there are any immature kernels or bad spots.

Cutting the kernels off the cob can be tricky. A corn cutter can be helpful. This round instrument has two handles. With the cob standing upright, place the cutter over the ear, squeeze, and push downward. You can also use a sharp knife to remove the kernels. Stand the cob in the hole of a Bundt pan. Cut down the sides of the cob with the knife, sawing as you go. The kernels will fall into the Bundt pan instead of scattering around the kitchen.

Creamed corn is a mixture made up of pieces of whole corn and a soup of corn "milk" and kernel hearts scraped off the cob. There is no real cream or milk in it.

Hominy is made from corn with its hull and germ removed. The hard kernels of corn are soaked in a weak lye solution to separate the hull from the rest of the grain. Hominy is quite soft, with large, swollen kernels. White hominy is made from white corn and yellow hominy from yellow. Yellow hominy is sweeter.

Cucumber is another fresh item that should be added to your shopping list. They have lots of fiber, vitamin C, potassium, and magnesium. It's especially valued in salads. Look for firm cucumbers that feel heavy for their size, with smooth skins and few blemishes or rough brown spots.

Since cucumbers have so much water in them, many cooks "purge" cucumbers before mixing them into a salad or dip. Slice the cucumbers and sprinkle them lightly with salt; let stand to drain for about a half an hour. If you skip this step, your salad will be watery.

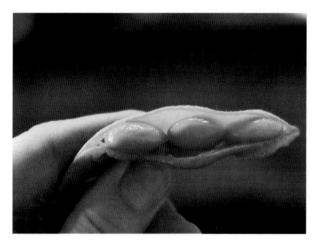

Edamame, or soybeans, are fairly new to the vegetable scene. They are popular in Asian cuisines. You can find edamame in the frozen foods aisle, completely prepared and out of the pod, or you can buy the fresh pods at farmers' markets. Simply boil the pods in salted water for a few minutes. To eat, squeeze the pods and they will pop open, revealing the crisp, edible bean.

Eggplant is an unusual vegetable, used mostly in Mediterranean cuisine. There are so many recipes and uses for eggplant. In Arabic countries, cooks make baba ghanoush by roasting whole eggplants over coals and then mixing with garlic and olive oil. The mash is eaten as a dip with warm pita bread. In Thailand, cooks use tiny round eggplants in curries and soups. Look for firm eggplants that are heavy for their size, with no soft spots or blemishes.

To prepare eggplant, wash it well and cut off the ends. Cut the vegetable in half, then place cut side down on the work surface. Cut into strips, then cut those strips into cubes. You can peel the eggplant or leave the skin on for more fiber. Some eggplants

are loaded with seeds and can be a bit bitter. To reduce bitterness, sprinkle lightly with salt after cutting the eggplant into strips. Let this mixture sit for 20 minutes and then blot away the liquid on the surface of the slices with paper towels.

Eggplants absorb a lot of fat as they cook. Don't be put off by this; that's just their character. They take on the flavors of the ingredients they're cooked with. To use large globe-type eggplants, sprinkle the cut pieces with salt and drain on a rack or paper towels for one hour. Rinse before using. Asian eggplants are longer and thinner than the Mediterranean variety. They're also less bitter, so advanced salting and draining are not necessary.

Endive is a member of the daisy family. This leafy vegetable is related to chicory and radicchio. Endive looks like tightly closed asparagus tips. It's used for arranged or composed salads and is also a great appetizer, when the leaves are pulled apart and filled with everything from chicken salad to a whole, perfect grilled shrimp.

Choose the smallest, whitest endive you can find (larger ones can be bitter), with moist, tightly compacted leaves with no brown discoloration at the tips. Arrange the nicest leaves on the plates artfully; thinly slice the remainder to use in salads.

Fennel is an ancient vegetable that belongs to the celery family. It is a large bulb with stalks and feathery fronds. Italians are well acquainted with *finocchio* (fennel). It has a mild licorice taste that mellows with cooking. The feathery leaves are added to salads and cooked in soups, while the bulbous white part is eaten raw or braised. Fennel is an underused vegetable in the United States.

Wash fennel under cold running water and remove any tough or discolored outer parts. Using a chef's knife, cut off the stalks and feathery fronds. Cut out the tough inner core of the bulb and the base. Slice the bulb into ½-inch pieces for braising or sautéing, slice it thinly on a mandoline, or use a sharp knife to cut the vegetable into matchsticks or cubes. Set the fennel fronds aside to garnish the finished dish. Use the fennel stalks to make a vegetable stock.

Try including fennel wedges or thin slices with any vegetable salad. Fennel can be grilled and served with olive oil and Parmesan. Eaten raw, slices of the white bulb are crisp and refreshing in salads or as crudités. Try paper-thin slices drizzled with a little olive oil, a few drops of fresh lemon juice, freshly grated black pepper, and shaved Parmesan as a summer salad with grilled foods.

Garlic is one of the most widely used vegetables. It is packed with nutrients that can help reduce the risk of cancer and heart disease, including selenium, manganese, vitamins B6 and C. People who eat garlic every day may have a reduced risk of some diseases, including heart disease and stroke.

Always choose very firm heads of garlic that have no green sprouts. Store garlic at room temperature in a basket, much as you would onions and potatoes. Sometimes a garlic clove will sprout; this is normal. Use it immediately and discard the sprouted areas.

Raw garlic is sharp and has a very strong taste, but it becomes sweet and buttery when roasted. To prepare, press on the garlic head with the side of a cleaver to separate the cloves. Then place each individual clove under a chef's knife and press down with the heel of your hand to crush the clove slightly. The peel will remove easily. Then chop, slice, or mince the garlic. Here's something to keep in mind: A single clove of garlic is three times stronger if pressed through a garlic press than if it's diced.

Garlic can be used in many ways. It is used raw in salad dressings and dips. Quickly sautéed, it becomes more mild. It can be braised alongside a pot roast or roasted all by itself until sweet and buttery.

To roast a head of garlic, rub the entire bulb with oil, wrap with foil, and roast at 350°F for an hour. You can also cover whole peeled cloves with oil and gently poach in a small pan until the garlic is completely soft.

Green onions, also called scallions, are used whole in hot pots, shredded into stir-fries, and minced for garnishes. They are the immature shoots of regular onions, pulled from the ground before a large bulb develops. Buy green onions with firm, bright green tops. The smaller and thinner the onion, the milder the flavor.

Leafy greens should be part of your everyday diet. The darker the green, the more nutritious the vegetable. Look for heavy greens with evenly colored leaves. To prepare them, wash and lay in an even layer on a dish towel or paper towels. Roll up and store in a plastic bag.

There are many types of lettuces available in today's supermarket:

Arugula, also known as rocket, is a leafy dark green that is an excellent source of antioxidants. It has a bitter, spicy flavor. It's used raw in salads.

Baby spinach is much more tender than regular spinach, with a delicate flavor. Always rinse spinach in cold water because it grows in sand. Then chop it roughly with a chef's knife. You can use regular spinach for a stronger taste. Frozen chopped spinach is an excellent buy; a lot of work goes into blanching, chopping, and freezing this leafy green.

Collard greens are a standard of Southern cooking. Collards, like kale, have a heavy stem and tend to be sandy. Collard greens need a fair amount of cooking. You can cook them in any kind of broth, though ham hock broth is traditional. Collards can be substituted for kale or turnip greens in soups and stews. They go especially well with ham or pork chops.

Escarole is a broad-leafed endive. Choose endive with crisp, pale green outer leaves with white stems. Escarole can be eaten lightly cooked as a side dish or raw in salads.

Iceberg gets its name from its crisp and cool character and great crunch. It has a sweet flavor that makes it ideal for salads and as a sandwich topping or base for seafood salads or even some stir-fries. Look for firm and heavy heads with white stem ends.

Kale is a superfood that is a member of the cabbage family, related to broccoli and cauliflower. It's an excellent source of vitamin A and beta-carotene. Kale's antioxidants reduce the risk of various cancers. Kale, unlike other leafy, more delicate greens, is cooked for 10 to 15 minutes in boiling water to become tender. It's also delicious sautéed in garlic-flavored olive oil.

Swiss chard is sometimes known as the "bottomless beet" because it looks so much like beet greens. Chard, like many dark sturdy greens, tastes better after it has been chilled by frost. It's often one of the last harvested vegetables. To prepare, immerse the greens in a sink full of cool water to remove all the grit. Shake off excess water, coarsely chop, and then cook in broth or olive oil.

Watercress can be eaten raw in a salad or cooked as a vegetable. It's delicious mixed into soups. Its unique peppery flavor is wonderful. Watercress is actually grown in water. It is found in small, cold spring-fed creeks and mountain streams. Many people forage for wild watercress in the springtime, especially on the East Coast.

Spinach and other greens can be tricky to wash, as the leaf folds often hide grit and insects. Soak greens that might hold insects in cold salt water (1 cup salt per gallon) for 30 minutes. Drain off the salt water and rinse with cold clean water. Really sandy greens may need several washings. Inspect the leaves as you wash, discarding thick stems and ribs and rotted or diseased areas.

If the leaves are big and coarse, remove the stems and tough cores and discard. Stack the leaves, roll them up, and slice into ribbons. Very tender greens such as spinach can be cooked whole.

Jerusalem artichoke is not actually an artichoke. It belongs to the daisy family and is commonly called a sunchoke or *topinambor* potato. The tuber is gnarly looking with a rough brown skin. Its fleshy white meat can be shaved and eaten raw in a salad, or it can be cooked like a potato. Varieties range from pale white to reddish purple.

Select firm Jerusalem artichokes with no visible blemishes and a firm texture. Store in a cool, dry place away from light. Jerusalem artichokes can last up to two weeks in the refrigerator. To prepare, peel gently to remove the thin outer skin. Then drop the chokes into cool water mixed with the juice of half a lemon to prevent browning.

Jicama is a very interesting vegetable used mainly in Mexican cooking. It is almost always eaten raw and is traditionally shredded and then tossed with a simple lime dressing. It is also eaten with radishes as an accompaniment to tacos. Some say it has the flavor of a potato crossed with an apple. It has a great crunch. Look for a jicama with smooth skin and no blemishes. Peel before cutting, as the skin is tough.

Leeks are a member of the onion family. They look like very large green onions

(also called scallions). Their flavor is milder than onions. Leeks are often used in French cooking.

Leeks are notoriously sandy and dirty because they grow in sand. If you don't clean leeks properly, the finished dish will be full of grit. Trim and cut the leeks into small pieces, then place in a very large bowl or sink full of water. Swish the leeks through the water so the sand falls to the bottom of the bowl. Pull the leeks out of the water; do not pour into a colander, as you will pour the sand back over them. Use a slotted spoon or tongs to take the leeks out of the water, leaving the sand behind in the bowl. Then prepare as the recipe directs.

Mushrooms are a great source of fiber, potassium, phosphorus, magnesium, and other essential nutrients. There are many more varieties of fresh mushrooms on the market today than there were 20 years ago. And there's a wonderful variety of relatively rare dried mushrooms such as morels and trumpets. You can usually find enoki, cremini, portobello, shiitakes, and other exotic varieties.

When choosing mushrooms, look for firm caps with stems that are securely attached. If you can see the gills, which are the feathery dark undersides of the caps, it just means the mushrooms are a bit older. Their flavor will be stronger, but that isn't a bad thing. Mushrooms are perishable, so store them in the fridge, well wrapped, and use them within a few days.

To slice mushrooms, wipe them with a damp cloth to remove any dirt. Trim off the end of the stem, which tends to dry out during storage. Then place the mushrooms, cap side down, on your work surface. Slice the mushrooms about ⅓ inch thick. Keep the slices uniform so they cook evenly.

Mushrooms are mostly water and so will shrink as you cook them. Mushrooms can be lightly sautéed or cooked until dark and rich. Heat oil in a skillet, then add the mushrooms. Stir them as they cook. For a concentrated mushroom flavor, brown them well. It takes a while for the liquid to evaporate off; just be patient.

Dried mushrooms include porcini, morels, shiitake, oyster, truffle, boletes, and black trumpet. They store very well as long as they are kept in an airtight container. The liquid you use to reconstitute them is very flavorful, but must be strained before use. To reconstitute dried mushrooms, place them in a medium bowl and pour boil-

Helpful Tip

It may look as though you have too many greens for just about any recipe. You don't. All greens cook down, and down, and down when heated. The trick is to start by cooking half of them, stirring until they reduce in size. Keep adding greens a handful at a time, until you've added them all to the pot. Cover and simmer until tender.

ing water over them. Let stand for 10 to 15 minutes until the mushrooms soften. Then cut off the mushroom stems, which are too tough to eat, and chop or slice the mushrooms.

Olives are a fruit that tastes dreadfully bitter fresh and deliciously savory when cured. They come in a variety of colors and flavors, from tangy green to salty black. You can buy olives already pitted or with the pit intact. Olives come stuffed with everything from pimientos to blanched almonds. They make an easy snack, as they require little prep work and can be stored for up to a year if they came in a jar. Loose olives stored in plastic should be consumed within a few weeks.

Onions are in the lily family. This root vegetable is primarily used as a seasoning.

Onions are best when fresh. You can easily find them in the produce section of the grocery store or at a local farmers' market. Buy firm onions with intact skins and no large tears or mold around the root area.

A whole onion needs no refrigeration. Onions will be fine for three to four weeks if kept in a cool, dry area. But, once you cut an onion, it must be refrigerated.

To prepare an onion, first cut it in half from pole to pole. Remove the papery skin and place cut side down on a cutting board. With the root end away from you, make lengthwise cuts across the onion, leaving ¼ inch of the onion still attached at the root end. This will hold the onion together while you cut. Rotate the onion 90 degrees and cut across the slices you just made for uniform cubes.

Peas are one of those vegetables everyone seems to love. Garden peas, or pod peas, must be removed from their shell before eating. Each pod has six to eight peas. They're usually found shelled and frozen in the grocery store. In fact, unless you grow peas in your garden, frozen peas are a better deal. The sugar in peas quickly turns to starch once the pods are picked. Frozen peas are shelled and processed right in the field for best flavor, nutrition, and texture.

Sugar snap peas and snow peas require very little prep work. These peas have an edible pod and are eaten whole. Simply rinse them under cold water in a colander.

Place the peas on a chopping block and, using a sharp chef's knife, trim off the ends. Be careful not to slice too far up the pod, or you'll cut into the peas themselves. If the peas have a tough string along the seam, pull it off before eating.

Potatoes are a popular starchy vegetable whose reputation has taken a beating over the past few years from the low-carb crowd. But potatoes are a nutritious and low-calorie food. They're full of fiber and are a good source of vitamin C and potassium.

There are several types of potatoes on the market:

Fingerling potatoes are about 4 inches long and slender. They do look like (relatively fat) fingers. They are delicious roasted or sautéed in butter.

Purple potatoes are really purple! Their skin is smooth, and their interior is a very deep purple. They have a mild, nutty flavor and retain their color after cooking.

Red potatoes, which are large and waxy, are good for potato salad because they keep their shape when cooked.

Russet potatoes are large and oval, with a relatively rough brown skin. They are perfect for baking or roasting because their flesh becomes fluffy when cooked.

Tiny, or new, red potatoes are perfect roasted or sautéed. These potatoes are delicate, so handle them gently. Rinse them off and dry before cooking. They may need a bit of scrubbing with a soft vegetable brush.

Yukon gold potatoes were released to the market in 1981. The flesh is unusually deep yellow in color. The potatoes have a creamy texture and buttery flavor. They're slightly lower in starch than Idaho, New England, or other russet potatoes.

White potatoes have a light creamy skin, white flesh, and mild flavor. They can be roasted, boiled, steamed, fried, or grilled.

When buying potatoes, look for firm potatoes that are heavy for their size. They should be fairly clean and smooth with no wet or soft spots. Avoid those with wrinkled skins, green or dark areas, or cuts or indentations. To prepare, all you have to do is scrub them under cool running water.

For the best mashed potatoes, make sure the potatoes are thoroughly cooked and tender. You can use a ricer to press the potatoes into tiny pieces or use a potato masher to crush them. Add the butter when you first start mashing to coat the starch so the potatoes don't become gluey. Beat in the milk, cream, or broth until the potatoes are smooth and fluffy. Never use a food processor or blender to mash potatoes or they'll be sticky and gluey.

To roast potatoes, preheat the oven to 400°F and place the rack in the center of the oven. You can roast potatoes whole or cut up. Coat the potatoes evenly with fat: oil, bacon fat, butter, and duck fat (the best!) are all good choices. Place whole potatoes directly on the rack. Toss cubed potatoes with oil and arrange in a single layer on a baking sheet. Roast whole or chopped potatoes for about an hour. Chopped potatoes should be stirred a few times while roasting.

To microwave potatoes, scrub them and then rub them with fat. Prick each one a few times with a fork. Cook on high for 5 minutes for one potato, 7 minutes for two, and 10 to 12 minutes for three. Let them stand for 4 to 5 minutes before serving.

Potato skins turn green when they're exposed to light. This area contains a toxin called solanine that can make you sick. Discard green-skinned potatoes. Potato sprouts are also poisonous, but you can break off the sprouts and discard them. Sprouted potatoes themselves are still edible but are lower in quality.

High-starch/low-moisture potatoes, which are best for baking and mashing, include the baking potato, white creamer, and russet. Low-starch/low-moisture potatoes include the fingerling, new potato, Red Bliss, red creamer, and white rose.

Radicchio is a lettuce-like vegetable that has been widely cultivated in Italy for hundreds of years. The most common radicchio available in the United States is the Chioggia variety, which is round and about 6 to 8 inches in diameter. It is a deep purplish red color with stark white ribs and veins running through it.

Treviso radicchio is long and resembles a Belgian endive. This long version is less common on the market. Radicchio is commonly used as a colorful lettuce added to other greens to provide color. It is also separated into "cups" and the leaves filled with sauces as a garnish.

Radicchio has a peppery, slightly bitter flavor and nice crunch. Rinse it well and tear or cut the leaves to use it in salads.

Radishes are valued in Asia for their crisp, peppery bite. Common globe radishes are available year-round, along with many other types. Radishes are usually used as an addition to an appetizer tray along with olives and pickles. They're also used as a salad ingredient. Daikon radishes, a white, mild-tasting Japanese variety that look like pale carrots, are used in cold dishes, pickles, and stir-fries.

You can cook radishes for an interesting change of pace. Cut off the tops and the root and scrub the radishes well. Peel off any tough or rough spots on the skin. Then slice them and stir-fry; or keep them whole, toss with olive oil, and roast in the oven until tender.

Shallots are still considered a gourmet item. This member of the onion family has a mild taste. Shallots are used in risotto, cream sauces, and wine sauces. Look for firm shallots with well-attached skin. To use, cut off the ends and then remove the brown

skin. Cut as you would an onion, either chop or finely dice. Shallots can be used raw in salad dressings and marinades or cooked as an onion substitute.

Sprouts were once considered a health food. They are very good for you, but have become more mainstream. There have been problems with contaminated sprouts sold in supermarkets and salad bars. It's best to grow your own. Buy a sprout kit and follow the directions.

Alfalfa, radish, and wheat berry sprouts are great additions to salads and sandwiches. Mung bean sprouts can be eaten raw, but most Chinese cooks add them to stir-fries or blanch and toss them with a dressing. Crisp sprouts with silvery white stalks will keep in the refrigerator for up to a week. Briefly soak sprouts in cold water, drain well, and store in a resealable plastic bag in the refrigerator.

Squash comes in two varieties: summer and winter. The summer squashes include zucchini, yellow squash, crookneck squash, patty pan and straight neck. They have soft skins that you can pierce with a fingernail. They're usually served raw in salads or as an accompaniment to an appetizer dip, but they're also good cooked in stir-fries and roasted. Just toss cubes or strips with olive oil and salt and cook until golden and tender.

Choose summer squashes that are heavy for their size, with smooth, unblemished skins. Wrap them in paper towels to extend their life in the fridge.

Hard or winter squashes include pumpkin, butternut, acorn, sugar pumpkin, Hubbard, confetti, and turban. They have a long shelf life. The skin and flesh of these vegetables are very hard. Winter squashes are loaded with beta-carotene, vitamin C, potassium, and fiber.

Cutting up a winter squash can be difficult. Use two knives: a very sharp one to make the initial cut and a serrated knife to saw your way through. A razor-sharp knife is safer to use than a dull one, which can slip during cutting. Wear a rubber glove to hold the squash steady as you work. To make squash easier to cut, microwave the whole, uncut squash on high for 1 to 2 minutes. This will help soften the skin.

Once the squash is cut in half, scrape out all of the seeds. Partially bake it at 350°F for 20 to 30 minutes, or microwave on high for 4 minutes on high to soften it. You can stuff squash with any number of delicious fillings. Or brush the flesh with oil, butter, or water and roast until tender.

If you want to cook a pumpkin, you will need to buy a "sugar pumpkin" or "pie pumpkin," which is small and heavy with a sweet pumpkin taste. If you can find it, a "cheese pumpkin" has the richest flavor, with the deep orange nuttiness most often associated with canned pumpkin.

Spaghetti squash is an interesting variety. Its flesh literally separates into strings when roasted, so it looks just like cooked spaghetti. Once it is roasted and cooled slightly, use a fork to scrape out the strands of squash from the tough, leathery shell. Toss with butter and Parmesan cheese or top with tomato sauce.

Sweet potatoes are an excellent source of beta-carotene and one sweet potato provides more than 250 percent of the recommended daily value of vitamin A. Sweet potatoes are also high in fiber, vitamin B6, potassium, and iron to promote cardiovascular and digestive health.

Sweet potatoes are not yams, and yams are not sweet potatoes, although the names seem to be interchangeable. Yams are starchy, large root vegetables native to Africa and are not sweet. Sweet potatoes soften when cooked, have a deep orange color, and taste sweet even without sugar.

Peel sweet potatoes and cut them into cubes as you would a russet potato, then toss with oil and roast. Or bake them whole and treat them as you would an ordinary baked potato. The flesh is also delicious as a casserole, cooked and pureed with brown sugar and spices.

Tomatillos, also called husk tomatoes or ground cherry tomatoes, are related to tomatoes. The fruit is covered with a papery husk and sticky coating that must be removed before eating. Remove the paper skin, rinse off the sticky coating, and use tomatillos cooked or raw.

A ripe tomatillo has light green and white flesh with small seeds. It is very tart with a grassy flavor. Tomatillos are used in salsa verde (green salsa) and chile verde (green chile stew) to give them their signature, tart flavors.

Tomatillos are small, ranging from a cherry

tomato to a golf ball. The smaller tomatillos are sweeter. Buy tomatillos that are firm to the touch with tightly closed husks. The tomatillo should fill out the husk, and the fruit should be touching the husk but not bursting through it. The husk should be a uniform green color with no yellowing. If a tomatillo is beginning to yellow, it is too ripe.

Tomatoes are technically a fruit, but they are legally classified as a vegetable. They are sweet and rich; used raw in salads, appetizers, and soups; and the basis for tomato sauce, ketchup, and barbecue sauce.

There are quite a few varieties of tomatoes:

Beefsteak tomatoes are the big tomatoes that are sliced and served on hamburgers. They have a rich flavor and are very juicy.

Cherry tomatoes are tiny. They're used in salads and can be stuffed for appetizers. Roasted, they become sweet and tender. A new type of cherry tomato, called the grape tomato, is even smaller and sweeter.

Heirloom tomatoes have not been hybridized, or genetically altered. They come in wonderful colors, ranging from green to yellow to purple to striped.

Plum tomatoes have a pear shape. They have less liquid and fewer seeds than regular tomatoes, so they're usually used to make tomato sauce. A common type of plum tomato is the Roma tomato.

Yellow tomatoes have a lower acid content, so they're a good choice for people who must avoid acidic foods.

Look for firm tomatoes that are heavy for their size. The skin should be smooth, not shriveled, and should be free of blemishes or rough spots. Store tomatoes at room temperature. The cold temperature of the refrigerator dulls the tomatoes' flavor and makes the flesh mushy.

To peel tomatoes, cut a small X in the bottom. Drop the tomatoes into boiling water and cook for 8 to 10 seconds. Remove the tomatoes and plunge into ice water for 1 to 2 minutes. The skin should peel off easily. Then cut the tomatoes in half, gently squeeze out and discard the seeds, and chop the flesh.

To chop tomatoes, wash them first, then cut them in half. Place them cut side down on your work surface and cut into slices. Then cut those slices into cubes.

Canned tomatoes are a great alternative to fresh during the winter months. You can find whole tomatoes, chopped tomatoes, tomato puree, tomato sauce, tomato juice, and tomato paste in cans.

Roasting tomatoes concentrates the flavor and color. To roast, cut tomatoes into pieces; toss them with onions, garlic, and olive oil; and bake until the tomatoes are shriveled. These shriveled tomatoes, while not beautiful, are packed with flavor.

Sun-dried tomatoes come in two varieties: dried and packed in oil. Dried tomatoes are hard and leathery and must be reconstituted in liquid for 20 to 30 minutes before eating. Tomatoes packed in oil can be eaten immediately. Their flavor is quite intense. The oil that the tomatoes are packed in is very flavorful.

STORING VEGETABLES

Storage depends on the vegetable. Some should be refrigerated, while others require room-temperature storage. Some vegetables freeze well, others don't. While your refrigerator's fruit and vegetable bins are designed to keep produce fresh as long as possible, there are some vegetables that are better kept in dry, cool areas such as basements or enclosed porches.

Follow a few simple rules to maximize your produce budget.

- Buy only what you'll use within a week to ten days. That's about the longest most veggies retain quality, although there are exceptions like cabbage, onions, and carrots, which may keep for several weeks.
- Never chop vegetables until you're ready to use them, as exposure to air and light speed nutrient loss.
- Plan weekly menus that incorporate the vegetables you've bought.

In general, root vegetables should be stored in a cool, dry place. Pumpkins and winter squashes should be stored at room temperature, as refrigeration can inhibit their flavor. Don't store your precious tomatoes in the refrigerator, either. The cold destroys their flavor. Always keep tomatoes in a sunny warm spot until they reach a point of perfect red softness, then eat them right away. Even green tomatoes will ripen slowly on the countertop, but they won't have the flavor of vine-ripened tomatoes.

Vegetables that are high in water content, including artichokes, leeks, greens, spinach, summer squash, bell peppers, celery, mushrooms, and peas should be refrigerated. Wrap them well before putting them in the fridge.

Refrigerator crisper drawers have special controls that help regulate temperature and humidity. Read the appliance's owner's manual to learn how to use the temperature and moisture controls in the drawers. Be sure to use the produce stored in those drawers every day. Examine the food for any sign of decay, and keep the drawers impeccably clean.

CLEANING VEGETABLES

How should you clean vegetables? Some people advocate plain old everyday tap water, while others swear by vegetable washes and even chlorine bleach solutions. Some say it's okay to not wash vegetables with inedible peels, while others insist that all vegetables must be washed. What's the real scoop?

Wash all vegetables, even those you peel before cooking and eating. As you peel vegetables, contaminants like pesticides or bacteria can get on your hands and be transmitted to the food you're preparing. The risk of contamination is highest for crops where the edible parts come in contact with the soil, such as potatoes, radishes, carrots, mushrooms, and leafy vegetables. Washing with clean water and peeling will remove most harmful contaminants.

This is the vegetable cleaning equipment you need:

- Colander or sieve
- Swivel peeler
- Vegetable scrub brush or mitt
- Sink spray nozzle attachment
- Paper towels
- Salad spinner
- Paring knife for cutting out bad spots

BUDGET TIP

Do those "green bags" that are sold to help keep produce fresh actually work? Tests shows they only extend the life of tender vegetables by a day or so. But if that day will help you use those bell peppers rather than throw them away, you may want to try them. Wash and reuse these bags instead of throwing them out.

IS FRESH BEST?

Most people believe that fresh vegetables are always superior to frozen and canned alternatives. This isn't always true. Frozen vegetables have some advantages over fresh. They're available when their fresh counterparts are out of season; they have a very long shelf life; and since they're processed quickly after harvest, they lose fewer nutrients in transit. Canned vegetables are generally a poor alternative to fresh and frozen. But there are times when it's acceptable to use them.

Keep these frozen vegetables on hand:

- Artichokes
- Broccoli
- Corn
- Green beans
- Peas
- Spinach
- Vegetable blends

Keep these canned vegetables on hand:

- Artichokes
- Beets
- Chickpeas
- Whole kernel and cream-style corn
- Pumpkin
- Sweet potatoes
- Tomatoes

> **Health Tip**
>
> According to the FDA, frozen fruits and vegetables provide the same essential nutrients and health benefits as fresh, because they're nothing more than fresh produce, picked at its nutritional peak, that has been blanched (cooked for a short time in boiling water or steamed) and frozen or canned within hours of being picked.

Vegetables like cabbage, eggplant, cucumber, lettuces, and radishes are only available in their fresh state. You won't find them frozen or canned, with the exception of sauerkraut. Frozen and canned carrots, potatoes, onions, and green beans lack the flavor of their fresh counterparts.

COOKING VEGETABLES

Cooking vegetables isn't difficult. There are several ways to cook them, depending on the result you want. For sweeter vegetables, cook them longer so the sugars caramelize. For crisp vegetables, just steam them briefly or stir-fry them. And there are lots of vegetables you can eat raw. Here are the methods for cooking (or not cooking) vegetables, in order from least cooking to most.

Why Eat Raw?

In recent years raw-food diets have received more and more attention. Those who advocate "going raw" cite many advantages to this radical departure from the normal Western diet. Cooking can destroy or reduce some nutrients. Raw vegetables provide many benefits for both our health and the environment.

Although many people try to adhere to this diet, in reality eating raw is very difficult. First of all, not all vegetables should be eaten raw. And second, studies have shown that cooked vegetables are not always nutritionally inferior to their raw counterparts. In fact, cooking makes many nutrients, such as beta-carotene and lutein in carrots, more available to the body.

On the other hand, raw vegetables have the best balance of water, nutrients, and fiber to meet body's needs. Raw vegetables are extremely rich in minerals, vitamins, trace elements, enzymes, and natural sugars, with no cholesterol or fat, making them naturally low in calories and high energy. And they're an important source of antioxidants, which aid in the prevention of chronic and life-threatening diseases like diabetes and cancer.

A safe raw vegetable snack bar would include the following:

- Baby spinach
- Bell peppers
- Carrots
- Celery
- Cucumbers
- Jicama
- Lettuces
- Summer squashes
- Tomatoes

Blanching

Blanched vegetables are partially cooked for freezing or make-ahead preparation. This easy technique is used to keep vegetables crisp and tender. Blanching makes skins easier to remove, reduces strong odors, and sets the color of vegetables.

When a green vegetable like broccoli is blanched, green gases expand and escape from the cells, bringing out the chlorophyll. So green vegetables are at their brightest after they've been blanched. Blanching prepares veggies for freezing, because it destroys enzymes that cause the loss of nutritional value and flavor. Onions, peppers, and herbs don't require blanching. Squash, sweet potatoes, and pumpkin should be fully cooked before freezing. All other vegetables, however, should be blanched for freezing. Bitter vegetables like brussels sprouts and broccoli rabe are often blanched to rid them of some of their sharp taste. Blanch string beans, broccoli, snow peas, and asparagus before grilling.

The trick to blanching is to boil the vegetables as briefly as possible. This can range from 30 seconds for greens to 3 minutes for broccoli and 7 minutes for artichokes. Blanching starts as soon as the vegetables hit the water, even if the boil stops temporarily.

Sweating

To "sweat" vegetables, cook them in a little bit of fat or liquid over very low heat to release their juices. The vegetables don't brown because the juices interfere with the Maillard reactions, which occur when sugars and proteins in food combine at high heat.

Sweating makes vegetable cell walls more fragile, so the flavors are drawn out. This also helps soften the vegetables so they're easier to combine with other foods and easier to eat.

To sweat vegetables, put a tablespoon of oil in a pan and place over low heat. Add the vegetables and a pinch of salt. The salt also helps bring out the water in the vegetables, which also prevents browning. Stir the vegetables often while they're sweating. When the veggies are translucent and fairly soft, you can continue with the recipe.

Steaming

Steamed foods are cooked by moist heat on a rack or in a steamer basket in a covered pan over boiling water. The gentle heat keeps the vegetables crisp without overcooking them. And it helps retain their color, flavor, and nutrients.

Various utensils are used for steaming. Steamer pots and baskets are designed especially for steaming, although a colander and a pot with a lid will do the job just as well. Microwave

Helpful Tip

Blanching is the process of quickly dipping an item into boiling water and then quickly chilling it by plunging it into ice water. Parboiling involves boiling something part way, but not chilling it. Parboiling is used to precook food that will then be cooked another way, such as braising, grilling, or stir-frying.

steaming is a convenient option, requiring little or no water; just place the vegetables in a microwave-safe bowl and cover them with plastic wrap, leaving one corner open to vent. Microwave from 1 to 2 minutes for peas and 7 to 8 minutes for brussels sprouts and zucchini.

To steam vegetables, wash, peel, and cut them into pieces. Then place them in a steamer or colander over simmering water. Cover tightly and let the vegetables steam until desired consistency. Obviously, hard root vegetables like carrots or parsnips will take longer to steam than delicate vegetables like bell peppers or sugar snap peas.

Sautéing and Stir-frying

Sautéing is a form of dry-heat cooking that uses a very hot pan and a small amount of fat to cook the food very quickly. Like other dry-heat cooking methods, sautéing browns the food as it cooks and develops complex flavors and aromas. Sautéing works best with food that's been cut into small pieces, making it an excellent cooking method for vegetables. To facilitate tossing, some sauté pans have sloped sides that make it easier to flip the contents within the pan and not all over the kitchen.

Stir-frying is the Asian version of sautéing. A traditional round-bottomed cast-iron or carbon steel pan called a wok is heated to a high temperature. A small amount of cooking oil is then poured down the side of the wok, followed by onion, ginger, and dry seasonings. As soon as the seasonings emit an aroma, the vegetables are added, stirred, and tossed out very quickly, usually within 1 to 2 minutes.

Roasting

Roasting is a dry-heat method of cooking that's similar to baking, but it's faster because the vegetables are tossed with a light coating of oil or butter, which speeds cooking while giving the vegetables a crisp, brown outer surface. A roasted vegetable is browned, caramelized, and crisp—a delight to the senses.

Roasting requires large pans. The pans should be shallow—no more than 2 inches deep. Baking dishes or sheets that measure 13 x 16, 13 x 18, and 11 x 17 are good sizes to use for roasting. You can also use two smaller pans. Place them side by side on the oven rack.

Cut all the vegetables the same size so they will cook at the same rate. Then arrange them in a single layer so the heat can circulate around them; don't stack them. If necessary, roast vegetables in two batches.

Grilling

Grilled veggies have a wonderful smoky edge and an intensified sweetness. They're delicious marinated or just lightly oiled and seasoned with salt and pepper.

While many vegetables grill well, some aren't cut out for it. You wouldn't want to grill celery, cucumber, or delicate greens (although grilled Romaine lettuce is fabulous in a Caesar salad). Tender vegetables such as tomatoes require a grill basket or mat. Tough root vegetables such as carrots, turnips, and potatoes must be blanched or parboiled before grilling. Most other raw vegetables can be grilled directly on a grill rack over hot or medium coals.

Helpful Tip

Different vegetables require different roasting times and temperatures. Baby artichokes roast in 20 minutes at 425°F. Beets can take anywhere from 45 minutes to 2 hours at 350°F, depending on their size. Allow 20 to 25 minutes at 400°F for sliced eggplant, 15 minutes at 425°F for fennel, 30 minutes at 375°F for winter squash, and 20 to 30 minutes at 425°F for carrots, parsnips, and turnips.

Frying

Fried foods tend to get a bum rap in our fat-phobic society. But properly fried foods can be high in nutrition and low in fat. When prepared correctly, fried foods should not be excessively greasy or fatty. In fact, that revered cooking authority Marion Rombauer Becker observed, "A serving of French fried potatoes properly cooked may have a lower calorie count than a baked potato served with butter."

Fried veggies may be coated in a thin batter for tempura or made into fritters, which are chopped vegetables held together in a batter. The secret to crisp fried vegetables is to heat the oil to the correct frying temperature, between 350°F and 375°F. This high temperature heats the water within the food, steaming it from the inside out. The moisture in the food repels the oil so the vegetables don't absorb it. If the oil temperature is too low, the food will absorb oil and be soft and greasy. Properly fried foods only absorb about 10 percent of the oil they are cooked in.

Oil temperature may be compromised by a number of factors. Adding food to hot oil automatically drops the temperature of the oil. The more food you add, the more the temperature drops. So never overcrowd the pan. And bring foods to room temperature before you fry them.

9

FRUITS

Fruits are, well, the fruits of trees and plants. A food is classified as a fruit if it contains seeds. Some vegetables, such as tomatoes and cucumbers, are scientifically classified as fruits, but they're legally classified as vegetables!

There's nothing like biting into a crisp apple on the first cool fall day or eating a ripe raspberry on a warm day in July. Fruits follow the seasons. Apples and pears are perfect for eating in fall, while berries are summer fruits. Exotic fruits like pineapples and mangoes have their seasons, too, even though they are available all year-round. You can buy raspberries in December from a locale like Peru, but they'll be much more expensive.

Perfectly ripe, fresh fruit doesn't need much preparation. But they're delicious in salads and in many baked dishes. Who hasn't enjoyed a fruit pie made with apples and cranberries or a strawberry shortcake on a summer evening?

Fruits are very good for you. They're a great source of fiber and many vitamins. They also are bursting with phytochemicals, those strange-sounding compounds such as anthocyanins and flavonoids, which scientists say help reduce your risk of developing heart disease and cancer. The USDA recommends three to five servings of fruit each day. So eat up and enjoy!

BUYING, STORING, PREPARING FRUIT

Ripe fruits are easily identified. Look for those that feel heavy for their size. They shouldn't be very soft or have any soft spots, holes, or dark spots. The skin should be firm and even.

Fresh fruit should be refrigerated, unless it isn't quite ripe. Keep fresh fruit well wrapped. The refrigerator is a very dry place, and delicate fruit can shrivel easily. Most fruits ripen well at room temperature, especially when placed in a bag together. The fruits give off a gas called ethylene, which hastens ripening.

When soft fruits like peaches and berries are ripe, they smell sweet. But there are other ways to judge ripeness. Peaches, pears, and nectarines will yield to gentle pressure, and the fruit flesh will be very shiny when peeled. Berries are picked when ripe and should be used as soon as possible. Melons and mangoes are ripe when they are fragrant and give slightly when pressed with the fingers.

Fresh fruit should be refrigerated, unless it isn't quite ripe. The refrigerator is a very dry place, so delicate fruit can shrivel easily. That's why you want to keep them well wrapped. Most fruits ripen well at room temperature, especially when placed in a bag together. The fruits give off a gas called ethylene, which hastens ripening.

There are different ways to prepare every fruit. Some fruits, like apples, pears, and berries, can be just rinsed off and eaten. But preparing a pineapple or a mango can be tricky. With a little bit of practice, you'll be able to cut up a pineapple or remove the flesh from a mango or papaya in minutes.

ALL ABOUT FRUIT

Apples really are the fruit of fall. If you've never visited an orchard, give it a try some crisp fall weekend. Apples trees, heavy with fruit, are very beautiful. And picking apples is a great family activity.

All apples—especially when eaten with the skin—are high in fiber. They are also high in phytochemicals, compounds that prevent cancer. Hence the old saying, "An apple a day keeps the doctor away."

Apples can be stored at room temperature or in the refrigerator. Chill them before eating to enhance their crisp texture.

Almost every variety of apple is suitable for

baking. You can use the Macintosh, a sweet/tart apple, or a much more tart apple, such as the Greening or Granny Smith, but there are hundreds of others from which to choose.

The best apples for baking have a strong sweet-tart taste and firm texture that doesn't become soft or mushy in the heat. These varieties include Granny Smith, Cortland, Empire, Golden Delicious (not Red Delicious), Jonathan, Jonagold, and Winesap.

You can peel apples or not; it's up to you, but always wash apples in cold running water before using them. Peel them with a swivel-bladed vegetable peeler or a sharp paring knife. Cut the apples in half or quarters. Then use a knife or coring tool to remove the core where the stiff membrane and seeds are located.

Apricots are stone fruits with a pit in the center. These fruits are very perishable and fragile, so handle them carefully. They have a sweet, floral flavor and aroma, with a slight tart aftertaste. Their season is quite short, from May through August. Canned or dried apricots are more readily available.

When buying apricots, choose heavy fruits that are smooth, with no soft spots or wet areas. Avoid very hard, pale yellow apricots, because they are unripe. Apricots taste best when they're tree-ripened. They have a fuzzy, velvety edible skin. The best way to peel an apricot is to poach it briefly in boiling water for 20 seconds, then plunge it into ice water. Peel off the skin.

Bananas are easy to spot when ripe because they turn bright yellow. You can buy green bananas; they will ripen easily and evenly. Bananas tend to taste best when they have little brown spots on their yellow skins. Store them at room temperature. You can refrigerate them, but the skins will turn black. Use overripe bananas in baking.

Bananas are easy to prepare! Just rinse them off, cut half of the top dark end off to make a little "tab," then use that tab to peel the banana. If you want to add bananas to a fruit salad or salsa, cut them into circles or cubes, then toss with a little lemon juice, because they turn brown quite quickly. And when they start to get too ripe, freeze them right in their skins. The skin will turn black and shrivel, but that's okay. When you have three or four frozen ripe bananas, use them to make banana bread.

Berries are delicious, beautiful, and highly perishable, but if you plan well, you can avoid waste and enjoy these delicious and nutritious fruits. Always store raspberries, blueberries, blackberries, and strawberries in the refrigerator and use them within a day or two. Never wash berries until you're ready to use them; when they're wet, they develop mold.

They are especially delicious in smoothies for breakfasts or snacks. Just whirl some berries with yogurt, a frozen banana or two, and a bit of milk until smooth.

To prepare strawberries, rinse them under cool running water. Use a knife to cut off the leaves and any white part. If there are any soft or bruised spots, cut them out with the knife. Then slice the strawberries.

To prepare raspberries, just rinse them under cool running water. Sort through them and remove any that are soft or squished. Then use them in recipes or eat them out of your hand immediately.

Rinse blueberries and sort over them to remove any that are too soft or soggy.

Blackberries are a bit sturdier than raspberries, but are still very perishable. Rinse them just before you're ready to eat them.

Cherries of the sweet variety are good for eating fresh, while tart cherries are delicious in pies and for juicing. Cherries have more disease-fighting antioxidants than any other fruit. These compounds include anthocyanins, which relieve inflammation and pain, and melatonin, which helps regulate sleep and mood.

Cherries are a sturdier fruit than berries and can be kept in the fridge for several days. Choose heavy, shiny cherries that are firmly attached to their stems.

Pitting cherries is messy work no matter how you do it. Cherry juice stains, so wear an apron or old clothes. Half-frozen cherries are easier to pit and are less messy. Set small batches in the freezer for 30 minutes before pitting if you'd like.

Single cherry pitters are very inexpensive. (An olive pitter works, too.) If you can't find one, use the tip of a potato peeler, a small crochet hook, or a nut pick to scrape the pit out. Or use a piece of rigid plastic drinking straw (the reusable kind) to push the pit through the cherry. A straightened-out paper clip is also a good pitter.

You can also just cut the cherries in half and pry out the pits. Or you can pull the cherry apart, but those cherries don't look as nice. Don't pit cherries ahead of time, as they can develop a brown hue.

Cranberries are very seasonal fruits. You can only find them fresh in the late fall, right after harvest. But they freeze beautifully. When you use frozen berries in baking, don't thaw them first.

Coconut that is dried, sweetened, and flaked, like the kind you buy at the grocery store, is no match for fresh coconut. Fresh coconut is moist and tender and not as sweet as its prepared counterpart. It can be added to fruit salads or eaten as a snack.

To prepare coconut, bake it for 15 minutes at 350°F. This will help loosen the meat from the hard, hairy shell. Let the coconut cool completely. Put the tip of an awl into one of the "eyes" on the coconut—those little indentations next to the stem—and hit it gently with a hammer. Repeat with another indentation and drain out the coconut water.

Hit the coconut itself with the hammer until it breaks into pieces. Work a knife between the white meat and the shell and pry the meat off. Peel it with a knife if any of the brown peel sticks to the white meat, then slice, cut it into chunks, or shred.

Dates, with their wrinkled skin and dark appearance, look like dried fruit. But they actually are fresh. They're the fruit of the date palm, a tropical tree.

Dates are sweet but with a floral undertone. The best ones are Medjools—the smoothest kind, with the richest flavor. Other date varieties include Dayri and Zahidi.

The date is one of the oldest cultivated crops in the world. They pack well, making them good for travel, which is why they're so popular in desert areas. And they can help you stay hydrated, since they're a good source of water and potassium. Dates are also very nutritious, with good amounts of fiber, vitamin A, and antioxidants. They also contain a lot of potassium, which helps reduce blood pressure.

You can buy dates prepared in several ways. Unpitted dates should be pitted before serving. Cut the date in half and remove the pit. Pitted dates are whole with the pit removed mechanically. These dates are good for stuffing. You can also buy chopped dates, but it's best to cut up dates yourself, as the cut variety can be quite dry. Avoid cut dates that have been rolled in sugar unless you're making gorp or a snack mix, because they are very hard and dry.

Dried fruits are nature's candy. They include dried figs, plums (also known as prunes), cherries, apricots, dates, raisins, currants, and cranberries. The sugars and other nutrients in the fruits are concentrated when they're dried.

Dried fruit is good for you. It's high in iron, fiber, and antioxidants and low in fat. While some of the nutrients are lost during the drying process, some dried fruits actually have four times the antioxidants of their fresh equivalents.

Helpful Tip

Be sure that every single cherry has every single pit removed. Pitting cherries is serious business. It's a good idea to pit them over a hard surface, such as a plate or the kitchen sink, so you can literally hear each pit come out of the cherry. Biting into a cherry pit will definitely hurt a tooth.

You can find dried fruits in the baking supplies aisle of your supermarket.

Figs are in season at the end of the summer but are enjoyed dried year-round. Most figs are sold dried, which look and taste very different from fresh figs. In fact, fresh figs are pretty rare and expensive, so if you find them, buy them! They should be smooth and heavy, with a firm skin and no soft or wet spots or bruises. A ripe fig should give slightly when pressed and should smell sweet and fragrant.

Figs are an excellent source of dietary fiber. They are delicious raw, but they can be roasted. Figs come in a variety of colors, from yellow and brown to purple, red, and black. Of course, most people have only experienced figs in Fig Newtons!

Grapes are actually berries, but their seeds are inedible. There are many varieties of seedless grapes; look for those in the supermarket. Buy grapes that are firm and heavy, have no soft spots, and are firmly attached to the stems. Make sure you buy seedless grapes, as seeded grapes are difficult to eat. Luckily, most grapes you find these days are seedless. Store grapes, well covered, in the refrigerator for several days.

There are several varieties of grapes: white grapes, also known as green grapes, are very light green. Red grapes are purplish in color and very sweet. Purple grapes are very dark blue and usually have some type of seed.

To prepare grapes, just rinse them under cool water. Pick them off the stems, discarding any grapes that are too soft or shriveled. Grapes can be eaten out of hand, included in fruit salads, or used in recipes like Chicken Veronique.

Grapefruit, a member of the citrus family, are quite large, with a sweet tanginess unmatched by any other fruit. They are available year-round but are at their peak in winter. Grapefruits are full of vitamin C, fiber, lycopene, and other phytochemicals. In descending order of sweetness, grapefruits come in red, pink, and white varieties. Buy heavy fruits with firm, thin skins. Store them at room temperature or well wrapped in the fridge.

To prepare a grapefruit, cut it in half through its equator. You'll see the sections surrounding a central white spot. A grapefruit spoon, with its serrated edges, can help coax out each section. Or you can use a grapefruit knife, which is serrated on both sides with a slight curve, to cut around each section so it can be scooped out with a spoon.

Healthy Tip

Grapefruit can interfere with some medications. If you are taking statin medications for high cholesterol, antiseizure medications, or some types of antianxiety or antidepressants, avoid grapefruits and grapefruit juice because they inhibit enzymes that make these medications work.

Lemons are one fruit that usually aren't eaten out of hand (although my little sister once ate a lemon that my mother had been saving to rinse her hair!). Every part of these yellow fruits can be used. The peel, which is rich in aromatic oils, is the most flavorful part of the lemon. The juice is sweet and tart and is excellent in recipes, salad dressings, and marinades. And the pulp can be used in baking and cooking.

Choose lemons that are heavy for their size and have thin skins. They should be firm, not puffy, with no soft spots or bruises. Store lemons at room temperature or well wrapped in the fridge. Wash lemons before you zest the skin, and be sure to remove only the bright yellow part of the skin. The white part between the colored skin and flesh is called the pith; it is very bitter. Using a microplane grater is the best way to avoid the pith. Rotate the fruit on the grater frequently for best results.

There are several ways to juice lemons. First, slice the lemon in half through its equator. Use a glass or plastic juicer and firmly twist the lemon over the core of the appliance. Or you can work a fork into each lemon half. Working over a bowl, twist the fork to break up the segments as you squeeze the juice out of the lemon. Or cut the lemon in half and squeeze out the juice using your hand. Whatever method you use, be sure to strain out the seeds or remove them by hand. Nobody enjoys biting down on a hard lemon seed.

Limes that you see most often in the grocery store are called Persian limes. These small green globes contain only 1 to 2 tablespoons of juice per lime, so if you're making a recipe that calls for ⅓ cup of juice, you'll need several limes. Choose limes that are heavy with no soft spots or dark areas on the skin. You may store them at room temperature or wrapped in the refrigerator.

Key limes are different and special. Found only in tropical climates, particularly the Florida Keys, these little citrus fruits are very tiny and yellow, not green. Once you experience the delicate sweet-and-sour taste of the key lime, you'll appreciate the difference. Some baking supply stores carry bottled key lime juice.

As with lemons, lime skin has lots of volatile oils that pack a lot of flavor. To obtain the zest, use a zester, grater, or microplane to remove only the green part of the peel.

Mangoes taste like wild peaches. When ripe, their flesh is soft and extremely juicy, with a wonderful sweet and tart flavor. Mangoes should smell sweet and give slightly when gently pressed. Don't buy a rock-hard mango at the store, or it may not ripen properly. Look for heavy fruits with firm, smooth skin. The color of a mango doesn't matter too much, although the fruits with a dark red blush are very beautiful.

Mangoes are notoriously difficult to cut. Don't peel the fruit; this will just remove much of the flesh in a stringy mess. Instead, there are a couple of different ways to cut a mango. For one, stand the mango upright and position your knife directly in the middle. Move the knife over ½ inch to avoid the large pit and cut off one "cheek." Repeat on other side. Score the flesh in a criss-cross pattern (don't cut through the skin) and then press up on the skin to "pop up" the mango cubes. Cut with a small knife or use a spoon to scrape the fruit from the skin.

For the other cutting method, first cut the mango in half and twist it to release one side. Cut around the pit, then slice off wedges. Remove the peel with a sharp knife. If you aren't going to use a mango immediately, sprinkle the fruit with lime or lemon juice to prevent browning.

Melons are grown all over the world. They have hard rinds; sweet, soft, and very fragrant flesh; and lots of seeds. Watermelon, cantaloupe (muskmelon), and honeydew are the common melons grown in gardens and found at stores. But there are some wonderful, uniquely flavored little-known melons. Try Ananas, Casaba, Canary, Charentais, Crenshaw, Christmas, or Galia melons. Seek them out in ethnic markets. Watermelon comes in red flesh but also orange, yellow, and white.

To test a melon's ripeness, the stem end should be slightly indented and smooth and it should feel softer than the rest of the melon. If it's rough, or if a bit of the stem sticks out, the melon was harvested too early. Also, pick them up and shake them. If you can hear the seeds sloshing around inside, they're ripe. If you gently rap the fruit with your knuckles, it should sound full rather than hollow. Ripe melons are heavy. The fruit should smell appetizing and sweet.

Here are some different kinds of melons:

Cantaloupe is an excellent source of vitamin A. This nutrient, along with beta-carotene, which is found in many orange fruits and vegetables, promotes eye health and can prevent some lung diseases. To prepare cantaloupe, first scrub under running water. Even though melons have thick rinds, they must be washed before cutting. Melons rest on soil and can easily pick up bacteria. This bacteria will transfer to the flesh when the melon is cut. Cut the cantaloupe in half and carefully remove and discard the seeds. Cut the fruit into fourths. Use a knife to cut along the base of the cantaloupe, in between the fruit and rind. Then cube the flesh.

Honeydew melons are green on the inside. Prepare them as you would cantaloupe. Other exotic melons are prepared the same way. Browse through your supermarket or farmers' market in the summer to look for exotic melons.

Watermelon is full of nutrition. This fruit has vitamin C and beta-carotene to help prevent heart disease. One cup of watermelon contains only 46 calories that are packed with phytochemicals such as vitamin A (important for optimal eye health), vitamin B6 (used to manufacture brain chemicals that help us cope with anxiety), and vitamin C (which helps bolster the immune system).Cutting watermelon can be a daunting task. Start by rinsing the rind. Using a sharp chef's knife, cut the ends of the melon off. Place the melon on its side, then slice down the middle. Cut each half into wedges. Using a paring knife, remove the flesh from the rind on each wedge. Cube the flesh.

Oranges are citrus fruits that are more sweet than tart. They are a great source of vitamin C and fiber. Oranges are usually eaten as a breakfast food, but they're great any time of day. There are several varieties of oranges, such as Taracco, the blood orange, with a deep red interior; Blondo Commune, the common orange; and clementines, a tiny, sweet, seedless orange.

To peel an orange, first rinse it, then use a knife to make a cut in the skin. Use your fingers to pull off the peel. Or you can slice off the peel. Slice a thin piece off the bottom of the orange so it stands upright. Then set it on your work surface. Cut the peel off with a sharp knife, following the shape of the orange.

For fruit salad mixes, you may want to "supreme" oranges and other citrus fruits. Use a sharp thin-bladed knife to cut just to one side of the membrane, and then to the other, holding each section of the fruit in place. Twist your knife a bit and the section will pop right out. When you're done, you'll be left holding the membrane, which is full of juice. Squeeze it over the orange sections.

Papaya was called the "fruit of the angels" by Christopher Columbus. Sweet, juicy, and healthy, papaya is one of the world's favorite tropical fruits.

In North America, there are two types of papaya found in supermarkets. One is

Health Tip

Always wash fruits before slicing to avoid passing bacteria from the skin to the flesh. All fruits can have bacteria on them from handling and shipping. Use a food-grade soap or washing solution and rinse thoroughly before you slice or chop.

very large and long (Caribbean type), while the other is quite small and rounded (Hawaiian type). Both are delicious when fully ripe. To make fresh papaya taste even better, drizzle a little lime juice over the cubed fruit.

Papayas are ripe when the skin turns orange, and the fruit feels soft when pressed. When buying papaya, look for skin that is turning from green to yellow. You should be able to indent the skin with your thumb.

To prepare papaya, wash it, then slice the fruit in half lengthwise. Crack open the papaya and scrape out the seeds. Scoop out the flesh or slice the fruit. Eat as you would watermelon slices, or cut off the skin and slice the flesh into cubes.

Passion fruit is native to South America and is cultivated in frost-free areas throughout Brazil, Peru, Paraguay, and northeast Argentina. The oval fruit has a shriveled appearance when ripe. Its interior is full of bright orange pulp and crunchy black seeds. Passion fruit can be cut in half and easily eaten with a spoon. Its natural flavor is very tart, so sugar is needed to soften its taste.

Peaches are fuzzy little fruits packed with beta-carotene, potassium, and heart disease–preventing lycopene, among other nutrients. Choose peaches that are firm and heavy for their size, with smooth skin. Like plums and other stone fruits (which contain a large, hard pit in the center), peaches should be ripened at room temperature until they smell sweet and give a bit under gentle pressure. They're delicious

Helpful Tip

Some people say that papaya seeds are edible; others say they are not. They are in fact safe to eat, although their flavor is quite strong and peppery. If you want the sweetness of papaya, discard the seeds.

eaten out of hand, in peach pie, and turned into salsa with some jalapeños and ripe tomatoes.

Peaches are short-season fruits, and when they are abundant in your area, stockpile as many as you can. Place unripe peaches on your countertop and cover with a dish towel for a couple of days.

Peaches are hard to peel unless you blanch them. Get a pot of water boiling and set a bowl of ice water near by. Cut an X into each peach, dip the peaches in the boiling water for about 30 seconds, then immediately transfer to the ice bath for a few minutes. The skins should slip right off. Place the peaches in a large food storage bag and cover with apple juice so they don't brown.

Pears can be stored at room temperature or in the refrigerator. Chill them before eating to enhance their crisp texture. Pears are the odd fruit that ripen best off the tree. When pears develop their mature color—which can be yellow, green, brown, or red—they are picked and allowed to soften for a few days. The most common pear varieties are Bosc, Anjou, and Bartlett, but you can often find other types in season, which runs from late fall to late spring. Pears contain the sweetest natural sugar, levulose, in a higher concentration than any other fruit, which is why they are very sweet.

To prepare a pear, rinse it, then peel it and cut it in half lengthwise. Using a paring knife, remove the stem. With a melon ball scoop, twist a circle around the core and gently remove it. You can leave the skin on the pear or peel it before use. When cooking pears, the skin helps hold the tender flesh together.

There are several types of fresh pears:

Anjou. These pears are fatter and rounder than Bartlett pears. They are quite sweet and very juicy. They come in a yellow green color with white flesh. They are good eaten raw or baked.

Asian. Asian pears are round like apples and never get as soft as regular pears. Since Asian pears are sturdier than their buttery European counterparts, they hold up well in steamed dishes, salads, and puddings. Shop for Asian pear varieties in the specialty produce section of your supermarket.

Bartlett. These pears are soft and sweet and are good for eating out of hand. You can find the ordinary green Bartlett and the Red Bartlett in stores. They are the classic pear shape.

Bosc. These pears are brown, with slightly rough skin. They have an elongated shape and their skin is often "russeted," which means it has some darker, cinnamon-colored areas. These pears are delicate and delicious.

Helpful Tip

Peaches come in two main varieties: cling and freestone. Cling peaches have pits that literally cling to the flesh. They can be very difficult to pit and are usually used for canning. Freestone peaches have pits that come out easily. Look for freestone peaches for the easiest preparation.

Comice. These round pears have a yellow skin and a rosy blush. If the pear is completely yellow, it's overripe. Look for heavy Comice pears with few bruises and firm skin.

Prickly pears. The Italian term for prickly pears or Indian figs is *fichi d'India*. They hail from the cactus family and are a bright fuchsia color. Prickly pears must be peeled to remove the small spines on the outer skin before eating.

Seckel. These tiny pears have a short season. They are very small, usually just about bite size. Seckel pears are green with a deep red blush. They are very delicate, so handle with care.

To find out whether a pear is ripe, smell it! Ripe pears should have a rich, fruity aroma. Then, using a paring knife, snip off a tiny bit of the fruit, right next to the stem. If the flesh is hard, the pear is not ripe. If the knife slides into the stem end easily and drips juice, it's ripe and ready to eat.

> ## Helpful Tip
>
> It can be hard to understand the description of pear texture as "smooth" or "buttery." All pears contain small cells called "stone cells," which give the fruit a slightly gritty texture.

Pineapple looks like the most tropical of fruits. Most of the pineapples sold in the United States are grown in Hawaii. Fresh pineapple puts the "sweet" in many sweet-and-sour dishes, including salads and stir-fries. Pineapple is a delicate tropical fruit that should be kept at room temperature and eaten quickly when ripe.

Pineapple is ripe when it smells ripe. Choose heavy pineapples, because they have lots of juice. A pineapple that feels soft is overripe. When shopping for a pineapple, look for flesh that is still firm but can be slightly indented with your thumb. When ripe the skin of the pineapple turns from green to yellow, so look for a pineapple that is between these two colors. One of the best tests for choosing a pineapple is to try lifting it by one of the uppermost leaves. If the leaf separates from the fruit, the pineapple is ready to eat. Store pineapple in the fridge or at room temperature.

There are several ways to cut a pineapple. You can simply slice off the skin and cut the fruit into chunks, discarding the core. Or you can slice off one side of the pineapple, use your knife to cut around the perimeter of the fruit, and then use a tablespoon to scoop out the fruit. You will be left with a hollow pineapple "boat" that can be used for serving.

In a third way to prepare pineapple, cut off the top and bottom inch with a sharp knife and cut off the peel. Then, using the tip of the knife, dig out any embedded eyes and cut the pineapple in quarters. The lighter-colored hard fibrous core should be visible on one edge of each quarter. Stand the quarter up and slice downward between the core and the flesh and then slice or chop the fruit.

Pomegranates are also very seasonal fruits. They should be firm, with no wet spots, soft spots, or dark spots on the skin. Buy heavy fruits, as they'll be juicy. Store pomegranates in the fridge. You eat just the seeds from the pomegranate.

Pomelo looks like a huge grapefruit and is one of the cultivars that contributed to the modern grapefruit. It is native to Southeast Asia and is used in Chinese cold plates and desserts. The flavor is milder and slightly sweeter than grapefruit.

The pomelo rind is extremely thick, but easy to peel. Slice the pomelo vertically into quarters. With a paring knife, cut through the pith at a corner and remove the peel. Pull off the inner membranes and cut the slices into chunks.

Rhubarb, a relative of buckwheat, has a supersour taste. Technically it's a vegetable, but it's legally classified as a fruit. It's available fresh only in spring and, even though it looks tough and hard, is very perishable. Buy firm, brightly colored stalks. Use it soon after purchase, and store it in the fridge.

Rhubarb must be cooked with sugar to be edible. It is often combined with strawberries. Both fruits are good sources of fiber and vitamin C. But be careful with rhubarb—while the stalks make delightfully tangy desserts, the leaves are toxic.

To use rhubarb, cut off the leaves and the stem ends. Wash the stalks thoroughly. You may want to peel the rhubarb if it is very stringy. Then chop it into the size called for in the recipe. Always cook rhubarb before eating it in sauces and pies.

Star fruit gets its name from the fact that it is shaped into five lobes and when cut crosswise looks exactly like a star. The technical name for this fruit is carambola. Star fruit is native to the Philippines. When ripe, it is mostly yellow with a bit of light green. It's a beautiful addition to fruit salads. The flavor is sharp and citrusy, with a mild sweetness.

To prepare star fruit, just wash it gently and cut across with a sharp knife. Sometimes the edges of the lobes have a brown line; this can be trimmed off using a sharp knife if you'd like. Remove the dark seeds with your fingers or the tip of a knife.

USING FRUITS

Fruits can be eaten out of hand or used in cooking and baking. Fruits are poached, blanched, frozen, or canned. Or they're used in baked recipes like quick breads, pies, cookies, and cakes. Fruits are also delicious paired with many meats.

Poaching

Poached fruits are a classic dessert. Choose firm fruits, preferably stone fruits like peaches or plums, or fall fruit like apples or pears. Whether you peel your fruits for poaching or leave them unpeeled is a matter of choice. If you choose to leave the peel on, remove a thin strip of the peel at the top of the fruit so the skin doesn't split in the heat.

Fruit can be poached in fruit juices, wine, or sweetened water. The poaching process turns hard fruits juicy and tender and adds a wonderful flavor. Serve with some ice cream or hard sauce for the perfect finish.

Blanching

Fruits are blanched so they are easier to peel and to prepare them before freezing. Blanching is far more efficient than peeling, which removes a great deal of fruit along with the skin. It also helps slow down the enzymatic browning process.

To blanch fruits, wash them well, then drop them into a pot of boiling water. Remove in 1 to 2 minutes. Then place them in a colander and run them under cold water to stop the cooking process, or place the fruit in a large bowl of ice water. Slip off the skins and cut the fruit in half. Remove the pits and slice the flesh.

Acidulation

Acidulation is a fancy term that just means brushing or soaking cut fruits with water mixed with lemon juice or vinegar. Apples, bananas, potatoes, peaches, and pears are fruits that will turn brown when exposed to oxygen, so they benefit from acidulation. The brown color is not harmful, but it is unappetizing.

Grilling

Many types of fruit are excellent when cooked on a charcoal or gas grill. When you grill fruit, leave the skin on. Brush the fruit with lemon juice. You don't have to grill fruit for a long time, just until it's very hot and picks up some grill marks. Because it's drier than baked fruit, grilled fruit should be dressed with a sauce, a bit of butter, or some honey.

Macerating

Macerated fruit has been "cooked" in ascorbic acid from citrus fruits. This is an easy way to prepare a variety of fruit. Mix together 4 cups of different prepared seasonal fruits, such as bananas and pineapples. Add ½ cup orange juice, 1 teaspoon curry powder, and sugar to taste. Toss to coat well. Let "cook" in the refrigerator for 1 to 2 hours, then serve.

Preserving

Jelly is made from strained fruit juices and is thick but nearly clear. Jam contains pureed fruit and sometimes seeds. It has a uniform consistency that is thick enough to spread. Preserves have larger, identifiable pieces of fruit and are softer than jam. Conserves are like preserves, but they have things like nuts and coconut added to them. Marmalades are like jelly with larger fruit pieces.

Gelatin Salads

Gelatin salads, once so popular at ladies' luncheons, are back in style. They are almost always made with fruits. Unflavored gelatin is very different from the luridly flavored gelatins you mix with water and chill. Unflavored gelatin is just pure gelatin—no water, no flavorings, no artificial ingredients. It comes in small envelopes in the baking aisle of the supermarket.

To prepare unflavored gelatin, first soften it in cool water. Then, after it "blooms," which takes about 5 minutes, add boiling water and stir to dissolve. Stir 4 to 5 minutes, until you can no longer see grains of gelatin in the spoon when you scoop up a small amount. If the gelatin isn't completely and thoroughly dissolved, the finished salad will be grainy. Don't boil gelatin, or it may become tough or lose its thickening power.

If you can find it, leaf or sheet gelatin is a great substitute for powdered gelatin. It comes in clear, stiff sheets that look like windowpanes. Just soak it in water to cover for a few minutes, then squeeze out the water from the soft mass and add the gelatin to the rest of the liquids.

To remove a gelatin salad from a mold, make sure it's very well set. Then remove from the fridge and place a serving platter on top. Drape a hot, wrung-out towel on the mold. Invert the mold and plate together and shake vigorously; the salad should slip right out. If it doesn't, repeat the hot towel application.

Freezing

All berries freeze well. Just freeze them on a cookie sheet first so they won't form one giant clump before transferring to a sandwich bag or lidded container. You can freeze fruit that is getting a little too soft for later use in smoothies or other recipes calling for frozen fruit, such as sorbet.

Berries need special care before they can be frozen. Wash them and then spread them in a single layer on a cookie sheet. Place the sheet in the freezer. When berries are frozen (after about an hour), remove and pack them into bags or containers. Label and date the bags and store in the freezer.

10
DAIRY

These days there are so many choices in the dairy aisle. Milk, eggs, cheese, yogurt, sour cream, whipping cream, and buttermilk are a few of the items you most likely buy every week. But you should take time to learn about these products. Dairy products are usually sold by their fat content. Milk comes in every fat content, from full fat, or whole milk, to skim. You can find regular sour cream, low-fat sour cream, and nonfat sour cream, and even nonfat heavy cream!

Always follow the use-by dates on dairy products. Throw away any product past its date. Keep dairy products except butter and milk in the body of the refrigerator, not the door, because the door area is warmer.

Keep milk, cream, buttermilk, yogurt, and cheeses tightly wrapped or sealed, because they can easily pick up stray refrigerator odors. Keep eggs in their carton, even if your door has those cute little hollows for holding eggs. If you buy pasteurized eggs for food safety reasons, remember they have very short expiration ranges. Pasteurized eggs are only good for a few days after purchase, so buy only what you need at one time. Butter lasts for a long time as long as it is well wrapped. Keep it in the butter shelf in the door.

DAIRY ITEMS AND FREEZING

Some dairy products freeze well, while other do not. Here's a quick guide:

Butter: Freezes well.

Hard cheese: Will freeze but is crumbly when thawed.

Soft cheese (cottage, cream): Does not freeze well.

Whipped cream: Can be frozen.

Heavy cream: Can be frozen if you add ½ cup sugar per quart, then heat to 170°F for 15 minutes before freezing.

Sour cream: Does not freeze well.

Whole milk: Can be frozen but will separate when thawed.

Buttermilk: Freeze like whole milk.

Homemade yogurt: Will freeze but may taste more acidic when thawed.

Organic dairy products are free of any bovine growth hormone (which makes cows produce more milk) and antibiotics (which are given to commercially raised cattle to ward off potential diseases). Organic dairy is slightly more expensive than commercial dairy, but the health benefits outweigh the minimal cost. Look for store-brand organic milk for the best savings.

BASIC DAIRY PRODUCTS

Milk is a popular drink among people of all ages. Children drink it without objection, and it is the classic accompaniment to a chocolate chip cookie. But not all milk is the same; there are many kinds in the dairy section of the supermarket. Here's how they differ:

Full-fat milk doesn't have a lot of fat, even though it tastes rich and creamy. It typically is about 3.25 percent butterfat.

Two percent milk has, well, 2 percent butterfat.

Low-fat milk has 1 percent butterfat.

Skim milk has 0 to 0.5 percent butterfat.

Many people are allergic to lactose, the sugar found in milk. If you or a family member is lactose intolerant, that doesn't have to mean giving up on a creamy glass of cold milk. Just choose almond milk, rice milk, or soy milk. You can also find goat's or sheep's milk in some specialty stores. And some specially processed lactose-free milks are also available.

Some people freeze milk to save it. Frozen milk may separate into a watery and a thicker layer when thawed. The milk can be blended back together and is perfectly safe. Freeze milk in freezer-safe glass or hard-sided containers for the best flavor. Don't freeze in cardboard cartons. Leave 1½ inches of space at the top of narrow-mouthed containers, ½ inch for pints, and 1 inch for quarts in wide-mouthed jars to allow for expansion. Frozen milk stores for about three months.

Dry milk is usually used in recipes. It can be rehydrated for drinking, but many people think it has a tinny and artificial taste. For better flavor, mix it with some fresh milk.

Evaporated milk is made by putting milk under a vacuum and removing half its water content. Then it's sterilized, homogenized, and sealed in cans. Evaporated milk is used primarily in cooking for creaminess and richness. The shelf life of evaporated milk is 1 to 2 years. Once opened, it has the same shelf life as fresh milk.

Buttermilk scares off many people because of the presence of the word *butter* in its name, but actually most buttermilk has very little fat. It's made from a combination of low-fat milk and lactic acid. If you can find real (not cultured) buttermilk, by all means use it. Real buttermilk is the liquid, or whey, left over when butter is churned from heavy cream. The fat goes into the butter! Buttermilk contains only about 1 to 2 percent butterfat.

To make homemade buttermilk for baking and cooking, place 1 tablespoon white vinegar in a measuring cup. Add enough milk to equal 1 cup and let sit 10 minutes. Voila! One cup of homemade "buttermilk" is ready for use. You can buy dried buttermilk powder on the market; just store in the pantry and reconstitute when needed.

Yogurt is filled with friendly bacteria for good digestive health. You can eat it straight out of the carton, use it in recipes, or use it as a substitute for sour cream or ricotta cheese.

While plain yogurt can be thin and watery, Greek yogurt is thick and creamy, because most of the whey has been strained out. It is a great way to enjoy low-fat yogurt. It's great to use in dips to replace sour cream for a healthier snack, as well as to eat on its own. Stir Greek yogurt into sautéed spinach for healthy creamed spinach or serve for dessert topped with honey and walnuts.

Not only does Greek yogurt taste completely different, it also boasts slightly more protein than regular nonfat yogurt. Plain nonfat Greek yogurt has 2.5 grams of protein per ounce, compared to 1.5 grams of protein per ounce of plain nonfat regular yogurt. And, while regular has a couple calories less than Greek yogurt, it also has twice as much sugar.

There are an infinite number of yogurts on the market today—experiment until you find one your family loves. It is most cost-effective to purchase a large tub of yogurt instead of many smaller ones. Remember that fruit-filled yogurts are often packed with sugar and even artificial flavorings and colorings.

Butter is a by-product of heavy cream. Cream with about 40 percent butterfat is churned or

BUDGET TIP

Strain your own yogurt instead of buying expensive Greek yogurt. Place yogurt in a cheesecloth-lined strainer, put over a bowl, then refrigerate until most of the whey, or thin liquid, drains out. The resulting yogurt, also called yogurt cheese, is thick and rich.

manipulated until it "breaks" and butter forms in the whey. The butter is removed, washed, and salted or not. It's used as a spread, in baking, and in cooking.

Unsalted butter is a fresher product than salted; the salt used acts as a preservative and increases the shelf life. If a recipe calls for butter, it is safe to use either salted or unsalted. However, if the recipe calls for unsalted butter and you use salted instead, taste the dish before adding the recommended amount of salt. Unsalted butter is a better choice when you're making sauces, because it tends to make a creamier sauce.

European-style butter (now available in many supermarkets) has a higher fat content and a more luxurious texture than America butter. It makes unbeatably tender baked goods.

Helpful Tip

Clarified butter, also known as drawn butter, is called for in some recipes. This butter has a higher burning point than regular butter because the milk solids are removed. To make clarified butter, melt butter in a saucepan over medium heat. Simmer until butter foams, then skim and discard the white froth. Carefully pour the remaining butter through a cheesecloth, leaving any remaining white sediment behind. You'll lose about a quarter of the volume by clarifying. Store in the fridge for up to a month.

Butter is one of the best dairy items to freeze. It will hold its texture and taste for at least nine months if packaged properly. You can freeze commercial sticks or blocks of butter by overwrapping them in freezer bags or freezer paper. You can also mold butter into forms with butter molds and freeze those. Little patties of butter can also be frozen if separated with pieces of parchment paper. Homemade butter can be pressed into containers and frozen.

When softening butter, the microwave oven can be tricky, because butter will usually soften unevenly and even melt in spots. This can change the texture of the finished product. In a pinch, you can use the microwave, but watch the butter very carefully. Microwave for 10 seconds at 30 percent power, let it stand 2 minutes, and then check the butter. Repeat one or two more times until the butter is soft to the touch.

Browned butter has a much more complex flavor than plain butter, with a rich nutty and caramel taste. The milk solids break down and recombine to form more compounds that give the browned butter a rich taste and deep caramel color. It takes about 8 to 12 minutes for butter to turn brown over medium-low heat. Watch it carefully and don't let it burn. If the butter does burn, you must throw it out and start over. Browned butter is used in frostings and as a flavoring. You can make browned butter a day or two ahead of time; just store it in the refrigerator.

Sour Cream is made from cream treated with a souring agent. It has 18 to 20 percent butterfat. You can find low-fat sour cream, which has about 12 percent butterfat, or nonfat sour cream, with 1 to 2 percent butterfat. You can substitute one for the other when topping a bowl of chili, but don't substitute the low-fat or nonfat varieties for regular sour cream when baking.

Crème fraîche, the silkier and more buttery cousin of sour cream, is delicious stirred into soups or sauces or served over vegetables or with fresh fruit. You can make a homemade version by combining 2 tablespoons cultured buttermilk with 2 cups heavy cream and heating the mixture to 85°F. Pour the mixture into a clean jar, cover partially, and let stand at room temperature for 8 to 24 hours, until thickened. Stir and refrigerate at least 24 hours before using. Homemade crème fraîche keeps for 2 weeks in the refrigerator.

Cream comes in two varieties: half-and-half, also called light cream, with 11 to 18 percent butterfat, and heavy or whipping cream, with about 36 percent butterfat. Double cream, a product used in England, can have 40 percent butterfat.

To whip heavy cream, be sure the cream, bowl, and beaters are all cold. Start beating at low speed, then increase the speed as the cream starts to thicken. Add powdered sugar as the cream whips. This product contains cornstarch, which helps stabilize the cream. Avoid ultra-pasteurized heavy cream. It takes longer to whip and sometimes will not whip to the proper consistency.

You can make whipped cream without sugar to use on very sweet desserts. Unsweetened whipped cream is used in many French savory sauces. You can freeze the whipped cream in small portions. Pipe or dollop some onto waxed paper, freeze until firm, and then let thaw in the fridge before topping desserts.

CHEESE

What would the world be without cheese? Every kitchen needs a good selection of cheeses. Cheese is made by separating milk into curds and whey with an acid and rennet, which is made from the lining of cows' stomachs. The type of cheese that's made is determined by how the curds are treated.

There are four basic types of cheese: fresh or unripe, soft and semisoft, semihard, and hard. Cheeses are also categorized by the milk used to make them. Most commercial cheeses are made from cow's milk, but sheep's milk and goat's milk cheese (also known as chèvre) are gaining in popularity.

Imported cheeses are more expensive than cheeses made in the United States. Cheeses in Europe are strictly controlled. France and Italy operate a system of regulations to protect certain cheeses under the acronym DOC (Denomination Controlled Origin). In 1955 the Ministry of Agriculture and a consortium of cheese makers agreed that cheeses with this stamp of approval could be made only in a specific region. Identifying and promoting specific cheeses this way help protect them from been copied while guaranteeing the consumer high quality.

Helpful Tip

To grate cheese it should be cold. Very soft cheeses will grate more easily if you put them in the freezer for 10 to 15 minutes (no longer). Make sure the grater has sharp holes. You can coat it with a bit of oil to make cleanup easier. Cut the cheese into manageable pieces and use it immediately after grating so it doesn't dry out.

An old-fashioned box grater does a fine job with semisoft and even some hard cheeses. You get a coarse grate, which is fine for some dishes. For grinding, use either a cheese grinder or the metal blade on your food processor.

Cheese Types

Here are the most common cheeses, from unripe to hard:

Cream cheese is a soft, unripened cheese. It has a unique ability to melt into dishes and provide fantastically creamy and luxurious textures. Cream cheese is often used in baking and makes very moist cakes as well as killer icing for carrot cake. Try melting 1 tablespoon into 2 scrambled eggs for an amazing treat. Or use in place of butter in mashed potatoes.

Soften cream cheese by just letting it stand at room temperature for an hour or two. Or place the cream cheese on a microwave-safe plate and microwave on 50 percent power for 1 minute. When combining cream cheese with other ingredients, avoid lumps by beating the cream cheese well first and then gradually adding liquids.

Ricotta is a popular soft cheese that is actually a cheese by-product. The name literally means "recooked." Made from sheep's or cow's milk, ricotta is created when the whey that's left over when cheese is made is cooked with more milk. Ricotta is grainier than cream cheese, with a lighter taste. Its shelf life is shorter than aged and salted cheeses. It's used in lasagna and many other Italian pasta dishes.

Mascarpone is a double- or triple-cream cheese made from cow's milk. It is fresh, not ripened. Mascarpone is very rich and smooth, with a deep milky flavor. This Italian soft cheese is used in desserts and cheesecake. With a fat content of 50 percent, it is mostly used for desserts.

Cottage cheese, the dieter's friend, is made from curds and whey that haven't been pressed. Its name probably comes from the fact that it was made in small villages by people in cottages from the buttermilk left over after the butter was made. Cottage cheese is classified by its curd size. Small-curd cottage cheese is made without rennet. Large-curd cottage cheese is made with rennet. Cottage cheese comes in full-fat, which is about 4 percent butterfat, to nonfat varieties.

Farmer's cheese or Pot cheese is really cottage cheese that has been pressed after the curds and whey are separated. It's a simple, semisoft cheese. Some people classify pot cheese as soft, while farmer's cheese is semisoft, since it's made from pressed pot cheese. The Mexican version of this cheese is called queso blanco.

Goat's milk cheese, also called chèvre (pronounced *shev,* the French word for "goat") is an entire classification of cheeses made from, well, goat's milk. Goat's milk cheese can be as soft as cream cheese, or it can be ripened into the dark brown Norwegian cheese known as Brunost, which is definitely an acquired taste.

Goat's milk cheese comes in as many types as cow's milk cheese, and it has the same fat content. Many people who are lactose intolerant can consume goat's milk with no problem. Babies and toddlers who have a hard time digesting cow's milk may tolerate goat's milk.

Brie is one of the great cheeses of France. This cow's milk cheese can be made with whole or partially skimmed milk. Creamy and rich, Brie can range from 30 percent to almost 90 percent fat content. The white moldy rind is supposed to be eaten, not peeled off and discarded. It has a mushroom flavor.

Brie will continue to ripen as it ages and become more runny and pungent. As Brie ripens the rind begins to take on a faint smell of ammonia. This is natural, and you should not be alarmed. However, if the ammonia smell becomes overwhelming, discard the cheese. For easier slicing, try putting it in the freezer for about 10 minutes.

Genuine mozzarella is made from the milk of the black water buffalo. It is usually sold as a snow-white ball, but can be purchased smoked. Fresh mozzarella is extremely perishable. It's at its best when eaten on the day it is made. Until modern food technology made possible the process of preservation, mozzarella was only a regional pleasure.

As a result of the huge demand for this fresh, soft cheese, it is now also made with cow's milk. Strictly speaking, this variety should not be called mozzarella but *fior di latte* ("milk flower"). Try serving it with freshly sliced tomatoes just picked from the garden, or use it to top a simple pizza.

Feta, a staple of Greek cuisine, is usually made with sheep's milk. It is a fairly soft cheese, although it can be hard enough so it crumbles easily. The flavor is sharp and fresh, with a tangy

Helpful Tip

The prized mozzarella made from buffalo's milk is called *mozzarella di bufala*. Mozzarella comes in a variety of shapes—rounds, braids, basket shapes, and balls, both large and small. The small balls of mozzarella are called *bocconcini*. The type of mozzarella that can be grated and comes in a block is called part-skim mozzarella. This cheese melts well on pizzas and lasagna.

aftertaste. It's either packed in a block in brine, or crumbled. You can find many flavors of feta cheese, seasoned with everything from sun-dried tomatoes to garlic.

Gorgonzola and Blue cheese. According to one legend, an innkeeper from Gorgonzola discovered that his Stracchino cheese had turned blue after a few weeks in his damp, cool cellar. Because he couldn't afford to lose money, he decided to sell it anyway. To his eternal gratification his customers demanded more. The vein in blue cheese is actually a variant of the penicillin bacteria.

More than eighty farmhouses, large and small, in northern Italy produce Gorgonzola. Some still follow the old way of using unpasteurized milk, exposing the curd to the mold naturally. Others use pasteurized milk to which the mold is added. The greenish blue veins of this cheese have a sharp flavor. The cheese is used for pasta, dressings, and salads.

Cheeses with blue veins that are not made in the Gorgonzola area of Italy or the Roquefort area of France are simply called blue cheeses. There's an excellent variety of blue cheese called Maytag Blue that's made in Iowa. These cheeses are used in cheese sauces and as garnishes for many recipes.

Fontina has a smooth, semisoft texture, which allows it to melt into a very creamy sauce. Fontina cheese may be hard to find in some markets. When looking for a substitute, look for cheeses that are firm but soft.

Havarti is a semisoft Danish cheese that has a buttery texture and rich, tangy flavor. It is delicious used in many recipes, especially as a melting cheese in sauces. It's often sold flavored with ingredients like dill or caraway seed. It pairs well with pears and grapes and is a good choice for a cheese board.

Swiss and Gruyère are two forms of Swiss cheese. Swiss cheese is a common cheese that has large holes created by carbon dioxide produced by the bacteria used to make the cheese. This same bacteria also produces acids that create its tangy and nutty flavor. The longer the cheese is aged, the more and larger holes it will have.

Gruyère is the Swiss form of Swiss cheese, made only in the Gruyère region of Switzerland. It's very rich and creamy with a nutty taste. Gruyère is usually used in fondues. Other forms of Swiss cheese include Baby Swiss, which is made from whole milk with small holes, and Lacy Swiss, made with low-fat milk.

Cheddar and Colby are used in many recipes and are excellent grating cheeses. Colby is just a milder version of cheddar. They are made with a process called cheddaring, which involves salting and draining the curd again, then layering it and pressing to form a cheese with a dense and smooth texture.

These cheeses are often colored yellow or orange, although you can find white cheddar cheeses. Cheddar cheese can be purchased in many varieties, from mild to extrasharp.

To cut cheddar cheese into cubes, first cut the block of cheese into ¼-inch slices. Next cut the slices in half lengthwise. Then cut the halves into ¼-inch strips. Finally, cut the strips into ¼-inch cubes.

Provolone is a cheese that hails from southern Italy, provolone is formed into a sausage-like shape. It is a semihard cheese made from whole cow's milk, aged for at least four months. Provolone comes in both plain and smoked varieties. The taste can range from mild to sharp.

Parmesan. Known as the king of cheeses, Parmesan, or Parmigiana Reggiano, is produced under the strictest rules. Only milk from cows from certain areas of Parma is used to make this ancient artisanal product. To carry the official Parmigiana stamp, the cheese must be certified by a government agency. The leftover whey from the cheese-making process is fed to pigs, which are used for prosciutto di Parma, which is considered the king of hams.

There are many different qualities of Parmesan cheese on the market, with Parmigiana Reggiano from Italy topping the charts in quality and flavor. Parmigiana Reggiano has thick waxy rind emblazoned with its name (so you will always know you are getting the real thing). Its texture is crumbly and a bit crunchy (from calcium crystals) and is best enjoyed finely grated over food or cut into little chunks to be nibbled slowly. There are many varieties of ordinary Parmesan cheese available that are perfectly fine when cooking and baking.

Pecorino is the generic name for cheeses made from pure sheep's milk. The smooth, hard rind ranges from pale straw to dark brown in color. Each is characteristic of a specific area and a particular breed of sheep. For centuries,

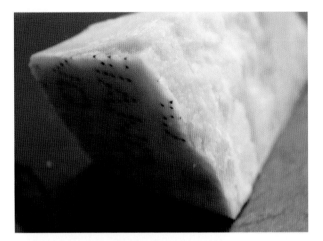

Helpful Tip

Parmigiano Reggiano's aroma is sweet and fruity; it's pale yellow in color, and the taste is fruity (like fresh pineapple), strong, and rich but never overpowering. It will keep in the refrigerator for months; it can also be frozen, and even grated when still frozen. The cows whose milk goes into the cheese are only allowed to eat fresh grass, alfalfa, and hay; this process guarantees the quality and the flavor of the cheese but drives the price for it higher.

Pecorino Romano was made in the countryside around Rome, and it remains virtually unchanged to this day. Each is characteristic of a specific area and a particular breed of sheep. This hard cheese is perfect for grating.

Cotija cheese is a hard grating cheese with a delightfully tangy, salty flavor similar to Parmesan but milder. It's an increasingly popular and versatile cheese.

EGGS

Eggs are one of nature's perfect foods. In fact, protein content of all foods is compared to the egg, which is given a perfect score of 100. Eggs consist of the white, or clear portion, surrounding the bright yellow or orange yolk. The little squiggly piece of dense material is called the "chalazae." It's a little structure that holds the yolk in the white.

For best quality, look for free-range, farm-raised eggs. If you can't find those eggs, look for cartons labeled "cage free" and certainly "no antibiotics." Mass-produced eggs have much less flavor and less nutrition. And the methods for raising mass-produced eggs can be cruel.

Eggs get a bad rap for their fat and cholesterol content, but much of the fat in eggs is unsaturated. Studies have shown that the "bad" (LDL) cholesterol in eggs may be offset by its "good" (HDL) cholesterol content. Eggs are a good source of vitamin A, iron, riboflavin, phosphorus, and calcium. You can find eggs in the market that have been enriched with omega-3 fatty acids for even more nutrition.

Before breaking eggs, wash them well in lukewarm water with a mild soap. Eggs are porous, so hot water may open the pores and allow microbes inside the egg. Don't consume eggs that are cracked in the carton; in fact, examine your eggs before you buy them and check them again before you use them and discard any that are cracked, crazed, or broken.

Cooking Eggs

Eggs can be cooked in many ways. They can be poached or fried, scrambled or hard-cooked. Omelets and frittatas are two different ways to cook beaten eggs, and the soufflé is the masterpiece of the cooking world.

Coddled eggs are really not cooked at all. They are used to make Caesar salad dressing. The egg is placed in simmering water for a minute or two to slightly set the white. Unless they're made from pasteurized eggs, coddled eggs aren't safe.

Health Tip

The FDA recommends that no one eat raw or undercooked eggs. That means if you want to have an egg over easy or poached, you'll need to use pasteurized eggs. Eggs are often contaminated with salmonella bacteria, so undercooked or raw eggs should not be served to anyone in a high-risk group. The very young, the very old, pregnant women, and people with suppressed immune systems should not eat undercooked or runny eggs. This is not to scare you; just be aware of this reality when you're cooking eggs. You can take your chances if you'd like, but it's best to play it safe.

Poached eggs are simmered in water until the white is set and the yolk is still runny. Poached eggs used in certain recipes should be runny, as the yolk becomes a sauce for the rest of the dish. You can also poach eggs until the yolk is firm. Remember to use pasteurized eggs if you're concerned about salmonella bacteria.

To poach an egg, bring a medium-size pot of water to a boil over high heat. Then reduce the heat to low. Add a teaspoon of vinegar to the pot to keep the egg in a nice compact shape. Crack an egg into a bowl, then carefully slide the egg from the bowl to the pot. Cook the egg for 3 to 4 minutes. Then, using a large slotted spoon, scoop up the egg, place the spoon on a folded kitchen towel to absorb excess water, and serve immediately.

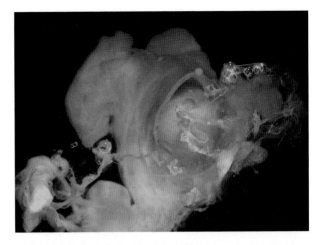

Fried eggs are cooked in melted butter until the white is set and the yolk is either runny, soft, or hard. Frying eggs can be a real art. If the egg is flipped while cooking, it's called over, as in over easy or over hard.

To fry an egg, first heat a skillet over medium heat. When it's hot, add a tablespoon or 2 of butter. Break the eggs, one at a time, into a small dish and slip them, one at a time, into the melted butter. Reduce the heat to low and cover the pan. Cook for 4 to 6 minutes, until the whites are set and the yolk thickened. If you used pasteurized eggs, you can serve them with a runny yolk; if not, cook until the yolk is firm.

To flip the eggs, first shake the pan to make sure the eggs aren't sticking. If they are sticking, gently run a spatula under them to loosen. Then ease the spatula under the egg and, using your wrist, flip the egg back into the pan. Cook for 1 to 2 minutes on the second side, then salt and pepper and serve immediately.

Baked eggs are also called "shirred." The eggs are broken into a cup and baked in the oven. The eggs can be baked until the yolk is soft or firm. Try lining the cup with a slice of ham and adding some grated cheese to the egg before serving.

Hard-cooked eggs used to be known as hard-*boiled* eggs, but as my seventh grade Home Economics teacher stressed, eggs should not be boiled. The eggs are brought to a simmer, the heat is reduced (or the pan taken off the heat), and then the

Helpful Tip

How can you tell if an egg is fresh? Place it in cold water. Very fresh eggs will sink to the bottom. Eggs that are a bit older (and perfect for hard-cooking) will stand on end, since the air pocket inside the egg has expanded while the eggs have been sitting. If the egg floats (or smells sulfurous) discard it.

eggs stand in the hot water until they are firm. Don't use very fresh eggs to make hard-cooked eggs, because they are difficult to peel. Store the eggs in the fridge for about a week before hard-cooking them.

To make hard-cooked eggs, place the eggs in pot of cold water on the stove. Turn the heat on high. When the water comes to a vigorous boil, cover the pan and remove from the heat. Let eggs sit for 10 to 12 minutes in hot water. Place the pan of eggs in the sink under cold running water. When they are cool, gently crack the shell of each egg under the cold water so the water can seep between the shell and egg. This will help the peel come off evenly. When all are cracked, peel them.

Don't overcook your hard-boiled eggs! If you do, the whites will be rubbery with an unpleasant greenish gray ring around the yolks, which happens when the sulfur in the egg white combines with the iron in the yolk. The ring isn't dangerous, it's just not pretty. Sometimes a hard-cooked egg won't peel easily because it's too fresh. Return it to the boiling water for a few seconds, then plunge it into ice water to shrink the egg. If your eggs turn into an irretrievable mess, looking moth-eaten and rough, just make egg salad.

Soft-cooked eggs are cooked in the shell in simmering water, like hard-cooked eggs, but for a shorter period of time. They are usually served for breakfast. You cut off the top of the egg and eat it by dipping toast points into the soft yolk.

To make soft-cooked eggs, place eggs in a saucepan; cover with cold water. Bring the water to a simmer, over medium high heat, then reduce the heat to low. Cook the eggs for 3 minutes. Remove the eggs with a slotted spoon and place them in an eggcup. Using a spoon, gently crack off the top of each egg. Sprinkle salt and pepper onto the egg and serve immediately. Remember to only use pasteurized eggs for this type of cooking if you are serving someone in a high-risk group or with a compromised immune system.

Deviled eggs are made from hard cooked eggs. The eggs are cooled and peeled, then sliced open. The yolks are removed and beaten until creamy with mayonnaise, paprika, and salt and pepper. The yolk mixture is then returned to the whites.

Scrambled eggs are best made over low heat and with gentle stirring. When eggs are scrambled fast in a hot pan, the proteins bind quickly and tightly, making the eggs tough. But when you lower the heat and gently stir them, the eggs maintain their creamy texture. Add a little extra fat to the whisked eggs before cooking them to maintain their soft texture. Never beat or season the eggs way ahead of time, or they will be watery.

Scrambled eggs are low in fat and high in protein and are quick, easy, and inexpensive. Use them as a sandwich filling instead of the more-involved egg salad.

To make scrambled eggs, beat the eggs and add 1 tablespoon milk or cream per egg. Heat a skillet over medium heat and melt 2 tablespoons of butter into the pan. Then add the beaten egg mixture. Reduce the heat to low and use a spatula to gently stir the eggs as they cook. Push the eggs around the pan, creating soft curds as they set. When the eggs are set but still look moist, they're ready to eat.

Omelets are beaten eggs cooked quickly in a pan. Making omelets isn't difficult, but lots of practice helps you perfect your technique. There are two kinds of omelets: flat or folded. Folded omelets are usually filled with ingredients, either cheese or cooked vegetables and meats. Flat omelets are like soft frittatas, served right out of the pan.

To make an omelet, beat the eggs with a bit of milk, salt, and pepper. For soft omelets, add 2 tablespoons of cold butter, cut into tiny cubes, to the egg mixture. Pour into a hot frying pan with 1 to 2 tablespoons of melted butter. As the eggs set, lift the edges with a spatula so the uncooked portion can flow underneath. Shake the pan frequently to make sure the omelet isn't sticking. Cook the eggs until the bottom is set but the top is moist. Add the filling and fold the omelet, either using a spatula or using the pan to help you fold it. Remember: An omelet should not be brown. Cook until the eggs are just set but still moist.

Omelet pans can help you perfect your omelets. This pan is hinged in a half-moon shape. You add the beaten egg mixture to both sides and cook until the eggs are set but fluffy. Add filling and put the two halves together quickly.

Frittatas are Italian open-faced omelets. Making a frittata is easier than making an omelet, because it's a sturdier dish. Whereas an omelet is fried, a frittata is partially fried and then broiled or baked to finish. Frittatas can be made in advance and served at room temperature or reheated and are an excellent way to use leftovers.

To make a frittata, beat eggs with salt and pepper. Cook the other ingredients, like chopped onion, bell pepper, and garlic in a pan with melted butter or olive oil. When the ingredients are tender, add the beaten eggs. Cook, moving the eggs around slightly, until they start to set. Then lift the edges of the frittata as it cooks, letting the uncooked mixture flow underneath. When the eggs are set but still moist, run them under the broiler or bake until the eggs are set and light golden brown.

Soufflés scare off many people, because they seem so ethereal and intimidating. But they're actually quite easy to make, once you've mastered separating eggs, beating egg whites to fluffy peaks, and the technique of folding.

It is helpful to understand the science behind egg whites before making a soufflé. Room-temperature whites beat up more quickly and fluffier than cold whites. An acid (cream of tartar, salt, lemon juice) helps the whites retain their stiffness (key when folding into other ingredients). Overbeaten whites will make a dry, clumpy soufflé. Use whites immediately after beating.

To make a soufflé, make a white sauce (See Chapter 14 for instructions) and add egg yolks and cheese. This sauce should be strongly flavored, since the egg whites really don't have much flavor. Let the sauce cool until it's lukewarm. Beat the egg whites, using cream of tartar as an acidic ingredient to help stabilize the eggs, until firm. Using a rubber spatula, fold about a fourth of the beaten egg whites into the base mixture to lighten and loosen it. To fold, cut the spatula through the mixture, draw it upward

> ## Helpful Tip
>
> Most people break eggs by tapping them on the side of a bowl. But this method results in broken egg yolks and can force the shell into the egg. The best way to crack an egg is to tap it quickly but firmly on the counter. This will break the shell but keep the yolk intact.

and toward you, then turn gently. Using the same motion, fold in the rest of the whites. Pour into a straight-sided baking dish and bake immediately until puffed and brown.

Separating Eggs

It's easy to separate eggs by hand. Crack the egg and gently separate the two halves of the eggshell. Place the egg into one hand. The white will leak through your fingers, while the yolk sits in your palm.

You can also use the eggshell to separate the egg. After the egg is cracked, tip it so that the yolk sits in the small end of the shell. Pour the egg white into a bowl. Slide the yolk back and forth between the two halves of the shell, letting the white drip into the bowl. Place the yolk into the empty second bowl. Examine the egg white carefully to make sure there is no yolk in it.

There are tools for separating yolks and whites. Place the separator over a cup or bowl and break the egg over it. The yolk remains in the separator while the white slips through the slits.

Beating Egg Whites

Beaten egg whites create a foam by holding air within a web of protein. Egg whites whipped and mixed with sugar are called meringue. There are countless uses for meringues, from individual cookies to pavlova to pie toppings.

To whip eggs whites into stiff peaks, the whites must be completely free of egg yolks and fat. The beaters and bowl must be free of grease and immaculately clean. The tiniest bit of yolk, grease, or fat on any part of the equipment will prevent peaks. To make sure the bowl is free of grease, cut a lemon in half and rub it over the bowl. The acid in the lemon will help stabilize the egg white foam, too.

To beat egg whites into a meringue, start the beater at low speed. When the egg whites foam, increase the speed. Add the sugar gradually so it dissolves and your meringue is smooth, not grainy. Feel a bit of the mixture between your fingers to make sure it's smooth. Beat until stiff peaks form. This means when you lift the beater, the egg mixture stands up in peaks.

⑪
FISH AND SEAFOOD

Let's face it: Seafood can be intimidating. Unlike a meat market, with its relatively few and familiar choices of beef, pork, and chicken, a well-stocked fish market has a bewildering display of several dozen different species of fish, mollusks, crustaceans, and cephalopods—often in their original state.

Some might require scaling, gutting, and boning. Others might require seemingly arcane tools and special techniques to prepare. And most are far too expensive to risk mangling or overcooking.

But seafood can be delicious and exciting. It cooks quickly in many ways. And fish is so good for you! It is high in protein, low in saturated fat, and the fatty or oily varieties (such as wild salmon, sardines, Arctic char, herring, and trout) are excellent sources of essential omega-3 fatty acids, one of the "good fats" that help your heart, joints, brain, and body function at their best.

As you work with fish, you'll gradually develop an eye for what is fresh. And you'll learn the types of fish you like most. Develop a relationship with your local fish vendor, whether it's the manager of the supermarket's seafood department or your regular fishmonger at the fish market. He or she can be a valuable source for information and practical advice on handling, storing, and cooking just about everything that swims. In addition, he or she often has access to a wide network of resources and can order anything you need, from the ordinary to the obscure.

Don't be afraid to ask questions about the characteristics of any fish or shellfish you're unfamiliar with, as well as any questions about source and quality. A good seafood dealer takes pride in his or her stock and will welcome your interest.

BUYING FISH

As a main course ingredient, fish is relatively inexpensive, if you know which kind to look for. Tilapia, catfish, and trout are environmentally friendly, farm-raised fish that are affordable. Fish is also a timesaver. In general, fish cooks much more quickly than meat, so it makes a quick after-work meal.

In a fish store or large supermarket, fish is available both whole and filleted. Judging the freshness of a whole fish is easier than it is for fillets, since the markers of freshness are still intact. If you have a choice, choose a whole fish and ask the fishmonger to fillet it for you for the freshest product.

Fish can be divided into three general categories: shellfish, round fish, and flat fish. Shellfish have, well, shells attached. They include lobster, crabs, clams, mussels, and oysters. Round fish have firm flesh and stronger flavors. They include salmon, cod, mahimahi, tilapia, and orange roughy. Flat fish are flat and broad. Examples of flat fish are halibut, sole, and flounder. They spend much of their time resting flat on the ocean floor. When cooked, flat fish are flaky and very white with a delicate flavor.

So how much fish should you buy? That depends on the type of fish you're cooking.

> ## BUDGET TIP
>
> High-quality frozen seafood can be an alternative if fresh is hard to find. Be sure to purchase a solidly frozen package. It should not have a fishy odor and only a minimum of liquid. Maintain frozen until you are ready to use it, thawing overnight in the refrigerator. Be sure to place the package on a plate to catch any drips. Never place frozen seafood in warm water or thaw at room temperature.

Whole fish: Count on buying 1½ pounds whole fish (before it's cleaned) per person. Have the fishmonger gut and scale the fish for you, as you don't want to do this at home!

Dressed fish: Buy about ½ to ¾ pound per person.

Fish fillets and steaks: Buy ⅓ to ½ pound fish fillet per person. Choose center-cut portions whenever possible; they cook more evenly than the skinnier tail pieces. Fish steaks (which are a cross section of the fish) are often less expensive than fillets, but they also have bones and skin still attached. Steaks are sturdy enough for the grill, but tender fillets are best browned in a nonstick skillet.

Shellfish: Buy ½ pound of shrimp, 10 to 12 clams or mussels, and 1 lobster per person. Buy 6 to 10 oysters per person, and 1 to 2 crabs, depending on their size.

The freshness of the fish you purchase is more important than any recipe you use. These are the criteria for choosing fresh fish:

- Look at the fish carefully. If whole, the eyes should be clear and full, not cloudy or sunken. Gills should be deep red and the whole fish should be very firm. Fish fillets and steaks should be firm and moist with no bruising or dark spots. The color should be the true color of the fish—sole will be white, salmon bright orange, mackerel grayish brown.
- Fresh fish is fragrant and does not smell fishy. Look for the pleasant smell of the sea. If the fish smells of ammonia or at all like the low tide, don't buy it.
- A fresh whole fish should be stiff, not floppy. Fish fillets and steaks should be firm. When you press the flesh with your finger, it should feel firm and spring back, leaving no indentation. The skin should be shiny and moist but not slimy. And the edges of steaks and fillets should be clean and smooth, with no browning. If the fillets or steaks are sitting in a pool of liquid, that means they may have been improperly handled or frozen and thawed too quickly.
- It's important to find a fish market you can trust. The people behind the fish counter should be able to answer all your questions on the fish they are selling. Fresh fish has a shelf life of about two days, if handled properly. Fish should always be refrigerated, preferably kept on a bed of crushed ice.
- When you buy fish, be flexible. Buy the freshest fish available, even if it's not the type of fish you had in mind for a particular recipe. Many different kinds of fish can be used in any given recipe. Shop around for the best quality and price. Try to buy fish that's in season. Also be adventurous—try a variety of species.

TYPES OF FISH

There are many types of fish available at the market. If you live close to a coastline, you'll have a better selection than people living inland. But good fish can be found in almost any market these days. Choose the fish you want to buy based on the result.

Fatty fish, which include halibut, salmon, and tuna, are rich and good for entertaining. White fish fillets are mild and light, good for quick lunches and casual dinners. Fish steaks are good for grilling and for a heartier meal. And shellfish can be served for any occasion.

These are the main types of fish found in the market:

Arctic char is similar to salmon, with a more delicate flavor. It has a fine texture and grills beautifully. Most char is farm raised, but it can vary in color from a creamy pinkish white to fiery red. It's only available fresh for a short period of the year (most often as fillets or whole fish), but char fillets can be found in individually quick frozen (IQF) form year-round. Score Arctic char by making shallow crosshatched cuts through the skin on both sides of each fillet. A very sharp knife is needed to make the shallow cuts, first in one direction and then in the other. Scoring helps tenderize the fish and helps the fillet keep its shape.

Baccala is dried and salted cod. In Portugal, it was a staple during the winter months. When you choose Baccala, make sure the piece is uniformly thick and the flesh pliable, not hard. Soak for 12 hours, changing the water three times. Baccala becomes very tender when soaked and cooked. You may need to order Baccala from your butcher. And you must follow soaking and rinsing times exactly or your recipe will be too salty. Make sure that you completely change the water when soaking the Baccala. The fish is too salty to eat as is, and even after a simple soaking in water it will be too salty. To make sure the fish isn't too salty, you can cook a small piece in a bit of butter until it's flaky, then try it. If it's still salty, change the water again and soak for another hour or two.

Basa, a large, meaty farm-raised fish similar to catfish, is becoming increasingly available in the United States as IQF fillets. The fillets are large, white, and tender. They take to almost any cooking method, from steaming in foil to panfrying to grilling. Basa is particularly good when paired with the assertive flavors and textures of Southeast Asian cuisines. This recipe incorporates the flavors of Vietnamese culinary traditions and shows off the best qualities of this up-and-coming fish.

Catfish is a sweet and delicious freshwater fish. Its natural habitat is muddy rivers, streams, ponds, or lakes—it loves mud. However, through aqua farming, catfish are now born and raised in clean water. Farm-raised catfish have no muddy taste. Traditionally, catfish is dipped in an egg batter and then a mixture of flour and cornmeal that's been seasoned. It's then fried in deep fat.

Cod is a fine, white ocean-going fish popular on both sides of the Atlantic. Young cod is called scrod. Cod may be fried, as in fish and chips. It can also be baked, broiled, poached for fish chowder, or ground up as the base for codfish cakes.

Flounder is a delicate white flat fish. Look for flounder fillets that are light in color and moist but not waterlogged. Avoid gray fillets or those with dried edges. Trim away any dark spots before cooking.

Grouper, a relative of the sea bass, is a highly prized fish. The flesh is dense, sweet, and quite flaky. Look for grouper fillets that smell fresh and are firm (not mushy) and pinkish white. Frozen fillets are available and very good. The grouper can be a giant fish, weighing 300 pounds, or a smaller variety, weighing 25 to 50 pounds.

Helpful Tip

Once considered a regional fish with an acquired taste, catfish has become one of the most popular fish in the United States in a short amount of time. Why? In a word: aquaculture. Farm-raised catfish from Alabama and Mississippi are of consistent quality with none of the muddy flavor found in wild-caught catfish. They're low in fat and their texture holds up to all types of cooking techniques.

Halibut is a very large flat fish that can weigh several hundred pounds. Its flesh is white and very lean, so take care not to overcook it or it will dry out. Choose halibut that is translucent white and fresh smelling.

Mahimahi fillets can vary in color, often appearing grayish with streaks of red. The texture should be fine and the flesh should have a clean sea smell. Avoid fillets that are brownish or mushy. Mahimahi is the Hawaiian name for dolphin fish, which has nothing to do with the mammal of the same name. Mahimahi means "strong-strong," in reference to the fight this fish puts up once caught on a line. Most mahimahi comes from Hawaii. The skin should be removed before broiling or sautéing.

Monkfish is a relative newcomer to the world of food fish. For years it was considered a "trash" fish with no market value, probably due to its unpleasant appearance and the fact that only the tail is edible. But the unique texture and flavor of monkfish have become appreciated. Monkfish is usually sold as a whole tail, but sometimes the tail is sold already cut into fillets.

If your monkfish tail has the skin attached, use a paring or boning knife to peel off the outer black skin. Remove the thin membrane that has small black spots beneath the skin. The fillets can be removed by slicing next to the bone on each side of the central backbone.

Perch fillets can be slightly gray, but they lighten as they cook. Look for fresh-smelling fillets and remove any dark lines for a milder flavor. Ocean perch is actually a rockfish. The best are caught along the Baja California coast north to the Bering Sea. Whole fish are best steamed or baked. Fillets are good braised, poached, in soups, and in stews. Avoid grilling, as this fish tends to stick. When cooked, perch is white with a fine flake. Its flavor is delicate and mildly pronounced. If you can't find perch in your local fish market, you can substitute tautog, black sea bass, scup, pollack, grouper, or red snapper. Perch is delicious paired with cucumber or asparagus or with a basil butter sauce. Perch can be used in a seafood version of the classic Italian dish known as saltimbocca, using mozzarella cheese for added flavor.

Pollack is another often overlooked fish with fine qualities similar to the more expensive cod. It is sometimes found fresh but more often frozen. Atlantic pollack is a member of the cod family. It's also called blue cod and Boston bluefish. In England it is used to make traditional fish and chips. A distant cousin, Alaskan pollack is mostly converted in Japan into surimi, which is used to make imitation crabsticks and commercially prepared foods such as fish sticks.

Salmon is a popular fish on today's tables and restaurant menus. It is very flavorful and loaded with nutrients, including omega-3 fatty acids. Atlantic salmon is the species that is typically farmed. Pacific salmon are usually caught wild. Most salmon found in the market are farm-raised Atlantic salmon. Wild Pacific salmon are very expensive.

Canned salmon has a mixed reputation because of the dry salmon cakes of old, but it is really quite moist and delicious. The large cans have some dark skin and soft bones included; these are completely edible, but unappealing, and the bones are chalky, so it's best to remove them. Small cans (and the newer foil packets) are usually boneless and skinless. Sockeye salmon is red salmon, which is the best quality of canned salmon; it's the most expensive with the richest flavor. Pink salmon is less expensive and will work just fine in burger recipes.

There are two kinds of smoked salmon: hot smoked and cold smoked. Both types are cured first in a mixture of salt, sugar, and water. Hot-smoked salmon is fully cooked and becomes firm and stiff. Cold-smoked salmon, commonly known as lox, is not really cooked because it only reaches a temperature of 80°F. It is soft and tender.

There are many different styles of smoked salmon. The most popular is Nova style, or Nova Scotia. It has a mild smokiness and is quite moist. Scottish style is much more deeply smoked and cured for slightly longer. It has a much stronger and dryer flavor and is popular in Europe. There are also unsmoked lox varieties, including Graved Lachs, which is a Scandinavian version marinated with dill, and Bell lox, which is simply salted salmon.

Sea bass is firm, moist, and lean, with a mild flavor that takes seasoning well. Whole sea bass should have clear moist eyes and resilient flesh; avoid any that feel mushy or limp. Take care to remove the spiny dorsal fin before prepping the fish, as it is quite sharp. Choosing fresh black sea bass is easy if you know what to look for. The fillet should be white, without dark spots or blemishes. It should have a mild ocean aroma, not a strong fishy smell. The skin should be shiny and intact. The flesh should feel firm to the touch and not soft or mushy.

Skate, a relative of the stingray, is not like other fish. It consists of two large "wings" around a smallish central body. Only the wings, which are two flat muscles on either side of a central cartilage, are edible. The flesh is arranged in long parallel lines and has a taste similar to scallops.

You can use small whole wings or sections of a larger wing. In either case have them skinned and filleted by a pro, as it's difficult to do yourself. An extrawide spatula called a fish slice is needed when cooking skate wings. This wide turner lets you remove the cooked skate wing from the pan without it falling apart. If you don't have a fish slice, use two spatulas held next to each other as you lift the skate wing.

Skate eat mollusks (which include clams, mussels, and oysters), and that gives this fish a wonderful sweet flavor. Skate wings become more tender if they are stored in the refrigerator for a few days before cooking. Soak the wings in water with a little vinegar or lemon juice for several hours before cooking.

Snapper has fine, white flesh and a sweet taste. Because of its low fat content, it takes to almost any method of cooking and is a perfect fish for spicy foods. There are several hundred species of snapper. The most common is red snapper. Snapper is usually sold in fillet form. Make sure the skin is still on so you can be sure you are buy-

ing snapper, which has pink to red markings on the skin. When panfried, the skin turns crispy and retains its reddish color. If you buy a whole snapper, leave the scales on so it won't stick to the grill.

Sole is very delicate, so it's important not to overwhelm it with strong herbs, spices, or aromatic vegetables, such as garlic. Sole (lemon, gray, or Dover) is good served plain, broiled, and dressed simply with lemon and parsley. Buy a 5- to 6-ounce fillet per person. Ask your fishmonger how best to prepare fish for cooking. Buy sole fillets that are nearly white and smell fresh and are not mushy. Sole is a delicate fish and needs to be handled carefully as flat fillets, but it's more durable when rolled.

Squid has a tendency to scare people, but many find themselves pleasantly surprised by calamari, which is another name for squid. Some are put off by tentacles, but you can easily enjoy squid without ever touching a tentacle. Frozen squid rings are already cleaned, detentacled, sliced, and ready to cook. They require nothing more than defrosting in the refrigerator. A simple coating and a short stay in hot oil is all they need to be delicious.

But there's an important rule to follow: Never fry calamari longer than 2 minutes. More than that will produce inedible rubber bands. Deep-fry rings just long enough to cook the coating, and your calamari will be perfect.

Swordfish steaks can vary in color from creamy white to pink to nearly orange. The flesh should be firm and resilient and should smell clean with just a hint of the sea. Any dark spots in the flesh should be reddish, not brown. There shouldn't be any iridescent shine on the surface (brown spots and iridescence indicate age). Frozen swordfish fillets should be defrosted slowly and completely in the refrigerator and patted dry before cooking. Avoid buying swordfish steaks that show signs of browning, which changes the flavor of the fish. Trim the swordfish steaks of any bits of skin and dark spots before cooking with a very sharp paring knife.

Tilapia is a lower-fat fish with a delicate flavor. It's one of the best species of fish to eat from an environmental perspective, as U.S.–farmed tilapia does not involve over-harvesting or a reduction in biodiversity.

Because tilapia is a vegetarian species of fish—unlike other oily fish—it subsists on seaweed rather than other smaller fish species and has lower levels of mercury. Tilapia is also lower in fat than other popular fish. Because of their fast growth rate, they are low in omega-3 fatty acids. Tilapia raised in North America, South America, and Mexico are of the highest quality. Tilapia, like catfish, is almost always farm raised. Though some tilapia is farmed in the United States, most is imported and can vary in quality. Tilapia fillets should be firm and moist, with almost no scent.

Tuna is the largest member of the mackerel family. Tunas range in size from the mighty bluefin, which can reach well over a thousand pounds, to the petite "little tunny," or false albacore, which weighs about 10 pounds. All tuna are edible, but not all have the red flesh prized by so many sushi lovers. Albacore or "white" tuna is usually canned because of its pure white flesh and non-oily flavor. You can also find tuna packed in pouches.

Most tuna has mercury, so very small children and pregnant women should consume it in small amounts and only occasionally. Pole-caught American yellowfin tuna or albacore from the United States or Canada are the best choices. Tuna is extremely nutritious, packed with protein, minerals, vitamins, and omega-3 fatty acids. Its light texture and flavor make it ideal cooking with other foods.

Whiting is a delicious, economical, readily available, but often overlooked fish. It is an affordable alternative for a large-grained white fish like cod. With the skin removed, the flavor of whiting fillets is very mild and sweet. Whiting can handle just about any cooking method other than grilling.

PREPARING FISH

Many people think fish is difficult to prepare, but it's actually very easy to work with. You just need to understand a bit about preparation, learn some doneness tests and cooking techniques, and get some experience. Most fish should be thoroughly cooked. Sushi fish is usually only served in restaurants, because experienced chefs know how to handle it and restaurants have suppliers who sell them impeccably fresh fish.

Every effort should be made to keep fish fresh once you've made your purchase. Put the fish in a cooler or insulated bag for the trip home. When you get home, unwrap the fish and rinse it under cold running water. Pat it dry and wrap it in waxed paper to store in the coolest part of the refrigerator, closer to the bottom, until it's time to cook. If you have a whole fish that you caught yourself, the fish should be gutted and cleaned before it is refrigerated. Keep freshly caught fish on ice for a maximum of two days.

Use fish within 48 hours. If you aren't going to cook the fish within this time, it should be frozen. If this is done quickly and correctly, the fish will be moist and flavorful when you thaw it for cooking.

Freeze fish in small quantities. Wrap it in freezer wrap as airtight as possible to prevent freezer burn. Mark the package with the type of fish and the date. In general, lean white-fleshed fish can be frozen for up to 6 months and oily fish for 3 months. Thawing the frozen fish unwrapped in the refrigerator will take about 12 hours. Many cooks recommend cooking the fish while it is still partially frozen, as this minimizes any loss in moisture.

Follow these steps to get your fish ready for cooking:

- Gut and clean freshly caught fish as soon as possible. Rinse the cavity thoroughly to remove any blood to help prevent spoilage. Rinse fish under cold running water to remove an ammonia smell, which sometimes occurs when fish is stored in plastic bags. A quick rinse will remove any scales that might still be clinging to a freshly caught fish.

- Next, examine the fish, checking carefully for bones of any kind. Don't just rely on your eyes. Your sense of touch is needed here. Run your index finger across the surface of the fish to detect any small bones. A pair of tweezers is a handy utensil for removing tiny bones.

- Check for ragged or discolored edges and trim them so the fish fillet or steak looks perfect. Use a very sharp small knife for this job. The scraps of raw fish can be frozen and used later to make fish stock.

- You can use a sharp knife to remove the fish skin. Place the fillet on a clean work surface, skin side down. Begin at the tail end, holding the skin firmly with your fingers. Run your knife between the flesh and skin, staying as close to the skin as possible. The flesh will separate from the skin as you press down firmly and move the knife away from the tail.

- With some fish, such as salmon steaks, it's a good idea to use butcher's twine to tie the thick slice of fish into a tidy bundle for easy cooking. The steaks will be moist because the edges did not dry out during the cooking process.
- Before cooking your fish, you need to season it. Very fresh fish needs little seasoning other than salt, pepper, and some lemon juice. But you can marinate fish for more interest. Marinating moistens and tenderizes fish and adds wonderful flavor. Marinades are made of oil, an acid, and herbs or spices. Marinate in a glass bowl or plastic bag. Delicate seafood actually starts to cook while in a marinade, so be careful not to marinate the fish for more than 10 to 20 minutes.

COOKING FISH

There are many ways to cook fish. You can poach it, steam it, fry it, stir-fry it, microwave it, bake it, roast it, and grill it. But there's one rule for cooking fish that applies across the board: Don't overcook it. Cook fish for 10 minutes per inch of thickness. This applies to all cuts of fish: steaks, fillets, and whole fish.

Baking fish is the easiest preparation method of all. Most fish is baked at a fairly high heat. Follow the recipe for 10 minutes of cooking per 1 inch of thickness, and your baked fish will be moist and succulent. If the fish is very thick, you may want to brown it under the broiler or sear it on the stove top and then bake it to make sure it's cooked through.

Frying fish is a staple of picnics and beach gatherings. But you can fry fish at home, too. The key to frying fish is to make sure the oil is at the right temperature. Most fish is fried at a temperature of 375°F. If the oil isn't hot enough, the fish will absorb the oil and be greasy. If the oil is too hot, the outside will brown before the inside has cooked through. Always use a food thermometer when frying fish.

Most fried fish is breaded or battered. To keep breading on the fish, let the coated fish stand at room temperature for 20 minutes to dry before frying. Use very fine crumbs for the breading and make sure the oil is very hot. Panko or Japanese bread crumbs create an outer crust that is very crunchy and most appealing.

A batter is quite different. This mixture uses beaten eggs, flour, and either baking soda or baking powder to coat the fish. Deep-fried fish and chips from England are

Helpful Tip

Holding onto raw fish is a slippery task! It's very easy to cut yourself when working with raw fish and a sharp knife (although a dull knife is even more dangerous). Grasp the fish with a paper towel to hold it firmly while you work. You can also dip your fingers in some salt to get a good grip. And there are some kitchen gloves that help you hold onto the fish while you're working.

often made with a beer batter. The Japanese pride themselves on their tempura dishes that feature seafood and fresh vegetables dipped in a batter made with cake flour. A batter made with club soda will give you light and crispy results, but this batter must be made at the last minute because the gasses in the soda dissipate quickly.

Grilling is a wonderful way to add flavor and color to fish. Since fish is delicate and the grill is a pretty rough-and-tumble cooking method, many cooks like to use grill mats to cook fish, especially fish fillets. These perforated nonstick mats go right on the grill rack. The fish won't stick to the mats, and smoke comes through the perforations, flavoring the fish. A grill basket is another good tool to use when cooking fish. The basket helps keep sticking to a minimum by separating the fish from the grill rack. And the basket helps keep smaller pieces of fish from falling through the rack onto the coals.

If you do want to grill fish right on the rack, make sure the rack is completely clean and well oiled. Let the fish cook on the first side until it easily releases from the grill. Then carefully turn it and cook it briefly on the second side.

Poaching fish creates a flesh that is both tender and moist. The key is to poach the fish very gently over low heat and just long enough to barely cook it through. Poaching in wine gives the fish flavor and gently firms the flesh. Leaving the skin on during cooking helps hold the fillets together and help them retain their natural juices. The skin is removed before serving.

Roasting fish is a delicious way to cook it. To roast a whole fish, despite its look, keep the head intact. There are delicious nuggets of fish in the head and collar region. Stuff the cavity with fresh herbs and citrus to perfume the fish. Roast at 400°F for 10 minutes per inch of fish; measure at the thickest part.

Sautéing fish is easy; just heat a sauté pan, add some oil or butter, melt, and then add the fish. Fillets will sauté very quickly, usually in only a few minutes.

Fish should be coated, or dredged, in flour before sautéing. To dredge the fish, take each skinless fillet and brush it with egg white. Place flour seasoned with salt and pepper into a long, shallow bowl or dish. Dip both sides of each fillet into the flour mixture. Brush off any excess flour before placing the fillets in the pan.

Let the fish cook on the first side undisturbed. If you move the fish too soon, it will tear. When the fish releases easily from the pan, turn it carefully using a large spatula. Cook for another 2 minutes, place on a prewarmed plate, and cover. Add some broth or white wine to the pan, along with a pat of butter, to make a sauce for the fish. You can also make a sauce with a cup of chopped fresh tomatoes, ¼ cup fish broth, and ¼ cup white wine. Add mushrooms, spinach, or almost any vegetable you enjoy. Pour the sauce over the fish and serve immediately.

Steaming is an ideal method for cooking fish. Simply place the cleaned, prepared, and seasoned fish in a steaming basket and place over simmering water. Cover and cook for 10 minutes per inch of thickness, until the fish flakes when tested with a fork.

You can also steam fish by enclosing it in a foil or parchment paper packet. The fish steams in its own aromatic liquid. You can vary the fish and the seasonings to make this a dish that you will never tire of. This method is derived from the French *en papillote*.

You can use aluminum foil or parchment paper to steam fish in a packet. Cut a large square of paper, fold it in half to crease it, and unfold. Set the fish on the right-hand side. Add other ingredients and fold the paper over the top. Seal edges by making a series of small, overlapping folds. Press firmly to seal each fold to hold the flavorful steam and liquid. The packets are then baked or grilled.

Stir-frying fish is a great way to cook it. You don't have to use Asian seasonings to stir-fry! Cube the fish and dust it with cornstarch and seasonings, then add to the skillet or wok as the recipe directs. Cook the fish quickly and keep it moving. It will be done in a few minutes.

FISH DONENESS TESTS

When is it done? The safe temperature to cook fish, according to the USDA, is 145°F. Many chefs cook it to a lower temperature; the choice is yours. To check for doneness, poke a chopstick into the flesh at the thickest part near the spine. The chopstick should easily pierce through the fish all the way to the bone. Any sign of resistance or pinkness near the bone means the fish is not fully cooked.

Helpful Tip

Whole fish can seem intimidating, but it is actually quite easy to prepare. Cooking fish whole produces the absolute best, most natural flavor by sealing the moisture inside. You don't have to be an expert on skinning or filleting, either; after cooking, the skin slips right off and the meat will come off the bones easily with a fork or chopsticks. You can also use a wide turner or spatula to lift the cooked meat in large sections right off the bones. Then turn the fish over and do the same to the other side. And don't worry about neatness—the process is inherently messy even if you're an expert. Just relax and enjoy the superior flavor.

Cookbooks used to say that fish is done when it flakes when separated with a fork. But some think that when a fish reaches that stage, it is overcooked. Determining doneness is up to you. If you do have a person in a high-risk category in your household, you may want to use the flaking test to check for doneness. To check whether fish

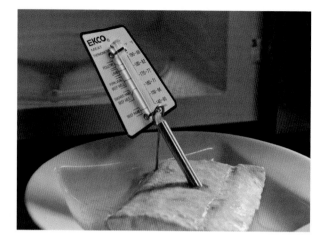

is cooked, insert a fork into the thickest part and gently pull back. If the inner flesh is soft and no longer translucent, the fish is cooked.

Some fish are served medium or medium-rare. Medium-done tuna and salmon are darkish pink at the center. White fish should look moist and opaque rather than translucent at its center. One way to identify cooked fish is to pierce it with a sharp knife. If it goes through with ease, the fish is done and should be removed from the heat immediately. Ceviche is a Spanish dish made with raw fish. The fish is "cooked" in an acidic mixture that turns it white and opaque. Ceviche is not safe for people in high-risk groups to eat.

Most people shouldn't eat raw fish unless they're at a sushi bar. If you do want to consume raw or undercooked fish, remember that frozen fish is inherently safer than fresh fish. The freezing process prevents some bacterial growth, but not all. In fact most sushi restaurants use prefrozen fish to comply with health codes.

SHELLFISH

Shellfish include crustaceans and mollusks, tiny shrimp, and giant crabs. The variety of these creatures is vast! Some cooks shy away from shellfish because of a lack of knowledge. It is important that you have an understanding of shellfish basics if you want to prepare it yourself.

Crustaceans such as crab, crayfish, lobster, and shrimp have an external shell and joints for movement. Mollusks include univalves, such as abalone and conch, and bivalves such as clams, mussels, oysters, and scallops, with two shells. Cephalopods, animals that carry their shells within their bodies, are also members of the shellfish family.

PREPARING SHELLFISH

There are several types of shellfish. Unlike fish, where it's hard to tell a fillet of cod from a fillet of orange roughy, shellfish are very individual and distinct. They have very specific preparation and cooking methods. These are the most popular kinds of shellfish:

Clams are bivalve mollusks. Anyone who has been to the beach has seen a clamshell. These animals live in the sand near salt water. There are two major kinds of clams from the east coast: hard-shell and soft-shell. Hard-shell clams have different names depending on their size. Littlenecks are the smallest. These tender clams are steamed. Cherrystone clams are the most common. They can be eaten raw or steamed, even though they're tougher than littlenecks. Clams should smell fresh and be tightly closed.

Chowder clams, or quahogs (pronounced ko-hawgs), are the largest. These tough clams are mostly chopped up for use in chowders. Soft-shells clams are sometime called longnecks, because of their shape, or steamers, because they're usually served steamed in their own broth with melted butter for dipping. Soft-shell clams have a soft shell that does not close completely.

To prepare clams, fill a large bowl with cold water. Rinse the clams and drop them into the bowl of water. Let stand 20 minutes. Remove with a strainer or a slotted spoon, being careful not to disturb any sand that has settled at the bottom of the bowl. Scrub the shells with a vegetable brush.

Opening clams is a skill that can be tricky and dangerous. When you're new to this kitchen task, work slowly and carefully. In fact, you might want to purchase a cut-resistant woven steel glove, found in kitchen supply stores, to protect your hands.

Open clams after they are well scrubbed and tested for liveliness. Hold a clam in a kitchen towel. Insert the blade of a clam knife into the crack. This takes skill but will go quickly after some practice. When the knife is between the two halves, twist it. Working over a bowl to catch the liquid, remove the top shell and loosen the clam by running your knife around the bottom shell.

Crabs are delicate and delicious. The flesh is incredibly sweet, perfect for eating straight or dipping in butter. Crabs are sold either live or cooked; there's no in-between. Look for crab legs with a sweet sea smell and minimal shell discoloration. Check that exposed meat looks moist and white. Let frozen crab legs defrost slowly and completely. You can grill, steam, or boil crabs.

Crab species vary by area. Blue crabs are indigenous to the east coast, stone crabs to Florida and the Gulf of Mexico. The Dungeness crab is a specialty from the Northwest, and the king crab belongs to Alaska. You can use blue or Dungeness crabs—they're both delicious—and any grade from the most expensive jumbo lump to economical claw meat. Just be sure to buy the freshest you can find. And don't forget to gently pick through crab for shell bits, which should be removed and discarded.

Crabs are purchased live and cooked live. Most of the meat is in the arms and claws. You can purchase cooked crab legs; they are extremely perishable and should be eaten as soon as possible. To cook crabs, just plunge them into simmering water. They're done when the shell turns color. A mallet, a crab pick, lots of newspaper on the table, and a bib are essential accessories when eating freshly cooked crab.

Soft-shell crabs are a unique treat full of sweet crab flavor. The entire crab is edible. The shell is very soft but fries up crisp. Some crabs shed their hard shell once a year;

they're caught before the new, hard shell is grown. Soft-shell crabs are only available fresh for a few weeks in spring, but they can be had frozen year-round. When buying fresh make sure they're alive before you have them cleaned and dressed. If frozen, defrost them slowly in the refrigerator to retain their sweet flavor.

Sautéed soft-shell crabs require just the tiniest bit of flour, not a lot of breading. Olive oil mixed with canola or peanut oil is the cooking medium of choice, not butter.

You can buy soft shell-crabs live, but then you have to clean them. It's easier to buy them precleaned.

Lobsters are the ultimate in luxury. Fresh lobster meat from the Atlantic lobster is wonderfully sweet, briny, and uniquely fragrant. Lobsters can be purchased live or cooked. Live specimens will be dark blue, green, or black. Cooked lobsters are bright red. Live or cooked, lobsters should feel heavy for their size.

When buying live lobsters, limbs should be intact and shells should be hard with no signs of discoloration. Live lobsters should be active and lively, not sluggish. A whole lobster may seem like a challenge, but they are actually simple to cook. Very large lobsters may look impressive, but are actually less tender and flavorful. It's better to serve two smaller lobsters than one large one. Some shellfish need to be cleaned before cooking, but not lobsters. Make sure the poaching stock barely simmers during the cooking time; high temperatures can toughen the lobster meat.

When you get home with live lobsters, keep them in a cool spot until you're ready to cook. A large sink is ideal for this. Keep the lobsters covered with wet newspaper.

Some cooks have no problem thrusting live lobsters into a pot of boiling water, while others believe that the most humane way to cook a fresh lobster is to first place the lobster in the freezer for 10 to 20 minutes. This desensitizes the lobster. Always ease the lobster head first into the simmering water and cover the pot with a lid.

Cutting open a lobster is definitely an acquired skill. First, pull the legs and claws off the lobster. Take the meat out of the claws by hitting them with a mallet to loosen the shell. Break off the shell and pull out the meat. Then put your knife into the lobster where the head meets the body and cut it in half along the spine. Pull off the tail, turn the lobster over, and cut completely in half. Remove the stomach and digestive tract along with the green liver.

Opening a lobster tail is much easier. Place the lobster tail on a cutting board. Hold the tail firmly in place. With a very sharp chef's knife, cut the tail in half lengthwise. Push the knife through the top shell and the body, but don't cut through the under shell. The tail can now be spread open to expose the lobster meat inside the shell.

Mussels have very sweet and tender meat. Most mussels in the market are farm raised and do not need scrubbing; but sometimes they do have "beards," which look like thin black strings and which are easy to pull off. The beards help the mussels cling to rocks or stakes. Mussels grow well along rocky shores and in bays, inlets, and areas where the water is clean.

Never, ever cook a dead mussel or those that are full of sand or have cracked shells. Live mussels open and close on their own. If you tap an open mussel against a closed one, it should close. Listen for a sharp click, not a hollow sound, when tapping mussels together. Find two that make a sharp click when hit, and use one as your control. If you get a hollow sound, the mussel is dead or slightly open. Set it aside; if it doesn't sound right, discard.

To ensure the safety of your mussels, find a fishmonger or retail outlet that you can trust. At home, inspect the mussels carefully. Don't leave them in a plastic bag—lack of air will kill them. When cooking mussels, give them all a chance to open.

One of the easiest ways to enjoy mussels is to steam two dozen in a mixture of white wine, butter, and garlic. Garnish the cooked mussels with freshly chopped parsley and enjoy.

Oysters have a rough layered shell, usually white to gray in color. They grow in nutrient-rich estuaries. Oysters are sold under a variety of names, which indicate their place of origin. They range from small to large with varying briny flavors. Eastern, Pacific, and Olympia oysters are the major species harvested in the coastal waters of the United States. Eastern oysters are traditional half-shell oysters, harvested from New England waters to the Gulf Coast. Pacific or Japanese oysters are found from northern California to British Columbia. Olympia oysters are indigenous to the Pacific Ocean. Belon oysters are farmed on both coasts.

If you want to eat raw oysters, go to a restaurant that specializes in them. And obey the R rule, which states: Avoid raw shellfish in months that do not have an R in them, such as June and July. During these warm months oysters are more prone to be contaminated with bacteria.

When buying raw oysters, choose moist, tightly closed oysters from a reputable purveyor. Oysters should be kept cool but not buried in ice (they'll freeze to death because they're sold live). Look for tightly closed shells and oyster meat that is shiny, moist, and plump.

Oysters need serious cleaning before use. Use a kitchen brush to get rid of sand and mud imbedded in the shells. Shucking oysters

Helpful Tip

There is a pretty intense controversy about whether soaking shellfish makes them expel sand or whether they hold much sand at all. Some subscribe to the theory of soaking shellfish in seawater; others use cornmeal in water. Neither is proven. There shouldn't be much sand in any cleaned shellfish. Just scrub the shells gently but thoroughly and rinse.

is a skill that can take years to perfect. You need a large heavy-duty glove and a shucking knife. In fact, this is another great use for that cut-resistant glove. There are even gloves made out of woven metal that really protect your hands. Scrub oysters first. Then hold the oyster in the glove and work the knife between the shells, near the hinge.

Twist the knife so the oysters open. Remove the shell and scrape the meat off. Work over a bowl to catch all of that liquid, called oyster liquor. Of course you can buy shucked oysters or ask the fishmonger to do it for you. Make sure he or she saves the oyster liquor. When opening oysters, keep the rounder shell on the bottom. This technique allows you to save as much of the oyster liquor as possible to use in sauces and broth recipes.

Most recipes for cooked oysters are baked, such as Oysters Rockefeller. It can be tricky to balance the oysters in their shell on the baking sheet. If they aren't stable, you can set them in a layer of coarse or kosher salt to steady them. Any oysters that don't open after 5 minutes should be returned to the oven for a few minutes more. Discard any that don't open after 10 minutes.

Prawns, a very close relative of shrimp, are becoming more available in the United States, as prawn farming continues to grow. The most popular farmed variety are freshwater Malaysian prawns. Their flavor is sweet and mild and they are quite tender.

What is the difference between shrimp and prawns? Shrimp are found in the ocean, while prawns live in freshwater. But to confuse the situation, jumbo shrimp are often called prawns. Prawns, which come from Hawaii and parts of Asia, are sweeter than shrimp and more perishable. Prawns are often available in fish markets in the Chinatown section of major cities.

Scallops are sweet and succulent and only get tough if overcooked. Most of the fresh scallops sold in the United States are from the Atlantic coast and are one of three types: the large deepwater sea scallops, the smaller inshore bay scallops, or the smaller semitropical calico scallops.

Bay scallops have the sweetest flavor. But be careful: Inferior calico scallops are sometimes passed off as bay scallops. Taste is a reliable test for the real thing. Bay scallops are uniform in size and small, with a delicate taste and texture. They're very expensive; expect to get 34 to 35 per pound. Scallops are usually sold shucked. They should be moist, with smooth edges and no gray or dark markings.

Cream-colored sea scallops are sold fresh and frozen. Sizes may run from 10 to 30 per pound.

The most popular methods for cooking scallops are sautéing, poaching, deep-frying, and broiling. Sometimes scallops come with a small, tough muscle attached to one side that should be removed. This muscle will be exposed if you run your fingers over the scallop. Just pull it off and discard.

Scallops cook quickly. In order to retain their natural tenderness, be careful not to overcook them. To test whether a scallop is cooked, make a cut into the center: The inner flesh should be opaque rather than translucent.

Shrimp is a delicious, versatile seafood that almost everyone loves. Shrimp are sold by size, according to how many of each size is needed to weigh 1 pound. There are about 70 tiny shrimp in 1 pound; 43 to 50 small shrimp; 31 to 35 medium shrimp; 16 to 20 large shrimp; and 10 to 15 extra-large shrimp. Jumbo shrimp are very big; expect to get 10 or fewer per pound.

When buying fresh shrimp, make sure they are firm with their shells well attached. Shrimp should smell sweet with no ammonia odor. If the heads are still attached, cook the shrimp the same day you buy them, for they deteriorate very quickly.

For best results, cook fresh shrimp within one or two days of purchase. Store cooked shrimp in the refrigerator for up to three days. Raw shrimp frozen in the shell maintain quality longer than frozen cooked shrimp. Thaw frozen shrimp in the refrigerator, allowing 24 hours for every pound of shrimp. For quicker thawing, place under cold running water. Never thaw at room temperature and never refreeze shrimp.

You will notice a black line running along the top of the shrimp. This "vein" is the simple digestive tract of the shrimp. Remove it by making a shallow cut along the shrimp and gently pulling the vein out with the tip of a small knife. Cultivated or

Helpful Tip

Here's an easy way to tell the difference between sea scallops and bay scallops: Bay scallops are from a bay, which is smaller than the sea, so bay scallops are smaller.

farmed shrimp usually do not have a visible vein, as the farms stop feeding the shrimp two or three days before harvesting.

Shrimp will be done in 2 to 5 minutes when stir-fried, sautéed, broiled, grilled, or deep-fried. Shrimp can be baked or roasted for a short time on high heat. The shrimp will be more tender and flavorful if coated with melted butter or olive oil. To bake shrimp, put them in a pan and place in a 400°F oven, stirring occasionally, until the shrimp are pink and their tails are curled, about 10 to 15 minutes.

Shrimp cook very quickly, so don't leave the stove while they are in the pan. Do not overcook shrimp, or they will become rubbery and unpleasant in texture.

SHELLFISH DONENESS TESTS

When a recipe calls for a variety of shellfish, they must be cooked in stages. The longest-cooking shellfish is put into the pot first; the shortest-cooking goes in last. Most recipes using shellfish are designed around this method. Seafood must always be carefully watched. It's too easy to ruin and too expensive to waste.

Doneness tests for shellfish include the following:

- Shrimp curl and turn pink or light orange.
- Mussels open. Discard any that do not open after cooking.
- Clams open. Discard any that do not open after cooking.
- Scallops cooked in the shell open. Shucked scallops turn opaque.
- Crabs change color.
- Lobsters turn bright red.
- Cooked oysters become firm and lose some of their gloss.

⑫
POULTRY

I f chicken is on the table for dinner, everyone will be happy. This bird and its relatives, like the turkey and Cornish game hen, are easy to prepare and adapt to the foods and flavors of any cuisine.

Chicken is available in a dizzying array of cuts and types, ranging from boneless, skinless breasts and thighs to thin cutlets, whole chickens, wings, and giblets. Whether you grill chicken, cook it in a slow cooker, stir-fry it in a wok, or cook it in a microwave, the tips and tricks in this chapter will ensure the best results, no matter what.

Chicken and turkey provide a great way to get the most out of your money at the supermarket. Chickens can be roasted whole (for the greatest savings), carved, and served as is or shredded for countless other dishes. Roasted chicken wings or dishes made from braised drumsticks and thighs utilize inexpensive cuts to create delicious meals. The dark meat is richer in flavor and moisture and is the best bet for both your palate and your wallet.

CHICKEN

Chicken is labeled according to its size and age. Young chickens can be prepared using any method, while older birds need special care to be tender and juicy. Because chickens have little fat and little connective tissue, they cook more quickly than other meats. A whole chicken, roasted in the oven, can be finished in about an hour, while the same size cut of beef needs several hours to become tender.

Types of Chicken

There are different types of chicken. They include the following:

Broiler-Fryers weigh 2 to 4 pounds. You can prepare them using any cooking method. The birds are 12 weeks old when harvested. They can be grilled, fried, stir-fried, or broiled. These are the most versatile of chickens and are most commonly found in the supermarket, whole or in parts. Dry-heat methods are used to cook this type of chicken. Marinades and sauces help enhance flavor.

Capons are castrated male chickens that are fed a fattening diet. They are about 8 to 9 months old and weigh about 6 to 10 pounds. The meat of the capon is very flavorful and tender; perfect for slow roasting. These chickens can be harder to find than regular broilers or roasters. You may need to special order them. Capons tend to have more white meat than dark.

Roasters are chickens that are a little older, about 3 to 4 months. They weigh 4 to 7 pounds. They have more flavor than broiler-fryers and a higher fat content, so they can be cooked longer. Dry-heat cooking methods, for a relatively short time, are best for this type of chicken.

Stewing hens are mature chickens at least 10 months old. They are larger, weighing about 5 to 7 pounds. The chicken is best used in stews, soups, or the slow cooker. The meat is tougher because the bird is older, but it is very flavorful. Stewing hens aren't often found on the market anymore; they were more common in the twentieth century.

Chicken Labels

When choosing a chicken, always read the label and check the expiration date. Look for chickens with clean whitish or yellowish skin with no visible bruises or blood on the surface. The chicken should smell good, feel firm, and have no tacky or slimy feeling to the skin.

Chicken labels can be confusing. The terms are vague, so it's important to know what they mean:

100 percent natural means the poultry doesn't have artificial ingredients, but it may have been fed grain mixed with preservatives. No government agency monitors this term.

Brine-injected chickens and other cuts of poultry are injected with a brine solution, made from water, salt, sugar, and additives or preservatives. This acts as an internal brine, which makes the chicken more moist and flavorful, but it also increases the sodium content of the chicken.

Farmed chickens are the typical chicken you find in the grocery store. They are raised in very small cages, indoors, and with no fresh air or sunlight. Their meat doesn't develop much flavor because they don't move around. These chickens are inexpensive to raise, but the meat is acceptable and safe to eat.

Free-range chickens are allowed access to the outside, fresh air, and sunshine. But they may have only been let outside once in their lives to qualify for this label term! The meat from these chickens is more flavorful, but it doesn't rise to the standards for organic or kosher meat.

Grain-fed birds were probably not fed animal products, but that fact isn't guaranteed. The chicken was fed grain, but it may have been treated with chemicals and mixed with antibiotics or hormones. This label doesn't tell you much!

Kosher chickens are prepared under very humane standards. The bird is kept as stress free as possible. Rabbinical inspectors check the birds to make sure they are healthy before slaughter. Chickens are fed grain, are free range, and aren't treated with antibiotics. However, their feed may have been treated with chemicals.

Organic chicken has to meet strict standards. The birds must be fed only organic grains and raised on a farm that has been free of

Health Tip

Do you worry about antibiotics and hormones added to the animals you eat? The USDA hasn't made a decision regarding any effects these chemicals have on human health or safety. In other words, we just don't know. If you are really concerned about health, look for organic and free-range meats that are raised without hormones and antibiotics. But you can be assured that all properly cooked chicken is safe to eat.

chemicals for at least three years. The chickens are not given hormones, drugs, or antibiotics to increase growth or size. And the birds roam outside, with access to fresh air and sunshine.

OTHER TYPES OF POULTRY

Chickens aren't the only birds in the poultry world. Other poultry you can find in the supermarket includes Cornish hens, turkey, poussins, ducks, and game birds.

Cornish Hens

Also called Cornish game hens, Cornish hens are a cross between a Cornish and White Rock or Plymouth Rock chicken. They are very small, less than 2 pounds apiece and 5 to 6 weeks old. Figure 1 bird per serving. These hens cost more than chickens do, pound for pound, as they are considered a specialty item.

Most Cornish hens are sold frozen. Defrost according to the package directions or thaw in the refrigerator for 24 hours. If you find fresh hens, use or freeze them within 1 day, as they are very perishable. Cornish hens usually serve one person, since the meat-to-bone ratio is fairly low.

Duck

Duck meat is very fatty, so during cooking you must remove fat that renders in the heat. Duck meat is much darker than the meat from other birds. It pairs well with red wine, port, spices, and rich fruits. The fat will float on the surface of the liquid in the casserole. Because duck has such a wild, rather gamy flavor, it is paired with strong ingredients like red wine, spices, and dried fruits.

Game Birds

Game birds include partridge, pheasant, and quail. These birds have quite a strong flavor, which is aptly described as "gamy." Game birds are usually a special grocery order, unless you have a hunter in the family. Because the birds are strongly flavored, they are cooked with ingredients like

oranges, onions, figs, and root vegetables. Be careful to remove any buckshot or birdshot if you're preparing a wild bird. These birds are often lower in fat than farm-raised birds, so they need added fat like bacon or butter for flavor.

Turkeys

Turkeys are rich and flavorful. They range from 10 to 25 pounds. The smallest turkeys are females, while the largest are males, also known as toms.

You can buy turkeys fresh or frozen. If you buy them frozen, you can cook them in that state (see "Cooking Turkey from Frozen" later in the chapter, page 218), or they can be thawed before cooking. Thawing a frozen turkey takes days in the fridge. Never thaw a frozen bird on the countertop. For quicker thawing, place the turkey in a sink full of cold water. Change the water every 30 minutes to keep it cold and allow 30 minutes per pound to thaw.

Overcooked turkey is unfortunately common. When properly cooked, turkey is juicy and delicious. Always use a meat thermometer when you're cooking a turkey and cook until the thigh meat registers 180°F.

POULTRY AND FOOD SAFETY

Chicken usually contains salmonella bacteria. Clean and sanitize all surfaces that come into contact with raw poultry. Be sure when the chicken is done, the deepest part of the thigh registers at least 170°F. The pop-up thermometers attached to some chickens can fail, so make sure the juices from the thigh run clear when the chicken is

pricked before you take it out of the oven, or test the doneness with an instant-read meat thermometer.

As a word of caution when cooking poultry: Most cases of salmonella come from cross-contamination, which occurs when people eat foods tainted with raw chicken, not from eating improperly cooked chicken. So when you are cutting raw chicken or handling it in any way, make sure you use a surface (like a thin plastic cutting board) that can easily be whisked to the sink and washed with soap and hot water or washed in the dishwasher. Clean each utensil used (and the sink!) before moving on to the next ingredient or preparing another dish.

There's no need to rinse chicken before you cook it. The chicken is thoroughly cleaned when it is processed. Rinsing simply spreads chicken juices, with all its bacteria, around your sink and kitchen. In fact, the USDA states, "Rinsing chicken will not remove or kill much bacteria, and the splashing of water around the sink can spread the bacteria found in raw chicken."

And never store raw chicken in the refrigerator on a shelf above items that are going to be eaten raw, such as fresh produce. The juice from the raw chicken can easily drip onto the fresh produce and contaminate it.

CUTS OF CHICKEN

Whole Chicken

A whole chicken is the best buy per pound at the supermarket. You can also be sure that the chicken is fresh when you buy a whole bird; cut-up pieces can be sitting in the display case for days before they are purchased. Whole chickens are quite perishable and should be cooked or frozen within two days.

Here's how to prep a whole chicken:

- Open the package over the sink, as there is usually quite a bit of liquid in the chicken.
- Remove the giblets, if any, and pat dry with paper towels.
- Stuff the bird, season it, or truss it, if you like.

You can roast a whole bird or cut it into pieces according to the steps below. Be sure to use a sharp, heavy knife and work slowly and carefully.

- Place the bird on a clean surface.
- To separate the legs and thighs, cut between the joints, through the cartilage.

- Pull the thigh away from the body and cut through the hip joint.
- Hold wings away from the body and cut through the shoulder joint.
- Cut through the ribs near the attachment to the spine and remove the back.
- Split the breasts down the middle or leave them whole.

After the chicken has been broken into parts, you can skin and debone pieces for quicker cooking. Use a sharp, thin-bladed knife for skinning and deboning. Follow these steps to skin and debone the pieces:

- Insert the tip of the knife under loose skin with sharp edge facing up. Slice through skin and lift off the meat.
- For breasts, slip the blade into the meat close to the bone and cut away from you. Some meat will remain on the ribs.
- Slice the flesh on thighs down the length of the bone, fold the meat back, and remove the bone.

Remember to save all of the scraps, and the backbone, neck, and carcass to make chicken stock. You can store these parts in the freezer until you're ready to use them. When you're finished skinning and deboning the pieces, clean the cutting area, your hands, and utensils with hot, soapy water.

Chicken Parts

When you buy chicken parts, you are buying a whole chicken minus the backbone. These parts are easy to season, cook, serve, and eat. You can purchase bone-in or boneless, skin-on or skinless chicken parts.

White Meat

Bone-in breasts are the most common chicken part. They are made of one whole breast split in half. The whole breast has two parts, separated by the breastbone. Bone-in chicken breasts have more flavor than boneless meat. When a recipe calls for a chicken breast, it means half a whole breast.

To prepare a bone-in breast, gently loosen the skin from the flesh and add salt and pepper, fresh herbs, spices, or condiments like mustard. Smooth the skin back over the flesh and cook the chicken breasts as usual.

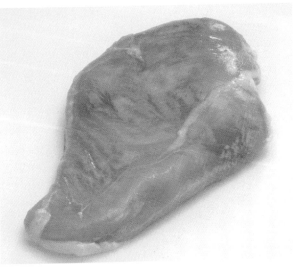

Boneless, skinless chicken breasts are ready to use as is or can be cut into strips or cubes. To prepare them, cut breasts into smaller pieces if the recipe calls for this. To make this step easier, freeze the breasts for 10 to 15 minutes prior to cutting. If marinating, add the chicken to the marinade, cover, and refrigerate for 8 to 24 hours. If the chicken spends more time than that in the marinade, the meat could become mushy or tough when cooked.

Cutlets are chicken breasts that have been cut into thinner pieces. The breasts are cut in half horizontally so they are the same width as the uncut breast but about half as thick. Cutlets cook much more quickly than a whole chicken breast. They can be breaded or coated in a seasoned flour mixture to help preserve moisture.

You can prepare your own cutlets. Just cut a boneless, skinless chicken breast in halves or thirds horizontally and then cut or pound each piece thin. If you pound them, they have a tendency to shrink when cooked. To pound cutlets, place the cut breasts between sheets of plastic wrap, smooth side down, and gently pound with a meat mallet or rolling pin. Work gently, starting from the inside and working out.

Chicken fingers are just breast meat cut into strips. They come from the breast itself or the tenderloin (the small piece of meat under the breast, closest to the bone). To make chicken fingers, if cutting the chicken yourself, use the tenderloin. Cut across each one to make shorter strips. Marinate the strips in buttermilk or a lemon marinade, then coat in flour and bread crumbs.

Chicken tenders are small muscles that run directly under the breasts of the bird. Do not confuse tenders with nuggets, which are sometimes made with ground bits of chicken scraps. Tenders also are not chicken fingers, which are cut pieces of the breast. Chicken tenders often have a strong white piece of thin tendon running through the meat. This will melt and disappear during cooking, but some cooks prefer to remove it with a sharp knife.

To prepare chicken tenders, marinate them or coat in breadcrumbs and bake, sauté, broil, or fry.

Dark Meat

Dark meat is less expensive than chicken breasts. Thighs, wings, and drumsticks are even great on the grill. They have more succulent meat and do not dry out as quickly as boneless skinless chicken breasts often do.

Dark meat does have slightly more fat and calories than white, but the difference is small. Dark meat depends on muscle use. Flightless chicken and turkeys have white breasts because they don't fly, and dark legs and thighs because they walk. Those muscles need more blood because they work harder. Ducks have dark breasts and legs.

Bone-in thighs are richer in flavor than wings or breast meat. They also tend to be far less expensive than wings or breasts, so you get a lot of food for your money. Bone-in thighs take the longest to cook of any chicken part. Cut off any excess visible fat before cooking.

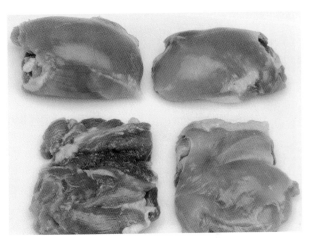

Boneless thighs are available prepackaged in the supermarket, but you can also cut the meat off the bone to save some money. And you'll have the bones and meat left on the bones to use to make chicken stock. Boneless thighs are meltingly tender when cooked. It's difficult to overcook them because they contain more fat. They're perfect to use in slow cooker recipes.

Chicken drumsticks are excellent for serving a crowd. Children love them because they come with a built-in handle. They also marinate well; the tender meat absorbs flavors easily. Whole drumsticks with skin should be cooked until the skin is crisp, unless you are going to remove the skin before serving. Remove the skin by grasping it with a paper towel and pulling gently but firmly.

Chicken wings are an inexpensive cut of the bird that can be cooked and flavored in many ways. Chicken wings are almost never skinned before use. The skin keeps the meat moist and tender and adds a lot of flavor. If you are going to slow cook chicken wings, you should brown or broil them, either before or after slow cooking, so the skin isn't flabby.

Whole wings are almost never served as is. They are typically cut into several pieces: the drummies, or the part with the most meat, with the thinner part and the tip cut off; another section, which doesn't really have a name; and wing tips. Keep in mind that wings weigh around an ounce each, which isn't very big. A serving of wings for an appetizer is 4 to 6 wings per person. If you want to serve wings as a main course, serve about ½ to 1 pound per person.

You can purchase chicken wings whole or already cut into drummies. The drummies, if you buy them separately, are more expensive per pound than the whole wing. To cut chicken wings yourself, use a sharp knife and keep these tips in mind:

Cut the wings through the joint.
- Don't splinter the bone, or you won't be able to serve the wings.
- Cutting the wings exposes more of the skin, making them cook evenly and providing more surface for breading and sauce.

Make drummies look like little drumsticks by pulling the meat off one end of the bone. Pull the meat over the bone and use your knife to scrape the bone clean.

Wing tips are usually not sold in the supermarket. You may ask the butcher for them, if the store sells drummies. Or cut the tips off whole chicken wings and save them to make chicken stock.

Other Chicken Products

Livers

Chicken livers are inexpensive and used to create pâté, a very luxurious treat, for very little money. You can purchase chicken livers very inexpensively or just freeze the livers that come inside a whole chicken until you have a pound (without spending a dime!). Chicken livers are also used in stuffing recipes. They can make an elegant entrée when sautéed with onions and garlic in a wine sauce. The livers should be trimmed of fat and any tubes before cooking.

Giblets

Giblets are the internal organs of a chicken or turkey. They usually include the heart, liver, neck, and gizzard. The liver can be used to make chopped chicken livers, a hearty and old-fashioned appetizer spread. And the other parts can be used to make stock or broth for giblet gravy. Giblets usually come in a paper package in the center of the chicken. They are more commonly found in whole turkeys.

Ground Chicken

Ground chicken is a healthier alternative to ground beef, pork, or bulk sausage. It cooks quickly, is low in fat, and can be substituted for any other ground meat in any recipe. Because it is lower in fat, it's lower in flavor, too, so it will need to be more highly seasoned than its red meat counterparts. You can find ground white meat chicken, ground dark meat chicken, or a combination of the two. Be sure to read labels carefully so you know which product you are purchasing. You need to cook ground chicken in some fat because it is so low in fat. It can be difficult to cook and can stick to the pan on its own.

You can buy ground chicken, or you can easily make it yourself from skinless breasts or thighs. Make sure they are very cold by putting them in the freezer for 30 minutes. Then just mince them finely, or pulse them in a food processor until they are roughly ground.

You can use ground chicken to make meatballs, patties, and even meat loaf. As with beef and pork meatballs and burgers, combine all of the filler ingredients before you add the chicken. Then when they are well mixed, add the chicken and work gently with your hands to incorporate everything.

Chicken Broth or Stock

Technically, broth is a liquid made from meat only, while stock is made from the meat and bones. Both are flavorful, but broth tends to be milder and more delicate.

It's easy to make chicken stock from the remains of a large roasted chicken, or you can pick up a few pounds of chicken necks and backs at the supermarket. They make wonderful stock and lots of it. Just add aromatic vegetables and herbs.

To make stock, place the bones (or necks and backs) in an ovenproof roasting pan. Broil until brown. Turn; brown the other side. Place browned bones in a stock-pot. Deglaze the roasting pan with enough water to dissolve and scrape bits off the bottom; add scrapings to the stockpot. Add remaining ingredients to the stockpot and bring to a boil on the stove. Reduce heat to a simmer, cover, and cook 2 to 3 hours. Cool the stock and skim off any fat. Remove bones. Strain; freeze for future use.

To make broth, use just the meat of the chicken. Simmer until the broth is fully flavored. The meat won't be usable, since all of the flavor and fat will have gone into the liquid to make a good broth.

For a rich and delicate chicken stock with lots of tender meat as a bonus, there's a special way to cook it: Simmer the chicken in water, with herbs, spices, and cut-up vegetables, for 1 hour, just until the chicken is tender. Then take the chicken out of the pot. Let it cool for 10 minutes, then remove the meat and return the bones to the pot to cook for another hour. Unlike other chicken stock methods, where the chicken is cooked until the flavor is entirely leeched out, this method will give you incredibly tender and moist shredded chicken.

CHICKEN COOKING BASICS

Cooking chicken can be tricky. Chicken breasts, because they are low in fat, can overcook easily and become tough and dry, even when cooked with wet heat. Cooking a whole chicken so the white meat is juicy by the time the dark meat is done is also challenging.

Doneness Tests

Doneness tests are the most important indicator of when chicken is perfectly cooked. You'll need an instant-read thermometer to safely prepare chicken. It must be cooked thoroughly, every single time. There is no such thing as a medium-well chicken. To observe chicken doneness, there should be no tinge of pink in the juices when the chicken is pricked or cut into. The meat should be firm and springy.

Chicken breasts must be cooked to 160°F. The chicken should then stand, covered, for 5 to 10 minutes so the temperature rises to 165°F. Dark meat—thighs and drumsticks—must be cooked to 170°F. Be sure to wash the thermometer between tests. Whole chickens should be cooked to a temperature of 180°F, as measured in the thigh and the thickest part of the breast.

Boneless, skinless chicken breasts should bake at 350°F for 20 minutes. Boneless, skinless chicken thighs should bake for 40 to 50 minutes. A whole cut-up chicken should bake for 1¼ hours. Bone-in, skin-on chicken breasts should bake for about 35 to 45 minutes.

Defatting Juices

Defatting the juices that render from the chicken as it cooks is an important step for a nongreasy sauce. You can simply skim the fat off the top of the juices or the stock with a spoon or ladle or use a fat-separating measuring cup. You can also cool the juice down; the fat will congeal on the top in a solid mass, making it very easy to remove.

Breading Chicken

Breading chicken requires a fair amount of flour and bread crumbs and eggs. Don't keep the leftover bread crumbs, eggs, or flour, since they have all been in contact with raw chicken.

Be sure you have all your breading ingredients ready and set up in three separate pans next to each other before you start, or you will have a mess on your hands. Try to keep a wet hand and a dry hand when breading food, unless you want all your fingers to be breaded like your chicken tenders.

Dip the chicken into the flour, which is the "glue" that makes the egg stick. Then dip into the eggs and immediately dip into bread crumbs. Use your dry hand to press the crumbs into the chicken so they stick. Let the breaded pieces stand for about 10 minutes, then bake or fry.

Stuffing Chicken and Turkey

Stuffing can simply add flavor, or it can create a side dish. You can stuff the cavity of whole chickens, turkeys, and Cornish hens with cut lemons, smashed garlic, and onion quarters to add flavor to the meat as it cooks. Add some sprigs of thyme or other fresh herbs, too.

Stuffing a turkey is traditional for Thanksgiving. And stuffed chickens and even Cornish hens make a delicious and fancy entrée. If you choose to stuff poultry, the stuffing mixture should be moist but not wet. The cavity is very moist, and the bird will release juices as it cooks. If the stuffing is too wet when you put it in the bird, it will be gluey when it's cooked through. Never pack stuffing into the cavity; it expands as it cooks and the bird may split if it contains too much stuffing.

There are a few ways to stuff chicken breasts. You can pound the boneless, skinless breasts so they are thin enough to wrap around the filling. You can also cut a pocket in the side of the breast and fill it. Or you can stuff the filling mixture between the skin and the flesh of skin-on breasts.

Drumsticks may not seem like a natural choice for stuffing, but they are. Loosen the skin and place the stuffing in between the skin and the flesh with a spoon or your fingers. Then pull the skin out and over the filling, smoothing it down as close as you can to the bone at the end. You

can stuff drumsticks ahead of time; just cover and refrigerate until you want to bake or grill them.

Cooking Turkey from Frozen

For food safety reasons, just because it's easier, and because you may have forgotten to thaw the turkey, you can roast a turkey from a frozen state. Here's how: Unwrap the turkey, rub it with butter, and roast at 325°F for 3½ hours. At this point, remove the turkey from the oven. It will have thawed enough so you can remove the giblets, stuff it if you want to, and return it to the oven. Roast 1½ to 2 hours longer, until an instant-read thermometer registers 180°F when inserted into the thigh.

Roasting Turkey Upside Down

The major problem with roast turkey is that it can produce dried-out breast meat. But if you cook the turkey upside down, the fat will run down into the breast and keep it moist as it roasts. This approach may look funny, but the result is a beautifully even turkey, with moist dark and white meat. Roasting a bird this way distributes the juices and ensures even heat distribution. The turkey is turned over toward the end of cooking time, about the last 45 minutes to an hour, so the breast can brown and the skin crisp.

You can also use this method to roast a whole chicken: Heat a large skillet over medium heat. Wipe the chicken dry and set breast up in hot pan. Then put the chicken in the oven for 30 minutes. Flip the chicken breast down and roast 20 minutes. Flip again breast up and roast another 10 minutes. Remember to let the chicken stand so the juices redistribute before carving.

Types of Heat to Cook chicken

There are two types of heat used to cook chicken: wet and dry.

Wet Heat	Dry Heat
Steaming	Baking
Boiling	Roasting
Poaching	Broiling
Slow cooking	Grilling
Braising	Panfrying
	Deep-frying

Wet heat is a good way to cook poultry, because no liquid will evaporate as it cooks. Some of the water naturally present in the bird will be squeezed out of the meat as the protein fibers shrink in the heat, but they will be reabsorbed into the meat as the chicken cools. Since water and steam are excellent conductors of heat, poached and slow cooker chicken can be cooked at lower temperatures, around 180°F to 190°F.

Chicken cooked in dry heat must be cooked at a higher temperature, at least 300°F. Air doesn't conduct heat as efficiently as water or steam, so dry heat methods need higher temperatures.

Remember that chicken can't be cooked to any stage other than well-done. Chicken flesh is less dense than beef or pork, so bacteria on the surface can travel all the way through the meat. Chicken breasts should be cooked to 160°F. Ground chicken should be cooked to 165°F. Chicken thighs and drumsticks should be cooked to 170°F. And whole chickens and turkeys should be cooked to a temperature of 180°F.

Cooking Techniques

Chicken can be cooked many ways. The microwave, stove top, oven, grill, slow cooker, and dual-contact indoor grill are all good methods to use. Once you learn how to prepare each cut and type of chicken perfectly, the sky's the limit. A simple panfried chicken breast, for example, can be transformed into a feast by the addition of pan gravy or some vegetables and fresh herbs.

Bake. Simply baked chicken is usually marinated or coated in herbs, crumbs, or a sauce to add flavor and moisture. You can "oven fry" at a high temperature to replicate deep-fried or panfried results. Typical coatings for baked fried chicken include bread crumbs, cracker crumbs, cornmeal, or crushed cereal.

For crisp baked chicken, place chicken on a rack in a shallow pan so the heat circulates evenly around the bird. This keeps the coating out of the juices that the chicken creates so it stays crisp on all sides.

You can bake chicken breasts in parchment paper for very moist and tender results. Place chicken breasts on sheets of parchment paper or on heavy-duty foil, 1 breast per sheet. Sprinkle with dried herbs to flavor the chicken, then top each with a thin slice of lemon or orange. Fold the parchment paper around the chicken and place on cookie sheets. Bake at 375°F for 20 to 25 minutes, until temperature registers 160°F.

Braise. Braised chicken is cooked in a pot with other ingredients. A chicken fricassee is made of pieces of chicken that have been browned, then cooked with vegetables to make a gravy. Add broth and wine to create deep, rich flavors. Braising requires a heavy pot.

Health Tip

Never thaw chicken or turkey and then hold it for days before cooking it. Thawed meat should be cooked as soon as possible. If you thaw a turkey quickly with the cold-water method, it's even more important to cook the bird as soon as it's thawed.

A dutch oven, either made of all metal or ceramic-clad metal, works beautifully for braising. The pot must have a tight lid to retain the steam. You can finish the braising process either on top of the stove or in the oven.

There are two types of braising: Brown braising is when the chicken is lightly covered in oil or butter before being braised in a flavorful liquid. White braising is when raw chicken is added directly to the cooking liquid.

Broil. Broiling poultry creates a crisp skin and moist interior. Most ovens have a broiler right in the oven cavity. The top heating coils turn on and stay on. There's really no way to regulate a broiler's temperature. You maintain control by changing the distance from the heat, and by turning and moving the food as it cooks.

You can get slow-broil results on a charcoal grill by banking the coals after they turn white and placing the chicken away from the direct heat. Be sure to cover the grill so that the inside of the chicken cooks thoroughly.

Deep-Fry, Sauté, Stir-fry. Everyone has had panfried, sautéed, deep-fried, or stir-fried chicken. This is the fastest way to cook chicken, and the finished dish can be high or low calorie, depending on the method. You can sauté chicken in some broth or other liquid or fry it in an inch of peanut oil for crisp results.

Properly fried food doesn't have to be full of fat. This dry-heat method cooks food quickly and evenly. If you keep the oil at a constant 350°F to 375°F, the food will absorb only about 10 percent of the fat by weight.

Deep-frying is a very satisfying way to cook chicken. The chicken is fried in 2 to 4 inches of hot oil. A deep-frying thermometer is needed to regulate the oil temperature. The temperature will drop about 25° when you add the chicken; keep an eye on the thermometer and raise or lower the heat as needed. Drain the chicken on paper towels after cooking; let stand 5 minutes so the juices redistribute. The chicken can be kept warm in a 200°F oven up to 45 minutes while you fry the rest.

To sauté chicken, make sure the skillet or pan is hot. Heat a couple of tablespoons of oil. Add the chicken pieces and, using a wooden spoon, stir them occasionally so that they cook evenly. Cook until done.

Stir-fried chicken is quickly cooked in a wok or large skillet. The chicken is always cut into small pieces and may be marinated before cooking. The marinade is often used as the sauce. To stir-fry chicken, heat oil in the wok until very hot. Add all of the chicken at once and fry, stirring constantly with a large spoon or spatula, until the chicken is evenly cooked. Proceed with the recipe as directed.

Grill. Grilled chicken can be a challenge to make. It's tricky to cook chicken thoroughly without drying it out. A graduated fire and indirect grilling are the best ways to brown the chicken and then cook it to juicy perfection.

It's a good idea to have different temperature areas on a grill. You can move the chicken around on these different areas as it cooks. Boneless, skinless chicken breasts will grill in about 10 to 15 minutes; bone-in will cook in about 20 to 30 minutes. Boneless, skinless chicken thighs will grill in 20 to 30 minutes; bone-in chicken will grill in about 35 to 45 minutes.

An instant-read thermometer, which is priced under $10, will take all the guesswork out of "Is it done yet?" You will never need to cut into your chicken again to see if it's cooked.

Microwave. Cooking chicken in the microwave oven can be a bit tricky and isn't recommended if you have a person in your family in a high-risk group. Most microwaves have hot and cold spots, which can lead to overcooked or undercooked chicken. For more evenly cooked chicken, cut it into smaller pieces before microwaving it. And let chicken stand for a few minutes after microwaving.

Poach. Poaching is a simple and flavorful method that yields a double result: moist, cooked food, plus a savory broth to make a sauce, soups, or stews. Season the poaching liquid with any aromatic vegetable and herbs: scallions, leeks, shallots, fresh ginger, fresh herbs (thyme, dill, and parsley), lemon or lime slices, whole peppercorns, or fennel or cumin seeds.

Poaching is an excellent way to cook boneless, skinless chicken breasts, because they can easily dry out with other methods. To poach boneless, skinless chicken breasts, place them in

a skillet with cold water to cover, with a halved onion and chopped carrot. Bring to a simmer; reduce heat to low until liquid barely moves. Poach for 10 to 15 minutes, until the internal temperature reaches 160°F. Let the mixture cool at room temperature for 20 to 30 minutes, then refrigerate the chicken in the liquid for the most tender and moist results. You can also poach chicken breasts in the oven. Place them in a deep pan, add boiling liquid, cover, and bake at 400°F for 30 to 35 minutes.

Roast. Knowing how to roast a chicken is a basic skill everyone should learn. Remove the giblets from the cavity of the chicken and trim any excess fat. Rub both the inside and outside of the chicken with olive oil or butter to moisten the skin and add flavor. Salt and pepper the chicken. Then, truss it if you'd like.

To truss a bird:

- Place breast side up on top of kitchen twine.
- Pull the twine over the wings and cross the twine.
- Wrap one end of twine around each drumstick and pull until the legs cross.
- Tie the twine and cut the ends short.

You can stuff the chicken before trussing, but be careful not to overstuff the chicken, or it may split during cooking.

Roast chicken is cooked at a moderate temperate, with the skin on, and is sometimes basted. Roasting a whole chicken is easier than you think—especially these days with the little pop-up thermometers telling you when it is done.

Place cut-up veggies in the roasting pan and put the chicken on top of the veggies and giblets. The vegetables will act as a rack, letting heat circulate around the chicken and adding flavor.

Slow cook. Slow cooking a chicken is just like braising. The chicken is cooked just at a simmer over low heat. Liquid doesn't evaporate in the slow cooker. Vegetables cook more slowly, so they are placed on the bottom. If you choose to cook chicken with the skin on, the meat should be browned first.

Newer slow cookers cook at a hotter temperature than older models, so some older recipes may have to be adapted to a shorter cooking time. With a new slow cooker, boneless, skinless chicken breasts cook in about 5 to 6 hours. Start testing them with a meat thermometer at that point.

> ## BUDGET TIP
>
> Roasting a whole chicken is a lesson in economy. You're buying the least expensive kind of chicken, and there are usually leftovers for another meal, along with a carcass to make chicken stock. Roasted chicken is also juicy, as the skin and bones baste and season the meat as it cooks, while protecting it from drying out in the hot oven.

The slow cooker is a wonderful way to cook dark meat. This cut of meat can cook for up to 9 or 10 hours, making it ideal for long-cooking recipes. You can start a recipe using chicken or turkey thighs or drumsticks at 7 a.m. and get home at 5 p.m. to a perfectly cooked dinner.

Panfried and baked. Some recipes call for chicken to be panfried to brown it first, then placed in the oven to finish cooking through. This helps keep the chicken moist while adding great flavor and color. Brown the chicken for a few minutes on each side, then bake it in a 350°F oven until a meat thermometer reads 160°F for white meat, 170°F for dark meat.

Resting time

After the chicken has reached the correct temperature on a food thermometer, it must rest. This allows the temperature to rise a few degrees, guaranteeing safety, and it lets the juices, which migrate to the chicken's surface during cooking, redistribute into the meat.

If you slice into a chicken before it has rested, the juices will run out of the meat and your chicken will be dry and tough. So cover the chicken with foil and let stand for 5 to 10 minutes before carving.

Carving a Whole Chicken

Carving a whole chicken is a skill, but it is very satisfying once you have mastered it. Place the chicken breast side up on a carving board. Pull on the leg and cut in between the leg and thigh, popping the joint. Repeat on other side. Using a sharp knife, cut directly down from the top of the breast, using a fork to help separate the meat away from the ribs. Cut breasts in half, if you like. Use the tip of the knife to feel for the joint where the wing joins the body. Cut through the center. You can cut the drumsticks and thighs into pieces to serve separately or serve them as chicken quarters. Arrange all the meat on a platter and serve immediately.

Seasoning Chicken

The spices and seasonings used in every cuisine around the world all pair well with chicken. The following spices are particularly good with this mild meat.

Basil has a spicy, lemony flavor. It's delicious with chicken breasts and whole chicken.

Curry powder is a blend of several different spices, including turmeric, coriander, cumin, salt, pepper, cinnamon, and cloves. It is delicious cooked with chicken, either as a curry or in soups or stews.

Health Tip

Don't cook a whole chicken in the slow cooker if you have family members with compromised immune systems. The chicken may not get hot enough, soon enough, all the way through to make it safe to eat.

BUDGET TIP

Freeze any leftover chicken pieces or parts and collect them in your freezer to make homemade stock. When you have about 2 pounds of parts, cover with water, add some chopped vegetables, salt, and pepper; simmer 3 to 4 hours.

Oregano is spicy and mildly hot, with an herby scent. It's delicious in barbecue sauce for any chicken or poultry product and is a classic in Italian dishes like chicken parmesan.

Thyme has a mild lemony flavor and sweet herbiness make it blend perfectly with chicken breasts, tenders, and whole chicken.

Here are some tips to keep in mind when you use spices and seasonings on chicken:

Use fresh herbs to season the chicken. Place the herbs in a pleasing pattern on the flesh of the chicken, under the skin. The pattern doesn't matter unless you're serving the chicken whole at the table.

Smooth the pattern down and then carefully pull the skin back over. Try to keep the herbs in place.

Dried herbs can be substituted for fresh, just use one-third of the amount. Crush them between your fingers to help release the flavorful oils before using them in a recipe.

Marinating chicken

To marinate chicken breasts for more flavor, first prick the chicken with a fork about 15 to 20 times so the marinade can soak in. Place the chicken in a large glass baking dish in a single layer and coat with the marinade. Turn each piece over and repeat on the other side. Cover the chicken with plastic wrap and refrigerate.

Brining Chicken

Brining your chicken will produce a juicier, more flavorful meat. Make sure that you choose chicken that hasn't been injected with a marinade or brine; read labels to make sure the ingredients list doesn't include water, salt, or flavorings.

Don't worry about the amount of salt used in a brine. The chicken flesh doesn't absorb much. It's the concentration of salt and sugar in the brine that forces liquid into the flesh.

To brine a chicken, combine ½ cup sea salt and ½ cup sugar with 3 quarts water. The chicken must be fully submerged in the brine. Place a heavy plate on top of the chicken to keep it under the surface. Soak for 1 hour per pound, or about 3 to 4 hours for a normal-size bird. Drain the chicken and pat it dry before baking, frying, or roasting.

Storing Poultry and Leftovers

Raw poultry should be used within 2 to 3 days. Ground chicken only lasts a day in the refrigerator. Cooked chicken can be refrigerated for 2 days. Wrap it well in plastic wrap or foil, or put it in a tightly sealed container, and refrigerate as soon as dinner is done. After 2 days in the fridge, wrap the chicken in freezer wrap, label it, and freeze up to 6 months.

Package chicken according to the way you use it. Chicken can be frozen whole, as a whole cut-up bird, or sorted into parts—breasts, legs, and so on. Leftover cooked chicken or any other poultry can be cubed or shredded, then packaged into freezer containers or placed in freezer bags and frozen up to 6 months.

Never defrost poultry, whether raw or cooked, on the counter. It should always be defrosted in the refrigerator. Plan for the extra time this will take. The larger the piece of poultry, the longer it will take to defrost. A whole chicken can take up to 3 days to defrost; a whole turkey or duck can take 5 days. Even if an improperly defrosted bird heats up to a temperature high enough to kill bacteria, they may have produced toxins that can make you sick. And those toxins aren't destroyed by heat.

BEEF, PORK, AND LAMB

13

Beef, pork, and lamb are considered red meats. That just means that the meat is a red color when raw. When cooked, beef is brown on the outside and pink in the center; pork is brown on the outside and white in the center, and lamb is brown and pink.

Many people are intimidated by these red meats, especially the big expensive cuts such as roasts. When faced with a beef brisket or lamb shoulder, most people would simply order pizza. But with a little care and some knowledge, you can turn these meat cuts into succulent dinners. If you know what kind of meat to buy and how to cook it properly, you've won the bulk of the battle!

The best way to save money on red meat is to know your butcher. Butchers are invaluable for answering questions about cooking and which cuts make good substitutions if you can't find the particular cut a recipe calls for. They can special order cuts that aren't always available, they can debone a roast that you'd rather not, and they can grind your meat on the spot so you know it is as fresh as possible. Just ask!

The best grade of meat is "prime" and is rarely found in supermarkets. Only the best butchers in big cities will have prime. Next is "choice," which is most common and the best all-around grade. "Select" follows and is generally of much lesser quality. When shopping, look for "choice" to fill most of your needs.

In the most general terms, tough, inexpensive cuts (like pork ribs, beef stew meat, brisket, lamb shoulder) require the longest cooking times in wet heat to soften their tough connective tissue to render them tender and moist. Steaks, chops, and tenderloins, whether bone in or boneless, are meant to be cooked with dry heat until just done.

There are a few countries in the world where beef is revered. The United States is one, but in Argentina and Japan, you'll find the best steaks in the world. In Japan the cattle that become Kobe beef are massaged by hand and fed organic grasses.

In Argentina, beef cattle are free range and graze on natural grasses. If you've ever had grass-fed beef, you understand the difference. The meat is rich and tender, with a full beefy flavor that's almost impossible to describe.

When possible, buy grass-fed beef. It is free of antibiotics and growth hormones and comes from cows that are raised in a pasture (hence, they eat grass). The meat is a bit leaner (and a bit more expensive, so you will have to budget yourself), so it cooks faster than conventional beef. It is also higher in omega-3 fatty acids. Grass-fed beef is lower in total fat, and can actually lower LDL ("bad") cholesterol levels.

If you can't afford grass-fed beef, look for pink meat that is finely and thoroughly marbled with white fat. There should be little juice in the package, and the meat should be firm and smell sweet. Never buy meat that's sitting in a pool of juice or meat that looks gray or seems dry.

Freezer burn is the number one cause of spoiled meats in the freezer, caused by dehydration. Never freeze meats in their original packaging. Remove meat from the original package and wrap in freezer paper, bags, or plastic wrap. Well-wrapped meats should be labeled using a grease pencil or waterproof marker. Use frozen meats within six months. To thaw meat, let it stand in the refrigerator overnight, or if you're going to cook it immediately, use the microwave.

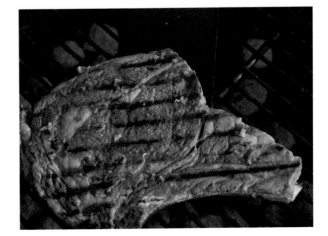

> ## Helpful Tip
>
> For storing meat, there should be specific "use-by" dates. Follow these to the letter. Meats should usually be used within a few days of purchase. Store them, in their original packaging, in the coldest part of the refrigerator.

BEEF

Steak

Steak houses have a secret for creating that rich, almost charred crust on their steaks: They add butter to the steak after it's cooked. The steaks are placed under an industrial broiler and broiled until the butter starts to char. You really can't replicate this at home, but melting butter onto a seared steak is delicious.

There are so many types of steaks available in the market that, unless you have some real knowledge, it can be difficult to understand what is what. Price is usually a good indicator of which steaks are the most tender. Cuts from the loin, such as T-bone, porterhouse, filet mignon (tenderloin), New York strip, and rib eye, are all excellent steaks. There are a few "value" steaks on the market these days, which are worth seeking out. One is hanger steak, also called the butcher's tender, and the other is flatiron steak. Both have excellent flavor and are tender when cooked medium or medium-rare and sliced thinly against the grain.

Types of Steak

These are the names of steaks you'll find in the supermarket:

Filet mignon is a slice of beef tenderloin, one of the most expensive and tender cuts of beef. The fat is intramuscular, marbled inside the meat, so it melts evenly for great texture. Filet mignon isn't the most flavorful steak. The filet mignon and tenderloin come from a part of the cow that doesn't bear weight and isn't involved in movement, so the meat is very tender.

Flank steak didn't become popular until recently. In the nineteenth century these cuts were considered throwaway meat and were usually given to ranch hands and cowboys in lieu of payment. Flank steak is the cut used in fajitas and is always marinated before cooking.

Flap meat is another cut from an area between the flank steak and the bottom sirloin. It's very similar in texture to skirt steak, but it's not quite as flavorful. This steak is usually marinated.

Flatiron steak or blade steak is a new cut of meat. University researchers looked at so-called "undervalued" meat cuts and discovered that if the gristle on the blade roast was removed, they could create the flatiron steak. This cut is almost as tender as the tenderloin, with more flavor. The flatiron steak, like the Flatiron Building in New York City, may have been named because it looks like an old-fashioned cast-iron flatiron when viewed from the top.

Hanger steak is a muscle that literally "hangs" between the loin and the rib on the cow. It's full of flavor but is fairly tough, so it must be marinated and sliced against the grain to be tender.

Rib eye steak is cut from the rib section of the cow. This steak is very flavorful and tender, since it's marbled with lots of fine fat. Rib eye steak is usually boneless. These steaks are also called Delmonico steaks. They don't need to be marinated before cooking.

Round steak is an inexpensive cut, easy to find in the supermarket. Look for well-marbled firm meat with little or no juices in the package. This steak is seared first, then braised or simmered over low heat for a long time to become tender.

Sirloin steak is from the short loin in the center of the cow, directly under the tenderloin. These steaks have good marbling and are boneless. They're cheaper than rib eye steaks or filet mignon, but they have the same good flavor. The top sirloin is considered better quality than the bottom sirloin. These steaks are usually marinated before cooking.

Skirt steak is from the tough belly area of the cow. It's very flavorful and slightly more tender than flank steak, but it often has a thin membrane that must be removed before cooking. Slide a sharp paring knife between the membrane and the meat. Use a slight sawing motion and pull the membrane up while carefully sliding the knife under it. After removing the membrane and any gristle, rinse the meat in cold water to remove excess bone fragments or membranes; pat dry. This steak should be marinated.

Strip steak is also from the short loin, close to the tenderloin. It's part of the T-bone and porterhouse steaks, but is also cut and sold on its own. It's also called a New York strip steak and top loin steak. It's not as tender as the filet mignon, but has more flavor. These steaks don't need marinating but can be marinated for more flavor.

T-bone and Porterhouse are from the loin area of the cow on its middle back. The steaks are made of a strip steak and beef tenderloin, joined by a T-shaped bone. Porterhouse steaks are larger than T-bone steaks because they have a larger portion of the tenderloin, but they have the same good flavor and tender texture.

Cooking Steak

A steak is considered one of the best meals, and a grilled steak the best of the best. Only the high, concentrated heat of the grill can make a crisp, caramelized crust on a juicy, tender steak. You can also cook steaks under the broiler or on the stove top. The most important rule is not to move the meat until the steak releases easily from the pan. This lets the steak develop a good sear, which creates that smoky, almost sweet flavor on a well-cooked steak.

Before you cook or marinate your steak, it should be trimmed. There must be some fat on your steak, because it carries the meat flavor. But if there is more than ¼ inch on the steak, trim off the excess. Use a sharp knife for trimming and be careful not to cut into the meat itself.

> ## Helpful Tip
>
> Let steaks stand at room temperature for 20 to 30 minutes before you put them on the grill. The steaks will experience less of a shock when placed on the grill and will be more tender.

Think of a marinade as a small science project. A marinade consists of an acid, oil, and flavoring ingredients. The acid breaks down the tougher fibers of the meat so it becomes tender. The oil seals in moisture, while the flavoring ingredients, well, add flavor! Any marinade can be used for the steak. There are lots of bottled versions on the market. Salad dressings are also good choices for steak marinade.

The tougher the steak, the longer it should marinate in the fridge. Flatiron steaks, rib eyes, filet mignon, and T-bone steaks don't need a marinade. The steaks that need

a marinade are the more inexpensive cuts, like round, skirt, blade, and hanger steaks. These steaks have a looser grain than the expensive tender cuts that have tight grains, so the marinade can penetrate the meat.

Resealable plastic bags make marinating meats neat and easy. Slide the steak into a gallon-size bag. Whisk together marinade ingredients and carefully pour into the bag. Add any aromatic vegetables, like onion. Seal the bag almost completely closed. Press excess air from bag and then seal completely. Place steak on its side, in the sealed bag, on plate or in a shallow baking dish in the refrigerator. Every couple of hours, flip the bag over to redistribute the marinade.

Make sure that your grill or pan is clean and well oiled before you add the steak. The grill or pan should be preheated so you hear a loud sizzle when the steak hits the heat. Be sure to pat the meat dry after it's removed from the marinade so the surface caramelizes and doesn't steam, which results in unappetizing gray meat. You won't be losing flavor; the first ¼ inch of the steak has already absorbed the seasoning.

If you want your steaks to have fancy grill marks, just arrange it in a certain way on the grill. *Quadrillage* is the French term that means "to quarter." It refers to the squares created by the grill grates when meats and other foods are cooked and then rotated in a certain pattern on the grill. Think of the steaks as being the straight hands of a clock set at 6 o'clock.

Place the steaks on the grill so they look like clock hands pointed at 10 minutes to 4; grill for 2½ minutes. Then carefully move the steaks, lifting completely off the grate with tongs, and place the steaks at 20 minutes to 2. Repeat this process on the second side. If you need to turn the steaks again, be sure to carefully align the marks with the grill so they are clear.

Meat doneness tests are straightforward. First, you can carefully time steaks and roasts. However, because oven and grill temperatures vary greatly, this can be unreliable. Second, use a meat thermometer to measure the temperature; this is the most accurate method.

Steaks deserve a rest after all that work! Cover with foil and let stand for 5 to 6 minutes while you finish other dishes. There are two good reasons for letting a piece of cooked meat rest before cutting into it. The first is to let it finish cooking, especially in the center. The second is to make the steak juicy. The meat reabsorbs juices when it's taken off the heat so they don't run out onto your plate.

When you carve a steak that isn't filet mignon, T-bone, rib eye, or sirloin, you must cut it "against the grain." The grain looks like lines running through the steak. Cut perpendicular to these lines to cut the fibers for a more tender bite. The steaks that should be carved against the grain include hanger steak, flap meat, flatiron steak, skirt steak, and round steak.

Beef Roasts

There's nothing like the aroma of a rich beef roast simmering on the stove top or in the oven. It smells like Sunday dinner at home. A roast is just a cut of beef that is at least 2 inches thick. Beef roasts are cooked two ways: with dry heat, simply roasted in the oven, or with wet heat, braised or simmered in liquid for hours. The roasts cooked with dry heat are called oven roasts; they come from the center part of the cow. The roasts cooked with wet heat are called pot roasts; they come from near the cow's legs, where the muscles are heavily worked.

Did you know that the same cut of beef can have many different names? It may be the whim of the butcher, the area of the country, or the directions from management, but this fact can be very confusing to experienced cooks and beginners. Talk to your butcher. Ask where the roast came from on the cow and how to cook it. He or she may even have recipes for you!

Helpful Tip

The size of the steak matters! A steak that is 1 inch thick will cook over direct heat in 8 to 10 minutes to medium doneness. A thicker steak should be cooked using direct and indirect heat. Sear the steak on both sides, then move over a drip pan to finish cooking. A 1½-inch-thick steak will take 12 to 15 minutes to cook.

Types of Beef Roasts

A good beef roast should be firm and hold together well with visible lines of fat. The color doesn't matter, as exposure to air can change the color. These are the main types of beef roasts:

Brisket. When you want some real beef, brisket is the best choice, as it has a lot of flavor. This cut is tough, though, so has to be cooked at a low temperature for a very long time. The cut has a lot of connective tissue, which has to melt before the meat is done. Choose a firm brisket with good marbling and a narrow rim of white fat.

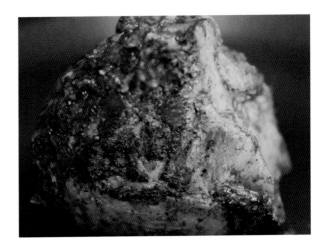

Corned beef. Traditionally served for St. Patrick's Day, this cut is made of a brisket or round steak that's cured in lots of spices and pickling ingredients. This meat can be tough, even when cooked correctly, so the slow cooker is the perfect appliance for it. The meat is thinly sliced against the grain for tender and melting results.

Chuck roasts. These are from the chuck or shoulder area of the cow. All of these cuts are tough and cooked with wet heat. Chuck roasts include the top blade roast, which is very flavorful; the 7-bone roast, which has great flavor; the chuck eye roast, which is tender and flavorful but quite fatty; and the chuck shoulder roast, which is relatively tough with only a mild flavor.

Rib roasts. These roasts are very expensive, since they're cut from the center of the cow. They are cooked with dry heat. Rib roasts include first cut rib roast, also known as prime rib, which is very flavorful and tender. The second cut is less tender and has a bit more fat. The rib eye roast is the cut from the area that produces rib eye steaks; it's perfect for roasting and is very tender and flavorful. Rolled rib roasts have been boned and tied into a roll.

Round roasts. Cut from the area right above the back leg, round roasts are usually cooked with wet heat because they're fairly lean. The cuts include bottom round, which is divided into bottom round roast and rump roast. This roast is flavorful and juicy; it is cooked with wet heat. Round tip roast can be roasted with dry heat. Eye of round is tough, but flavorful, so it's usually braised. Round tip roast can be cooked with dry heat since it's near the sirloin.

Short loin. These are very tender and mildly flavorful roasts cooked with dry heat. The tenderloin is the main short loin roast; filet mignon steaks are cut from this roast. The tenderloin doesn't have a lot of beef flavor, but it is very tender and juicy. The top loin roast is cooked with dry heat.

Sirloin roasts. These roasts are cut from the top of the animal, right in front of the back legs. They are flavorful but not quite as tender as rib roasts. Top sirloin roast is very flavorful and juicy, with a tender texture, but it does have a large amount of gristle. The tri-tip roast has a triangular shape, which makes it difficult to roast evenly. This roast is usually cut into sirloin tips, which are used in stew and braised dishes.

Cooking Roasts

The best cuts of beef for pot roast include chuck, top round, bottom round, rump, and brisket. These cuts are full of flavor and tough unless cooked in low, moist heat.

It's important to season these large chunks of meat well. Enough salt is the secret to the best-tasting meat and gravy. Don't go overboard, but up to 2 teaspoons salt for a 4-pound piece of meat is appropriate. Trim off excess fat before seasoning.

Dry-heat cooking methods. Roasts cooked with dry heat are expensive and naturally tender. Just season them with salt and pepper and place in the oven. They can be browned first to create a caramelized crust before roasting. Place the roast on a rack in a shallow, heavy roasting pan with the fat on top. Don't cover the roast and don't add liquid.

These roasts are cooked like steak, either to rare, medium-rare, or medium. If the roasts are cooked to medium-well or well-done, they can be tough. Use a meat thermometer to check the temperature; in fact, with a large roast, it's a good idea to invest in an oven-cooking thermometer. This device has a probe that's inserted into the meat and a long ovenproof cord that comes out of the oven and attaches to a temperature readout. You can set the desired temperature, and the device will sound an alarm when the roast has reached that temperature.

After roasting, these cuts must stand, just like steak, to let the juices redistribute and allow the meat to reach its final temperature. Place on a solid surface like a cutting board and cover tightly with aluminum foil. Because these roasts are so large, they should stand for 15 to 20 minutes before serving.

Wet-heat cooking methods. Wet-heat cooking of roasts is quite different from dry-heat cooking. The beef is cooked in a lot of liquid, usually with lots of vegetables and seasonings to add flavor. The final temperature of these roasts should be 210°F. That sounds high, but it's high for a reason. These cuts have a lot of gristle and connective tissue that must melt before the roast is edible. That's why a pot roast falls apart when it's cooked. The meat is so tender because it's gone beyond the well-done stage of cooking.

> ## Helpful Tip
>
> To prepare a rare roast, the meat should roast for about 15 minutes per pound, to a final temperature of 135°F. For medium-rare, roast for about 20 minutes per pound, to a final temperature of 140°F. For medium roasts, cook the beef for 25 to 30 minutes per pound, for a final temperature of 145°F to 150°F.

To braise (or pot roast) a roast, brown it first to provide caramelization for flavor and appearance. Brown the meat well on both sides in a heavy skillet. Then place it in a casserole, dutch oven, or large roasting pan. Deglaze the pan used to brown the meat with stock or wine, scraping up all those brown bits. Pour this mixture over the roast, cover, and cook over very low heat on the stove top, bake in the oven, or cook in the slow cooker.

Pot roast really isn't pot roast unless it's cooked with lots of root vegetables. The vegetables add wonderful flavor to the meat and add fiber and vitamins. Root vegetables such as parsnips, potatoes, carrots, and onions are traditionally used with pot roast. They become meltingly tender in the moist environment and long cooking time. You can cut them into chunks or slices as you prefer.

It can be difficult to brown such a large chunk of meat. Use a large pan and take your time. Some heavy tongs will help you turn the meat. Be sure you don't move the meat until it releases easily from the pan. Those pan drippings, or fond, contain a lot of flavor, so deglaze the pan and add the liquid to the pot.

Bone-In or Boneless?

Bones add a lot of flavor to food while it's cooking, so opt for the bone-in cut when possible. If a recipe calls for boneless, you can substitute bone-in, but you'll need to increase the cooking time by about a quarter to accommodate the bone. Save leftover bones (cooked or uncooked) for making flavorful stock.

Ground Beef

Ground beef is an excellent way to get beefy flavor and nutrition in any recipe for very little money. Ground beef is made of the less tender cuts of beef, like chuck and round, and the trimmings from steaks and roasts. It's categorized by its fat content:

- Ground beef has 70 percent meat and 30 percent fat.
- Ground chuck roast has a high fat content, so it makes deliciously juicy meat loaf and hamburgers with 80 percent meat to 20 percent fat.
- Ground round is leaner, so it makes ground beef with 85 percent meat to 15 percent fat.
- Ground sirloin is the most expensive type of ground beef because it has the most flavor. It has 90 percent meat to 10 percent fat.

Ground beef is considered "lean" if it has 20 percent or less fat content by weight. That's still a lot of fat, and while that's good in a meat loaf, you don't want that much fat in other recipes like casseroles, pasta sauces, or soups. So brown the beef and drain it well before continuing with the recipe unless you're making meat loaf, meatballs, or hamburgers.

If you are feeling industrious, grind your own meat. Choose a good-looking roast or shoulder cut and ask the butcher to grind it fresh. If you have a standing mixer, a grinding attachment is available and easy to use. Freshly ground meat should be used immediately or frozen for later use.

When you use ground beef to make hamburgers, meat loaf, and meatballs, the meat must be handled carefully and with certain precautions. The bacteria present on all surfaces of beef cuts is mixed throughout the ground beef when the meat is ground. Ground beef must be cooked to well-done (although you'll find a method for making safe medium-rare burgers later on in this section). The less you handle ground meat, the better—overwork it, and you'll end up with a tough burger, meatballs, or meat loaf.

Meat Loaf

Meat loaf is an easy and comforting dish most people love. But everyone has had a bad meat loaf that was tough and dry or flavorless. To make a tender, juicy, and flavorful meat loaf, follow these rules:

- Use a variety of ground meats when making a meat loaf. The standard mix is equal parts beef, pork, and veal. This mixture has a more complex flavor than 100 percent ground beef.
- Mix all of the additions to the ground beef before you add the ground beef. This ensures that the ingredients will be evenly mixed throughout the meat for a tender loaf.
- The more you handle ground beef, the tougher the final product will be. Handle gently. Work with your hands, gently but thoroughly, just until everything is combined.
- Bake meat loaf on a broiler rack to keep it out of the fat that will render as it cooks.
- When the meat loaf is done, with an internal temperature of 160°F, remove it from the oven. Immediately cover with a sheet of foil and let the meat loaf stand for 10 minutes. This lets the juices redistribute and the internal temperature rise to a safe 165°F.

Meat Sauces

Ground beef is delicious in meat sauces served over pasta. The beef must be browned before the sauce is made. Place the ground beef in a pan and turn the pan to medium. Use a fork to break up the beef as it cooks, turning the beef so the uncooked portion comes into contact with the hot pan.

For a lower fat version, cook the beef, drain it and rinse it under hot water, and then return it to the pan. You can brown the ground beef ahead of time, as long as it's fully cooked before you refrigerate it.

To prepare a quick meat sauce, brown 1 pound ground beef, turkey, or pork (or a combination) and then add a 28-ounce can crushed tomatoes, 2 crushed garlic cloves, a pinch of oregano, and salt to taste. Simmer uncovered until thick, about 20 minutes.

Burgers

Almost everyone loves a juicy burger hot off the grill. It's one of the joys of summer. And a grill filled with sizzling burgers is a great way to entertain. For juicy, tender burgers with lots of flavor, follow the same instructions for making meat loaf, with a few exceptions, of course!

- Handle the beef as little as possible for the juiciest burgers. Combine all the additions to the meat first, then add the beef and mix gently but thoroughly with your hands. To shape the burgers, form the meat into round patties about ¾ inch thick. Shape the edges so they are smooth and firm. Don't press the meat together.

- Press an indentation into the center of the burgers so they'll remain flat when cooked. If you don't make the indentation, the burgers will puff up and not sit on the buns or hold condiments.
- When the burgers are cooking, never press down on them with a spatula. That will squeeze the juice right out of the meat as it cooks. The burgers are ready to turn when they release from the grill. If they stick, keep cooking. Watch the burgers carefully on the grill. Move them to lower heat if they are cooking too quickly.

Small hamburgers are the newest trend in incarnations of the grilled hamburger. These burgers, called "sliders," are 2 inches in diameter and served on cocktail or small sandwich buns. The burgers are prepared just like larger variations but must be handled more carefully. Use a grill basket or a smaller rack placed over the main grill rack so they don't fall through and burn up in the coals.

Most people stopped eating rare burgers when the FDA recommended they be cooked to a final internal temperature of 165°F. But you can have medium-rare burgers using a special method explained here. You grind your own meat after it's blanched.

You don't need to add much to these burgers, as the quality of the meat is the focus. So buy sirloin or chuck steak with about 20 percent fat and good marbling. Prepare and preheat the grill and all other ingredients. Chill 1¼ pounds meat and the grinding equipment. Bring a large pot of water to a boil. Drop the steak into the water. Leave it in water for 20 seconds and remove.

Cut the steak into 1-inch cubes and place on ice. Grind in batches to a coarse grind, then grind all together again to a medium grind; add 1 teaspoon salt and ½ teaspoon steak seasoning. This meat must be cooked as soon as it's ground; don't do this ahead of time. Add any extra ingredients you'd like when grinding the meat. Form the ground meat into burgers; grill over direct heat to 135°F. Add cheese and cover for 60 seconds, then place on grilled buns, add condiments, and dig in.

Meatballs

Meatballs are the perfect convenience food. The precooked frozen meatballs you find in the supermarket are delicious and easy, but they can be very high in sodium and preservatives. Meatballs are

easy and fun to make on your own. Meatballs freeze very well; cook them completely and freeze, then you can use them as you would the processed type.

To make meatballs, follow these tips:

- As with meat loaf and burgers, don't handle the meat for meatballs much. Mix all the other ingredients first, then add the meat. And make the meatballs the same size so they cook evenly.
- To form meatballs quickly and evenly, use a small ice-cream scoop. A 2-tablespoon scoop is just about the right size. Dip into the ground beef mixture and form a ball; smooth out the edges with your hands.
- To fry meatballs, pour 1 inch of oil—such as canola, grapeseed, or peanut—into a frying pan. If you use a deep-fat fryer with a basket, you will need more oil. But don't fill it too full; the oil bubbles up and expands when hot. Bring oil temperature to 350°F. Don't add meatballs all at once; start with two, bring oil back to temperature, turn meatballs over, and add two more. When completely browned, drain meatballs on paper towels, turning so that the oil drains off.
- To bake meatballs, put them in a baking pan or shallow roasting pan. Bake them in a preheated 400°F oven for 20 to 25 minutes until browned and cooked through. The temperature of the meatball should be 160°F. You will need to drain baked meatballs, especially if you used ground beef with 20 percent fat or more.

If you are going to store unsauced meatballs, cool them completely. Place them on an aluminum foil–covered cookie sheet, making sure they are not touching. Freeze meatballs solid. Put them in a resealable plastic bag and store in the freezer, using as needed.

Beef Ribs

Beef ribs are less common than pork ribs, but they are still very delicious, with tender meat and lots of flavor. When properly cooked, these ribs are so tender, the beef falls right off the bone.

Beef ribs are cut from an area near rib eye steaks. They are well marbled, but they are tougher because they get more of a workout on the cow. Beef ribs are either roasted very slowly for a long period of time with dry heat, or they are cooked for hours with wet heat. There's no way to cook beef ribs quickly and get a tender result. Marinating beef ribs can help make them tender. Most beef ribs have a thick membrane that must be removed before you marinate or grill them.

There are two kinds of beef ribs: back ribs and short ribs. The short ribs are meatier, while back ribs are more tender. In the back rib cut, the meat lies between the bones and there's not much of it. Back ribs must be cooked to well-done, just like a pot roast, to be tender. Short ribs have meat lying on top of the bones. There's more meat on this cut. Short ribs can be cooked with dry heat to medium or medium-rare, although most recipes call for braising them.

Veal

Veal is simply baby beef. Some people object to eating or buying this cut of meat because the methods to raise veal can be controversial. Veal is very popular in Italy, especially in the northern regions. Calves are milk fed and then butchered when only a few months old so they are very tender. Because veal is almost flavorless, the success of a veal dish depends on the sauce, seasoning, and stuffing used.

Veal is available in roasts, chops, steaks, and ground meat. The cuts that can be cooked in dry heat include cutlets, cube steaks, arm steaks, chops, veal shoulder, veal roasts, and blade steaks. The cuts that need wet heat include boneless breast, riblets, cross cut shanks, and rib chops.

Beef Doneness Tests

These doneness tests apply to cuts of beef, not ground beef. The temperature will rise 5 degrees after standing to the safe recommended temperature.

Rare. Internal temperature of 135°F. Not recommended for those in high-risk groups. The steak feels very soft, and the juices run dark pink.

Medium-rare. Finished cooking temperature of 140°F. The steak feels soft when pressed with fingers. The juices are pink.

Medium. Finished cooking temperature of 150°F. The steak feels slightly springy when pressed with fingers or a tong.

Medium-well. Finished cooking temperature of 155°F. The steak feels almost firm when pressed. The juices are light pink.

Well. Finished cooking temperature of 160°F. The meat feels firm when pressed, and juices run clear with a tinge of pink.

PORK

Pork is a mild and naturally tender meat, which takes beautifully to any flavor from any cuisine. Think about recipes and cuisines that you love and use the flavors to create your own recipes. For Asian pork, combine soy sauce, hoisin sauce, grated gingerroot, and a bit of honey for a marinade. Tex-Mex pork chops could be made with brined chops that are glazed with a mixture of taco sauce, olive oil, chili powder, and adobo sauce. For French pork, combine herbes de Provence with olive oil, chicken broth, and balsamic vinegar. Greek pork would be delicious with a marinade of lemon juice, olive oil, chopped fresh oregano, and salt and pepper. Top the pork with feta cheese as it stands after grilling or roasting.

Pork is a good source of high-quality protein, iron, zinc, B vitamins, selenium, and phosphorous. The leanest cuts of pork, such as fillets and tenderloins, have less than 6 percent fat. Pork contains more unsaturated fat and omega-3 fatty acids than beef. Trim all visible fat from most pork cuts and use healthy cooking techniques like grilling, roasting, or stir-frying to prepare this lean meat.

Many people are paranoid about eating pork that is remotely pink or juicy because of trichinosis. However, the disease of trichinosis is almost never found in pork these days. Trichinosis was caused by pigs being fed garbage (which is now illegal) and is almost unheard of today. Pork that is slightly pink and juicy is so much more flavorful than the dry, overcooked pork chops Grandma made. Pork should never be served rare, but that doesn't mean it has to be cooked to the point of dryness.

Pork isn't graded into prime, choice, and select as beef is. Apparently, to the USDA, pork is pork! Cook pork to an internal temperature of 145°F to 155°F, then let it stand before carving. The meat will continue to cook a little while resting.

Pork Roasts

A pork roast is a delicious cut of meat that easily serves a crowd. Choose a loin roast; it has the most flavor and is the most tender. It's very easy to cook; just season it, place it in the roasting pan, and turn on the oven. Pork loin is one of the leanest meats available. Since it doesn't have much fat, be careful not to overcook it. Don't trim off the thin fat layer; it's there to provide flavor.

Try brining the pork loin overnight with a few peppercorns to infuse flavor and juiciness when roasting. You can season the roast with any herbs or spices that you'd

like. Spice blends like curry powder or chili powder, especially if homemade, add wonderful flavor.

The secret to the best roast pork is to make sure it's not overcooked. The internal temperature should read 145°F to 150°F. Let the pork loin stand 10 minutes before slicing to allow juices to redistribute.

A standing rib roast is a spectacular cut of pork perfect for special occasions. This roast has bones attached. Ask the butcher to "French" the bones. This means that all of the meat and fat are cut off the bones so they are clean for a nice presentation. These roasts are tied together, because the meat can separate as it cooks.

Just trim off excess fat, season the meat, then place it on a rack in the oven. Roast, uncovered, until the temperature reaches 150°F to 155°F. Cover the roast and let stand for 15 minutes, then cut between the bones to serve each person an individual chop.

Pork Ribs

Pork ribs are the stuff of old barbecue joints and backyard parties. These flavorful and tender cuts of the pig are fun to cook and fun to eat. But they're very fatty, so there are some tricks to make them juicy and tender without being greasy.

Pigs have 14 ribs that are attached to the spine and divided into five cuts, in order: baby back, spareribs, St. Louis, rib tips, and country style. As you move farther away from the spine, the bones get bigger and straighter with more meat between them.

When you buy ribs, look for firm, deeply colored meat with an even layer of fat and marbleizing. For all ribs, remove the membrane that covers the bottom of the ribs.

Start cutting it away with a sharp knife, then grab the membrane with a paper towel and pull it off. Season ribs with a dry rub before cooking or marinate them in the fridge.

Here's a description of each type of rib:

Baby back ribs are the most expensive type of rib because they're the most lean and tender. The meat comes from the loin. The name comes from the fact that they're shorter than spareribs, not that they're cut from baby pigs. These ribs are curved with lots of meat. Baby back ribs can be cooked directly on the grill over low coals for hours. They're also delicious braised in the oven; they can be finished on the grill to brown and crisp them.

Country-style pork ribs are not really ribs at all; they are pork chops sold in a rack. These ribs are cut from the blade end of the sirloin near the shoulder and do not contain bones. You can find country-style pork ribs as a slab, but more often they are cut into thick strips. Country ribs are leaner than regular or baby back ribs, but they are thicker and fattier than spareribs or baby back ribs. If the ribs are fatty, trim off some of the visible fat. You could brown the ribs in a skillet for a few minutes. You may need to drain some of the fat three-quarters of the way through the cooking time.

Rib tips are the meat cut from spare ribs when making St. Louis–style ribs. They don't have bones; cartilage holds them together. They are an inexpensive cut with a lot of meat. Brine them, or marinate, then grill.

Spareribs got their name because the meat on them is, well, spare. The meat is very flavorful and tender, but there's just not a lot of it. These ribs have their tips exposed. They're cut from the side of the rib cage nearest to the belly. Trim the ribs of excess fat before cooking them, but leave some on to flavor the meat. Spareribs should be simmered on the stove top or baked in the oven before being grilled to remove excess fat.

St. Louis ribs are made of spareribs without the rib tips. This cut is very flat, so the ribs can be cooked in a pan on the stove top. They're also good grilled. This cut is good smoked, if you have a smoker.

Cook ribs in the slow cooker before finishing them on the grill to get really tender and juicy results. The sauce caramelizes on the grill to form a rich crust. Just make sure the slow cooker is large enough, and be sure to brown the ribs to give them color before cooking. Remove excess fat before you put them into the slow cooker.

Pork Tenderloin

Pork tenderloin is one of the more expensive cuts of pork, but there is absolutely no waste and very little fat. Tenderloin is such an overlooked cut of meat. It's perfect for grilling and quick cooking on the stove top.

Pork tenderloin is cut from the full loin. It is, as its name suggests, very tender. You can find plain pork tenderloins in the market, as well as

> ### Helpful Tip
>
> When meat cooks, the juices move around the fibers of the meat. If the meat is cut prematurely, the juices will run out. Resting the meat allows the juices to pull back into the meat. There will always be some juices that escape, and they should be saved to add to the sauce.

Helpful Tip

Sometimes there is a membrane over the tenderloin called the silver skin; pull this off with a paper towel before slicing or cubing. Look at the tenderloin carefully before you start cooking. If there's a thin, shiny skin on the meat, remove it. The silver skin will shrink as it cooks, squeezing juice out of the meat.

tenderloin that has been premarinated. Tenderloin should be pink, with just a little fat, and should be firm and smell sweet. Cook tenderloin to 150°F.

Medallions are cut from the larger tenderloin, then sometimes pounded so they are quite thin and will cook quickly. Simmer ½-inch-thick medallions 15 minutes, until just slightly pink inside. Because the medallions are quite small, serve 2 or 3 per person. Use a large skillet so the medallions brown evenly and don't steam in their own juices. The ends of the tenderloin are tapered, so they don't work well for medallions. Cut them off and freeze them to use later in stir-fries.

Pork Chops

Pork chops are delicious and succulent when properly prepared. Not all pork chops are created equal, however. Different cuts have more flavors and are more tender than others. Loin chops, because they're cut from a muscle that isn't frequently used, are more tender than rib or blade chops. Look for center-cut boneless pork chops for ease in preparation.

Brine pork chops for tender and juicy results. The meat absorbs the salt, which helps retain moisture during cooking. To brine, in a large container combine ½ cup kosher or sea salt and ½ cup cold water with ¾ cup boiling water. Add 3 quarts cold water; stir well. Add herbs, whole spices, citrus peel, or any other flavorings to infuse the flavor. Brine pork chops 12 to 24 hours in the refrigerator. Remove from solution, rinse twice, pat dry, and cook.

Marinating pork chops adds flavor and makes them very tender. Use any standard meat marinade or have fun experimenting using your own favorite flavors. Don't marinate pork chops longer than 24 hours, or they will become mushy.

For panfrying, purchase thin chops; they cook more quickly and stay juicy. If they are not available thin, just pound boneless chops or cutlets lightly with a rolling pan until thin.

Stuffed pork chops are a delicious and fun recipe. You cut a pocket into the side of the chop and stuff it with a flavorful mixture made of seasoned bread crumbs and cooked vegetables. Use a small sharp knife to cut the pocket in the chops and work slowly and carefully. Be sure that your knife stays parallel to the chops so you don't poke holes or make weak spots in the meat. Make the opening as small as you can, and move the knife back and forth to enlarge the pocket.

Meaty pork chops benefit from being cooked in a two-step process called brown braising. First, the chops are browned to create a caramelized crust, which adds sweetness and a visually pleasing exterior. Then the chops are finished by braising them in tomato or wine sauce, which adds moisture to the chops.

Hams

All hams are made from the pig's hind leg. When the meat is fresh, it's called, logically enough, a fresh ham. This is prepared like any other pork roast. But to be a ham, the meat is brined, cured, smoked, and aged. This isn't something you can do at home. The method for making ham is strictly regulated by the USDA.

Prepared hams are fully cooked and can be eaten right out of the package. You can heat it up, of course, but it's equally good cold. To heat a ham, you can use several methods: grilling, slow cooking, or baking. If there are directions for heating the ham, follow them, because they are developed for that particular product.

To heat a fully cooked ham, place it, cut side down, in a roasting pan and add some liquid. You can use chicken broth, cola, water, or fruit juice. Cover the ham tightly and heat it at 325°F for about 12 minutes per pound. To slow cook a ham, put it in a large slow cooker on low for 6 hours. To grill ham, cook it over indirect heat using a drip pan; baste the ham frequently.

Spiral-cut hams are fairly new on the market. A savvy butcher invented a way to literally cut a whole ham into a spiral so it's very easy to serve. These hams are heavily glazed with a sugary crust. To reheat, follow package directions.

Authentic Smithfield hams—also known as country hams—are dry cured, hickory smoked, and aged. The result is ham that packs a lot of taste in a thin sliver. These hams are usually soaked in many changes of water, because they're so salty, then are baked for the best flavor.

> ### BUDGET TIP
>
> Ham steaks can be purchased boneless or bone-in. They are slices of ham cut about 1 inch thick. They're much less expensive than large hams. Try to find a ham steak that's more than 1 inch thick. Thinner steaks will dry out quickly on the grill. The ham steak is fully cooked so only needs to be heated. Because the ham is so simple, you can have fun with glazes, sauces, and accompaniments.

Leftover ham should be used within three days. If you have some left over after that time has passed, freeze it. But ham doesn't freeze well for a long time. Use frozen ham within a month.

Sausages

Sausages are extremely versatile. They can be grilled, roasted, panfried, or removed from their casings and sautéed. There are many different types of sausages, both cooked and uncooked. They have many different names, depending on their country of origin and who makes them. For instance, Spain has many different names for chorizo, which is a heavily spiced sausage. And Germany has tons of wursts, such as bratwurst and knockwurst, that are different pork sausages.

Fresh sausages are not cooked when you buy them. Because they take some time to cook through, precook them on the stove top or oven before grilling. Then finish them on the grill for a crisp smoky crust bursting with grill flavor. Cooked sausages are simply reheated. You can grill them to add a crisp crust and even more smoky flavor, or you can boil or cook them on the stove top.

The following are the fresh sausages that must be cooked before serving. But these names can be deceiving. Always read the sausage package before you buy to check if it must be cooked before serving, or if it can be eaten out of hand. All packages will have these directions.

Boudin is a fragile fresh sausage popular in the Deep South, especially around New Orleans. This sausage must be cooked carefully or it will burst. Prick the boudin sausage several times with the tines of a fork to help release juices as it cooks. Cook the boudin slowly in a heavy skillet over medium-low heat until it is firm.

Bratwurst is a classic German sausage. It's usually made of veal or a mixture of veal and pork. The flavor is rich and not too spicy, with a juicy and slightly rough texture. Cook bratwurst on a grill or on the stove top following the directions for Italian sausage.

Breakfast sausage is the generic name for any mildly seasoned raw sausage. It can be purchased in links or in patties. Cook these fresh sausages in a skillet over medium heat, turning them frequently, until they are browned and cooked through. They're also good grilled or broiled.

Chorizo is a fresh pork sausage that originated in Spain and arrived in South America with the Spanish colonists. Chorizo sausage is garlicky and delicious. It has a high chile and spice content. This sausage is drier and firmer than most fresh sausages.

Italian sausage comes in two varieties: sweet, which is fairly mild, and hot, which is spicy. It's delicious grilled or cooked on the stove top. To keep it moist and tender, start the sausages in a pan with about ½ cup water. Let the water simmer so the sausages firm up. As the water boils off, the sausages will start to brown. Cook, turning frequently, until they are brown and crisp.

Knockwurst, another classic German sausage, is softer than bratwurst and made of beef and pork. It has a large amount of garlic and seasonings in the recipe. The sausage has a casing that makes a "crack" when it's bitten into; that gives the sausage its name.

Should you pierce sausages before cooking? Piercing won't let out all the fat and juice; it just prevents splitting in the heat. Pierce only about ¼-inch deep with a sharp fork in two or three places, then cook the sausages however you like.

These are the types of smoked or cooked sausages that can be eaten straight out of the package:

Andouille is a firm smoked sausage. You can slice andouille sausage before you cook it to release more of the fat and juices.

Braunschweiger is a very soft spreadable sausage. It's fully cooked and used as a sandwich spread. It's also known as liverwurst.

Hot dogs are pork sausages, although some are made of beef. They are fully cooked. You can simmer them in water, beer, or broth; fry them on the stove top; steam them; or grill them. The only way to ruin a hot dog is to overcook it. Keep an eye on the grill, since hot dogs do cook quickly.

Kielbasa or Polish sausage is a fully cooked and smoked sausage with a deep color and rich taste. The two names are interchangeable, although kielbasa is often formed into a ring shape. Sometimes it's sold fresh, so be sure to check the label before you prepare it. Some types are smoked and others aren't. It's delicious heated on the grill and served with mustard.

Linguica is a cured sausage seasoned with paprika, onions, and garlic. It is available in the United States in areas where there is a strong Portuguese heritage, such as southeastern Massachusetts, Rhode Island, and California. If not available, try substituting a mild smoked Italian sausage.

Mortadella is a smoked, dry sausage made of cubes of pork fat and beef, flavored with garlic, anise, and peppercorns.

Salami is a highly seasoned, dried, and cured sausage that's ready to eat. You can fry strips of salami to mix into scrambled eggs for a delicious and hearty breakfast. Salami is available in sausage shape or as lunch meat.

Spanish chorizo is a cooked sausage. It gets its deep red color from the dried smoked red peppers used to make it. While it is a totally different type of sausage, you can use Spanish chorizo in place of Mexican chorizo to add flavor and color to many recipes. Cut the Spanish chorizo into ¼-inch pieces and cook them just long enough to heat through.

Summer sausage or cervelat is a cooked smoked sausage. It's made of pork, beef, mustard, spices, and garlic. Reheat it on the grill or on the stove top and serve in buns with horseradish or mustard.

You can sometimes find cooked varieties of bratwurst and knockwurst in the grocery store. Read the label directions carefully. These sausages need only to be heated for a bit before they're ready to eat.

Sausages are one of the easiest foods to grill. With precooked sausages, you don't have to worry about doneness or undercooking. But that doesn't mean these sausages aren't flavorful! Brush them with glazes and mops as they grill, top them with everything from salsa to honey, and grill them over herbs or wood smoke.

Because these sausages can dry out on the grill, keep a pan of beer or stock on the grill. As the sausages finish cooking, add them to the hot liquid and they'll stay hot and juicy for an hour. Grill them again for a few seconds just before serving to crisp.

Fresh sausages can be frozen when you get them home from the store. Wrap in freezer wrap or place in freezer bags, label with the contents and date, and freeze up to 6 months. To thaw, let stand in the refrigerator overnight; never thaw at room temperature. Cook thawed sausages just as you would fresh ones.

Ground Pork

Ground pork can be used in place of ground beef in many recipes, such as lasagna or meatballs. It's also used in combination with ground beef in many meat loaf recipes to lighten the texture and add more flavor. Treat it as you would ground beef. It's very perishable, so use within a day or two of purchase. Ground pork must be cooked to 165°F, just like all ground meat.

Meatballs made with pork have a slightly lighter texture than beef meatballs. They will be spicier if you make them from pork sausage, which is usually heavily seasoned. Remove the meat from the casings by slicing the side. Push the meat out and discard the casings.

Health Tip

Although bacon and turkey bacon have been cured and smoked, the possibility of bacteria and food-borne illness is real. Always make sure you thoroughly cook bacon and clean and sanitize any utensils that have come in contact with raw bacon.

Bacon

Bacon is truly one of the world's most amazing foods. It's made from the cured and smoked belly of the pig. Most bacon we buy is presliced, but bacon can be bought in one piece; this is called slab bacon. The curing process can include all manner of spices and sweet components including honey, maple syrup, and molasses, but most bacon we buy has been cured in simple salt and sugar. In Italy the most popular bacon is not smoked and is called pancetta.

Some recipes call for wrapping raw bacon around an item before broiling or grilling. To make sure the bacon is crisp and completely cooked, panfry the bacon until some of the fat is rendered out but the bacon is still pliable. Wrap around the food and proceed with the recipe.

To cook bacon, place it in a cold large, shallow pan in a single layer over medium heat. Cook until it releases easily from the pan. Keep turning the bacon until it's brown. You'll know the bacon is done when the hissing and spitting almost stop. Drain the bacon on paper towels, then crumble using your fingers to break it apart.

You can also bake bacon! This is the easiest cooking method, since you don't have to turn it or fuss about doneness. When the bacon looks done, it is done. To prepare bacon this way, just place it on a rack in a shallow pan and bake it at 400°F for 12 to 17 minutes until it's brown and crisp. Drain on paper towels, then use.

There are quite a few varieties of bacon on the market. You can buy plain bacon, thick-cut bacon, smoked bacon, and bacon that has been coated with cracked pepper. Use your favorite type in any recipe calling for plain bacon.

Thick-cut bacon is actually deep-fried, because it cooks in the large amount of fat it renders. Spoon off some of the fat as the bacon cooks. When the bacon is an even brown color and the sound has really reduced, remove to a stack of paper towels. Let the bacon stand for a few minutes, then cut the bacon with a knife into small pieces to use in recipes, or serve as is.

Bacon fat is an excellent flavor enhancer. When you brown meat in bacon fat, the flavor permeates the recipe. Just cook the bacon until crisp, then remove from the pan, drain, and refrigerate until it's ready to add to the recipe. Drain off a bit of the fat, add some olive oil, then cook the rest of the recipe.

Helpful Tip

A staple in Italian cooking, pancetta, often called Italian bacon, is the salt-cured pork from the belly of the pig. It is rolled and sometimes spiced with pepper, cloves, nutmeg, fennel, hot peppers, and garlic. Some varieties are much like American bacon. Pancetta rigatino is a lean pancetta from the region of Tuscany in Italy. You can find pancetta in the deli section of Italian food markets.

Ham Bone

A ham bone is a wonderful thing. It looks raggedy and unappealing, but the flavor it adds to soup is incomparable. It's really only used as a flavoring for soups or stews. Paired with split peas in a classic soup, this inexpensive wonder will help warm you up no matter the weather. There isn't a lot of meat on a ham bone. You can usually get about a cup to a cup and a half of diced meat from the bone after it's cooked. The bone adds rich flavor to soup and thickens it. Cut the meat from the bone after cooking, dice, then return the meat to the soup. Discard the ham bone.

LAMB

Many cultures embrace lamb as a staple protein. However, for those who didn't grow up eating lamb, the meat can be an acquired taste. For the mildest flavor, buy young, farm-raised lamb and trim off all visible fat.

Lamb is a very tender meat when properly cooked. The most common cuts include shoulder roast, leg, chops, and loin. Fresh lamb should be firm and have a pink or red color with even white marbling running through the meat. It may have a coating of fat; leave this on, as it adds flavor.

Lamb should be cooked medium-rare to medium. It will be a light pink color inside. Lamb is a delicate meat, but must be prepared with certain ingredients for best results.

Lamb tastes so rich because its fat has a low melting point. That's why it coats your mouth as you eat it and why it is served with rosemary, mint, garlic, and lemon. Those types of foods with a sharp taste cut through the fat and counteract its richness.

These are the common types of lamb found in the market:

Lamb chops are tender and delicate. They can be cooked like pork chops, but they should only be cooked to medium for best flavor and texture. If you're used to pork chops, you may be surprised at how small lamb chops are.

The best types of lamb chops are sirloin, loin, or rib chops. Butchers don't always keep them in stock, so you may have to order them ahead of time. Look for chops that are firm and finely textured with white fat. Buy chops that are about an inch thick for the most even cooking.

Flavor lamb chops with anything from garlic to mint and honey. Marinate them if you'd like, but keep the marinating time (in the refrigerator) to a few hours. Panfry, broil, or grill the chops to 140°F. Remove them from the heat and cover. Let them stand for 4 to 5 minutes to let the juices redistribute, then dig in!

Leg of lamb isn't just for Easter anymore. When marinated and grilled, it's flavorful, tender, and juicy. A boneless leg of lamb, also called a lamb roast, is easiest to grill. The leg should be butterflied so you can add a paste or rub over the largest area. You can grill the lamb as is or roll and tie it for longer cooking.

Rack of lamb is also known as lamb rib roast. Eight ribs serve two to three people, so for 6 servings buy 16 to 24 ribs. Have the butcher crack the chine, or backbone, so the ribs are easy to separate after they have been grilled. Also ask the butcher to clean the ribs for a nice presentation.

Buy a rack of lamb that is firm, with smooth, creamy fat. There shouldn't be too much fat on the ribs, and the meat should be firmly attached to the bone. Lamb should be cooked medium-rare to medium. The final temperature is 135°F to

150°F. A single rack of lamb is the perfect amount for serving two people. For serving more people, buy more racks. Baby rack of lamb doesn't need marinating and needs very little trimming. It's broiled and then baked.

Lamb shanks are a very flavorful cut of meat. Shanks can be tough if not cooked correctly; they must be braised for a long period of time. The lamb shanks you buy in the store should be "cracked." That doesn't mean the bone is cracked—the butcher makes some cuts in the meat so they don't curl up tightly while cooking.

SAUCES, ROUX, AND DRESSINGS

14

Sauces and dressings are the finishing touch to most meals. In fact, good restaurants devote a lot of time to making these recipes. Good sauces use the flavor developed when cooking meats and vegetables to finish the dish. Roux is the thickener for many classic sauces. And dressings are what bring out the flavors of salads.

Making true sauces from broths and stocks takes many hours and huge bubbling pots filled with meats and veggies. In professional kitchens there is usually someone specifically assigned to this task, and it is a full-time job. Thankfully you don't have to do all this work.

Long and slow preparation of almost anything is bound to be superior to supermarket shortcuts, but we live in a fast-paced world, which often demands the use of shortcuts. By all means, learn how to make perfect stock when you have the time. The lesson learned will be an excellent baseline of flavor and texture that will allow you to use shortcut methods most effectively.

SAUCES

Everyone who cooks needs to know the basics of sauce making. If you can whip up a sauce, you can turn everyday dishes into amazing creations. There are five "mother sauces" in classic cooking. They are béchamel, or white sauce; veloute, which is a white sauce made with stock or broth instead of milk; espagnole, a rich brown sauce also known as a demi-glace (and whose scope is beyond this book!); hollandaise or béarnaise, an emulsification of eggs and oil; and tomato or pasta sauce.

Many sauces employ the technique of reduction. The sauce is simmered until thickened. The whole point to reduction is to concentrate and increase flavor. So you must start with high-quality ingredients. Use homemade or boxed stocks and don't be afraid of herbs and spices. When reducing a sauce, watch it carefully. It can go from burnished and perfect to burnt in seconds. Taste frequently and adjust seasonings as needed.

White Sauce, also called béchamel, is very easy to make with a couple of tricks and tools. First, always use a whisk when making a white sauce to prevent lumps. A well-made white sauce is the perfect finish for vegetables, and it can be flavored to complement chicken, seafood, or any other meat. White sauce is the base of many creamy soups.

There are several different types of white sauces:

White sauce. This basic sauce is made of flour sautéed in fat. Milk is added and the mixture is cooked until thick.

Alfredo sauce. This sauce is a white sauce made with cream instead of milk. It's used in Italian cooking and in many pasta dishes.

Cheese sauce. Add any type of shredded cheese to a finished white sauce to create a cheese sauce. This is used as a finishing touch for many vegetables, and is the basis for mac and cheese and scalloped potatoes.

Mornay sauce. Shredded Swiss and Parmesan cheese added to white sauce, with a touch of nutmeg, creates this flavorful sauce.

> ## Helpful Tip
>
> There are many ways to change the flavor of a white sauce. Add sautéed mushrooms for an excellent sauce for chicken. Adding chopped pieces of cooked chicken gives you chicken á la king. Two tablespoons of Parmesan cheese will also transform this sauce.

To make a white sauce, heat butter in a saucepan over medium heat. Stir in minced shallot or onion and cook until softened. Whisk in flour and cook, stirring until well blended with the fat, about three minutes. Don't skip this step! The flour must cook in the fat so its starch granules soften and swell so they can absorb the liquid. Then add warm milk, stirring constantly with a wire whisk to prevent lumps. Mix in salt and pepper to taste. Reduce heat to low and stir until very smooth and creamy.

If you don't sauté the flour prior to adding the milk, you will end up with a lumpy sauce and a raw flour flavor. If you add cold instead of warm milk to the sauce, you may get lumps. When adding lemon juice, do so just before serving, or the sauce will curdle (i.e., separate).

Veloute is made by adding stock or broth to the mixture of cooked flour and fat instead of milk. The stock or broth used is usually light, either a beef stock made from unroasted bones, or a chicken or fish stock.

This sauce is excellent when flavored with wine. Always use a good wine when you're cooking. Avoid cooking wines, which have been heavily salted to make them unsuitable for drinking. When you're cooking, always use a wine you'd like to drink.

A veloute made with beef stock is also called a brown sauce. Brown sauce is superb with all sorts of meats. Vary the flavor by adding 1 tablespoon dry red wine to the brown sauce. Adding ½ cup roasted, peeled, and chopped chestnuts will make the brown sauce perfect for roast beef or venison. To make a spicy, hot sauce, simply sauté 1 chopped jalapeño pepper.

Pan sauce is made using drippings left in the pan from sautéing and searing meats and vegetables. For the easiest sauce, just swirl a bit of broth and butter into the brown bits and juices left in the pan after cooking meat. This step is called deglazing. Chefs consider the drippings left in the pan the essence of the food. Wasting them is simply not done.

To make the simplest pan sauce, follow these directions.

- Take all the juices from the meat and return them to the skillet.
- Turn heat to medium-high and add a little sweet wine or broth and a dash of salt. Chicken broth or stock is one of the best liquids for making a pan sauce, but you can use marinades or milk or cream for a rich and thick pan sauce.
- Let the mixture bubble and reduce a little, scraping the pan to release the browned bits, pour over sliced meat, and serve.
- For a rich pan sauce, finish with butter. Just swirl a pat or two of cold butter into the pan sauce just before you take it off the heat. This will help finish the sauce, give it a nice gloss, and help it thicken a bit.
- If you want a thicker sauce, add a cornstarch slurry: a mixture of cornstarch and cold water. Blend it well so it's completely smooth before adding to the pan. A couple of minutes of cooking and the sauce will be thick and glossy.

Helpful Tip

Always have boxed or canned chicken broth, beef broth, and vegetable broth in your pantry. Choose low-sodium versions to avoid salty finished products. While you can make your own broths and stocks, as you learn to cook, these products can save you lots of time. The boxed stocks seem to be of better quality than canned.

Gravy is a slightly more complicated pan sauce. Nearly every beginning cook has had the experience of struggling to make a gravy for the Thanksgiving turkey while all the other food gets cold. But making gravy is just as easy as making pan sauce.

To make a gravy for chicken or turkey, follow these steps.

1. While the bird is roasting, rinse the giblets and place in saucepan.

2. Add water, onion, garlic, salt, and pepper and bring to a simmer.

3. Reduce heat to very low and simmer for 2 to 3 hours, adding more water if necessary.

4. Strain broth, reserving giblets. Discard the neck; chop the remaining giblets finely.

5. Melt butter or pan drippings in saucepan. Add flour; cook and stir until light golden brown. Or add a slurry of flour and water to the drippings; just whisk together flour and water to make a smooth sauce. Simmer for a few minutes.

6. Skim the fat from the turkey or chicken juices left in the pan or use a fat separator.

7. Add enough of the broth to the drippings and flour in the pan to make a smooth gravy. Stir in giblets; simmer 10 minutes.

8. Season with salt and pepper. In fact, the secret to the best gravy is salt. Keep tasting while you add salt. When you've added just the right amount, the gravy's flavor will suddenly bloom and intensify.

Helpful Tip

Bases are like bouillon but more moist and easy to stir into liquids. They are available in many grocery stores and online. Bases come in many flavors, such as crab, chicken, beef, and vegetable. Use a blend of bases when making sauces. For instance, if you're making a white sauce, use chicken, vegetable, and mushroom bases. Bases can be a bit salty, so taste the sauce before adding salt.

Glazes can be made from a sauce that has been reduced to a syrupy consistency. A glaze is shiny and highly flavored. It can be used on any meat or vegetable. Glazes usually have some type of sugar in the recipe so they will brown and thicken.

Tomato sauce is a classic Italian sauce that is the base for many recipes, including spaghetti with meatballs and pizza. It's made by cooking onions and garlic in butter or olive oil, adding chopped tomatoes, and simmering until smooth and thick.

You can use canned or fresh tomatoes in a tomato sauce. Before adding fresh tomatoes, remove the skins. The skins can take on an unpleasant texture when cooked for hours in the sauce. Blanch tomatoes in boiling water for a few seconds, then plunge into ice water. Remove the core and scoop out the seeds and tomato jelly, because these parts can make the sauce watery and bitter.

For a basic tomato sauce, use 5 pounds tomatoes or three (28-ounce) cans crushed tomatoes. Cook 1 onion in ¼ cup olive oil with 3 cloves garlic, minced. Add the tomatoes and stir. Add 1 cup dry red wine, dried basil and oregano, and salt and pepper to taste. Simmer for 30 to 40 minutes until the sauce is thick. Refrigerate for up to 5 days or freeze for longer storage.

Barbecue Sauce is just dressed up tomato sauce. This sauce starts with a base of tomato sauce, paste, pureed tomatoes, or ketchup. Spices are added, along with sweeteners like honey, molasses, brown sugar, or maple syrup. Some people like to add mustard to barbecue sauce, and hot sauce and chiles may be added for some kick.

You can dress up a purchased barbecue sauce to add your own twist. Taste the sauce and see if you think it's missing something. Add honey, brown sugar, hot sauce, cooked onions, garlic, cayenne pepper, or any herbs or spices in your pantry.

ROUX

A roux (pronounced *roo*) is a blend of flour and fat used to thicken soups and sauces. All classes of sauces begin with a roux. There are several different types of roux, based on how long the flour is allowed to cook in the fat.

Helpful Tip

For a homemade barbecue sauce, cook 1 onion, chopped, and 4 cloves garlic, minced, in 1 tablespoon butter. Place in a 2-quart slow cooker. Add 1 cup ketchup, ⅓ cup vinegar, ¼ cup brown sugar, 1 teaspoon salt, 2 minced jalapeño peppers; cook on low for 7 to 8 hours. Refrigerate up to 5 days or freeze up to 3 months.

White or light roux is used in white sauces. It doesn't provide any flavor but is just used to thicken a sauce.

Blond roux is a bit darker than white roux. It is made by cooking the flour in the fat until it colors slightly.

Medium roux is slightly darker, like the color of peanut butter. The flour is cooked until light brown, about the color of oak wood.

Brown or dark roux is made with flour cooked until brown. This adds a great deal of flavor to the sauce and is mostly used in Cajun and Creole cooking. Gumbos are made with a brown roux.

The proportion of roux is usually one part fat to one part flour. The fats can be bacon fat, butter, olive oil, peanut oil, or schmaltz. The flour used is almost always white all-purpose flour. You can make a quantity of roux, then refrigerate or freeze it in ⅓-cup portions up to 6 months. Let thaw in the fridge, then add to the recipe. This is a great shortcut if you make lots of dark and rich stews and gumbos. The mixture may separate as it sits; just whisk it for a minute and it will recombine.

A blond roux is cooked for 10 to 15 minutes, until the flour is slightly toasted. It will smell like popcorn. Brown roux is used in gumbos and chowders. It's cooked for 25 to 30 minutes, until it is the color of peanut butter. And dark brown roux is cooked for 40 to 50 minutes. The flour starts to lose its thickening power as the roux is used for flavor. Don't overcook the roux or let it burn; if it burns, you'll have to start over. If you like gumbo or other Cajun dishes, make a lot of roux at once.

The roux will spatter quite violently when you add vegetables, so be careful. Add a batch at a time and stand back. When you add the chicken broth and beer, use a wire whisk to help incorporate the liquid into the roux.

MARINADES AND BRINES

Marinades and brines tenderize meats and add flavor. Marinades use acid to tenderize protein. Brines are solutions of water with salt and sugar. They force water into the meat to make it juicy.

Marinades combine an acidic ingredient like buttermilk, vinegar, or lemon juice with herbs, seasonings, and a bit of oil. The acid in a marinade (whether it is citrus juice, vinegar, yogurt, or wine) breaks down tough connective tissue. Herbs and other ingredients, like lemon zest, orange zest, and minced garlic, add flavor.

Here are a few tips about marinades:

- You must follow food safety rules when marinating meats.
- The marinade can be discarded after use, or used to make a sauce or glaze. Before you can serve a marinade, it must be boiled for at least 2 minutes.
- Always marinate chicken, pork, and beef in the refrigerator, even if the marinating time is only 30 minutes.
- Cover the dish tightly with plastic wrap or foil so the flavors don't transfer to other foods in the fridge.
- You can marinate meats in a plastic bag. Place the bag in a dish so it won't leak in the refrigerator. Turn the bag over several times while the meat is marinating to ensure full contact with the marinade.
- Never let cooked meat come in contact with uncooked marinades.

Pat the meats dry before grilling for best caramelization. A wet steak or pork chop won't caramelize on the heat; it will just steam as the marinade boils.

Brines are weaker marinades used to force moisture into food. Make sure the food you brine is natural, not enhanced, since enhanced meats are already injected with brine. You can brine steak, roasts, pork chops, turkey, and chicken. Some people brine shrimp and other shellfish, but this isn't as common. It's easy to make those tender foods tough with too much brine.

To make a brine, combine 1 cup of salt and ½ cup of sugar in a large pot big enough to hold the chunk of meat. Add at least 3 quarts of water and stir until the salt and sugar dissolve. Then add the meat and refrigerate. Small pieces of meat, like chicken breasts, will be done in 30 minutes. A large turkey can take 12 to 24 hours to brine.

Don't worry about the health effects of salt in brines. The food doesn't absorb much sodium, because the salt concentrations between the brine and flesh must equalize, drawing liquid into the meat.

DRESSINGS

Dressings are the finishing touch for many salads. There are quite a few types of dressing. Vinaigrettes are simple combinations of oil and vinegar, with herbs, salt, pepper, and other ingredients like honey or mustard. Mayonnaise is an emulsification of oil and egg yolks. Emulsifying is the blending of oil and liquid. All of these recipes are easy to make, tastier than store-bought dressings, and cheaper than store-bought, too.

Mayonnaise is a French invention, which is nothing more than oil emulsified in egg yolks. Almost no other condiment is as widely used. Homemade mayo has a milder flavor and creamier texture than store-bought versions. The egg yolk acts as a natural emulsifier, because it contains lecithin, a binding agent. Since mayonnaise contains lemon juice or vinegar, which bacteria don't like, it is protected against spoilage for a short period of time. Use the freshest eggs and best-quality oil to produce top-notch results. For food safety reasons, you should use pasteurized eggs in homemade mayonnaise.

To make mayonnaise, separate 1 pasteurized egg; freeze the white and place yolk and 1 more whole pasteurized egg in a blender. Blend in 2 tablespoons lemon juice. Then, with the blender on, slowly drizzle in 1¼ cups olive oil until the mixture is thick and creamy. Store, covered, in the fridge up to 5 days.

For the mayonnaise to blend properly, the oil must be added very gradually. Some emulsions can be fixed if they break by adding a bit of hot or cold water or even re-emulsifying with a bit more protein from more egg yolk.

Mayonnaise is easy to flavor. For a roasted garlic mayonnaise, just cut ¼ inch off the top of a garlic head. Drizzle cut edges with olive oil and wrap head in aluminum foil. Roast at 400°F until soft, about 45 minutes. Squeeze out soft garlic and mix with ½ cup mayonnaise. Or you can add chopped herbs, mustard, or honey. Some people like to cut mayonnaise with lemon or lime juice to use as a simple salad dressing.

Helpful Tip

If you want to flavor whole chickens or turkeys without the mess of a brining solution, try a dry brine. Sprinkle the chicken or turkey with a generous amount of salt. Let chicken rest, uncovered, in the refrigerator for 5 or 6 hours. A turkey should sit for an hour per pound. Rinse the bird thoroughly, dry it off, then roast.

Olive oil labeled as "grown, pressed, and bottled" in a single country is considered the best olive oil (the label "product of Italy" only means the oil was bottled there). The label "cold pressed" means the oil was never subjected to heat, which creates the best flavor. Extra-virgin olive oil is essential to the taste of most vinaigrettes. It has a rich and fruity flavor. Extra virgin oil comes from the first pressing. Virgin olive oil (the second pressing) and plain olive oil (the third) are often mixed with other oils and aren't as desirable for vinaigrettes.

Sesame oil is extracted from sesame seeds. Raw sesame seed oil is clear to pale amber in color, with a subtle flavor. Dark sesame oil is made from toasted seeds. That wonderful flavor is volatile and dissipates during long cooking times, so add it just before you serve the dish. A tiny bit adds great flavor to vinaigrettes.

Vinaigrette is just a combination of oil and vinegar or lemon juice. This dressing is the simplest of all. It's perfect drizzled over fresh baby salad greens. It can be flavored many ways or served as is, seasoned with a bit of salt and pepper. Oils and vinegars are the crucial ingredients in vinaigrettes.

To make a vinaigrette, place vinegar or lemon juice in a small glass jar with a tight lid. Add seasonings like salt, pepper, mustard, herbs, spices, or minced garlic. Then add the oil. Use three parts oil to one part vinegar. Close the lid tightly and shake until blended. You can also combine the ingredients in a blender or food processor; blend or process until smooth and thickened. You can season the dressing any way you'd like. Add lots of fresh herbs or use spice blends like curry powder or chili powder to add a bit of a kick. Vinaigrettes can be made ahead of time. Store in the fridge, but don't keep it longer than four days.

Homemade vinaigrettes are only temporary emulsions. Mustard and honey can be added to your vinaigrette to add flavor and to help keep the vinegar suspended in the oil.

Vinegar is not just for salad dressings; its acidic bite helps sharpen the flavors of many foods. Cooked greens benefit tremendously from a splash of vinegar (red wine and apple cider are best). Add a teaspoon of balsamic or wine vinegar to a pan sauce for the best flavor.

In Asia, rice vinegar has been in use for millennia. There are three types: red, white, and black. The red and black are used as condiments, while white is used for cooking. In Thai cooking there is a further option: coconut vinegar. If you can find it, use it in place of rice vinegar. Otherwise, a good Western substitute is apple cider vinegar, which offers many health benefits.

Raspberry, cherry, and other fruit vinegars are best in salads and in sauces. Tarragon, bay, and rosemary vinegar are particularly good on fish and salads.

While balsamic is a fine choice for salad dressing, its strong, sweet flavor often overpowers more delicate lettuces and milder dishes. Sherry wine vinegar can be added to soups and salad dressings for a milder taste.

Salad Dressings are a bit more complex than vinaigrettes. They often include ingredients such as egg yolks, mayonnaise, mustard, shallots, onions, and herbs and seeds. Mixed dressings, like Caesar salad dressing and green goddess dressing, are a blend of mayonnaise and citrus or vinegar, along with other seasonings.

Helpful Tip

A genuine balsamic vinegar is at least fifty years old, sweet in taste, and used very sparingly because of its high price. It's often used on desserts or other delicacies like fresh strawberries. Balsamic vinegar is made from the best grapes available, just like the best wines, and the process is very labor-intensive. For ordinary use, buy regular balsamic vinegar, which is rich in flavor, not too acidic, and not too sweet. Use the pricey stuff for drizzling on fruits or meats for a special occasion.

When you do make your own salad dressings, feel free to store them in an empty salad dressing bottle from the store or a jam jar with a lid that can be shaken up before serving.

Salads made with lettuces and other tender greens like spinach are dressed when cold or at room temperature. Fruit salads are usually refrigerated before serving. But when you're dressing pasta and potato salads, add the dressing to hot ingredients. By adding the hot ingredients to the salad dressing, the food will absorb the flavors of the dressing.

Hollandaise is a special sauce that is a variation of mayonnaise. It's made of egg blended with melted butter, some lemon or vinegar, and salt and pepper. Hollandaise is served over eggs Benedict and steamed asparagus.

Classic hollandaise can be tricky to make, as it breaks, or separates, easily. Blender hollandaise is easy to make. Just put 3 (pasteurized) egg yolks in a blender or food processor. Add a pinch of salt and pepper. Melt 2 sticks of unsalted butter and turn on the blender. Add the butter in a very thin stream, slowly, while the blender is running. Add 2 tablespoons lemon juice and blend until thick.

Coulis is an uncooked fruit sauce. Making coulis is easy with a blender. You can make a coulis by pressing the fruit through a fine sieve. Use any seasonal fruit, such as mangoes with a bit of lime juice. Strawberries, blueberries, and blackberries are also possibilities. Peaches are very good and can be used as a sauce on pork or duck.

For a savory coulis, add spices and/or herbs to the fruit sauce. For a terrific coulis to serve with roasted chicken or duck, make this recipe: Mix 1½ cups fresh raspberries with 1 tablespoon fresh rosemary and 1 teaspoon hot sauce or curry powder. Or

blend 1½ cups cut-up ripe pears (skins on) with 1 tablespoon lemon juice and 1 cinnamon stick to produce a fresh sauce that's delightful on chicken or turkey.

OTHER SAUCES

There are many different types of sauces from around the world that will add delicious flavor and an elegant finish to your cooking.

Adobo is a sauce made with chile peppers, vinegar, and garlic. Chipotle peppers in adobo are one variation of the condiment. Adobo has a rich and deep flavor from long cooking time and a complex combination of ingredients. You can't make adobo sauce at home, but it's readily available in the ethic aisle of general supermarkets and at specialty stores.

Chimichurri sauce is an Argentinean green sauce used with fish, chicken, steak, and vegetables. It's also used as a marinade. Chimichurri usually combines parsley, garlic, vinegar, and red pepper. You can also add other spices and herbs such as paprika, cumin, oregano, thyme, and bay leaf.

To make a chimichurri sauce, combine 1 cup parsley, ⅓ cup chopped cilantro, 3 cloves minced garlic, ½ cup extra virgin olive oil, 3 tablespoons white balsamic vinegar, 1 tablespoon fresh oregano, ½ teaspoon salt, and ¼ teaspoon crushed red pepper flakes. Blend until combined, then refrigerate until you're ready to eat.

Compound butter is the simplest sauce. It's just a mixture of butter and other ingredients like cooked garlic, herbs, spices, and cheeses. You can use it to top grilled chicken, pork, or seafood. Don't store compound butter in the refrigerator more than

2 days, because butter is a low-oxygen environment. This is the ideal place for botulism spores to grow. Discard after two days or wrap and freeze for two weeks.

To make compound butter, just beat softened butter until creamy. Add washed and finely chopped herbs, garlic, or sautéed vegetables. Form the butter into a roll and wrap in waxed paper. Refrigerate until firm. To use, thinly slice the butter and place on top of hot cooked meats or vegetables.

Fish sauce, also known as *nuoc mam,* is literally made from fish, accented with herbs and spices and fermented. Anchovies are commonly used because they have such an intense flavor. A little bit goes a long way. Most recipes call for only a tablespoon.

Hoisin sauce is made from soybean paste, sugar, chile peppers, and a variety of seasonings. It's the usual accompaniment for Peking duck and mu shu pork. Like many Chinese sauces, hoisin has sweet-and-sour aspects. It's a reddish brown, thick sauce that can be used to glaze roasted or barbecued meats.

Peanut sauce is made with ground peanuts or peanut butter, an acid like vinegar or lemon juice, and broth. The sauce for sesame noodles is made of equal amounts of tahini, peanut butter, sesame oil, soy sauce, and rice wine vinegar. Make a thinner version, using less tahini and peanut butter, more vinegar and soy, and a little canola oil, and use it as a salad dressing.

Shred green cabbage and make a slaw by tossing it with this peanut sauce. Include a little minced fresh ginger in the sauce. Or use the sauce as a dip for crudités, including daikon radish slices.

Salsa is a blend of chopped vegetables that can be cooked or uncooked. Your salsa can be chunky or almost smooth, depending on how you prepare the vegetables. In Mexico, home cooks consider their personalized salsa recipe a point of pride. Salsa keeps well in the refrigerator so don't worry if you have lots leftover. Store in a lidded container.

Soy sauce, comes in two traditionally brewed varieties: shoyu and tamari. Shoyu is made from soybeans, roasted wheat, and sea salt, along with mold spores to cause the fermentation. Tamari is a wheat-free liquid made from pressed soybeans, sea salt, water, and *koji,* a product made from wheat. Shoyu is best for everyday use, while

tamari, with its stronger flavor, is used in smaller doses in cooking. Look for traditionally brewed in either case.

Tzatziki is a cooling side dish used in hot Middle Eastern and Mediterranean countries. It's just a mixture of yogurt, chopped cucumber, some minced garlic, and a bit of lemon juice. In Indian cooking, this sauce is called *raita*. It is used as a dip for fresh and toasted pita, as a sauce for grilled meats, and as part of a meze tray.

To make *tzatziki,* either use thick Greek yogurt or drain plain yogurt first. To drain yogurt, place it in a cheesecloth-lined sieve over a bowl in the fridge for a few hours. The whey will drain out of the yogurt, leaving a thick mixture. Combine with seeded and finely minced cucumber, garlic, lemon juice, pepper, salt, and fresh dill.

⑮ STOCKS, BROTHS, AND SOUPS

S *oup.* The word conjures up images of comfort and home. It is a universal food, loved around the world. Soup can be simple or complex, a flavorful broth or a complicated one-dish meal. But how many people have enjoyed a true homemade soup instead of one reconstituted from a box or a can?

Soup is not difficult to make. Most of the best soups require two things: good ingredients and time. But even that time is spent letting the food bubble away on the stove, in the oven, or in a slow cooker or pressure cooker. The actual work time you invest in a good soup is minimal.

Broths and stocks are the basis for soups. They're both made the same way, by simmering ingredients in water for long periods of time to extract all the flavor and nutrition. Stocks contain bones, while broths do not.

BROTH

Broth is invaluable in the kitchen. It's used as the base for soups and stews, for gravy, and for cooking meats and vegetables. Broth can be a soup in itself. Simply heated broth, sprinkled with a few fresh herbs, is an elegant first course recipe. Broths are lighter than stocks but can be very flavorful.

> ### Health Tip
>
> Soups and broths are so good for you! Chicken soup, sometimes known as "Grandma's penicillin," contains proteins that can help lower blood pressure, along with anti-inflammatory ingredients that stop the release of chemicals that make you feel sick.

There are several different types of broth:

Beef broth is made from beef meat and lots of vegetables. Onions and garlic add depth of flavor and sweetness to the broth, while carrots and celery add floral notes.

Chicken broth is one of the easiest recipes to make, yet its quality and flavor are essential for the best soups. All you need for chicken broth is some chicken, filtered water, and a few vegetables.

Fish broth or seafood broth is made from seafood and vegetables. This is one of the lighter broths.

Vegetable broth is made from lots of vegetables and water, along with herbs and whole spices. It's used in vegetarian soups and stews and often in seafood soups. It's also the least expensive broth. Root vegetables are most often used to make vegetable broth. Their rich flavor and deep colors help make the stock taste and look rich.

Good broth is made from good-quality ingredients. Beef stew meat is used because it is a cut that is full of flavor but inexpensive. Browning the meat before simmering the broth adds flavor and color to the finished product. Use any vegetables or herbs you'd like to flavor your broth and enjoy the delicious soups you make from it. Making your own broth allows you to adjust the seasonings and salt in the broth. It's economical, too; you are turning waste into something valuable. After all, you can use vegetable peelings from other recipes to make broth.

Broth should cook long and slow to intensify the flavors. Just wash vegetables, cut them into pieces, cut the meat (if using) into pieces, perhaps brown the meat and vegetables in a bit of fat, add water, and let it simmer away.

Stir the broth occasionally as it cooks and break up any large meat pieces. Adjust the salt to your taste or leave it out altogether. Black or red pepper, powdered onion, and garlic are good seasonings for most broths. Celery seed, celery leaf, or parsley and minced rosemary are excellent for chicken broth. Don't add sage—it turns bitter.

A pressure cooker is a good way to get more flavor out of all of those vegetables and herbs than just simmering, and it's faster, too. A slow cooker is a great way to make broth.

STOCK

For the richest and deepest stock, it's important to brown the meat very well before cooking. The bones add body and richness to the broth that you can't get with just meat. The bones add a bit of gelatin to the stock, making it slightly thicker than broth. You can make the recipe without browning the meat first; the stock will still be rich, but it will be lighter in color.

Beef stock is made from the meaty bones, either leftover from another recipe or purchased from your butcher. If you have a friendly butcher who will save you some meaty beef bones, you're lucky. Otherwise, buy short ribs or oxtails for beef stock. Or, if you've done a large standing rib roast, you have the basis for excellent beef stock. For the best beef stock, brown the bones with some of the vegetables before simmering or roast them in a hot oven until golden brown. Don't let the bones or vegetables burn, as this will ruin the stock.

Chicken stock is made from the meat and bones of the bird. Stock is richer than broth, since the bones add lots of flavor. You can make chicken stock from the remains of a large roasted chicken, you can pick up a few pounds of chicken necks and backs at the supermarket, or you can use leftover chicken bones. Freeze those leftovers after removing the meat. When you have enough, make stock! Just add aromatic vegetables and herbs.

Fish stock or seafood stock is made from fish bones, shrimp shells, and lobster shells. Seafood or fish stock can be difficult to find in stores, even specialty or gourmet stores. If you make a lot of seafood soups, it's a good idea to make your own and keep it in the freezer. If you don't have shrimp shells or bones, or can't find them at the market, just simmer shrimp until they turn pink, shell, freeze the meat, then use the shells for stock. Do the same thing with fish steaks or whole fish. You can improve any seafood stock by simmering it for a few minutes with reserved shrimp shells. The best vegetables for seafood stock include onions, garlic, celery, and bell peppers—the same vegetables used to make gumbos and jambalaya.

For best flavor, simmer stock, don't boil it. Simmering is defined as just below boiling. The bubbles will float gently to the surface and break softly. The food doesn't move much when simmering. You want the broth to cook slowly to extract all the flavor from the meat and vegetables.

Helpful Tip

To clarify any broth or stock, prepare and strain the mixture. Return to a clean stockpot or saucepan. Add ¼ cup cold water and 1 egg white. Bring to a boil and then remove from heat. Let stand five minutes; strain the broth through cheesecloth. You can also use eggshells; bring to a boil, let stand, and strain.

BUDGET TIP

Some recipes tell you to cook whole chickens to make chicken stock. But you don't have to waste all that meat. Instead of simmering the entire chicken in the water for hours, which will render the meat tough and inedible, cook the chicken just until the meat is tender. Then remove the meat and freeze for later use. Return the bones, fat, and trimmings to the stockpot and continue simmering. You'll still get all the flavor from the chicken, but the meat won't be wasted.

Don't forget about the fond when you brown meat, bones, and vegetables for stock. Always deglaze the roasting pan with water. Scrape up the little browned bits—the fond—and add everything to the stockpot.

To prepare homemade chicken stock, combine 2 pounds chicken pieces with 3 quarts water, onions, garlic, and carrots. You can roast the chicken, onions, garlic, and carrots in a 400°F oven for 45 minutes until browned before cooking in the stockpot. Add salt, pepper, and herbs like thyme and tarragon. Simmer for 2 to 3 hours.

The foam, or scum, on the top of the broth or stock that forms as it simmers consists of protein combined with fat and impurities in the food. If you don't skim it off, the soup will be cloudy. Use a large flat spoon and carefully remove the scum. Discard it in the sink; it doesn't add any flavor or nutrition to the soup.

Then cool and remove all of the large pieces of food with a slotted spoon or sieve. Pour the broth through a strainer into a large pot. Refrigerate the broth overnight, remove the fat that has solidified on top, and freeze the stock or broth in small containers.

Removing Fat from Stocks and Broths

When making stocks and broths, you may want to remove the fat before freezing. There are several ways to do this.

The fat in a broth or stock will always rise to the top as the soup cools. When you chill a soup overnight, in the morning you'll find a layer of fat has risen to the top and solidified. Gently break the fat and peel it off. If there's a thicker clear layer under the fat, keep that; it's gelatin, which thickens the soup. Chilling may make the broth jellylike.

To remove fat by skimming, you have to have a clear broth or stock that hasn't been combined with a slurry or roux for thickening. Skimming broths and stocks manually can take some time. The fat will appear as clear puddles on top of the liquid; scoop it off carefully using the side of a large flat spoon.

Manual separators are probably an essential piece of equipment if you make lots of stocks and broths. They're easy to use and inexpensive.

SOUPS AND STEWS

Soup recipes are very tolerant; that is, they will be delicious no matter what you add to or subtract from the recipe. They're an ideal choice for the beginning cook. You can change the vegetables, use different meats, add more herbs, or change the proportions, and the soup will still be delicious.

When making soup, measuring accurately is only important for the seasonings. Other ingredients can be measured more casually. There are only two guidelines you should follow when making soups and stews: Don't overseason your soups and stews, and don't overload the pot! If your slow cooker or pot simmers over onto the stove top, you'll be left with quite a mess on your hands.

Types of Soup and Stews

Soup is usually defined as a combination of broth or stock and solid ingredients. Soups can be chunky or pureed smooth. These are the different types of soups and stews:

Bisques are the richest soups for more formal occasions. They are thickened with egg and cream and usually pureed. Bisques can be served hot or cold. The flavor of a bisque is quite intense, so the ingredients used to make it should be top quality. Like chowders, bisques are usually made with seafood, although they can be made with any meat.

Chili is a stew made with beans, tomatoes, and meat. Although "true" chili doesn't use any beans, the chili we all love includes legumes, usually kidney beans. Chilies are always highly seasoned. Dried and fresh chiles (note the different spelling), cayenne pepper, and chili powder (which is a blend of chiles and other seasonings) add distinctive flavor to this thick stew.

Chili can be garnished with lots of flavorful foods. Place shredded cheese, sour cream, guacamole, chopped raw onions and bell peppers, jalapeño peppers, or crumbled tortilla chips in bowls and let each diner garnish his or her own bowl.

Chowders are thicker than soups. They are usually, but not always, based on seafood, with some milk or other dairy products included in the recipe. The soup is thickened with milk and cheese. Potatoes are usually included in chowder recipes.

Most clam chowder that you find in a can or even a restaurant isn't very heavy on the clams. Make your own to add as many clams as you'd like. Throw in a couple of cans, or use part diced and part whole clams. Some people like their clam chowder so thick that a spoon can stand up in it. If that's your idea of bliss, add more flour. Or mash a few of the potatoes to thicken the soup.

Clear soups are the simplest soups. A homemade broth or stock can be a perfect first course

or a soothing treatment for a cold. Float a few herbs and chopped vegetables in the broth for garnish. Egg drop soup is a good example of a clear soup.

Consommé is a clear soup that has been clarified with egg whites and filtered with cheesecloth. This rich and elegant soup is quite complicated to make. When consommé is chilled, it thickens because of the gelatin present in the stock.

Gumbos are the thickest soups. Classic gumbos are made with a roux, which is a mixture of flour cooked in oil, and file powder for thickening. It originated in the Gulf coast area of the United States. Gumbos always start with the "holy trinity" of vegetables: celery, bell peppers, and onions. The soup includes sausage and seafood.

The roux thickens gumbo and adds a deep flavor that can't be duplicated with any other ingredient. File powder, the classic thickener for gumbo, is made from sassafras leaves. The roots and bark of that plant contain a carcinogenic ingredient called *safrole*. Older copies of *The Joy of Cooking* claim file powder should not be used. But the leaves, when harvested very young, do not contain safrole, so they are safe.

File powder should not be cooked, so it is added last, after the soup is removed from the heat. You must stir as you add the file powder, as it starts to thicken when heated. Sprinkle the powder evenly over the gumbo and stir constantly. You can also dust the soup bowls with file powder and add the gumbo; it will thicken as you eat.

The classic way to serve gumbo is to cook some medium grain white rice until tender. Spoon the gumbo into a bowl dusted with file powder, then top with a scoop of the rice and dig in.

Pureed soups are some of the easiest to make, since you don't have to worry too much about cutting ingredients into uniform pieces. The key is to make sure the ingredients are completely soft so the soup will be silky smooth. If your soup has some lumps, you can strain it through a fine sieve. If you use a conventional blender for any pureed soup, make sure to cool the soup before pureeing. Hot liquids expand when pureed in a blender or food processor.

Stews are simply thick soups. Stews are thickened with a slurry of cornstarch and flour or with flour used to coat the meat. Stews are often thickened by long simmering in an uncovered pot so much of the liquid evaporates. Stews can be thickened with vegetable purees or with pureed legumes or split peas, too.

Thick soups usually have a slurry of cornstarch or flour added to thicken the broth or stock. Lentil soup is a classic, easy, and inexpensive thick soup that is nourishing and delicious. You can make the soup as smooth or as chunky as you'd like. Blend it partially or completely.

COOKING METHODS

There really aren't very many cooking methods for making soup, although there are a few good appliances to use. Making soup is easy; just combine all the ingredients in some type of container and simmer until the ingredients are tender. There are several ways to cook soup. The stove top is the obvious method, but soups also cook well in slow cookers, pressure cookers, and the microwave. And there are soups that can be made in the food processor or blender. Each requires a bit of finesse and different instructions.

A soup is only as good as its ingredients. Never use wilted vegetables or fruits or poor quality meats. Long cooking soups, especially, concentrate the flavor of the ingredients. Poor quality ingredients mean a poor quality soup. Don't be afraid to use canned or frozen produce in your soup recipes. These products are processed very soon after harvesting, so they can retain even more vitamins and minerals than fresh produce that's been shipped across the country or around the world.

Preparing Soup Ingredients

Preparing ingredients for soup is simple. Most meats and produce are just peeled and chopped, sliced, or diced, then added to the soup at different times according to how long they take to cook. For a quicker cooking soup, cut everything into small dice. For long-cooking soups or soups made in a slow cooker, cut the food into larger pieces.

A soup is only as good as its base. Usually, aromatics like onions, garlic, and spices are cooked in oil or with meat to start the soup. Then water or stock or other liquid is added, and ingredients like pastas are added at the end of the cooking time.

Making Soups and Stews in a Slow Cooker

Soups cooked in the slow cooker are very flavorful, as the ingredients' flavors blend beautifully in this appliance. There's almost no evaporation, so all the flavors concentrate; volatile flavor compounds are kept in the appliance along with the food. Since there is no evaporation, don't fill the slow cooker with liquid. The vegetables will give off liquid as they cook.

If you want deeply flavored soups cooked in the slow cooker, it's important to brown the meat and some of the vegetables before you fill the appliance. Heat fat in a pan and coat the meat with seasoned flour. Cook until browned, turning a few times. This should take about 5 to 8 minutes. And be sure to deglaze the pan with water or broth to pick up all of the rich fond. Fill the slow cooker one-half to three-quarters full.

If your soup or stew isn't as thick as you'd like at the end of the cooking time, add a cornstarch slurry, stir well, and cook for another 15 to 20 minutes. Or turn the slow cooker to high, remove the lid, and cook for a half an hour or so. Cornstarch is the best quick thickener for soups cooked in the slow cooker; flour takes longer to thicken.

If you want to make stock in the slow cooker, just place ingredients in a 3- to 4-quart appliance. Cook on low 7 to 8 hours, skimming the surface occasionally, until the stock tastes rich.

Making Soups and Stews on the Stove Top

A soup simmering on the stove top is a wonderful, comforting thing. This is a much faster cooking method than making soup in a slow cooker; you can usually make a soup in about 30 minutes, although it can simmer for hours.

Soups don't have to cook for a long period of time to be high quality. Some quickly made soups include beer cheese soup, fruit soups, and egg drop soup. The key to short-cooking soups is to use a full-flavored broth; that makes the soup taste as if it cooked for hours. Just follow the recipe and use heavy, quality pots and pans.

Making Soups and Stews in a Pressure Cooker

A pressure cooker is a great way to quickly cook deeply flavored soups and stews. One of the best things about making soup in a pressure cooker is its ability to cook dried beans and peas quickly and evenly. Even after overnight soaking, sometimes these products don't get soft enough with regular cooking methods. The pressure cooker eliminates that problem.

Whichever type of pressure cooker you use, be sure to follow the manufacturer's instructions to the letter. The pressure cooker can't be opened until the pressure is reduced through the release of steam. Always use care around the pressure cooker: Steam can burn. Timing is important. Vegetables can overcook in the time it takes some meats to cook.

Most soups convert well to the pressure cooker. Always fill the pressure cooker one-half to two-thirds full. Reduce the liquid in soup recipes by about half. In an old-fashioned pressure cooker, there will be some evaporation due to steam release. Most pressure cooker recipes take 20 to 40 minutes.

Making Soups and Stews in the Oven

Soups and stews can be baked. If you don't have a slow cooker, this is a great way to make a soup that is rich and easy. Soups will bake in the oven just about as long as they cook in a slow cooker. The temperature of the oven is usually very low, around 300°F. Make sure the liquid is simmering before you set the dutch oven or ovenproof pot in the oven. Use a large ovenproof pot or stockpot. The soup doesn't need to be watched or stirred as it bakes.

Heating Soups and Stews in the Microwave

Most soups aren't cooked in the microwave oven; but it's a great way to reheat them, especially those that are frozen. Place a frozen block of soup in a microwave-safe container. Try to break it up with a knife. Microwave, uncovered, for 4 to 5 minutes on 30 percent power. Remove and check if you can break up the soup. Return to the microwave. Microwave on 50 percent power for 3 to 4 minutes longer; remove and stir. Continue microwaving at 50 percent power for 2- to 3-minute intervals. When the soup is thawed, microwave until the soup starts to bubble.

The microwave is a good way to cook ingredients to add to soups. Onions, garlic, mushrooms, and other hard root vegetables cook well in the microwave. This is a good way to speed up preparation if you want to make a soup quickly but want to use longer-cooking ingredients.

Making Soups and Stews in a Food Processor or Blender

Food processors and blenders not only speed up preparation of the ingredients that go into the soup, they can make a cold soup from start to finish. For soups like gazpacho and chilled pea or melon soups, just coarsely chop the ingredients, peel when necessary, and add to the processor or blender. A few pulses, and you can serve the soup immediately or chill it to let the flavors blend.

Processors and blenders are also used to puree hot soups. Use care when pureeing boiling hot mixtures. Never fill a food processor or blender more than two-thirds full with a cold liquid or half full with a hot liquid. Add the cover securely and then hold a folded thick kitchen towel on the cover to prevent hot liquid from spurting out of the processor or blender.

Some soups are partially processed; that is, some of the solid ingredients are pureed in a food processor and then returned to the soup. This thickens the soup naturally, without using roux or slurries of flour or cornstarch.

Thickening Soups

There are a few ways to thicken soup. Slurries, reduction, roux, and vegetable purees are the most common. In addition, adding mashed potatoes to a soup, or even bread crumbs, can thicken the broth nicely.

Beurre manie, or "kneaded butter," is a mixture of flour and fat and is one way to thicken a soup at the last minute. To make beurre manie, flour is mixed with butter until smooth. Then the mixture is added in small amounts to the soup or sauce and simmered for just a minute or two until the liquid thickens.

Bread crumbs are a good way to thicken a soup, add fiber, and use up leftover bread. Just stir them in and simmer until dissolved. A soup called *ribollita,* from Tuscany, is made using dry leftover bread.

Cheese is often used to thicken soups and stews. As the cheese melts into the liquid, it thickens and adds wonderful flavor. When you add cheese to a soup, coat it with flour or cornstarch. This helps prevent the cheese from melting into a single glob and further thickens the soup.

Be sure to not let the soup boil or cook too longer after adding cheese. Natural cheeses, especially, can curdle or break, making the soup unpleasant to eat. Processed cheeses, which contain emulsifiers and stabilizing agents, are an easier way to thicken soup.

Cornstarch or flour slurry is a good way to quickly thicken a soup at the last minute. These mixtures are made from a combination of broth or water and cornstarch, potato starch, arrowroot, or flour. Use a cool or cold liquid to make a slurry. You don't want to start cooking the flour or cornstarch when it's first mixed with the liquid; you just want to dissolve the thickening agent.

Helpful Tip

Salt is essential to the taste of most soups. When you add the cornstarch or flour slurry, or when you're adding delicate ingredients at the end, taste the soup. Add salt a pinch at a time, tasting the soup after each addition. When the flavor suddenly blooms, you've added the perfect amount.

Be sure the cornstarch is thoroughly dissolved in a small amount of cold liquid before you add it to the soup. If the cornstarch isn't dissolved, the soup will be lumpy. Cook for at least 5 minutes, stirring frequently with a wire whisk, to activate the cornstarch.

The ratio of thickening agent to soup is about 1 tablespoon for every 2 cups of soup. If you like a thicker soup, or are making a chowder, you can increase that to 1 tablespoon for every cup of soup. But don't go beyond that proportion or the soup will be too thick.

Egg yolks are natural thickeners. But they can't just be added to the soup; they must be tempered first. Beat the yolks with some of the hot liquid to bring the temperature of the yolks and the soup closer together. This may seem like a fussy step, but tempering the egg yolks will prevent curdling and lumps.

Pasta can help thicken soups, because it releases starch as it cooks. When pasta cooks in a flavored liquid, you won't believe the difference in taste. Pasta absorbs flavors as it cooks. When cooked in soup, the pasta has a firmer texture.

When pasta is cooked in soup with tomatoes, the acid in the tomatoes keeps the pasta from becoming very soft. It will have a wonderful al dente texture, with a slight bite in the center. When you cook pasta in liquids other than water, the cooking time changes. Make sure you adjust the cooking time for each type of pasta you use. Add about 2 to 3 minutes to the cooking time listed on the pasta box and keep checking until the pasta is al dente.

Purees are the most pure method for thickening soup, because they intensify the flavor. You don't add any more calories or fat, and the soup retains excellent color and aroma. Choose an ingredient already in the soup to keep the flavor consistent.

Purees are just blended vegetables, peas, or beans. You can make a puree several ways. First, you can drain a can of beans, peas, or vegetables, add them to a food processor or blender, and then process them until smooth, or you can mash the vegetables, peas, or beans with a potato masher until mostly smooth. Stir this puree into the soup and simmer until thickened. Or just puree part of the soup right in the pot using an immersion blender.

Helpful Tip

You may have heard a chef speak of a sauce or soup "breaking." When something "breaks," the fat separates out of the solution and becomes a congealed mess. The cheese in many soups contains fat, and if it gets too hot it will break or separate. So don't overheat soups or stews after you add cheese. If your soup does break, there is no way to fix it; you must start again or go out to dinner!

You can also remove cooked beans, peas, or vegetables from the almost-finished soup, puree them in a food processor or blender, and then return the puree to the soup. A few minutes of simmering are all it takes to thicken the soup.

A rough-textured soup can be rustic. However, if you want smooth soup, you need a fine blend. If blending doesn't get all the particles out of the soup, press it through a fine sieve.

Reduction is the easiest method for making a soup thicker. Reducing a soup makes the texture thicker and concentrates the flavor. The downside is that it will increase the calories of the soup, because there is less water.

Reduction does take a bit of time. Bring the soup to a fast simmer, not a boil, and cook uncovered for 30 minutes to an hour. Stir the soup occasionally to make sure it isn't burning on the bottom. Taste the soup. If it tastes rich and you like the texture, you're done! If not, keep simmering until the soup looks and tastes how you want it.

You can use the power of reduction to improve a canned broth or stock. Just add some chopped vegetables and a bit of water to a canned soup and simmer until it's reduced and rich.

Roux, the French word for "red," is a classic way to thicken soup. It's simply a combination of flour and fat, heated so the starch in the flour expands to absorb liquid. A roux stabilizes the soup so it won't break. There are several different types of roux. A wire whisk is an essential tool for making a roux. It's almost impossible to make a smooth roux without it. For more information about roux, see Chapter 14.

Helpful Tip

You can reduce soups on the stove top, obviously, but also in the oven and in the slow cooker. In the oven, bake the soup with the lid off for 1 to 2 hours. In the slow cooker, remove the lid and turn the heat to high. Cook for 30 to 40 minutes, until the soup is reduced.

CHILLING AND FREEZING SOUP

It's a good idea to make a large batch of soup and refrigerate or freeze some of it for a later time. This is a great way to save money and make another meal.

To chill soups safely, transfer them while still hot to a large, fairly shallow container. The larger surface area and shallow container will help the soup cool quickly to get it through the danger zone of 40°F to 140°F. This also helps preserve the flavor, texture, and color. Let the soup cool for about an hour at room temperature, then transfer the container to the fridge.

To cool soup very quickly, place it in an ice-water bath. Fill a large container with cold water and add ice. Place the pot of soup in the ice water. Make sure the ice water doesn't lap over the edges of the soup pot. To cool the soup even faster, fill a clean bottle with ice water and use that to stir the soup while it's cooling.

When the soup is cold, cover the container or transfer to smaller containers, seal tightly, and refrigerate up to three days. For longer storage, freeze up to three months Soups are more forgiving of freezer burn; if it does happen, add more water and reheat slowly.

Always label the containers holding your soup with the name of the soup, reheating instructions, any ingredients and garnishes that need to be added to the soup , and the date it was made and frozen. Place the soup in the coldest part of the freezer. And be sure your freezer is set to 0°F; use a freezer thermometer to make sure.

You can freeze stock in ice-cube trays for use in sauces, or in 1-cup containers, or by the quart. After you've frozen a couple of ice-cube trays' worth, place the cubes in plastic ziplock bags. Then, when making sauces, add the cubes as you need them. Try to keep a couple of quarts of chicken stock and beef stock in your freezer for making quick soup.

To thaw a frozen soup slowly, place it in the refrigerator for 8 to 24 hours. Not all of the ingredients may be thawed, but they will reheat in the warming step. Never thaw soup at room temperature.

To thaw soup quickly, microwave it. When you microwave soup to thaw it, you must cook and serve it immediately. Don't thaw partially in the microwave and then refrigerate for eating later. The microwave creates hot spots that can bring some of the food into the danger zone of 40°F to 140°F.

The simplest method for thawing and heating is on the stove top. Just place the frozen block of soup in a saucepan. Add a little water or whatever broth you used to make the soup. Heat on low, breaking up the soup as it warms. Then slowly bring the soup to a simmer; simmer until all the ingredients are hot and tender.

ETHNIC SOUPS AND STEWS

Every cuisine in the world has a special type of soup. These soups may use different ingredients, but they all have one thing in common: They're delicious! Once you learn how to make simple broth, stock, and soups, broaden your horizons with some of these classic choices.

Egg drop soup is a classic Chinese recipe. This delicate soup is made with beaten egg drizzled into clear hot broth just before serving. In a soup as simple as this one, the quality of the broth is very important. If you haven't made broth from scratch before, this soup is the time to try it. Other ingredients like mushrooms add flavor to the soup, but the broth must be very flavorful to begin with. The egg mixture is added to the broth at the last minute. The easiest way to add the egg is to put the egg into a squeeze bottle, then stir the soup and squeeze the egg into it to create fine threads of cooked egg. This soup must be eaten immediately.

Gazpacho is a Spanish soup, traditionally made with stale bread, olive oil, garlic, and vinegar. Tomatoes and other vegetables were added later in the soup's history. This cold soup is perfect for a hot summer day. All you need are some good quality fresh vegetables, olive oil, perhaps some broth, seasonings, and a food processor or blender.

Minestrone is a thick Italian vegetable soup. Most people have heard of the classic minestrone, or "big soup," named because of the variety and amounts of vegetables that go into it. Usually this soup is eaten hot, but in some regions of Italy, such as Campania, the soup is eaten at room temperature during the summer. Each region adds its own flair to the soup. In the Veneto region of Italy, rice is added. Tuscans make a hearty minestrone thickened with beans and bread. Romans drop a mixture of egg and Parmesan cheese into the hot soup, while southern Italians love stylish *ditalini,* a tiny round pasta, in their soup.

Miso is a classic Japanese soup consumed for breakfast, lunch, and dinner. Miso is soybean paste fermented with salt. It adds a rich and salty flavor to the soup. The soup is made by adding miso to dashi, or Japanese soup stock, made from dried foods like bonito flakes, sardines, kelp, or shiitake mushrooms. Dashi granules are like chicken bouillon cubes, but they have more flavor.

Miso paste addresses what food scientists call the "fifth taste": umami. In addition to salty, sweet, sour, and bitter, umami taste buds detect a meaty taste from glutamates, compounds found in meat, mushrooms, vegetables, and soybeans. *Umami* is a Japanese word that means "savory" or "delicious."

Pasta e fagioli, which many people pronounce *pasta fazool,* is a thick and rich soup that is so good for you. The name literally means "pasta and beans." This soup was originally peasant food, since it's made from inexpensive and readily available ingredients. You can make this soup with any bean, pasta, and vegetable combination. It often calls for a ham bone, but you can leave it out and add some cubed round or sirloin steak, use chicken thighs, or omit the meat altogether. This is a very versatile recipe. For a thicker soup, add more pasta; for a thinner soup, use less. Serve the soup with some hot garlic toast, a mixed green salad with a Parmesan dressing, and red wine.

Ragout is a simple French stew of meat and vegetables, seasoned with herbs and spices. It can be made with any meat, but typically is made from lamb or beef. The French term *ragout,* or in Italian, *ragu,* means "a stew or sauce heavy with long, slow-cooked vegetables." This type of food is perfect for the slow cooker. This is where root vegetables shine. Think about using less common types of vegetables, like turnips, rutabagas, and parsnips, in these types of recipes.

Ribollita is a Tuscan soup made of vegetables, thickened with stale bread. Make any rich vegetable soup as directed, omitting the cheese. Add 1 tablespoon tomato paste. Cool the soup and refrigerate. The next day, stir in 2 cups cubed stale crusty Italian bread, then reheat the soup until the bread dissolves and the soup thickens. Serve with Parmesan cheese and drizzle with extra-virgin olive oil.

Scotch broth is a rich soup made from lamb or beef bones and root vegetables such as carrots and onions. Barley is the grain usually used in Scotch broth, but lentils are a good substitute. They make the soup slightly more cloudy than barley.

You can use more unfamiliar root vegetables, like parsnips, turnips, and swedes, also known as rutabagas, in this soup. They add a sweet and earthy taste.

Swedish fruit soup is a staple of Scandinavian countries. During the long, cold winters, when fresh summer fruit was impossible to get, Scandinavians made do with dried fruits. Fruit soup was considered a dessert.

Today a cold fruit soup is an excellent summer lunch entree. Use dried apricots, fresh or dried peaches, or a mixture of dried fruits, as was used in the "old days." Once you start making fruit soup, you can vary it with the seasons. Melon soup, made with honeydew or cantaloupe and spiked with lime juice and ginger, is delightful. Add dried cherries or cranberries on top for a fine garnish. Garnish fruit soup with fresh mint leaves, basil leaves, toasted nuts, or fresh berries. A dol-

lop of low-fat yogurt or sour cream is also nice.

Vichyssoise, the soup with the fancy name, is cold potato soup, but much more than that. Onions, leeks, and garlic cooked in butter make a flavorful base for this elegant soup. When the soup is well seasoned and served with a sprinkling of chives, it's fit for the fanciest party. It's also an excellent soup to serve on a hot summer day. The soup is very inexpensive, especially if you omit the leeks and use another onion and another clove of garlic.

SOUP ADDITIONS

One of the nicest things about soup is that it's fun to garnish. You can add so many things to a soup for texture, color, nutrition, and flavor. For great contrast, think about serving a cold topping on a hot soup or a warm topping on a cold soup. Toppings can add crunch to a smooth and suave soup or cool down a spicy mixture. Croutons are an obvious choice, but little crackers, fresh herbs, grated cheese, sour cream, popcorn, gremolata, or salsa are all excellent options.

Dumplings. Dumplings are just quick breads, made of water, liquid, and some fat for flavor and tenderness. They cook through in minutes, adding a hearty touch to soup. The secrets to the best dumplings are to use a light hand with the dough, to drop the dumplings onto simmering stock or soup, and to leave the lid on until the dumplings are completely cooked through.

You can make dumplings from scratch or use a baking mix. There are even dumplings mixes available on the market. Ethnic names for dumplings include gnocchi and spaetzle; look for those mixes in the supermarket.

As with all quick breads, handle dumpling dough gently. Stir dumplings just until the dry ingredients are moistened. Work quickly when dropping the dumplings into the soup or stew. Use a tablespoon measure and drop batter from the side of the spoon. Keep the dumplings the same size so they cook evenly. And remember to space them evenly around the pot.

To test for dumpling doneness, cut a dumpling in half. The texture will be even and fluffy all the way through. The dough will be very hot; internal temperature should be around 180°F. Dumplings will float when they are properly cooked. To serve, ladle the stew into a bowl and top each serving with two to three dumplings.

Cheese popcorn. Pop ¼ cup popcorn kernels in 2 tablespoons butter. Cover pan and shake until popping slows. Place popcorn in bowl, removing unpopped kernels. Sprinkle with ¼ cup grated Parmesan cheese, ¼ cup grated Romano cheese, and 1 teaspoon dried Italian seasoning; toss and serve.

Curried croutons. Cut 3 slices oatmeal bread into cubes. Melt ¼ cup butter; add 2 teaspoons curry powder. Drizzle over bread cubes and toss to coat. Sprinkle bread with mixture of 2 tablespoons brown sugar and 2 tablespoons sugar. Bake at 400°F 8 to 10 minutes, until crisp.

Garlic croutons. Cut ten 1-inch-thick slices of French bread. In small saucepan, combine ⅓ cup olive oil and 4 minced garlic cloves; simmer for 5 minutes. Drizzle over bread; toss to coat. Sprinkle with ½ teaspoon salt and ⅛ teaspoon pepper. Bake at 350°F for 10 to 15 minutes until brown; remove and cool.

Herbed oyster crackers. In bowl, combine 2 tablespoons dried parsley, ¼ cup instant minced onion, 1 teaspoon garlic salt, 1 teaspoon onion salt, 1 teaspoon dried dill, and ⅛ teaspoon pepper with ½ cup oil. Mix and drizzle over 4 cups oyster crackers. Bake at 275°F for 20 minutes until browned.

Honeyed pecans. On baking sheet, place 1½ cups small whole pecans. Drizzle with 2 tablespoons melted butter, ¼ cup honey, and ¼ cup brown sugar. Bake at 350°F for 15 to 20 minutes until glazed. Sprinkle warm nuts with ½ teaspoon salt and cool.

Matzoh balls are made from a mixture of matzoh meal, chicken stock, eggs, and seasonings. They are a type of dumpling made without flour. You can also make them from a soaked matzoh cracker. These dumplings aren't light, but shouldn't be heavy and dull either. When properly made, they are dense and slightly chewy but tender enough to cut with a fork.

Sparkling water is the secret ingredients for lighter matzoh balls. The water adds some carbon dioxide to the batter, much like baking powder, without the aftertaste. Rinse your hands with cold water every time you form a matzoh ball; otherwise they will stick to your hands. Drop the balls into the stock as you work. To check for doneness, cut one open; when cooked through, the texture will be even. The matzoh balls should float when they are done.

Pesto. In food processor, combine 2 cups fresh basil leaves, ½ cup shredded Parmesan cheese, ½ cup toasted pine nuts, 2 cloves garlic; process until finely chopped. Add ⅓ cup extra virgin olive oil and 2 to 3 tablespoons water; process. Store in refrigerator.

🔢 **16**

DESSERTS

No matter how many diets our nation tries, one thing never changes: We still want rich, delicious, and accessible recipes for dessert. We crave chocolate desserts for Valentine's Day, an elegant cake for birthdays, and an array of perfect cookies for Christmas. A good report card, a telephone call from an old friend, and even the first day of spring all give us reasons to celebrate, too, with perfect peanut butter brownies, a cool fruit fool, or some homemade pudding.

Once you understand a bit about the science of baking and have learned some techniques, you will see that baking isn't difficult. As you gain confidence, you can expand your repertoire and create beautiful pies, tarts, cakes, and even candies and ice cream with ease.

When you start baking, begin with the easiest recipes. The easiest dessert recipes are trifles and parfaits, where you just layer ingredients. The next easiest are quick breads and muffins. Then try bar cookies. Once you've mastered those treats, move on to fruit desserts like crumbles and crisps, then try cakes and pies. Yeast breads are the "final frontier" for baking. Once you've made a fragrant and light loaf of yeast bread, you'll be a real baker.

DESSERT FLAVORS

When you think of desserts, you almost always think of something sweet. Chocolate, caramel, vanilla, and fruits are all sweet flavors. Sugar plays an important part in flavor and texture, but there are other flavors that make desserts delicious. To make the best desserts, you need to know about these flavors and how they interact.

Sweet and Salty

Sugar has many functions in dessert recipes besides flavor. Sugar is hygroscopic, which means it attracts water. This keeps desserts moist after they're baked. Sugar crystals help form the structure of cakes and cookies. The sharp crystals cut pockets in butter or shortening, which are filled with carbon dioxide from the leavening. Sugar also helps cakes and cookies brown.

There are many different types of sugars. Granulated sugar is the one most commonly used in desserts. Brown sugar is granulated sugar that has some molasses added for richer flavor. It must be measured by packing into a cup. Powdered sugar is finely processed granulated sugar with some cornstarch added. It dissolves quickly for use in frostings and glazes. Sanding, or demerara, sugar is used to decorate desserts because the crystals are very large.

Honey and other syrups—including corn syrup, maple syrup, and molasses—are used to create a soft texture and smoothness. You can't directly substitute honey for sugar in most recipes because honey adds water to the formula. If honey or other syrups crystallize, warm the jar in a saucepan of water over very low heat. There are several grades of honey, maple syrup, and molasses, from light to dark. Keep a variety on hand.

Fresh, frozen, and canned fruits all have their place in dessert recipes. The sim-plest dessert is just some perfectly ripe fruit, drizzled with a simple syrup and topped with mint or other herbs. Choose ripe fruits for your desserts. Don't use overripe produce in any recipe, unless you're making banana bread or banana cake. Many frozen fruits are used frozen (when baking a pie, for instance); others are thawed. Fruits can be peeled, chopped, or pureed before being adding to a recipe.

Salt is an unusual chemical. It enhances other flavors. Salt can make chocolate taste richer and strawberries seem sweeter, and it

brings out the flavor of extracts and spices. The newest trend in desserts is sweet and salty together: Think of a caramel sprinkled with some *fleur de sel,* a fancy salt with excellent flavor.

Salt has other functions in desserts. It strengthens gluten formation in doughs and makes egg whites foam stronger. Measure salt carefully; if you add too much, the recipe will be salty or may not work.

Tart and Spicy

If desserts were just sweet, they wouldn't be very interesting! Even the sweetest recipes, such as chocolate and caramel dishes, have other flavors for balance. We may be born with a sweet tooth, but there are foods that are too sweet.

Some foods are naturally tart. Fruits, especially citrus and stone fruits, have a tart or sour aspect to their flavor. This tart flavor enhances the sweetness of the fruit for a more enjoyable taste.

Lemons, limes, and oranges are used in many dessert recipes. The pulp, juice, and zest of these fruits add tart flavor and floral fragrance. Always choose citrus fruit with smooth skin, heaviness for its size, and plumpness. Avoid wrinkled or shriveled fruit. Always wash citrus fruits with food-safe soap before zesting to remove pesticides. These fruits can be substituted for one another.

Tart fruits add nice flavor contrast to many desserts. The tartness level will vary with ripeness and variety. Tart apples include Granny Smith, Jonathan, Northern Spy, Pippin, and Winesap. Rhubarb is technically a vegetable but is classified as a fruit. It is very tart and must be cooked with sugar. Dried fruits such as currants and raisins have a slightly tart taste.

Spices are an integral part of baking. Gingerbread cake or cookies must include ginger, cinnamon, nutmeg, and sometimes cardamom. These spices provide a bit of heat on the tongue and create wonderful aromas.

Scientists are discovering that some spices have medicinal qualities. The latest scientific research shows that spices, especially cinnamon and ginger, have health benefits. Cinnamon can help lower cholesterol and stabilize blood sugar, as well as improve memory and brain function. Ginger may help prevent cancer and reduces inflammation. Cloves have antibacterial properties, and nutmeg helps relieve stress. All of these spices have antioxidant properties.

The best spices are the freshest. Most ground spices have a shelf life of 3 to 6 months. Smell the spices before you use them in your recipes. If they don't have a very strong aroma, discard them and buy fresh. You can purchase whole spices—cinnamon sticks, gingerroot, and whole nutmeg—and grate them yourself. Use a microplane grater or a spice grinder reserved solely for this use.

DESSERT TEXTURE

Texture is almost as important as flavor in desserts. Always take texture into consideration when contemplating a dessert or baking recipe. Think about biting into a pecan bar or an apple crisp with crunchy oatmeal topping. You expect the food to snap between your teeth and create a moderate amount of crunch.

Crunchy

Food scientists measure the crunchiness of foods with displacement curves. A crunchy food produces a curve with lots of peaks and valleys. The more peaks and valleys, the crunchier the food.

When you eat a dessert, the way it feels in your mouth is called, logically enough, mouthfeel. Crunchy foods should resist the first bite, then shatter. There are several ways to make foods crunchy. Nuts are toasted, cookies are baked until golden brown, and streusels are made with oatmeal and butter. Baking, broiling, grilling, and toasting all produce crunchy products. The opposite of crunchy is soggy.

Making good desserts also means knowing how to store them. Storing crunchy desserts correctly is crucial. If you refrigerate a dessert that shouldn't be chilled, crunchy toppings and crusts can become soggy, as they absorb water.

Streusel is made of a combination of flour, sugar, and butter for a crunchy topping on many desserts. The dry heat of the oven literally fries the mixture as it bakes, creating the crunchy texture. Streusel is used to top cakes, cupcakes, pies, and tarts. It is also used as a filling for coffee cakes. The word *streusel* is a German term that means "sprinkled or scattered." When stored, streusels will become less crunchy.

Helpful Tip

There are several vinegars that play a role in baking and desserts. Plain vinegar is used to sour milk or to help egg whites keep a firm foam. Vinegar makes the interior of a pavlova soft. The simplest dessert is a very good balsamic vinegar drizzled over sliced ripe fresh fruits.

Helpful Tip

Unless you're making peanut brittle or toffee, most dessert recipes have other textural characteristics, most notably creamy, chewy, and crisp. Measuring, mixing, and baking techniques are all designed to maximize these textures, so follow them carefully.

Nuts are naturally crunchy. When toasted, their crunch factor increases. You can toast nuts in the oven, in the microwave, or on the stove top. Different nuts have different levels of crunch. Pecans are less crunchy than almonds, and pine nuts are crunchier than walnuts. There are two ways to roast and toast nuts. You can use a hot skillet, preferably a heavy, cast-iron frying pan. When the pan is hot, add the nuts; keep them moving and stir often. Or you can bake nuts in a 325°F oven for 10 to 15 minutes.

To coarsely grind nuts, pulse in a food processor, pausing to scrape down the sides of the bowl. Or grind nuts coarsely by placing them between sheets of waxed paper and pounding them with a meat mallet. For finely ground nuts, pulse in a food processor for a few seconds, then whirl the nuts on high. Chop nuts before you toast them, or toast and cool completely before you chop them or they'll be mushy.

Creamy

A creamy and smooth dessert is comforting and satisfying. Of all the dessert textures, creamy is the most indulgent. Think about spooning a rich rice pudding or chocolate fondue into your mouth. The creamy mouthfeel is described as rich, melting, thick, and smooth. Fat is usually a prime component in creamy desserts. Creamy foods coat the mouth, which allows you to taste the food longer. That's why a creamy chocolate dessert tastes more intense than one that is crisp or crunchy. No wonder we associate creamy foods with comfort!

To achieve a creamy consistency, lots of stirring or beating is required. A wire whisk is an excellent tool when making sauces and puddings. Lumps and graininess have no place in a dessert that is supposed to be creamy and smooth. Melting and cooking ingredients for creamy desserts must be done carefully. Chocolate can seize, or become grainy, when overheated, and cream and other dairy products can curdle.

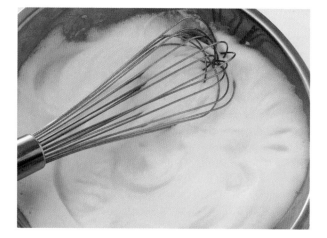

Chocolate is often the first food we think of when we hear the word *creamy*. Creamy chocolate puddings, frosting, pies, and ice cream are all treasured desserts. Chocolate is a truly universal food these days, and its comforting and complex richness has reached all corners of the globe. Milk and dark chocolate have a melting point of just about 98.6°F, the same temperature as your mouth. That's why chocolate has such a creamy texture when you eat it.

To melt chocolate quickly, chop it into small pieces. Use a large knife and cut into the chocolate on a cutting board. Melt the pieces in a microwave oven or in a double boiler. Watch the chocolate carefully when it is melting and stir frequently.

Chocolate must be handled carefully and kept within a certain temperature range. When chocolate develops a white or grayish covering or streaks, it's been stored at high temperatures. This coloring is called bloom. Bloom doesn't affect the quality of the chocolate. It disappears when the chocolate is melted.

Cooked pudding is a good example of a creamy dessert. The mixture of fat, sugar, flour, and liquid gives it its creamy texture. Puddings and other creamy mixtures must be stirred constantly over heat so they thicken evenly.

Fillings are made of whipped cream; a frosting-like mixture of fat, sugar, and liquid; or other ingredients such as cornstarch and eggs. Cooked fillings are either cooked on the stove top or baked in the oven on some type of crust. A filling can be made of any mixture that includes fat, sugar, and some type of thickener. When baked, creamy fillings thicken as they cool, so be careful not to overbake them.

Whipped cream adds a creamy consistent to any dessert. Only heavy whipping cream will whip to form a foam that is creamy. Make sure you read labels in the supermarket. The cream, beaters, and bowl should be very cold for best results. Chill everything in the refrigerator for several hours before beating the cream. The cream can then be folded into other mixtures. You can flavor whipped cream with brandy, powdered sugar and vanilla, caramel, or chocolate.

Peanut butter is one of those ingredients with mystical properties. It can be sweet or savory and used in desserts, sauces for grilled meats, or eaten out of the jar at 3 o'clock in the morning. Of course classic sandwiches—such as peanut butter and jelly; peanut butter and banana; and, for those who don't know, peanut butter and bacon—are among the greatest culinary creations ever.

Nutella is wildly popular in Europe, where it is usually spread on bread and eaten for breakfast with a good cup of coffee. Nutella was a

Health Tip

Low-fat products can be substituted for full-fat ingredients in desserts. However, when you're making a creamy dessert, never use all nonfat ingredients; the texture of the dessert will not be creamy and satisfying. Combine low-fat and nonfat substitutes for best results, or substitute nonfat ingredients for some of the full-fat products.

1940s invention of Pietro Ferrero, who owned a pastry business in Italy. Because cocoa was rationed and chocolate was hard to produce, he added hazelnuts to his chocolate, and that was it.

Crisp

Crisp foods shatter in the mouth, adding another dimension to a recipe. Food scientists differentiate crisp from crunchy in a specific way. Crisp foods break apart in a single stage, but crunchy foods have several stages of disintegration. The sounds you hear when you eat a food affect your opinion of it.

A piecrust is crisp, as is a shortbread cookie, a flaky cereal, or a fresh apple. Crisp food is easy to bite. There is very little resistance to pressure, and the food stays crisp until it's swallowed.

Techniques to make desserts crisp include frying, layering fat with flour, baking meringues, and using crisp fruits. There is little moisture in crisp foods, a characteristic they share with crunchy foods. Crisp foods can become soggy or tough if they absorb moisture, so proper storage of these foods is critical. Store them in airtight containers. You can bring some crisp foods back to the proper texture by baking them for a short time to drive out moisture.

Phyllo, filo, or fillo, is a paper-thin dough made of flour and water. It's difficult to make at home. Buy phyllo dough in any large supermarket in the frozen pastry aisle. Thaw it overnight in the refrigerator. To make phyllo crisp, layer the dough with melted butter and other ingredients such as ground nuts and sugar. Baking at a high temperature removes moisture from the dough, and the butter fries the dough,

making it crisp. Phyllo dough is used to make baklava, the classic Greek dessert layered with nuts and syrup, and turnovers, which are filled with cooked fruits.

Meringues can be soft and tender, chewy and melting, or crisp. Meringue starts out full of moisture. Crisp meringues, used as dessert shells or fat-free cookies, are baked at a low temperature until all the moisture is removed. This sets the foam into an airy and brittle web. Follow directions for making meringues carefully and store them tightly covered at room temperature.

Shortbread crispness is created when flour is layered with fat, either by cutting butter into dry ingredients or by folding dough. The dough must be high in fat or the flour in the gluten will develop, making the shortbread tough. Shortbread should be handled gently and baked at a relatively high temperature. It should also always be stored in a tightly closed, airtight container at room temperature.

BAKING EQUIPMENT

Like every other art, baking requires special equipment. You must measure ingredients accurately, have the equipment to mix and aerate the batters so they will rise in the oven, and use the correct equipment to hold the batters and doughs as they bake.

Measuring Equipment

Since baking is an exact science, tools for measuring ingredients are very important. All recipes are fairly tolerant—that is, the measurements can vary slightly, within a few teaspoons, but larger variations will cause the recipe to fail. You need proper measuring tools to bake desserts correctly. See Chapter 2 for more information about the measuring tools and equipment you need.

Baking recipes are not like cooking recipes. When you're cooking soups, creating casseroles, or making salads, you can substitute ingredients or change proportions with very little problem. Baking recipes are precisely calculated formulas that need a certain balance of solids, sugars, fats, liquids, and leavening ingredients. Making a change to this formula increases your chances of failure. It's possible to change recipes slightly but only after you understand how they work.

Pans and Sheets

Cake pans, saucepans, tart pans, and cookie sheets are all important in dessert recipes. As with other utensils and equipment, buy the best you can afford. Cheap pans (not inexpensive pans, but cheaply made) can warp in the oven's heat, which will deform the food and ruin your dessert. It's also important to have a good variety of this equipment so you can make different desserts.

Cookie sheets can be found in any grocery or hardware store. But if you venture into a baking supply store, you'll find a lot more choices. Cookie sheets can be made with aluminum and stainless steel and with nonstick coatings, and some are double-layer insulated sheets that stop cookies from burning on the bottom.

Tart pans and tube pans have removable bottoms for ease in serving. These pans have to be handled carefully, but they create excellent products. Pie pans are just one piece and can be found in glass, ceramic, and metal varieties.

Helpful Tip

Never measure ingredients over the large bowl that contains the rest of the ingredients. It's too easy to slip and add much more of an ingredient than you want. For instance, if you're adding one-half teaspoon of salt to a recipe and your hand slips, the finished product is going to be a lot saltier than you want.

Tart pans with removable bottoms and tube pans are unique utensils. You must handle them carefully and lift them only from the sides when they are filled with batter, or they can fall apart. These pans make it easy to serve tarts and large cakes. Remove the side from the tart pan and serve from the base. Run a knife around the tube pan and push the cake up, then remove the base.

Bundt pans are specially shaped pans with fluted sides. These pans must be carefully and thoroughly greased before you add batter. Spray them with nonstick baking spray containing flour, or grease them using a paper towel. Then sprinkle the greased surface with flour so the cake won't stick.

BASIC RULES OF BAKING

A baking recipe, such as that for a cake or a cookie, is not the same thing as a cooking recipe, such as a soup or a salad. Moist cakes, tender cookies, fluffy meringues, and soft sweet rolls need accurate measurement, specific combinations of ingredients, and baking in the right pans with calibrated ovens.

Baking recipes are precisely calculated formulas with a certain balance of solids, sugars, fats, liquids, and leavening ingredients. Making a change to this formula increases your chances of failure. It is possible to change recipes slightly but only after you understand how they work. If you add too much liquid, a cake will never set; too little and it will be dry. Add too much sugar and the recipe will be too sweet and may overbrown.

Make sure you measure all of the ingredients correctly and have them at room temperature so they combine easily. Don't microwave butter to soften, because parts of it almost always melt, which will change the structure of the baked goods. Let the butter stand at room temperature for an hour before using.

Usually fat and sugar are combined to begin the recipe. Then eggs and flavorings are added, and finally flour and liquid ingredients are stirred in, sometimes in a particular way. The last step in putting together a baked product is often folding in beaten egg whites. All of these steps—performed in the correct order—are critical to the recipe's success.

Helpful Tip

Do not use self-rising flour unless a recipe calls for it specifically. This type of flour, which is a mixture of flour, baking powder, and salt, is used primarily in the South. One teaspoon baking powder and ½ teaspoon salt is added per cup of flour. This is usually too much salt for most baking recipes. If you use this flour when the recipe doesn't call for it, the recipe will fail.

When baking a traditional cake or cookie, the creaming method is standard. Creaming is when butter is beaten with sugar. The sugar creates tiny holes in the fat, and these holes help form the structure of the finished product. This step is very important in creating a fine, even crumb, or texture, in the finished cake or cookie, so don't skimp on this process.

Eggs are added to baking recipes to provide protein for structure, along with moisture and flavor. For best results, have the eggs at room temperature by letting them stand at room temperature for 1 hour, or place them in a bowl of lukewarm water for 20 minutes. Break the eggs, one at a time, into a shallow saucer and add to the batter so you can make sure every egg is perfect. If some eggshell gets into the egg, use another piece of eggshell to remove it.

Adding liquid and dry ingredients alternately to a cake batter helps build the structure. Beat the batter well to full incorporate the dry ingredients and then the liquid into the butter-sugar-egg mixture before adding more ingredients. An electric mixer is the best appliance for this job, but you can beat it by hand.

Cakes

Cake batters are scientific formulas, so follow the recipe to the letter. Measure carefully, using calibrated measuring cups and spoons. Don't skimp on beating time when making cake batters. Even if you're using a mix (which is perfectly acceptable), the beating time is critical to aerate the batter and form the structure.

For layer cakes, an equal amount of batter in each pan is important to the finished product. Weigh the pans as you pour the batter for the most precise results. Place the pans on a scale and zero it. Then add batter. Or you can use a measuring cup.

Make sure your pans are well greased and floured. Baking spray containing flour does an excellent job. But you can grease the pan using unsalted butter or shortening and then spoon in a bit of flour and shake and tap the pan until the flour coats the fat. Tap out any excess flour and add the batter. Your cakes will come out of the pans perfectly.

Never let the cake stand in a pan longer than 5 to 10 minutes. If the cake sticks, you can hold it over a burner briefly to melt the cooking spray. Run a knife around the edge of the pan. Then gently shake the cake back and forth. Place a wire rack atop the cake and invert with the pan. Tap the pan bottom; the cake should drop out.

There are few types of cakes that deserve special mention.

Angel food cake, a classic low-fat dessert, is airy, sweet, and fluffy. Before there were mixers, making this cake required a lot of strength. The cake is made of egg whites, beaten with sugar until stiff. A bit of flour and flavoring is folded into the egg whites, then the batter is baked in a tube pan. Angel food cakes are cooled upside down so the proteins in the egg whites don't shrink as the cake cools.

Boston cream pie is a misnomer. This recipe isn't a true pie; it's a layered cake. It got its name because New England bakers made cakes in pie tins. This dessert was originally made in the 1800s at the Parker House Hotel. When properly made, this cake is an elegant and delicious dessert. Tender vanilla sponge cake is layered with a rich vanilla-scented cream, and a satiny chocolate glaze finishes the top.

Flourless chocolate cake is exactly what it sounds like. There is no flour in this recipe, which makes it a wonderful dessert for those who cannot eat gluten. The protein

in eggs forms the structure of this dessert. When the eggs are beaten with the other ingredients, the proteins unwind and form a web that holds everything else in suspension. The cake is very flat and dense, almost like a truffle.

Molten chocolate cake was invented by a chef in New York or one in France in the 1980s. It is very simple, very rich, and the perfect ending to a special meal. The little cakes have a liquid, or literally molten, chocolate center that oozes out when the cake is cut.

There are several ways to make this cake. In one, a truffle is made and put in the center of a thick cake batter. In another, the cake is simply underbaked slightly so the center is undercooked. Like a soufflé, this dessert should be served as soon as it is made. The key to success in this dessert is to not overbake the little cakes.

Cookies

The quintessential American after-school snack is a fresh-baked cookie and milk.

To make perfect cookies, measure the flour carefully. Most people scoop the measuring cup into the flour; this usually results in too much flour, which makes tough cookies. Lightly spoon the flour into the measuring cup, then level it off with the back of a knife. Also, don't overmix cookie dough, or the cookies will be tough.

Chilling cookie dough makes tender cookies, because the protein in the flour has a chance to relax and the flour abosorbs the liquid. In fact, your cookies will be very tender if you omit a couple of tablespoons of flour *and* chill the dough before baking. For the most even cookies, use a small ice-cream scoop to scoop out the dough. A 1-tablespoon scoop is a good size.

When making cut-out cookies, try to cut out as many cookies as possible from the first roll. When you reroll the scraps, gluten forms and the cookies will be tougher. It's easiest to just cut the dough into squares or rectangles. Use a wavy-edged pastry cutter for a pretty look or use a shaped cookie cutter. You can also press the dough into a rectangle on the cookie sheet and cut out the shapes about an inch apart from each other. Peel away the scraps and bake your perfectly formed cookies. For tender roll-out cookies, sprinkle your work surface with powdered sugar instead of flour. This adds a touch of sweetness and helps the cookies brown.

Watch cookies carefully in the oven. They should be just done when you remove them—barely set in the middle. Let the cookies stand on the baking sheet for 2 minutes, then remove with a spatula to a wire rack to cool completely.

A few unusual cookies deserve mention here.

Bar cookies are simply cookies that are made in a pan and cut into squares or other shapes when baked. Bar cookies are great time-savers. You make a dough and press or pour it into a large pan, bake the cookies, then cut them into squares. Bar cookies can be fudgy like brownies, cake-like, or layered.

The most famous bar cookies are brownies. To make cake-like brownies, which are less dense and thicker, just add an extra egg and bake the brownies for a few more minutes. Fudgy brownies are best a bit underbaked. For the best bar cookies, follow the recipe, measure the ingredients carefully, and be sure not to overbake the cookies. Grease the pan thoroughly and let the bar cookies cool completely before cutting.

Biscotti. If you've become addicted to expensive biscotti from your favorite coffee shop, make your own! They're much less expen-

Helpful Tip

There is a recipe that's easy for beginning bakers that doesn't depend on cold dough. For an easy piecrust made with the hot-water method, try this recipe: Combine ½ cup butter and 6 tablespoons solid shortening in a bowl. Combine ¼ cup water and 1 tablespoon milk in a saucepan; heat until steaming. Add this to the butter mixture and mix with a fork until fluffy. Add 2⅓ cups flour and ½ teaspoon salt; mix until a dough forms. Roll out between sheets of waxed paper.

sive, fun to make, and so much better. The word *biscotti* comes from the Latin for "twice cooked." The cookies are literally baked two times to create the crunchy and dry texture characteristic of the product.

Macaroons are simple cookies made of egg whites, sugar, and either coconut or ground almonds. These cookies are quite sweet, with a chewy and moist texture. Macaroons can also be light and crisp like a meringue. The cookies are a great choice for Passover, as they do not contain any leavening. Coconut macaroons are the most common. They are made from sweetened egg whites and flaked or shredded coconut. Almond macaroons are usually made with almond paste. They are slightly less sweet and chewier.

Pies

The best pies have a good piecrust. Piecrust takes a "light hand." That means you should handle the dough as little as possible. A standard piecrust recipe should be kept cold. Nest its bowl in a larger bowl filled with ice water (yes, water with ice cubes floating in it) to keep it cold. Chill the pie dough before rolling it out to allow the gluten to relax.

When rolling out piecrust, use a firm hand and roll evenly from the center to the edges. When you put the crust into the pan, don't pull or stretch it, or the crust will shrink in the heat of the oven. Add the filling as the recipe directs, then top the pie with the second crust (or add a streusel topping, which is easier), and bake as directed.

You can also top the pie with meringue. Beat egg whites with sugar until stiff. Spread the meringue on the crust and make sure it touches the edges of the crust so it doesn't shrink in the oven's heat. For a pretty look, use the back of a spoon to make peaks and swirls in the meringue.

You may want to put a cookie sheet underneath the pie, especially if you're making a fruit pie. The juices from the fruit will bubble up as the pie bakes, and these juices have a tendency to run over the edge of the pie and drip onto the oven floor, where they will burn.

DONENESS TESTS

Beautifully browned cakes, tender and delicate cookies, and crisp and flaky piecrusts all have one thing in common: They have been baked to perfect doneness.

Doneness tests in baking are important, because underdone cakes can fall, while overdone cakes are dry and tough. Underdone cookies will fall apart, while cookies baked too long can burn or become dry.

Use the baking and cooking times given in recipes as general guidelines. Start checking the food about 5 minutes before the earliest time. If the recipe isn't done, continue checking at 4- to 5-minute intervals until it is finished. Make sure to write down the final baking or cooking time on the recipe so that you can be more accurate next time.

Some recipes call for more than one doneness test to make absolutely sure the recipe is baked or cooked correctly. This helps ensure the accuracy of the recipe.

Toothpick test. Insert a clean toothpick into the cake or torte, at the center or near the center of the food. Pull it out. If the toothpick is dry and clean, the recipe is done. If moist or wet crumbs stick to the toothpick, keep baking, but remember that some recipes call for moist crumbs on the toothpick as the perfect doneness. Don't reuse the toothpick; use a clean one each time you perform the test.

Finger touch. Lightly touch your finger to the top of a cake or cookie. When it's done, the cake will spring back with no indentation. Don't press down too hard on the cake, or the test will not be accurate. If you do press down too hard, and the cake is not done, return it to the oven

immediately. The part where you pressed your finger might not expand in the oven, even when the cake is properly baked. Just fill with frosting.

Internal temperature. Any recipe that contains raw eggs should be cooked to an internal temperature of at least 160°F for food safety reasons. Custards, puddings, and cheesecakes should reach this temperature. Cakes are finished when their internal temperature reaches 200°F. All foods will continue cooking slightly after they are removed from the oven. This is known as residual cooking, which stops after a few minutes out of the oven.

Observation test. The doneness test for brownies, especially those that are fudgy or include additional ingredients like chocolate chips, is to observe a shiny, dry crust.

Cakes are done when they are evenly golden brown and the sides pull away from the pan. Cookies are done when they are light golden brown. The centers of the cookies should still be moist. Cheesecakes will look set, with golden edges, but the center will jiggle slightly when the cake is moved.

TYPES OF DESSERT

There are many different types of desserts beyond cakes, cookies, and pies. These recipes come from different ethnic cuisines, but they have one thing in common: They're all delicious. These desserts are not difficult to make once you understand the basic rules of the kitchen. Follow the recipe carefully, look up any words or terms you don't understand, and remember to enjoy the process. Dessert is one thing that makes life worthwhile.

Bananas Foster first appeared in Brennan's Restaurant in New Orleans in the 1950s. Bananas were imported into the United States through the port of New Orleans, and the restaurant wanted to feature them in a new dessert. This simple, yet elegant dish is made of sliced bananas sautéed in a butter-and-sugar mixture, flavored with spices, and sometimes flamed before being spooned over ice cream.

Betty is a simple fruit dessert topped with a sweetened and buttered bread mixture. The dessert is sometimes made with applesauce instead of the whole fruit and sometimes with bread crumbs instead of cubed bread. This is an economical dessert, designed to use up stale bread. You can use any type of bread for the topping, but cinnamon swirl or raisin bread makes the dessert a bit more special.

Bread pudding is the ultimate comfort food. It was originally developed as a way to use leftover bread in more frugal times. But it's been upgraded to an elegant dessert with the addition of ingredients like chocolate, dried fruits, and sauces. Use any type of bread in this recipe, except for very soft, fluffy processed bread. The bread should have some type of texture so it stands up to the creamy custard it bakes in.

The bread slices should be dry to absorb some of the moisture from the custard. Pour the custard slowly over the bread. Push the bread down into the custard mixture as it stands for a few minutes, then bake it. The top should be crusty and nicely browned when the pudding is done, which makes for a wonderful texture contrast.

Clafouti is a French dessert made with cherries baked in a sweetened and spiced cake batter. The batter is poured over the cherries, and the whole thing is baked until the cake has a nice golden crust and the cherries are softened and sweet. This dessert is traditionally served warm out of the oven, with heavy cream or ice cream.

Cobblers are deep-dish pies with a cake topping on a fruit filling. Juicy fruits like peaches, pears, and berries provide a sauce to accompany the cake. Cobblers were originally invented by settlers and farmers as a way to use fruits and turn them into a hearty and filling dish. Other names for this classic American dish include buckle, slump, grunt, and pandowdy.

Crème brûlée is a grown-up pudding, flavored with vanilla bean and topped with a crisp, glassy crust of burnt sugar. The best crème brûlée is silky smooth, with a deep and rich vanilla flavor. The dessert is heavy with cream and egg yolks, yet it should melt on your tongue. The crisp and brittle sugar coating is made by melting brown or granulated sugar with a small propane torch or by placing the chilled custard under the broiler until browned.

Crepes are simply very thin pancakes. They have a higher liquid-to-flour proportion than typical breakfast pancakes, so the batter spreads out more in the pan.

The trick to crepes is getting the batter to evenly coat the pan as soon as it's added. The batter should be the consistency of heavy cream. Add to the pan and swirl and twist the pan to coat. Let the crepes cook until you can move them with a spatula. Then flip and cook for a minute on the other side. Cool the crepes on kitchen towels. Don't stack them until they're cool, or they'll stick together and you'll never get them apart! Fill crepes with everything from ice cream to pudding to sautéed fruits.

Crisps are a combination of baked fruits and streusel topping made with flour, oatmeal, butter, and brown sugar. Granola can be used as a shortcut. Crisps can be made with almost any fruit that tastes good baked. Pear crisp, peach crisp, and blueberry crisp are some good options.

Custard is the original comfort food. It's a simple combination of sugar, eggs, milk, and vanilla mixed and baked until silky smooth and set. Baked custards are thicker and slightly denser than custards and puddings cooked on the stove top or in the microwave oven. Most custards are baked in a water bath. The water helps shield the custard from the heat of the oven so the outside edges don't overcook before the center is set.

Flan is a custard baked on top of melted sugar. The melted sugar creates a hard shell on the baking dish and softens as the custard bakes to make a caramel sauce. This sauce then spills down over the flan when it is unmolded.

The combination of caramel, with its complex flavors, and the silky custard is really spectacular. Melting sugar isn't difficult, but it does take some patience and constant

surveillance. It will seem at first like the sugar will never melt, but it will start softening around the edges. When this happens, stop stirring and just swirl the pan occasionally. Then the edges liquefy, and the sugar gradually develops a deep brown color. When it is completely liquid, quickly pour it into the custard cups.

This alchemy happens because the liquid from the custard reacts with the melted sugar in the heat of the oven, gradually softening it. This sauce also makes it easier to unmold the flan after baking.

Floating island is made of fluffy meringues poached in water until they set, served in a velvety custard, and drizzled with a caramel sauce. The soft meringues look like islands floating in the custard, hence the name. This dessert originated in France, Poland, or another part of southeastern Europe.

To poach the meringues correctly, keep the water at just below a simmer. If the water boils, the meringues will become tough. Regulate the heat carefully. When you remove the meringues from the water, let the slotted spoon rest briefly on a towel to remove excess moisture.

Fondue for dessert is a relatively new phenomenon. It started appearing in restaurants and cookbooks in the 1960s. It quickly caught on and is now considered a classic chocolate dessert. The rich and silky chocolate mixture is easy to make as long as you follow a few rules. Melt the chocolate over low heat, stirring constantly while it melts. Do not use Sterno to keep the fondue mixture hot while serving. A small slow cooker turned to the warm setting is the perfect way to serve this dessert. Use your imagination and have fun with the dippers. You can use any cookie, fresh fruit, or cake cut into squares. For a larger party or a dessert buffet, make several different flavors of fondue and offer lots of dippers.

Fool is an old-fashioned word for an old-fashioned dessert. Traditionally fools were English. They first appeared in the 1500s, made with pureed fruit folded into whipped cream. They can be made with any fruit, but gooseberries were originally used. The word may have been derived from the French word *fouler,* which means "to crush."

Grilled fruit is an easy and elegant dessert. The fruits that grill best include apples, pears, pineapple, peaches, nectarines, strawberries, and oranges. Very delicate berries like raspberries, blueberries, or blackberries don't take well to the high heat of the grill. Bamboo skewers, soaked in cold water for 30 minutes, are the best choice for this easy dessert. A bit of sugar adds a caramelized crunchy crust.

Poached fruit has been a staple of French cooking for at least 200 years. There are countless recipes with all manner of flavorings added to the poaching liquid. The common ingredient is always sugar, which adds flavor. Look for firm, almost ripe fruit to poach, as very ripe fruit will fall apart when cooked.

Fruit salad is a refreshing and healthy choice for a quick and easy dessert. You can top it with a sweet sauce if you'd like, or you can just drizzle it with honey and add fresh herbs for an exotic taste. Herbs are delicious with fruit salads. Mint is the obvious choice, but thyme and basil bring out the sweetness of the fruits. For dessert, you want the most luscious fruits you can find. Peaches, nectarines, strawberries, blueberries, and raspberries are the obvious choices. During the winter, make a delicious dessert salad from apples, pears, and canned exotic fruits like mangoes or kumquats. For a finishing touch, use ice-cream toppings or just a dollop of whipped cream.

Icebox desserts are old-fashioned desserts that are very easy to make and impressive and elegant to serve. To make one, you need plain, crisp chocolate wafers or cookies, such as the Famous Wafers brand. The cookies are layered with sweetened whipped cream, then the whole thing is refrigerated overnight. The cookies gradually soften in the whipped cream to create a cake-like texture.

When serving this dessert, cut 1-inch-thick slices on the diagonal. That way the cookies will all be sliced, and they will create a pattern in the whipped cream mixture reminiscent of a zebra stripe.

Ice cream comes in several different types. All are delicious and easy to make if you have an ice-cream freezer. These are the different types of ice cream:

Gelato, a dessert from Italy, is richer than ice cream because it contains less air. The gelato is churned at a slower pace in special machines. Technically, gelato has less fat than American ice cream, but it tastes richer because it's denser.

Ice cream is made from a custard base with the addition of heavy cream and sometimes eggs. In fact, the best ice cream is made of just three ingredients: cream, sugar, and flavoring, usually the seeds from a vanilla bean.

Sherbet is an ice made with milk or other dairy products. Sherbet comes in almost as many flavors as sorbet. The terms *sherbet* and *sorbet* are often used interchangeably, even though they are not technically the same thing.

Sorbet is an ice made of fruit-flavored liquid or fruit juice that's stirred while freezing to add air. Making your own sorbet is easy with an ice-cream maker.

If you don't have an ice-cream maker, you can still make these treats. Place the cold sorbet, sherbet, or ice-cream mixture in a freezer container or a baking pan. Place in the freezer. When it begins to freeze, whisk the mixture with a fork. When the mixture is quite stiff, break it up, put it into a blender, and blend it until smooth. Return the ice cream to the freezer. When the mixture is frozen, place it in a plastic container and keep it frozen until ready to serve.

Ice cream on a stick is a delicious treat that kids love. Freeze your favorite smoothie for tasty smoothie pops. You'll need a freezer pop tray for this treat. If you don't have one, pour the smoothie mixture into a regular ice-cube tray for mini smoothie pops.

Meringue is made with egg whites beaten with sugar until very stiff, then formed and baked in the oven until they are dry. It can be used as a piecrust for those who need to avoid gluten, or it can be made as cookies or tartlets.

Meringue tarts can be baked on cookie sheets or in individual tartlet pans. They bake for a long time in low heat. Meringues cookies are baked on a flat cookie sheet to make small, individual cookies. They can be spooned onto the sheet or piped to make fancy shapes. Meringue pie shells are spooned into a traditional pie pan, then formed to create a shell.

For the best meringue, beat the egg white mixture until it stands in very stiff peaks and the sugar is dissolved. Rub a bit of the meringue between your fingers. If you feel any grains of sugar, keep beating. To make the crust even more interesting, fold ¼ cup ground nuts into the stiff egg whites. Another good addition is fresh lemon or orange zest.

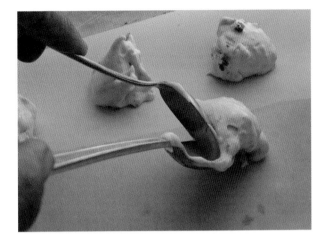

For the best meringue, the eggs must be room temperature. The bowl must be immaculately clean, with no drops of egg yolk. Granulated sugar is used for best results; superfine sugar makes a glossy, high-volume meringue. Add a pinch of cream of tartar to aid whipping. Once beating begins, do not stop until the process finishes. A mixer will make this process easier.

Mousse is a fancy chocolate pudding. The mixture is light and airy because heavy cream—and sometimes meringue—is folded into the creamy chocolate mixture. If a recipe uses eggs, use pasteurized eggs for food safety. The heavy cream provides the fat and creamy mouthfeel.

Parfaits are an elegant dessert. They are very easy to make if you keep just a few ingredients on hand. All you need is something fluffy, something sweet, and something for texture such as fruit, chopped candy, cookies, or cake. Fluffy ingredients include silken tofu, yogurt, whipped topping, puddings, whipped cream, ice cream, and flavored gelatins. Pantry items for making parfaits include fruit preserves, cookie crumbs, granola, canned fruit, dried fruits, and pudding mixes. To make the prettiest parfaits, use tall, stemmed goblets or invest in some attractive parfait glasses. Small, long-handled spoons make eating this fresh dessert fun.

Pavlova, originally called "pavlova cake," was named after the famous Russian ballerina Anna Pavlova. Legend has it that the dessert was created in her honor when she toured Australia or New Zealand in the early 1900s. This dessert is beautiful, with a fluffy marshmallow-like meringue topped with whipped cream and fresh fruit. You can use any single fruit or any combination you'd like. This dessert must be made ahead of time, so the whipped cream mixture can help soften the meringue a bit and the fruit mixture can flavor the cream. Vinegar

Helpful Tip

Meringue tarts are spectacular. But if you live in a humid climate, make the crust at the last minute. Humidity in the air will soak into the meringue, making it gummy.

and cornstarch are added to the meringue in this recipe. These ingredients change the pH of the mixture so the inside of the meringue stays soft.

Pots de crème—pronounced *po deh kremm*— is an elegant and rich French dessert that is the perfect finish to a fancy meal. It is served in small quantities because it is so rich. It is served with small spoons too, for the complete elegant experience. The name *pots de crème* refers to the rich chocolate custard as well as to the small cups that hold it. Most pots de crème are flavored with vanilla or chocolate. This custard is thicker and denser than regular baked custards or flans. Don't substitute light cream or artificial products for the heavy cream and egg yolks, or the recipe will not work.

Rice pudding is another classic comfort food. It should be creamy and thick, with very tender rice. To create the most tender pudding, the rice is cooked twice. First it's cooked in water to rehydrate it until it is tender, then it is cooked with cream, sugar, egg, and flavorings. This double-cooking process extracts more starch from the rice, making the pudding creamy and thick.

Semifreddo sounds like an exotic dessert, but it is very simple and easy to make. This is a very rich dessert, made with an egg custard combined with meringue and whipped cream. Semifreddo is a molded dessert similar to ice cream, but you don't need an ice-cream maker. The fat content keeps the mixture soft and creamy even when frozen in an ordinary freezer. The meringue and whipped cream add air, replicating the ice-cream mixer's aeration.

Shortcakes are wonderful desserts made with the best berries of summer. Flaky shortbread is split and layered with whipped cream and slightly sweetened sliced strawberries. Shortcake is called short because the pastry is high in fat. It makes the pastry flaky and crumbly. On a side note, this is why hydrogenated fats are called shortening.

You can make strawberry shortcake with everything from pound cake to leftover biscuits from breakfast. But if you make it yourself, remember that it's important that the butter is cold. When the pastry bakes, the butter melts and creates a flaky, tender shortcake texture.

Soufflés can strike fear into the hearts of the most accomplished cook or baker. But these ethereal concoctions are fairly foolproof when you understand the science. Soufflés rise because the air trapped in egg-white protein bubbles expands in the oven heat, so a well-whipped meringue makes it rise. A sturdy sauce adds flavor.

When you bake a soufflé, put it directly into the oven after you fold the egg whites into the base. Keep the oven door closed so the temperature remains constant. And don't bang the oven door or thump the finished soufflé down on the table. Finally, serve the soufflé immediately from the oven; it won't wait for guests! It does deflate easily, and will last only about 5 to 7 minutes after it's removed from the oven. Still, even if it does fall, it will taste divine!

Summer pudding is a classic English dessert made of bread soaked in berry juice, then pressed into a bowl and refrigerated until set. Even though the generic English word for *dessert* is pudding, this recipe isn't a pudding in the American sense of the word. Summer pudding holds together because the fruit and bread meld into a sweet and tart dessert with a texture somewhat like, well, pudding.

Trifle is the name of a dessert in England, and it's called tiramisu in Italy. Whatever you call it, this dessert is delicious. It was invented to use up leftover cake. A light angel food cake (or dense pound cake) is layered with fresh fruit and a fluffy, creamy mixture, then chilled. The cake soaks up the juices from the fruit, and the whole thing blends together into a wonderful fresh dessert. The recipe traditionally uses liqueur, but you can omit it if children are eating the dessert. Substitute orange juice for Grand Marnier or raspberry juice for framboise.

Use a glass bowl to display this beautiful dessert. Since it must be made ahead of time, it's the perfect choice for entertaining. Kiwi fruits, raspberries, blueberries, and peaches can all be used in this dessert. Garnish with mint just before serving.

Tiramisu is the Italian version of English trifle. The ingredients are a bit different, but the end result is similar. The Italian version uses ladyfingers, a soft cake-like cookie, along with mascarpone cheese and espresso.

Frostings

Broiled frosting is one of the easiest finishes for a cake, aside from topping a cake with sifted powdered sugar or serving it plain. A mixture of butter, sugar, cream, and nuts or coconut is spread onto a baked cake, then broiled until the mixture bubbles. This cooks the mixture and melts the sugar, making a moist, creamy, and flavorful topping. This frosting was developed in the 1950s, when cooking and baking were changing dramatically. Cake mixes were introduced to homemakers, and everyone was looking for shortcuts. The only trick to broiled frosting is to watch it carefully when it's under the broiler. The frosting can go from perfectly cooked to burned in seconds.

Buttercream frosting is the classic frosting recipe. It's just a mixture of butter, sugar, and cream, flavored with a bit of salt and vanilla. The key to making the best buttercream is to beat it long enough. Even powdered sugar, as fine and powdery as it is, needs to dissolve in the frosting for it to be fluffy and creamy. This takes time. The butter must be thoroughly softened, but not melted, for best results. Let the butter stand at room temperature for 2 to 3 hours before starting the frosting.

Seven-minute frosting is a cooked meringue with a consistency similar to marshmallow crème, but it's much fluffier and less sticky. It's made of egg whites, sugar, and water, beaten in a double boiler over boiling water. The egg whites cook as they turn into a meringue, which makes the frosting stable enough to frost a cake. This frosting doesn't last long. In a day or two (sooner if the weather is very warm or humid), the cake will begin to absorb the frosting. So make this recipe only when you're sure the cake is going to be devoured the same day it's made.

Conversion Chart

Metric U.S. Approximate Equivalents

LIQUID INGREDIENTS

METRIC	U.S. MEASURES	METRIC	U.S. MEASURES
1.23 ML	¼ TSP.	29.57 ML	2 TBSP.
2.36 ML	½ TSP.	44.36 ML	3 TBSP.
3.70 ML	¾ TSP.	59.15 ML	¼ CUP
4.93 ML	1 TSP.	118.30 ML	½ CUP
6.16 ML	1¼ TSP.	236.59 ML	1 CUP
7.39 ML	1½ TSP.	473.18 ML	2 CUPS OR 1 PT.
8.63 ML	1¾ TSP.	709.77 ML	3 CUPS
9.86 ML	2 TSP.	946.36 ML	4 CUPS OR 1 QT.
14.79 ML 1 TBSP.	3.79 L 4 QTS. OR 1 GAL.		

DRY INGREDIENTS

METRIC	U.S. MEASURES	METRIC	U.S. MEASURES
2 (1.8) G	¹⁄₁₆ OZ.	80 G	2⅘ OZ.
3½ (3.5) G	⅛ OZ.	85 (84.9) G	3 OZ.
7 (7.1) G	¼ OZ.	100 G	3½ OZ.
15 (14.2) G	½ OZ.	115 (113.2) G	4 OZ.
21 (21.3) G	¾ OZ.	125 G	4½ OZ.
25 G	⅞ OZ.	150 G	5¼ OZ.
30 (28.3) G	1 OZ.	250 G	8⅞ OZ.
50 G	1¾ OZ.	454 G 1 LB.	16 OZ.
60 (56.6) G	2 OZ.	500 G 1 LIVRE	17⅗ OZ.

Glossary

Acidulated water: Water that has some lemon juice or vinegar (acid) added to it in order to use as a batch to keep foods such as cut apples from browning.

Aioli: A garlic mayonnaise made in France's Provence region, used as a condiment or sauce.

Al dente: An Italian phrase meaning "to the tooth" describes doneness of pasta.

Altitude: Height above sea level.

Amandine: Prepared or cooked with almonds.

Bake: To heat food rapidly, using dry heat, as in an oven.

Baking powder: A leavening agent used in baked goods, made of baking soda and an acid such as cream of tartar.

Baking soda: A leavening agent used to make baked goods rise; bicarbonate of soda.

Basmati: A long-grained Indian rice that is hugely popular. It is readily available in white or brown and imparts a fragrant aroma with light, fluffy texture when cooked.

Baste: To brush cooking food with a liquid, keep it moist as it roasts or bakes.

Beat: Manipulating food with a spoon, mixer, or whisk to combine.

Béchamel: A béchamel sauce is just a white sauce made with chicken broth instead of, or in addition to, milk or cream.

Bisque: A soup thickened with cream and sometimes egg, pureed to velvety smoothness.

Blanch: To briefly cook food, primarily vegetables or fruits, to remove skin or fix color.

Blend: To mix ingredients together thoroughly, either by hand or using a mixer.

Blind bake: To bake a piecrust without a filling. The crust is filled with pie weights or dried beans to keep its shape and prevent puffing while in the oven.

Braise: To cook for a long period in liquid to tenderize and soften.

Bread: To coat food with crumbs or crushed crackers, before baking or frying.

Brine: A mixture of salt, sugar, and water used to season chicken and turkey before cooking.

Brining: Soaking food in a brine, or salt solution.

Broil: To cook food close to the heat source, quickly.

Broth: Liquid extracted from meats and vegetables, used as the basis for most soups.

Brown: Cooking step that caramelizes food and adds color and flavor before cooking.

Butterflying: To cut a piece of meat in half, then spread it open to increase surface area.

Caper: The small pickled unopened flower bud of a Mediterranean bush. Used mostly in sauces and condiments.

Caramelize: A chemical reaction catalyzed by heat that combines sugars and proteins to form complex flavors and colors in grilled food.

Charcoal: Real charcoal is made by burning solid wood in a controlled atmosphere without carbon; it becomes almost pure carbon.

Chiffonade: Translates from French into "made of rags"; a way to finely cut food (mostly leaves such as basil) into very fine strands.

Chill: Refrigerate a mixture or place it in an ice-water bath to rapidly cool it.

Chimney starter: A metal container with a handle that is used to start briquettes or lump charcoal before adding it to the grill pan.

Chop: To cut food into small pieces, using a chef's knife or a food processor.

Chowder: A soup thick with vegetables and meats, usually seafood, thickened with cream and cheese.

Coat: To cover food in another ingredient, as to coat chicken breasts with bread crumbs.

Cream: To mix together a fat and sugar, usually the first step in baking. It is also a dairy product with a high amount of fat. Heavy cream usually has 40 percent fat content.

Cut in: A process of working fat such as butter or shortening into flour and other dry ingredients to produce a fine mixture.

Cutlet: A thin cut of chicken or turkey, either pounded thin or cut very thin to cook quickly.

Deep-fry: To cook quickly in a large quantity of oil heated to at least 350°F, in a deep pot or deep-fryer, as opposed to shallow-frying, in which the food is fried in a few inches of hot oil in a skillet or frying pan.

Deglaze: Adding a liquid to a pan used to sauté meats; this removes drippings and brown bits to create a sauce.

Devein: The process of removing the "vein," which is really the digestive tract of shrimp.

Dice: To cut food into small, even portions, usually about ¼-inch square, smaller than cubes.

Direct grilling: To cook food directly over a heat source, whether a burner, coals, or burning wood.

Divan: Any recipe named *divan* means cooked with broccoli in a creamy béchamel sauce.

Dock: To mark a piecrust or pastry with a docking tool or a fork to prevent puffing.

Dry rub: Spices and herbs rubbed into meats or vegetables to marinate and add flavor.

Enzymes: Proteins in foods that control complex biochemical processes; they can be inactivated by heat, such as by blanching.

Extract: Concentrated flavorings derived from foods usually by distillation or evaporation. Extracts are often used in baking.

Fiber (dietary): Also referred to as roughage, which comes from plants and legumes and aids in digestion.

Flake: To break into small pieces; canned meats are usually flaked.

Fold: Combining two soft or liquid mixtures together, using an over-and-under method of mixing.

Fond: The brown bits and fat left behind in a pan after meat or vegetables have been seared, panfried, or sautéed.

Frittata: An open-faced omelet with other ingredients, such as meat or vegetables, cooked first in a skillet and then finished under the broiler.

Fry: Submerge food into hot oil to cook for a crunchy exterior texture and moist interior.

Ganache: A mixture of chocolate and cream, melted together over low heat and used to coat baked goods. It's also used as frosting and as the base for chocolate truffles.

Garnish: A decorative yet edible addition to a finished dish.

Gazpacho: A cold soup, usually made of tomatoes, that is pureed without cooking.

Gluten: The main protein in flour, produced in the presence of water. Gluten consists of two protein molecules, glutenin and gliadin.

Grate: A grater or microplane is used to quickly cut food or peel into small even pieces.

Gratin: A casserole dish with a topping of bread crumbs, grated cheese, and dots of butter, broiled or baked until light brown.

Grill: To cook over coals or charcoal, or over high heat.

Grill pan: A skillet with ridges, used on the stove top to simulate grilling.

Herbs: The fragrant parts of plants used in cooking.

Indirect grilling: To cook food over an area on the grill where there are no coals, usually over a drip pan.

Induction cooking: A method of transferring heat by electromagnetic energy. It is a relatively new cooking method.

Instant-read thermometer: Slim tool with a digital read or clock face that will tell you more-or-less instantly the temperature of the food.

Julienne: To cut into thin strips, as in julienned carrots.

Jus: Usually refers to the juices derived from roasting meats.

Knead: To work dough by mixing, stretching, pressing, and pulling it.

Kosher salt: The coarse, flaky salt preferred by chefs and cooking professionals. It's called "kosher" because its flat surface is ideal for koshering (drawing blood from) meat. Its crystals don't melt right away when sprinkled on food (unlike table salt), making it less likely that you will oversalt your food.

Low sodium: Any food that has 150 milligrams or less of sodium per serving.

Mandoline: A kitchen utensil that slices food when it is slid over a series of blades. It's generally operated by hand.

Marinade: A seasoned liquid into which a meat or vegetable is placed for a specific period of time to flavor it. To *marinate* is to undergo this process.

Marinate: To soak meats or vegetables in a mixture of an acid and oil to add flavor and tenderize.

Melt: To turn a solid into a liquid by the addition of heat.

Mezzaluna: A chopping tool that has a curved blade attached to two handles. You hold onto the handles and rock the blade over the food.

Microplane grater: A perforated steel tool for grating and grinding ingredients, such as nutmeg seeds and gingerroot, or for zesting citrus fruit.

Microwave: An appliance that cooks food through electromagnetic waves, which causes molecules to vibrate, creating heat.

Mince: To cut a food or herb into very small and even pieces, about ⅛-inch square.

Mop: Both a thin mixture placed on food as it is grilling and a tool like a floor mop, used to apply marinades and glazes.

Nonreactive cookware: Pots and pans whose surfaces do not react with the strong acids in certain foods, like tomatoes and wine. Stainless steel and enamel-coated cast iron are both nonreactive.

Olive oil: The oil derived from pressing ripe olives and separating the oil from the liquid. The first cold pressing is referred to as extra virgin.

Pan drippings: The juices and fat left in a pan after meats have been roasted; also called fond. They are used to make gravies.

Panfry: To cook quickly in a shallow pan in a small amount of fat over relatively high heat.

Peel: To remove the skin of a fruit or vegetable. As a noun, the peel is the skin of a fruit or vegetable.

Poach: To cook at a temperature just below a simmer.

Preheat: To heat up an oven to a predetermined temperature before cooking.

Quadrillage: A way of placing food on the grill to create crosshatch marks.

Reduce: To boil down a liquid, reducing it in quantity and concentrating its taste, as for sauces.

Roux: A cooked mixture of butter or oil and flour, whisked into a paste and used as a base for thickening sauces.

Rub: A mixture of dry ingredients, usually spices, pepper, and salt, that is rubbed onto food to season before grilling.

Santoku knife: A knife from Japanese kitchens that looks like a chef's knife, but it has small divots pressed into the blade near the cutting edge. These divots, called *kullens,* hold juices as you cut, which reduces the drag on the food so cutting is easier.

Sauté: To cook a food briefly in oil over medium-high heat, while stirring it so it cooks evenly. The terms comes from the French word *sauter*, meaning "to jump."

Scallop: A layered dish, usually of potatoes or another vegetable, baked in a white sauce, often with cheese and bread crumbs.

Sear: To brown the surface of a food over high heat, usually with little oil or fat so a visible sear is achieved. This cooking technique is often used to seal in juices when cooking meat.

Seasoning: To add herbs, spices, citrus juices and zest, and peppers to food to increase flavor.

Seize: When chocolate is overheated or when water is accidentally added to melted chocolate, it can become thick and grainy—that is, seize.

Shred: To use a grater, mandoline, or food processor to create small strips of food.

Silicon baking mat: A great way to avoid greasing and cleaning baking sheets when baking cookies, biscuits, or breads. This nonstick and reusable mat is made of oven-safe silicon and lasts virtually forever. One brand of silicon baking mats is Silpat.

Simmer: A state of liquid cooking, where the liquid is just below a boil.

Skewer: As a noun, a skewer is a sharp metal or wooden stick threaded with food. As a verb, it means to place food on a skewer to make kabobs.

Skim: To remove the foamy film floating on the surface of a heated liquid with a spoon or ladle. Soups and sauces are often skimmed.

Slow cooker: An appliance that cooks food by surrounding it with low, steady heat.

Smoke point: The stage at which heated fat begins to emit smoke and acrid odors and impart an unpleasant flavor to foods. The higher its smoke point, the better suited a fat is for frying.

Soufflé: A light, fluffy baked dish made with egg yolks and beaten egg whites combined with various other ingredients and served as a main dish or dessert.

Soup: A mixture of solids and liquids, served hot or cold, as a main dish or part of a multi-course meal.

Spices: The edible dried fruits, bark, and seeds of plants, used to add flavor to food.

Steam: To cook food by immersing it in steam. The food is set over boiling liquid.

Stir-fry: To quickly cook food by manipulating it with a spoon or spatula in a wok or pan over high heat.

Tagine: A two-part casserole dish used in North African cooking, most commonly in Morocco, consisting of a bottom plate and a removable conical-shaped lid.

Tempering: To bring two mixtures of different temperatures closer together in temperature so they can be combined easily with no lumps or separation.

Timbale: A custardlike dish of eggs, cheese, chicken, fish, or vegetables baked in a drum-shaped pastry mold of the same name.

Toss: To combine food using two spoons or a spoon and a fork until mixed.

Vegan: A person who eats no animal foods or products made from animals. Some vegans will not even eat honey, as it is produced by bees.

Verjuice: An acidic, sour liquid made from unripened grapes and/or other fruits. It is mostly used in salad dressings.

Whisk: Both a tool, which is made of loops of steel, and a method, which combines food until smooth.

Zest: The colored part of the skin of citrus fruit used to add flavor to food. Zesting is the action used to remove the skin of citrus fruit.

Photo Credits

Emily Heller: p. 92, p. 95, p. 104 (bottom), p. 106, p. 108 (top), p. 132, p. 144 (top), p. 161, p. 164 (top), p. 168, p. 261 (top, bottom); *Francisco Ramírez:* p. 164 (bottom), p. 232, p. 240 (top), p. 260 (bottom); *Debi Harbin:* p. 26, p. 30, p. 36, p. 43, p. 44, p. 49, p. 50, p. 52, p. 53 (top, bottom), p. 55, p. 94, p. 97, p. 123, p. 197, p. 201, p. 206 (all), p. 208 (top, bottom), p. 209 (top, bottom), p. 210, p. 211, p. 212 (top, bottom), p. 213 (top, bottom), p. 214, p. 215, p. 217 (top, bottom), p. 220 (all), p. 221, p. 222, p. 230 (bottom), p. 236, p. 245, p. 263, p. 264 (top, bottom), p. 267 (top, bottom), p. 268 (top, bottom), p. 269 (top, bottom), p. 270, p. 272, p. 273, p. 274, p. 275 (top, bottom), p. 277 (top, bottom), p. 278 (top, bottom); *Christopher Shane:* p. 87 (top), p. 88, p. 115 (bottom), p. 120, p. 190, p. 191, p. 192 (top, bottom), p. 202 (top, bottom), p. 203, p. 252 (top), p. 253, p. 255; *Liesa Cole:* p. 10, p. 25 (top, bottom), p. 35, p. 47, p. 48, p. 71, p. 108 (bottom), p. 115 (top), p. 117, p. 124 (center), p. 126, p. 159, p. 162, p. 167, p. 181 (bottom), p. 183 (center, bottom), p. 198, p. 230 (top), p. 237, p. 239, p. 261 (center), p. 262 (bottom); *Jackie Alpers:* p. 74, p. 104 (top), p. 107, p. 109, p. 110, p. 136 (top), p. 156, p. 160, p. 173, p. 182 (top, bottom), p. 226, p. 227, p. 231, p. 240 (bottom), p. 241, p. 254 (bottom), p. 260 (top), p. 292 (bottom); *Dana Devine O'Malley:* p. 177, p. 179 (top, bottom), p. 238, p. 250, p. 252 (bottom), p. 254 (top); *Peter Ardito and Susan Byrnes:* p. 13, p. 18, p. 45, p. 99, p. 111, p. 119 (bottom), p. 124 (top), p. 127, p. 128, p. 129, p. 131, p. 133, p. 136 (bottom), p. 137, p. 140, p. 143, p. 144 (bottom), p. 145 (top, bottom), p. 147, p. 148, p. 150, p. 151 (top, bottom), p. 152, p. 153, p. 155, p. 163, p. 185 (top, bottom); *Viktor Budnik:* p. 14, p. 16, p. 22, p. 23 (top, bottom), p. 29, p. 31 (top), p. 32, p. 33 (top, bottom), p. 34, p. 46, p. 58, p. 63, p. 65, p. 80, p. 87 (bottom), p. 90, p. 91, p. 116, p. 119 (top), p. 121, p. 124 (bottom), p. 157, p. 158, p. 165, p. 169, p. 175, p. 181 (top), p. 183 (top), p. 248 (top, bottom), p. 256 (top, bottom), p. 257, p. 262 (top, center), p. 280, p. 281 (top, bottom), p. 283, p. 284 (top, bottom), p. 285, p. 286, p. 288, p. 289, p. 290, p. 291 (top, bottom), p. 292 (top), p. 293 (top, bottom), p. 294 (top, bottom), p. 295 (top, bottom), p. 296, p. 299 (top, bottom), p. 300 (top, bottom), p. 301 (top, bottom), p. 302

Extra:

P. 8 (top): Courtesy of Fisher Paykel; p. 8 (bottom): Courtesy of www.brokstone.com; p. 15: Bret Kerr/Globe Pequot Press; p. 27: Courtesy of Polder; p. 31 (bottom): Courtesy of Oneida, Ltd, photo by James Demarest; p. 37: jocicalek/shutterstock

Index

barley, 120

bulgur (cracked wheat), 120–21

oats, 121

polenta, 121

quinoa, 122

to stock, 7

wheat berries, 122

whole, 7, 119

See also breads; pasta; rice

grapefruit, 160

grapes, 66, 81, 160

graters and knives, 30–32

gravy, 253

green onions, 138

greens, leafy, 138–39

grilling indoors, 56–57

grilling outdoors, 48–56

adding flavor, 53–54

building fire, 50–52

charcoal grills, 50–51

cleaning grill, 52

common foods, 54–56, 153, 168, 196, 221

controlling temperature, 52–53

direct grilling, 53

gas grills, 52

grill-frying and grill-roasting, 48–49

indirect grilling, 53

marinades, rubs and, 88

organizing space for, 49

packets, 55–56

reducing carcinogens, 88

safety, 49–50

tools, 49–50

wood chips and smoking, 53–54

grills, 36–37, 50–52

grinders, 36

grocery shopping, 17–20

children and, 20

coupons for, 19

efficiency tips, 19–20

list for, 8, 19

store options, 18–19

grouper, 189

Gruyère cheese, 178

gumbos, 268

H

halibut, 190

ham bone, 247

hams, 243

handful, defined, 26

handling food, 71

hard-cooked eggs, 181–82

Havarti cheese, 178

"healthy" labels, 74

herbs, spices, and seasonings

bruising herbs, 104

for chicken, 223–24

in desserts, 282–83

dried vs. fresh herbs, 99–100

freezing herbs, 11

grinding spices, 36, 104

growing herbs, 93

herb varieties, 92–95

herb-and-spice blends, 103

lifespan of, 83

matching with foods, 100–103

neutralizing excess spices, 72–73

other seasonings, 105–10

pantry items, 7

preparing, 103–5

seasoning to taste, 72

seed flavorings, 98–99

smell testing, 71

spice varieties, 95–98

storing, 11, 13, 16, 103–5

toasting seeds, 105

See also salt (sodium); *specific herbs/spices/seasonings*

hoisin sauce, 261

hollandaise sauce, 259

holy trinity, 128

hominy, 135

honey and sweet syrups, 281

honeydew melons, 163. *See also* melons

I

ice cream, 11, 298

iceberg lettuce, 138–39

icebox, 297–98

immersion blenders, 35–36

induction burners, 39

ingredients

measuring, 67–68

quality of, 71

reading labels, 73–74

shopping for, 17–20

See also specific ingredients

instant-read thermometers, 27, 29, 221

international seasonings, 108

Italian seasoning, 103

J

jelly, 169

Jerusalem artichokes, 139

jicama, 139

K

kale, 139

kitchen safety. *See* food safety; safety

in pressure cooker, 270–71
slow cooking, 270
stocks/broths for. *See* stocks
    and broths
on stove top, 270
thawing, 275
thickening, 272–74
types of, 267–69
sour cream, 82, 172, 174–75
soy sauce, 262
soybeans. *See* edamame; tofu
spaghetti, 124
spaghetti squash, 145
spatulas and turners, 29, 49
spices. *See* herbs, spices, and
    seasonings
spinach, 138, 149, 173
spoons and ladles, 29
sprouts, 144
squash
    about, 144–45
    cutting and preparing, 144–45
    grilling, 56
    spaghetti, 145
    summer, 144
    winter (hard), 144
    See also zucchini
squid, 192–93
staples and value-added
    foods, 3–12
    freezer, 10–12
    pantry, 4–8
    refrigerator, 8–10
star anise, 97–98, 102
star fruit, 167
steaming, 59, 151–52, 196–97
stewing, 59
stews. *See* soups and stews

stir-frying, 47, 49, 152, 197, 221
stock pots, 22
stocks and broths
    broths, 215–16, 263–64
    curdled, fixing, 72
    removing fats from, 266
    stocks, 215–16, 265–66
    See also soups and stews
storing foods
    fresh vs. frozen vs. canned,
        13–14
    lifespan of foods and, 80–83
    vegetables, 10, 147
    See also freezers; pantry;
        refrigerators; staples and
        value-added foods; *specific*
        foods
strainers or sieves, 27
streusel, 283
stuffing poultry, 87–88, 217–18
sugar, 83, 281
summer savory, 94, 101
sweating vegetables, 151
Swedish fruit soup, 277–78
sweet potatoes, 67, 145, 149
Swiss chard, 139
Swiss cheese, 178
swordfish, 193

T

tarragon, 95, 101
tart pans, 287–88
tea, 16
temperatures
    converting Fahrenheit to
        Celsius, 65
    doneness tests and, 74–77
    food safety and, 79

teriyaki sauce, 110
thermometers, 27, 30, 49, 75, 79,
    86–87, 221
thickening soups and stews, 61,
    272–74
thyme, 95, 101, 224
tilapia, 193
timers, 27
tiramisu, 301–2
toaster ovens, 37
tofu, 116–17
tomatillos, 145–46
tomatoes
    about, 146–47
    buying, 146
    canned, 146, 149
    chopping, 146
    frozen, 12
    lifespan of, 81
    peeling, 146
    refrigerating, 13
    roasting, 147
    sauces, 253–54
    sun-dried, 109, 147
    types of, 146–47
    yields, 67
tongs, 30, 49
tortellini, 124–25
trifle, 301
tube pans, 24, 287
tuna, 193
turkey
    buying, 209
    cooking temperatures and
        doneness, 77, 79, 209, 218
    fresh vs. frozen, 209
    frozen, cooking, 218
    ground, 13

About the Author

Linda Larsen is a cookbook author and home economist who has created and tested recipes for major food companies like Pillsbury and Malt-O-Meal since 1987. She is the Guide for Busy Cooks at About.com (http://busycooks.about.com), providing cooking lessons, recipes, menu ideas, and information about food science and food safety.

She was a member of the Bake-Off staff at Pillsbury, manager of search in 1992, and manager of Internet recipe cearch in 2000. She developed original recipes, conducted tolerance tests, presented recipes to taste panels, styled food for photography, and conducted trend research. At Malt-O-Meal, Linda developed quick and easy recipes and held cooking demonstrations for health food fairs.

Linda has written articles for *Woman's Day* magazine, and her recipes have appeared in Good Housekeeping's *Quick and Simple Magazine*. Linda has been interviewed on several radio programs, including the *Ask Heloise* nationally syndicated show. In summer 2007 she was a panelist for About.com's Under One Roof event, meeting editors from magazines and publishing houses.

She has written *The Joyce Lamont Cookbook* and *Back of the Box Recipes* cookbook, among others.

Linda holds a degree in biology from St. Olaf College, and a degree with High Distinction in food science from the University of Minnesota.